EBURY PRESS

MAVERICK MESS.

Ramesh Kandula is a journalist based in Hyderabad. He holds an MA in English literature from Hyderabad Central University and an MA in politics from Andhra University. In a career spanning three decades across the media spectrum—print, television and the web—he has been associated with various organizations, including *Eenadu*, *Deccan Chronicle* and the *Tribune*.

PRAISE FOR THE BOOK

'Excellent political biography of NTR. I enjoyed reading it. There is a lot of good stuff here'—Sanjaya Baru, author and political commentator

'A very objective, lucid, truthful biography. It is a dispassionate account of a politician's role in shaping the public life of his state and the nation. Eminently readable'—Dr Jayaprakash Narayan, founder, Lok Satta

'This is not an adulatory work. I wouldn't have liked it if it were one. It is fair, even-handed and objective in assessing NTR's political journey . . .' —Parakala Prabhakar, author and political commentator

'Found it impossible to put down the book till I completed it' —K. Padmanabhaiah, chairman, Administrative Staff College of India

'Ramesh Kandula's political biography of N.T. Rama Rao is a marvellous narrative'—Carolyn Elliott, Professor Emeritus, the University of Vermont

'NTR found an ideal biographer in Ramesh Kandula, who combines the sympathy of an admirer with the critical eye of a political journalist' —The Wire

maverick messiah

A POLITICAL BIOGRAPHY
of N.T. RAMA RAO

RAMESH KANDULA

EBURY
PRESS

An imprint of Penguin Random House

EBURY PRESS

USA | Canada | UK | Ireland | Australia
New Zealand | India | South Africa | China

Ebury Press is part of the Penguin Random House group of companies
whose addresses can be found at global.penguinrandomhouse.com

Published by Penguin Random House India Pvt. Ltd
4th Floor, Capital Tower 1, MG Road,
Gurugram 122 002, Haryana, India

Penguin
Random House
India

First published in Ebury Press by Penguin Random House India 2021

ISBN 9780143460176

Typeset in Adobe Caslon Pro by Manipal Digital Systems, Manipal
Printed at Gopsons Papers Pvt. Ltd., Noida.

www.penguin.co.in

For my wife, Vijaya Lakshmi, and daughter, Manasa

Contents

Act III

Act IV

Act V

Foreword

Nandamuri Taraka Rama Rao (1923–96) was not just a film star who challenged the mighty Indira Gandhi and knocked out the one-party rule in Andhra Pradesh (AP). Elected thrice as the chief minister of united AP, the actor-politician redefined the political culture in the region and scripted a new political idiom.

His subnationalism was constructive, and his identity politics was devoid of parochial undertones. His brand of regionalism celebrated the pluralistic idea of India. A patriot to the core, NTR proudly wore his Teluguness on his saffron sleeve, but without privileging it over other identities.

An outsider to the political establishment, NTR displayed an instinct for political mobilization. The way politics was played in AP underwent a profound change after NTR's arrival on the scene. Power, in NTR's case, was truly drawn from the people.

However, his rather dramatic entry into politics, the profound impact he left on the people of AP and the vital role he played in national politics during his relatively short political life have not received deserving recognition. His fight for strengthening the federal character of our Constitution and the emphasis he laid on the welfare role of the governments remain relevant in today's India when regional aspirations are on the rise, and crony capitalism is in command.

This first comprehensive political biography of NTR is an attempt to provide a 360-degree view of the most charismatic personality that the political churn in the country produced in the second wave of regionalism of the 1980s.

NTR was a man of fascinating contradictions. He was a commanding personality but resorted to baffling theatrics and bewildering sartorial predilections. He was considered orthodox by many, but he displayed radical tendencies that caused a furore in the establishment. Though outwardly religious, he was staunchly secular. A leader who fought on the plank of regional aspirations, he remained a committed nationalist throughout. A man of no known ideological persuasion, he was able to come up with his own brand of populism and a clearly enunciated doctrine on Centre–state relations.

A fighter to the core, NTR liked to punch above his weight. His contribution to the Opposition unity at the national level was a pioneering effort, and NTR would have played a more substantial role as the National Front chairman in the 1990s but for a quirk of fate.

The most colourful personality in the drab world of politics, NTR never ceased to amaze because of his complexities. The element of drama was deeply embedded in his rather momentous life. In his last days, the personal and political got merged in his life in an unusual mix, resulting in a tempestuous climax that has few parallels in modern Indian politics.

Maverick Messiah: A Political Biography of N.T. Rama Rao captures these different facets of NTR in all their multifold hues and puts in perspective the significant contribution of the actor-politician to the ever-changing Indian political tapestry.

* * *

Though he played such an important role at the regional and national level, NTR's political life, surprisingly, did not receive the attention it deserved as is evident from the dearth of informed works on him. Except for the first authentic biography written a year after he entered politics by S. Venkat Narayan, there has not been a serious book on NTR's politics. Narayan's slim volume continues to be the only authentic work on NTR's early life and times. His tenure as the chief minister, his path-breaking initiatives, the controversies that surrounded him, his bold foray into national politics and the rather dramatic end to his political career and life remained unexplored. Some sketchy accounts of NTR's life, academic articles on his electoral victories and some discussions of his policies are available, but an exhaustive narrative or an analytical chronicle of his rather eventful political career in its entirety has been sorely missing.

This book is intended to fill such a void. However, it was not my intention to come up with a hagiography of NTR. In this book, I tried not only to recount and recreate the historic role NTR played in his rather brief political career but also attempted to provide an objective analysis of his politics, its relevance and its impact. NTR was a volatile politician with a strong political personality, and it would be puerile to present him without his glaring faults, warts and all.

My personal interactions with NTR were not too many, but I followed his political life closely as a journalist since 1986. I covered many of his press conferences and interviewed him while he was in the Opposition. I had the opportunity to speak to him regularly at the fag end of his life after he was toppled as chief minister. I met him even on the last day of his life, and he spoke about his future political plans. By the time my report appeared in newspapers, he was no more. I was one of those who witnessed this rather grim period of his life from close quarters.

In writing this biography, I have chosen a style that is neither too pedantic nor too dramatic. NTR's political life broadly falls into five parts—his stunning entry, the unexpected toppling, dramatic resurrection, devastating defeat and his triumphant comeback which culminated in a catastrophic finale. I have broken them down into five acts, reflecting the theatrical nature of NTR's political life. While maintaining the historicity and authenticity, I have tried to tell the story of NTR through an engaging account. I have incorporated various views—both academic and non-academic—to understand NTR's politics in a broader perspective.

It is my wish that NTR is restored to his rightful place in the country's political history. If this biography can serve this end, I consider my effort fulfilling.

Ramesh Kandula
Hyderabad

Act I

A Thriller Unfolds

The warm winter sun was losing its burnished glow behind the seven peaks of Tirumala. The temple town of Tirupati, nestled in the foothills of the Eastern Ghats, had just drawn curtains over one of the most dramatic election campaigns in the history of the south Indian state of Andhra Pradesh (AP). Prime Minister Indira Gandhi, the country's most powerful and popular leader, had wound up her exhausting election tour moments ago. After concluding her last speech at the municipal school grounds in the midsized town, a tired Indira slumped into the back seat of her car. She sank into deep thought as the VVIP cavalcade whizzed through. This was the last day of her blistering roadshow across the length and breadth of the state that had always been on her side.

It was not the first time that the entire burden of leading the party to victory rested solely on her capable shoulders. But the assembly polls of January 1983 unexpectedly turned out to be a litmus test for her political pull and personal charisma.

AP had been the Congress's favourite state in general and Indira's in particular. No other party had come anywhere near capturing power here since Independence. It was the reason why she had stood like a rock during 1969–71 when two successive

1

separatist movements—Separate Telangana and Jai Andhra—
had rattled the state.[1] AP was the country's fifth largest state
with a population of nearly 56 million at this time. She did not
want such a large state that had been continuously returning her
party to power to be torn into two. She was especially mindful
that AP had come to her rescue when she needed it the most.
When the entire country rejected her in the 1977 elections, AP
won her party forty-one out of the state's forty-two Parliament
seats, with an astonishing 57.4 per cent of votes. After the veteran
leader touched her lowest political ebb post-Emergency, it was AP
that secured her political comeback. Her newly founded Congress
(Indira) Party formed the state government in 1978 on the freshly
issued hand symbol. The resounding victory in AP when she was
out in the cold in Delhi boosted her confidence and foretold her
imminent return to power at the Centre.

A lot of water had flowed under the Yamuna since then.
Indira, now the president of the Congress (I) Party, wrested
back power at the Centre in the midterm elections of 1980 and
emerged more powerful than ever.[2] The personality cult around
her grew phenomenally. The sealed cover culture ruled the fate
of the leadership in the states. Chief ministers were like pawns
on the chessboard, to be moved in and out at Indira's will. Those
were indeed the days of 'Indira is India and India is Indira'. She
enjoyed absolute power but did not feel secure. The recent loss of
Sanjay Gandhi, the heir apparent, in a helicopter crash had made
her shaky. She became more assertive in her position than ever.
The defeat in West Bengal and the split verdict in Haryana and
Himachal Pradesh in the May 1982 assembly elections, widely
interpreted as early signs of weakening of the once formidable
politician, made her restive.

It was against this backdrop that the assembly elections to AP
and Karnataka were being held. Both had Congress governments,
and Indira had set her eyes on retaining the two states. AP, the
apple of her political eye, was even more coveted. So grateful was

the iron lady to AP for her political resurrection that she chose to keep Medak parliamentary constituency in the state after the 1980 election victory, giving up her other seat—Rae Bareli in Uttar Pradesh—which was a family heirloom. But an unexpected hurdle presently threatened to play spoilsport in the Congress fairyland. She had taken care of umpteen Opposition parties such as the Janata Party, Lok Dal, the BJP and various Congress splinter groups with political skill. But a brand-new party that had all the hallmarks of a south Indian masala movie was rising on the horizon in AP.

She was not sure of the new party's popularity, or its ability to make inroads into the Congress's bastion. When she first heard that a film actor was looking to make a bid for power, Indira considered the development, according to her close friend Pupul Jayakar, a 'political joke'.[3] Her state party leaders gave her little reason to fear anything untoward. They told her, in one voice, that while the newcomer was a famous movie star, the people who thronged his meetings were mere fans, eager to get a glimpse of their screen idol. They assured her it would be impossible for a fledgling party, which lacked organizational structure or political machinery, to convert the frenzied crowds into bankable ballots.

But Indira was no greenhorn in such matters. The seasoned leader got an inkling of the turn in the popular tide during her campaign in AP. She left nothing to chance. She conducted one of the most elaborate electioneering for this poll. No prime minister, or for that matter national leader, had campaigned as extensively as she did in the state. She had been flying non-stop and conducting roadshows since 15 December 1982 for the elections in three states—AP, Karnataka and Tripura.

Today, 3 January 1983, was the last day. The tireless campaigner had addressed 300 public meetings in the three states. 'Seldom has Mrs Gandhi campaigned so hard in State elections as on this occasion in Karnataka, and especially in AP,' observed the *Indian Express*.[4] Except for Christmas, the prime minister was on the move without a break from early morning till late night every single day for the last nineteen days. Having realized the challenges ahead, she had spent ten days in AP alone. This was the first time that the PM was away from Delhi for such a long time.

The queen of the Congress party still attracted crowds in good numbers. But it didn't remotely compare with the madding masses that thronged the impromptu meetings of the upstart founder of the new regional party. She could see the tepid enthusiasm of the people at her own gatherings, especially when state Congress leaders spoke. She missed the earlier spark that characterized her election rallies. But she went on with her campaign resolutely, with the new scion of the dynasty, Rajiv Gandhi, too making his foray into the bitter battle. The mother–son duo showed no sign of let-up in their furious wooing of voters. Indira was now at the fag end of the exhaustive campaign trail. Tirupati, famous worldwide for its richest temple in India, was the last post in this battle of votes.

In a curious coincidence, the temple town turned out to be the stage for a dramatic climax to the high-voltage electioneering. Nandamuri Taraka Rama Rao, popularly known as NTR, too was rounding off his whirlwind campaign at the same place and on the same day. A film star with a cult following, he was known in almost every household through his memorable portrayal of various social and 'Puranic' (Hindu mythological) characters. NTR chose to end his campaign here since he was contesting from the local assembly seat of Tirupati on the banner of the newly floated Telugu Desam Party (TDP), created barely nine months ago. This was also the place from where he had kicked off his last leg of the campaign. Indira Gandhi had selected Tirupati for her last stop as she was to inaugurate the seventieth Indian Science Congress scheduled in the town the same evening.

The pilgrim town sported a festive atmosphere with two of the most charismatic personalities camping here in a do-or-die battle. The hold of Indiramma (Mother Indira, as she was affectionately addressed across rural AP) on public imagination had been unparalleled till date. Anna (Brother, as NTR was fondly called) was the new kid on the political block. But he had already left a deep imprint on the Telugu consciousness through his long and illustrious film career. The political novice was mounting a serious challenge to the seasoned leader's claim on the territory. This face-off had attracted the attention of not only the people and press in AP but the entire nation. The polls aroused curiosity even internationally, since it was widely seen as the first credible challenge to Indira Gandhi's popularity.

Having covered Gudivada in Krishna District, his other constituency in coastal Andhra region, NTR reached Tirupati the same day. The prime minister was resting at the vice chancellor's guest house in the Sri Venkateswara University campus before getting ready for the last public meeting. NTR was already burning the rubber in a breakneck tour of thirty-six villages surrounding Tirupati. The atmosphere in the pilgrim town had turned electric with the news of NTR's arrival. His 'Chaitanya Ratham' (chariot of awakening), a refurbished Chevrolet van from the 1950s, had already left the surrounding villages hysterical. Crazed fans and curious onlookers were eagerly waiting to spot the Chaitanya Ratham in the town itself.

At the guest house, the prime minister walked out to the waiting cavalcade after a light lunch and told the retinue of officials and local party leaders that she was ready for the public meeting. As they scurried around the convoy, she inquired whether the crowd had gathered at the venue. The local leaders told her that people were still trickling in at the municipal grounds. She considered for a moment and then asked to be taken around the town in a roadshow. A few minutes after the police confirmed that security was in place for the prime minister, the caravan left for the town. Indira stood up in an open jeep and tried to connect with people lined up on either side of the streets, waving and smiling at them.

The crowds responded enthusiastically, and a fatigued Indira's face lit up briefly.

Meanwhile, information reached them that the size of the crowd at the venue was decent. When the entourage entered the grounds, the Congress leaders seemed relieved to see around 10,000 people gathered for the meeting—many brought in by local leaders with some effort. The local Congress (I) candidate was the outgoing assembly speaker, Agarala Eswara Reddy. He spoke briefly, asking the people to not be carried away by the upstart regional party. NTR's son-in-law, Nara Chandrababu Naidu, a serving junior minister, was a Congress contestant from the neighbouring Chandragiri constituency. He called upon the audience to vote for the Congress (I) party for development and prosperity.

Indira, in her thirty-minute speech in English, tried to hit the nail on the head by telling the assembled crowd to not get carried away by glib talk. 'I too like a good farce, but only for entertainment. Showmanship has no place in politics,' she said, indirectly referring to NTR's film aura. Political experience and understanding, not films and drama, were required for tackling the intractable issues facing the nation, she asserted. A slight note of despondency struck her tone as she exhorted, 'I am not worried over who wins or loses in this election; I am concerned that inimical forces are poisoning people's minds.'[5] But her strenuous effort did not seem to have much effect. Many in the audience, especially women, started leaving the venue in the middle of her speech after news of NTR's Chaitanya Ratham rolling into town spread like wildfire. Attempts by the organizers to make the eager beavers sit through the meeting failed as half the venue vacated.

Outside the municipal school grounds, where the prime minister was speaking, Tirupati was in a frenzy. Crowds gathered out of nowhere and started running behind NTR's Chaitanya Ratham. It was by now a familiar sight to the observers of this election. The whole town was euphoric, and everyone—men, women, the old and the young—was straining their necks to get a peek at the legendary actor-turned-political messiah. NTR, who had a mesmerizing presence both on and off screen, did not look like a glamorous actor. His face was tanned because of the continuous exposure to elements during his relentless campaign. The weather-worn look only added to his raw appeal. The ordinary folk were awestruck by the directness of his approach—a hero always under arc lights choosing to reach out to them with disarming simplicity and earnestness. Beaming faces everywhere—street corners, housetops, treetops—lustily cheered him. By the time NTR reached the venue, it was overflowing with crowds, an estimated one hundred thousand plus. A sense of jubilation appeared to have pervaded the audience. They were all ears to whatever NTR was going to say. He, of course, wouldn't disappoint them, neither in histrionics nor in grandiloquence.

By now the brand-new terminology that he had brought into his campaign speeches had become popular. He would not take any names but lambast the Congress party with the choicest abuses. He called its leaders looters of public money and powerless dummies who danced to Delhi's tunes. These leaders wouldn't think twice before mortgaging the self-respect of 6 crore Telugus at the altar of power politics.[6] He would passionately talk about the glory of the Telugu language and culture, its history and heroes. He would lament how the state was denied its glorious future due to a rotten political system that survived only on corruption and nepotism. These by now were NTR's familiar claims, but they elicited a thunderous response every time he said them with a theatrical flourish. His style was attacking, but his language was always highfalutin. His dramatics entertained, but his sincerity touched chords in people's hearts.

The next morning, twenty-four hours before the most historic election was to happen in AP, NTR went up the Tirumala hill. He got his head tonsured before having a darshan of Lord Venkateswara, the most popular god in the state. Indira Gandhi delivered her inaugural speech at the Indian Science Congress held at Sri Venkateswara University the same evening. After a puja early the next day on the Venkatadri hill, she left for Renigunta Airport with officialdom and party leaders in tow. As she was about to step on to the VIP aircraft, a local Congress leader approached her and thanked her profusely for the visit. Her vigorous campaign would ensure victory for the party, he told her reassuringly.

A sombre-looking Indira Gandhi glanced at him sharply, and shot back, 'I don't think so.'[7]

A Self-made Star

The man who emerged from nowhere to scare the iron lady of India in her citadel was himself a steely character shaped by adversity. His present involvement in public life, however, was rather unexpected and dramatic. A person with absolutely no political background deciding to float a party at the ripe age of sixty was unheard of in Indian politics.

Born on 28 May 1923 to a peasant family in a remote village in Krishna District of the erstwhile Madras presidency,[8] NTR worked his way to the top with determination and a strong work ethic. His parents, Venkataramamma and Laxmaiah, gave him up for adoption to the latter's brother, Ramaiah, and his wife, Chandramma, who were childless. NTR had his early education in Nimmakuru, his native village, where he studied up to class V. His foster parents moved to nearby Vijayawada for him to continue his education, and he passed the matriculation examination in 1940. The family faced financial difficulties during this time. While doing his intermediate course in SRR and CVR College in Vijayawada, he supplemented the family income by supplying milk to hotels on his bicycle. In 1942, following the practice in Telugu families, he was married to Basavatarakam, the daughter of his maternal uncle. He was twenty years old at the time. He failed twice in the intermediate course, did some odd jobs for a couple of years, but eventually cleared the backlog. He then joined Andhra Christian (AC) College in Guntur, 30 km away, for a bachelor of arts course in 1944, commuting each day by train.

NTR was bitten by the acting bug in his intermediate days. He formed an amateur drama group, National Art Theatre, with the help of his friends in AC College and staged plays regularly. Most of the stalwarts in the Telugu cinema industry hailed from the coastal region, which during this time was flourishing in artistic endeavours. Telugu cinema based out of Madras was at the cusp of embarking on its classical period.[9] NTR was five feet nine inches tall with a sculpted face, clear complexion and sharp looks. No wonder, he was spotted by the first generation of creative film-makers in Madras, the capital of the Madras Province. He, however, turned down an offer from the famous Telugu director C. Pullaiah to act in the film *Keelu Gurram*. He was concerned with completing his college degree.

Because of his poor family circumstances, NTR considered a career in acting as too much of a risk. He looked for a stable job. He successfully appeared for the Madras Service Commission examination for the sub-registrar's post and took up the position in Mangalagiri in 1947. But he felt unhappy in the job, which denied him an opportunity to fulfil his artistic urge. 'I am forced to sell my soul and art in this office,' he wrote in a letter to his friend Kongara Jaggaiah (who also later became a famous actor) in October 1947. Even as he was feeling stifled in government service, luck smiled on him in the form of another film director. B.A. Subba Rao was making his directorial debut, *Palletoori Pilla*. Subba Rao saw NTR's photograph in well-known director L.V. Prasad's album and selected him for the lead role despite the latter's apprehensions. Prasad had earlier offered NTR a small role of a police sub-inspector in his film *Mana Desam*, which the latter had refused because he wanted to play only a lead character. Following Subba Rao's offer, NTR resigned from his job and took a train to Madras. It was a turning point in his life. He now accepted, on

Subba Rao's suggestion, the part of the sub-inspector in *Mana Desam*. It became his first film, which was released in 1949. *Palletoori Pilla*, in which he was the protagonist, was released the following year and proved a commercial success.

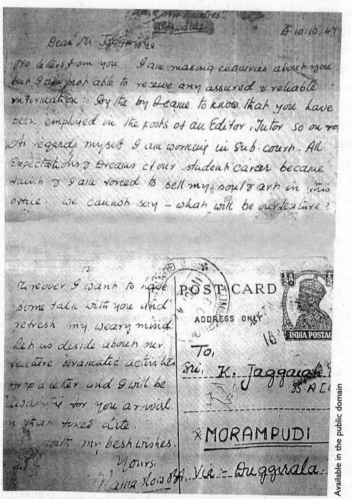

Though he was gainfully employed in the sub-registrar's office, NTR felt distressed at his inability to pursue his acting career, as is evident in this letter written in 1947 to his friend Kongara Jaggaiah.

He had his share of rough patches, but NTR never looked back. In no time, he became a sought-after actor with directors and producers finding him to be a disciplined, hard-working, dedicated and talented actor. The folk film *Pathala Bhairavi* (1951) gave him his first break as a hero of the masses. *Malliswari,* released in the same year, achieved cult status. He continued his success with *Missamma* (1955) and the all-time classic *Maya Bazaar* (1957), in which he played Lord Krishna for the first time. All four films were produced by Vijaya Vauhini Studios with which NTR had a contract. Soon the film industry recognized him as a versatile actor who brought finesse to Puranic characters on celluloid. He went on to play a variety of roles during the 1960s and 1970s based on Hindu mythology, carving a niche for himself.

By 1962, NTR had completed 100 films and firmly established himself as a successful lead actor. Along with the mythological films, his social and folk movies were a big hit too. He also donned the role of producer and director, making several movies under his home banner, National Art Theatre. The thespian directed seventeen films during his career. The Government of India bestowed the fourth-highest civilian award, Padma Shri, on NTR in 1968. Andhra University felicitated him with the 'Kala Prapoorna' award. He continued to be the leading hero into the 1970s, acting in eleven films in 1978 alone.

Meanwhile, the Telugu-speaking regions of Madras Province were formed into the first linguistic state of Andhra in 1953. Then, with the merger of the Nizam's Telangana, AP came into being in 1956. But NTR continued to rule in Telugu cinema from Madras, now the capital of Tamil Nadu. He had also acted in twenty direct and dubbed movies in Tamil, while four of his early films were dubbed into Hindi. After 1971, NTR entirely concentrated on Telugu movies.

His performances in more than 300 films over three decades turned NTR into a household name for Telugu-speaking people across the world. Such has been the imprint of his movies over generations that a CNN-IBN poll survey conducted in celebration of 100 years of Indian cinema named NTR the greatest Indian actor of all time.[10] He lived and breathed films throughout his life. 'I was so engrossed in my film career all the while that I did not have any time to read either newspapers or books,' NTR told his biographer S. Venkat Narayan in 1983.[11] For such a man who knew no other world except the celluloid one, the precocity with which he took his political plunge and the impact he created within a short period of time appeared almost cinematic.

Indira Gandhi was, after all, a leader with her ears firmly to the ground. The local Congress leaders who depended on her charisma for their political sustenance might have refused to believe that a political novice could really take her on. But Indira could see that NTR's challenge was no bluster. She had never thought that a film star from AP who had been living in Madras for the last three

Available in the public domain

A still from *Pathala Bhairavi* (1951). The film based on a folklore catapulted NTR into stardom in Telugu cinema.

and a half decades would make a severe dent in the impregnable Congress fortress in such a short period of time. But she did sense that a shift was in the offing.

Indira experienced first-hand the immense popularity of the star. But outside of the state, few seemed to have anticipated from AP, the Gandhi dynasty's fiefdom, the rise of a non-Congress force. Even within the state, NTR's foray evoked more curiosity than serious consideration in the early days. The reason was not difficult to fathom. While the rotten situation in AP was ripe for a new political experiment, nobody had an inkling that NTR would be the one to jump into the fray. That was because, in his long and eventful career in the movie industry, he had never exhibited an interest in the state's politics. His filmography, too, had little to do with political content or social issues affecting AP. It was a quirk of fate that NTR thought about public life on a cold September day of 1980 in Ooty, where he was shooting for the film *Sardar Papa Rayudu*.

It was not unusual during this time to invite film reporters to outdoor shooting locations for interactions with the actors. During one such press interaction, NTR was casually asked about his approaching sixtieth birthday.[12] 'As you are going to celebrate your *Shashtipoorthi*, would you consider doing something lasting for the public which has patronized you for decades with great love and affection?' asked a reporter. NTR, initially taken aback, gathered himself and replied in his lofty style that he would take up 'public service' after his sixtieth birthday, which was in May 1982. He did not directly refer to politics. However, this news soon made its way into mainstream Telugu newspapers, and rumours started floating around about NTR's likely political entry. At the same time, developments in the ruling Congress government hastened NTR's foray into the state's politics.

Nadendla Bhaskara Rao, an ambitious politician, rose very quickly in the ranks of Congress politics. Originally from Tenali in coastal Andhra, he studied law in Hyderabad. While practising

as an advocate in the AP High Court, Nadendla became close to
the veteran Congress leader Marri Channa Reddy and sided with
Indira Gandhi during her post-Emergency setback. Nadendla
claimed he was the one who pushed Devaraj Urs in Karnataka
and Marri Channa Reddy in AP to back Indira and her breakaway
faction, the Congress (I), when most of the senior Congress
leaders deserted her.[13] He became the AP Congress (I) general
secretary as Channa Reddy's protégé when there were few takers
for the party in the state. Later, when the party surprised everyone
by securing a majority in the 1978 assembly elections, Nadendla
became a minister in Channa Reddy's cabinet.[14] He developed a
good rapport with power brokers in Delhi. His meteoric rise was
resented by many Congressmen in the state. However, Channa
Reddy soon began to suspect that the upstart had ambitions of
replacing him.

Nadendla took care of much-needed party funds.[15] He was
widely seen as having developed proximity with Sanjay Gandhi,
who was said to be calling the shots in the Congress (I). In fact,
it was for this reason that Channa Reddy started keeping him at a
distance. Sanjay's sudden death, meanwhile, wrecked Nadendla's
position in Delhi. Subsequently, T. Anjaiah replaced Channa
Reddy as chief minister and removed Nadendla from the cabinet.
Even after Bhavanam Venkataram took over as chief minister after
Anjaiah stepped down, Nadendla failed to secure a place in the
ministry. He suddenly felt like a pariah in the back-room politics
of the Congress in Delhi.

Chafing at the insult, Nadendla began toying with the idea
of floating a new regional party. He resigned from the Congress
on 21 March 1982.[16] It was the same day that NTR held a press
conference in Hyderabad to declare his intention to soon devote
his life to public service. In his autobiography *Walking with
Destiny*, Nadendla claimed that he had been working on forming
a regional party for some time by then. He procured from Madras
the constitution, rules and regulations of the Dravida Munnetra

Kazhagam (DMK) and the All India Anna Dravida Munnetra
Kazhagam (AIADMK) parties and studied them. NTR and
Nadendla were in contact during this time. While Nadendla was
already set on launching a regional party, NTR was still in two
minds about his course of action.

Nadendla said NTR called him through Daggubati
Chenchuramaiah (NTR's son-in-law Venkateswara Rao's father)
and expressed interest in meeting him. During the meeting, when
Nadendla conveyed his plans, NTR was not overly enthusiastic.
'I won't consider any such move till I have celebrated my
Shashtipoorthi,' NTR told him. This was at the beginning of
1982. However, according to Nadendla, NTR kept calling him,
seeking details about the progress of his proposed outfit.

After several meetings between the two, NTR finally chose
to begin his political journey much before his sixtieth birthday.
NTR, who was cautious by nature, was clearly emboldened to
transition to politics after his interactions with Nadendla. The
latter's interest in NTR was because of the realization that
despite his political acumen and connections, he would not be
able to succeed on his own. He was a first-time MLA and lacked
political capital or personal charisma to pull off a regional party
on his own strength. Well-wishers urged Nadendla to attract
people who could help turn the tide. What better choice than
NTR who a few months earlier had declared his intention to
take up public service?

It is difficult to pinpoint the exact reason for NTR's sudden
interest in politics. 'I really hate politics. Never had plans for a
political foray. I am here because this is the only way for public
service,' NTR told the well-known policeman H.J. Dora when
he, as intelligence superintendent of police, met the thespian soon
after his party announcement.[17] He was not known to be close to
or comfortable with politicians during his long career in the film
industry. He never made any attempt to make friends with chief
ministers or ministers, even though he had been the most popular

actor and a celebrity for decades. He, of course, knew many AP leaders, from Neelam Sanjiva Reddy to Kotla Vijayabhaskara Reddy. Even Kasu Brahmananda Reddy was a fan. However, he was not given to cultivating friendships with any of them. In fact, he would chastise crew members on studio floors for indulging in political gossip, calling it a waste of time.[18]

NTR's real connection to politics occurred when he got his daughter Bhuvaneswari married to a serving Congress minister. Nara Chandrababu Naidu was a self-made, unassuming politician from Chittoor District. The marriage was solemnized in Madras on 10 September 1981. The Nellore-based sociopolitical weekly *Zamin Ryot* reported that there were more politicians than film personalities at the wedding held at Kalaivanar Arangam on Mount Road. Chief Minister T. Anjaiah and former Union Home Minister K. Brahmananda Reddy were among the guests. Later, NTR attended his son-in-law's swearing-in ceremony as minister at Raj Bhavan when Bhavanam Venkataram replaced T. Anjaiah as chief minister on 24 February 1982. Bhavanam was NTR's classmate in college in Guntur during 1944–47.

Curiously, NTR announced his political party barely a month after attending Venkataram's induction as chief minister. He had clearly been mulling over his political entry during this time. In the backdrop of rumours about his political plans, NTR was apparently sought to be appeased by the Congress through a nomination to the Rajya Sabha.[19] A confident Bhavanam told the Congress high command, which was concerned over rumours of the film star's political ambitions, that NTR would not launch a political party as long as he was the chief minister. However, that was not to be.

One reason Nadendla offered for the actor's sudden interest in politics was that despite his nearly cult status as a film star, NTR, for a long time, had felt slighted by political leaders. During his visits to districts in his native state, he could see the power exercised by politicians. Well-known film-maker and lyricist Mallemala

Sundara Rami Reddy (known as M.S. Reddy) had a fascinating anecdote in this regard.[20] NTR was invited to inaugurate a movie complex of three theatres. Krishna, Kaveri and Kalyani had been built by the liquor businessman (who later turned politician) Magunta Subbarami Reddy in Nellore, a three-hour drive from Madras. While NTR was under the impression that he was the chief guest, N. Janardhana Reddy, a senior Congress politician and a serving minister from Nellore, had also been invited. Mallemala recalled how he was terrified when he saw the invitation card, which mentioned Janardhana Reddy as the chief guest. Fearing that NTR would take umbrage, he convinced Subbarami Reddy to print another set of a hundred cards separately. The new cards mentioned NTR as the chief guest and were distributed within the film industry.

But as feared, things did not go smoothly. When NTR was getting ready for the function in the restroom of the local government guest house, Janardhana Reddy walked in and was angry to learn that NTR was inside. 'This guest house is reserved for me,' the minister said curtly. It was loud enough to be audible to NTR. Without saying a word, NTR came out, got into the car and left for the venue. Once the programme was over, NTR refused to even have lunch and took off for Madras in a huff. This was on 27 July 1980. The next morning, Mallemala met a sullen NTR at his house and found him wearing saffron clothes in the manner of Vivekananda. The conversation went thus:

> Mallemala: What is this new get-up, sir?
> NTR: Didn't you see Janardhana Reddy's behaviour and his arrogance yesterday? Isn't it because of political power? I have come to a decision—to launch a political party. Vivekananda will be my inspiration for this . . .

Even as NTR considered public life, he was hesitant about a direct political entry. He was a cautious man and spent a good amount of time brooding over the repercussions of his moves. While he got in touch with Nadendla, he was initially reluctant to jump headlong into the sphere without an understanding of the depths of politics. He resisted Nadendla's offer at the beginning of 1982, saying he would consider the option after Shashtipoorthi. But NTR kept calling him, seeking to know how things were progressing. Nadendla said he was a little annoyed and questioned him point-blank as to why he would want to know the details if he wasn't interested in being a part of it. By February 1982, NTR firmed up his decision to join politics and kept inviting Nadendla to his film studio at Hyderabad to exchange ideas.

Interestingly, NTR's family members were not thrilled at his proposed political foray. Nadendla recalled their reaction when he once visited the studio. They expressed annoyance in his presence about why NTR, a reigning film star, was being dragged into the murky world of politics. Daggubati Venkateswara Rao, NTR's son-in-law, a medical doctor by training, confirmed the lack of support from within. He recalled that he chose to stay with NTR for the proposed outfit as not many relatives or friends were ready to come forward to work for the party in the initial stages.[21]

But the driving force behind NTR's decision to turn to politics was indeed to make a difference. Living in Madras, he had witnessed how the Dravidian parties were able to protect the interests of Tamil Nadu. Whereas, in AP, the national party was treating its chief ministers as doormats. He was undoubtedly influenced by M.G. Ramachandran (MGR), a good friend who was already a chief minister, making a mark in Dravidian politics. H.J. Dora recalled the brewing angst in NTR for a Telugu renaissance. 'Telugus have lost their identity. We have been reduced to being care-of-Madras. Why should we allow ourselves to be belittled? I want to show what stuff Telugus are made of. I want to awaken them, arouse them,' a fired-up NTR told him soon after founding the party.[22]

However, the decision to launch the party was not made on the spur of the moment. NTR had for some time debated with himself whether he had what it took to make a new beginning in politics. And whether he was ready to entirely devote time to his new calling and make a clean break from his film career and family obligations. Having seen highs and lows in the cinema industry, he was also concerned whether he could really make an impact and succeed in this new field.

During his first press conference at Ramakrishna Studios on 21 March 1982, NTR appeared undecided on his course of action, only broadly hinting at his intention to be part of the political process. The actor said that he would step into his sixtieth year on 28 May 1982, and from then on, he would like to give up his film career and serve people. For this purpose, he might float a political party. However, at this stage, he was not clear about his proposed party, which he wanted to call for the time being only an 'organization'. But a week later, he made the formal announcement of the Telugu Desam Party (TDP). Evidently, Nadendla's influence did prevail over NTR's initial hesitation in firming up plans for the regional party far ahead of his May deadline. But once on board, NTR was a transformed man. He acknowledged in his first few press conferences that after he took the decision, he became a possessed person. 'A new power has overtaken me,' he said.

One of the reasons for NTR's initial hesitation was finance. He was not comfortable with the idea of collecting or spending funds to gain political support. NTR was known in the film industry as being tight-fisted with his hard-earned money. He was also averse to seeking money gratis from others. So, his main worry seemed to be the need to take up fundraising, which he abhorred. He was also not prepared to spend his personal wealth for political influence. NTR sincerely believed that he was already sacrificing his life for the public good, and that it was below his stature to seek political power in lieu of money. Known for his impeccable planning in film production, he spent time trying to figure out the kind of funding and resources required to launch and run a political outfit. He felt assuaged when Nadendla told him that he would take care of the financial aspects. In any case, the TDP did not spend a significant amount of money on the election campaign. NTR was the only top leader who campaigned for the party across the state, taking care of his own needs, which were rather modest.[23]

NTR's expenses were minimal as he travelled in his own refurbished Chevrolet van. It was his mobile home as well as his entire campaign paraphernalia. The trailer was sparsely furnished and not even air-conditioned. Even then, at one point of time during the campaign, NTR was upset as the party did not have money for publicity material. Nadendla claimed that NTR turned so despondent at the situation that he was almost ready to give up. Soon, donations started to pour in, even from ordinary people. Alapati Sivaramakrishnaiah, a freedom fighter from Guntur District, gave his house, 100 square yards of land, and Rs 200 monthly pension to the new party.[24] The party, however, did not rely on money for its politics. To this day, the TDP remains a rare exception that fought its debut election with an absolute disregard for funds. NTR had a healthy contempt for buying the support of voters through monetary offers.

Despite the favourable response in the early days, NTR was unsure of what lay ahead. He was not willing to risk anybody's career for the sake of the new party since he was not sure of its fate in the elections. NTR discouraged Parvathaneni Upendra, a public relations officer in Indian Railways based in Delhi, when he expressed his wish to resign from his job and join the TDP campaign. 'The mass of the people is supporting us. But our party is still untested. I don't advise that you should take a risk at this stage,' NTR told him.[25] He was also not keen that his son-in-law Chandrababu Naidu, already a minister in the Congress government, should face the uncertainty of the new party.

First Shot

NTR's first interaction with political reporters was on 21 March 1982, when he still seemed to be in two minds. When the call from Ramakrishna Studios came for a face-to-face meeting with the fabled N.T. Rama Rao, there was expectedly an air of anticipation and excitement among the reporters. NTR was known to many as a screen idol, but few had seen him in flesh and blood, let alone interacted with him. No one had any information about what the actor intended to say, though they had a whiff of his recent interest in politics. The eager scribes were served snacks under the watchful eye of his elder son Jayakrishna. NTR, wearing white dhoti-kurta in quintessential Telugu style, walked down the stairs and assuredly took charge of the proceedings.

After recapitulating the enormous love and affection people had showered upon him during the three decades of his film career, a calm and collected NTR opened up about his plans to retire from films on his sixtieth birthday. He said he was contemplating devoting himself to public service. However, he did not specify whether he would join a party or float one. Veteran journalist Kalyani Shankar, who was present on the occasion, described her impression of NTR's debut press briefing:

> NTR was the master of ceremonies himself and handled the show without the usual hangers-on. It appeared to be a well-rehearsed speech. He took everyone by surprise when he said that he was calling it a day for his film career. However, he proposed to join politics after his 60th birthday on May 28 and begin a new chapter in his life. He did not say he was going to float a party. He made eloquent noises about the poorest of the poor and how he wanted to serve them, and repay his debt to the society, from which he had indeed reaped rich benefits. The time had come, he declared, for him to do something in return.[26]

What was remarkable about this press conference was how NTR was unruffled and kept his balance despite some provocative, even offensive, questions posed to him. Shankar was 'quite impressed by his chaste, if somewhat superfluous Telugu, his sonorous voice, his effective delivery and above all, his dominating personality'.[27] When asked point-blank whether he would give part of his wealth to the poor, NTR, though taken aback, replied that it would be a drop in the ocean, even if he did. He was also open about his plan to distribute his wealth among his children so that they would not be a burden on society. The response was characteristic, because NTR would never resort to guile in such matters for the sake of political convenience.

While he made it clear that he would not join any existing party, NTR, however, also clarified that he would consult well-wishers and assess his strengths and weaknesses before reaching a decision. Indicating that he was still testing the water, NTR said that it might take two to three months before he could come up with a manifesto for his proposed outfit, which he was averse to call a party at this juncture. He also made it clear that he did not consult his industry colleagues like Akkineni Nageswara Rao (ANR) or political acquaintances like Kasu Brahmananda Reddy for advice on his plans. Neither did he ask his son-in-law Chandrababu Naidu to join him. He appeared undecided on various issues such as whether he would take part in elections, if held early. He was unyielding in his response to repeated questions about launching his own party, recalled I. Venkata Rao, a senior journalist who covered the press conference.[28] Despite NTR's squeamishness, newspapers across the state announced the star's imminent entry into politics. Interestingly, it only took a week for him to go the whole hog, and on 29 March 1982, he was all set to formally launch the Telugu Desam Party.

The dramatic quality that became the hallmark of NTR's party was clear from its inception. Before its launch, several names were considered for the new political outfit. A day before the formal announcement, Nadendla divulged some of the names under consideration. They were Andhra Congress, Telugu Congress, Visalandhra Congress, Jai Telugu Nadu and Telugu Velugu. Evidently, these were suggested by Nadendla and others, as NTR would never agree to having Congress in his party's name. During a meeting at Ramakrishna Studios to discuss the probable names, NTR acknowledged everybody's suggestions but did not seem enthused. He kept scribbling on a white paper.[29] Later in the afternoon, at the first political meeting organized at the new MLA quarters, NTR took out a small piece of paper from the side pocket of his white kurta and announced the name of the party—Telugu Desam (Telugu Nation/Land). It was a somewhat unconventional title for a political organization. Even Nadendla didn't have a clue about the impending announcement.

Later, NTR explained the reason why he had named his party Telugu Desam. With some leaders in the past provoking parochialism in the name of 'Jai Telangana' and 'Jai Andhra' for their own self-interest, 'Andhra' had become contentious, dividing Telugus. To convey a sense of oneness of all Telugus, he had named the party 'Telugu Desam', he explained. He also proposed to change the name of the state from 'Andhra Pradesh' to 'Telugu Nadu' to reiterate this sense of belonging among all Telugu-speaking people.

There was criticism of the party's name both within and outside. The next day, when he met the inner circle, many expressed their reservations. Some thought it was not proper to call a political party 'Desam'. Tomorrow, somebody might come up with Urdu Desam, one critic said. Some found fault with the pairing of the Dravidian 'Telugu' with the Sanskrit 'Desam'. Feeling a little uneasy, NTR cross-checked with his writer-friend and Jnanpith awardee, C. Narayana Reddy. He wanted to know whether Telugu Desam was a corrupt compound (*sankara samaasamu*), as many were alleging. Reddy told him that the two words occurred in the famous verse of Vijayanagara Emperor Krishnadevaraya's classic *Amuktamalyada*.

He even quoted the line: 'Telugadela yanna Desambu Telugu [Why compose in Telugu? Because this country is Telugu].' A relieved NTR went ahead with the name.[30]

The meeting at the MLA quarters in Himayat Nagar where the outfit was formally launched, and its name announced, on a sunny Monday morning was indicative of how the party's affairs would unfold thereafter. It was intended to be a small gathering of enthusiastic supporters-cum-delegates of the proposed party in a small room on the second floor of the conference hall at the legislators' quarters. NTR flew in from Madras and from the airport went directly to Nadendla's house in Jubilee Hills. A big crowd had gathered at Begumpet Airport to welcome NTR and followed his convoy all the way to Jubilee Hills. There he was introduced to a few MLAs who had resigned from the Congress party. After tea, NTR drove to Ramakrishna Studios, where he sat with party sympathizers to discuss the course of action. At 2.30 p.m. as scheduled, he reached the new MLA quarters for the closed-door meeting in which he was expected to announce the party. However, the gathering swelled so quickly that there was no way to carry on the business inside the small hall. The meeting was immediately shifted outdoors to the lawns where thousands had gathered to listen to NTR. Several MLAs and their curious family members too had come to watch the proceedings.

While about 300 delegates were expected to attend the meeting, the venue was packed with more than a thousand people. Except for a hurriedly fetched mic and a small table, there was little paraphernalia put together for the meeting. NTR made his first political speech in his familiar baritone voice, explaining the need for a political party that could save AP from the current stagnation. He spoke of what propelled him to jump into the political arena and what he intended to do through his party. He addressed the audience for about fifteen minutes and then announced the name of the party. 'I am a Telugu and from this moment on I dedicate myself to the glory of my language, culture and my state,' he concluded. It was a scintillating experience for the audience, including the journalists who had grown up watching his films, to lay their eyes on and listen to NTR.

Ramakrishna Studios became the temporary office of the party. NTR was still living in Madras then, as it was the hub of the south Indian film industry. He, however, had started buying properties in Hyderabad from 1962, beginning with the NTR Estate at Abids.[31] He built the first deluxe air-conditioned theatre in AP, Ramakrishna 70 mm, in 1968, which was inaugurated by the then chief minister K. Brahmananda Reddy. MGR opened Ramakrishna 35 mm in the same complex. Later, NTR established Ramakrishna Studios in Musheerabad in 1978, three years after ANR founded Annapurna Studios in Jubilee Hills. While ANR moved base to Hyderabad, NTR continued to stay in Madras. But once he began work on the party in 1982, NTR made Ramakrishna Studios his camp. This was where the party activity continued to be carried out until after the August crisis of 1984.

The 29 March 1982 meeting defined the future contours of the party as well as its leadership. Nadendla, who was the initiator of the idea of the regional party and had worked towards its realization in earnest, became secondary on the very day of its foundation. Nadendla thought he could use NTR's services as a crowd-puller but wield the strings himself. However, the thespian seized the initiative in a way Nadendla could never have imagined. From giving the party its name to establishing its anti-Congress ideology on the very first day, NTR was able to leave his distinct stamp on the new outfit. His magnetic personality was already working magic.

The meeting provided enough indications that NTR would not be a mere showpiece but one who would lead the party from the front. Nadendla would have sensed the shape of things to emerge. However, he was still confident that he could turn things in his favour once the immediate goal—of capturing power—was achieved. Besides, he could not have gone back even before he started, especially given the spontaneous and massive public response the new party generated. This instantaneous response from the crowds, with little or no effort at mobilization, became the hallmark of the party in later days. The fact that Ramakrishna Studios became the headquarters for the party strengthened the perception that the TDP was essentially NTR's baby.

On the day of the formal launch, another development in Delhi hit headlines across the nation: Maneka Gandhi leaving her mother-in-law Prime Minister Indira Gandhi's official residence following a falling-out with her. The two events happened on the same day. Maneka leaving Indira's house was big news nationally. NTR launching a new party did not get any attention. Soon, Maneka would launch her own political party, Sanjay Vichar Manch, and in a curious turn of events enter a tie-up with the TDP in AP.

Within days of the party's launch, hundreds of local leaders, especially those from the Lok Dal, the Janata Dal and many former socialists, made a beeline for the TDP. In the party's early days, socialists such as K.V. Satyanarayana, Tummala Chowdary and Turlapati Satyanarayana ran the party office. Many of the second-rung Congress district leaders, disillusioned with the party's functioning, saw the new party as a ray of hope. NTR cut down on his shooting schedule, and kept the momentum going by addressing the press frequently. He focused on the omissions and commissions of the Congress party, which became the thrust of his campaign throughout:

> State leaders are acting like lackeys of the Centre. They go to Delhi even to brush their teeth. They can't stand up to the Delhi queen even when the state's interests are compromised. Why should they nod their heads sheepishly for anointed chief ministers who are but high command's rubber stamps? What happened to Telugu self-respect?[32]

Soon, yellow, the party flag's colour, which symbolized prosperity in the Telugu culture, fluttered everywhere. NTR, in his early interactions with the press, stated that the outlines of his new outfit's policies were subsidized food, free primary education, promotion of vocational training and protection of minority rights. He attacked the endemic corruption in the political system and the widespread immorality in politics. These remained his pet topics throughout the campaign. Knowing the importance of momentum, NTR called for a public meeting in Hyderabad. The first public meeting of the TDP, held at Nizam College grounds, barely twelve days after the formal announcement, saw one of the biggest crowds witnessed during those times. It was evident that the fledgling party was not going to be a short-lived affair, as many in the ruling party had hoped. The TDP was here for the long run.

Interestingly, almost all the leading actors of the Telugu film industry showed little enthusiasm for the new political party. NTR himself was not too keen on inviting actors into his party. He had sought the good wishes of his 'elder brother' MGR, the chief minister of Tamil Nadu, before embarking on his political journey. But the latter did not make any public statements in favour of NTR. This was due to the controversy a certain section of the media had created over NTR's remarks on Madras. Asked about NTR's political entry, MGR said that there was no comparison between him and NTR. 'I had a long history before launching AIADMK. Tamil Nadu can't be repeated in AP,' he replied.[33]

Fellow actor ANR was against NTR's political entry from day one. According to Nadendla, NTR invited ANR for dinner one day and sought his opinion about his plans for a new political party. ANR discouraged him and gave him a lecture on the rough and tumble of politics. Another actor with some following in the state, Ghattamaneni Krishna, father of present-day actor Mahesh Babu, was consistently opposed to NTR's politics. His brothers, who produced many of his films, were office-bearers in the Congress party. Soon after the TDP was launched, fans of Krishna came out openly against NTR and his party.

Like ANR and Krishna, many actresses were close to the Congress party through T. Subbarami Reddy, an industrialist who was also a film producer. Jamuna, a well-known heroine of yesteryears, became active in the Congress at this time and even held positions in the Congress government. M. Prabhakar Reddy, a character actor, was also part of the Congress establishment. Another actor, Vijay Chander, a grandson of Tanguturi Prakasam, was a bitter critic of NTR.

Thus, few film personalities chose to sail with NTR on his political boat. The only ones to embrace NTR openly in his political journey were Ravu Gopala Rao, a popular character actor, and D.V.S. Raju, a respected producer and prominent film personality. According to Yalamanchili Sivaji, a senior political activist who was an early entrant in the TDP, NTR was not keen on film actors joining the party. In fact, more film personalities joined politics and supported the TDP after Chandrababu Naidu took over the party in the 1990s.

From early on, NTR adopted a friendly approach towards the existing Opposition parties, even while reserving the harshest diatribe for the ruling Congress. Even then, the Opposition parties, especially the communists, adopted a hostile attitude towards the TDP. They were a divided lot and the Janata Party, Lok Dal, Congress (R), the Communist Party of India (CPI) and Communist Party of India (Marxist) (CPI [M]) were fighting against the Congress without much unity. The Bharatiya Janata Party (BJP), a newer version of the Jana Sangh which was founded in 1980, was another anti-Congress party in the state. While the Janata Party and Lok Dal leaders were a little soft on NTR, the communists were belligerent from day one.

'The new regional party is another poisonous development in state politics,' CPI (M) leader Puchalapalli Sundarayya lambasted. Before the new party completed a month of its existence, he bemoaned in a resolution passed at the CPI (M)'s state executive meeting held in Vijayawada, 'This party looks like one of those regional outfits that threaten the integrity of the nation.'[34] The CPI, too, was unkind. 'TDP is trying to capture power by provoking people. This party will only help Congress (I),' declared Neelam Rajasekhara Reddy, an executive member of the CPI, at a public meeting in Vijayawada.[35] Janata Party leader Babul Reddy was a little considerate. An alliance with the new party was possible, he said, only if the TDP publicly declared that it would fight against Indira Gandhi's dictatorial rule.

All these 'national' parties felt that a regional outfit promoted by a film star could not be more than a flash in the pan. Some seasoned politicians looked at the enthusiasm of the masses as a passing fad and thought it was below them to partner with NTR. The very next day after the first public meeting that drew massive crowds, though, the Janata Party and the Lok Dal took note of the TDP's visible popularity and sent word to NTR requesting a meeting. However, these parties were not inclined to be seen courting a new player. So NTR himself went to meet Janata leader Babul Reddy and Lok Dal leader Gouthu Latchanna.

These parties had a bloated sense of their electoral importance in a state where they never had a significant presence. The two parties wanted to contest in 150 seats out of the 294 in the AP assembly in an alliance with the TDP. Not unexpectedly, NTR left the discussion open-ended. There was another attempt at a coalition before the polls, which also failed. Later, the Left parties, too, were ready to talk. It was too late in the day by the time the communists came forward to accept fifty seats for the alliance with the TDP. By this time, NTR and his party were on a high, with the masses everywhere going gaga over the new star on the state's political horizon. NTR was confident that the TDP would secure enough seats to form the government and he would be able to deliver on his promises to the people.

Caste-based Party?

Critics sought to discredit the TDP at its very inception by dubbing it as a 'Kamma Party', the caste to which NTR belonged. There was a historical background to this charge and a political reason why this depiction was plausible.

During the independence movement, it was the educated and socially mobile Brahmins who led the masses in the state. The leading lights of the Congress party in the Andhra region included prominent leaders such as Konda Venkatappayya, Tanguturi Prakasam, Ayyadevara Kaleswara Rao and Pattabhi Sitaramayya. Closely following them were a few leaders from the socially and economically emerging Reddy and Kamma communities. However, the ways of these two caste groups diverged politically in the decades leading to India's freedom. While a few Kamma leaders of stature, such as N.G. Ranga, Kalluri Chandramouli, P. Rajagopala Naidu and Kotha Raghuramaiah, continued with the Congress party, many radical youths from the community were attracted to the communist parties.[36]

In fact, this landowning community, which was growing economically prosperous since the early decades of the twentieth century, soon became the backbone of the Communist Party of India in Andhra. 'Since the founding of the Communist Party in 1934, the party leadership has been the property of a single sub-caste, Kamma landlords, who dominate the Krishna-Godavari Delta,' remarked Selig S. Harrison, a scholar on South Asian affairs, in his study of Andhra communists.[37]

According to the well-known Indian sociologist M.N. Srinivas, the two castes—Kammas and Reddys—fell apart after pushing the Brahmins out during the days of the Justice Party in the 1930s and 1940s. 'One joined the Communists, and the other the Congress,' stated Srinivas in his seminal work *Caste in Modern India: And Other Essays*.[38] Thus, at the time of India's Independence, the Congress was increasingly led by the Reddys with the support of the Brahmins (who lost their previous hegemony over power). The CPI (and later Marxist Party) had several important Kamma leaders at the helm.

The communists emerged strong enough to challenge the Congress in the first polls in independent India. In the general election of 1952, out of the 140 seats from Andhra in the Madras Legislative Assembly, the Congress could secure only forty-three, while the CPI bagged forty of the sixty seats it contested. However, the Congress managed to form the government through alliances, and over time, the hold of the communists on the electorate began to decline.

When a separate Andhra state was formed in 1953, following the death of Potti Sriramulu during a fast for the cause, Tanguturi Prakasam became its first chief minister.[39] Later, the efforts for a larger state by combining the Telugu-speaking parts of Hyderabad State fructified, and AP came into being in 1956 with Neelam Sanjiva Reddy as the Congress chief minister. From then on, the Kamma-dominated communist party[40] gradually faced erosion in the electoral base, while the Congress became the de facto ruling party of AP till 1983.

The Congress in power meant the Reddys in power. While the Congress had nine chief ministers from its ranks during this time, as many as five were Reddys—and no one from the Kamma community.[41] The Reddy stranglehold on the Congress was comprehensive. The Kammas had lost their political influence after the 1950s with the shrinking base of the CPI and the CPI (M). Their decision to sail with a non-Congress ideology ensured that they were cut off from political power for more than three decades after Independence. But the Kamma community continued to make significant progress in other spheres, including agriculture, business, trade, education and cinema. Social and political commentator K. Balagopal said the Kammas prospered due to the 'pushing commercial enterprise of this class'. He also underlined the caste's progressive trait due to its exposure to radical

movements—from socialism to radical humanism.[42] By the time
NTR launched himself into the political arena, the Kammas had
emerged as an important community socially and economically.
However, they lacked the political wherewithal to capture power.

So, it was neither surprising nor unanticipated that the new
development was seen by many as an expression of the Kamma
urge to make a mark on the state's politics. While the Reddys
of the Congress themselves did not directly use the 'Kamma' tag
for the TDP, it was not left unsaid by their colleagues. The state
Congress president at this time was Gaddam Venkataswamy,
a veteran Dalit (a member of the Scheduled Castes) leader. He
liberally threw the dig 'Kamma Party' at the TDP as soon as it
was launched. NTR was forced to address this charge in the first
few days of announcing his party. At the public meeting at the
Nizam College grounds, he vehemently denied it. He asserted,
'This party is not a Kamma party. TDP is not for any caste, it is
for all the Telugus irrespective of caste, creed or religion.'[43] Telugu
Desam leaders countered Venkataswamy's criticism, saying that
all 'big Kamma dons' were with the Congress.[44]

However, the temptation to brand the TDP a Kamma
party, especially when it was pitted against the Reddy-
dominated Congress, remained strong for many commentators.
Interpretations based on caste dynamics of the TDP dominated
the writings of political analysts and were widely referred to in
academic papers. Quoting several earlier works, K.C. Suri, professor
of political science in Hyderabad Central University, summed up
this narrative succinctly:

> According to this analysis, the Kammas never had a chief
> minister in the state even though an elite section among them
> grew economically powerful by accumulating surpluses in
> agriculture, business, industry, etc. The increasing disjuncture
> between their economic power and their failure to capture
> the highest political office alienated the Kammas from the

Congress. As a result, they aligned their financial and political support behind NTR, who was a Kamma.[45]

It was mainly the political class in power that gave much currency to the notion of the TDP being a Kamma party. That may have been one way to ensure that the Congress remained a Reddy-dominated party. The Kammas, too, bought into this formula in the later years, especially the middle-class Kammas, who over time identified with the TDP in their political consciousness. In fact, it is from the current view that such description seems justified, because this caste assertion was nearly absent during the party's birth. In fact, as soon as it was formed, the TDP attracted a good number of Reddy leaders. They included Bezawada Papireddy, Nallapareddy Srinivasulu Reddy, Anam Venkata Reddy, Budda Vengala Reddy, Byreddy Seshasayana Reddy, S. Ramamuni Reddy, Challa Ramakrishna Reddy, S.V. Subba Reddy, Tatiparthi Jeevan Reddy, Kunduru Jana Reddy and Gutha Mohan Reddy. In 1983, the number of Reddy MLAs in the TDP legislature party was nearly the same as Kamma MLAs.

As Suri pointed out, the growth of a neo-rich class was not exclusive to Kammas. Besides, although a vast majority of Kammas might have voted for NTR in the TDP's first elections, their proportion in the total electorate—roughly about 5 per cent—was not significant enough to ensure the party's victory. No party could hope to win the election in the state if it identified itself with a single caste. Like Balagopal pointed out, the Kamma connection was evident, 'but to stop there would be to read the story by halves'.[46]

The Kamma political class at the time, in fact, was not particularly enthusiastic about the new party. Many of them already had some play in the Congress system and did not want to upset the apple cart. For example, Chandrababu Naidu, who was a minister in the Congress, kept away from the new party. In the run-up to the 1983 polls, not many Kamma leaders in other parties, especially the ruling Congress, were drawn to the party. Rayapati Sambasiva Rao, a powerful industrialist from Guntur, continued to sail with the Congress and was elected to the Rajya Sabha during the March 1982 election. K.L.N. Prasad, the Kamma founder of *Andhra Jyothy*, a regional newspaper, was also sent to the Rajya Sabha on a Congress ticket in the same election. P. Rajagopala Naidu, a senior Congress leader, criticized the TDP as a haven for anti-progressive forces. Kommareddy Suryanarayana, a veteran Congress leader, vehemently opposed NTR's Telugu nationalism.[47] The Boppana family in Gudivada (Krishna District) and the Mullapudi family in Tanuku (West Godavari District) spent money in the 1983 polls to defeat the TDP.[48]

Several senior Kamma leaders of the Congress party, such as Gottipati Brahmaiah, Paladugu Venkata Rao and Pinnamaneni Koteswara Rao, brushed aside the TDP as not worthy of politics. Gottipati said that regional parties were dangerous and only the Congress could work with people. As Gottipati, a Padma Bhushan awardee, enjoyed goodwill in the community, NTR himself responded to him. 'Brahmaiah should realize that the state remained poor because of the Congress rule. This is not the real Congress of the Independence movement,' he clarified.[49] Paladugu Venkata Rao, another leader known for his integrity and then minister for marketing and rural development, decried the TDP as a party that had neither history nor social philosophy. Thus, the status-quoists among Kammas were inimical to the new party, even as the TDP made every conscious effort to steer clear of caste dominance by appealing to the broader electorate.

The support extended by the press baron Ramoji Rao of *Eenadu*, the leading Telugu newspaper, to the TDP was often quoted as an illustration of the Kammas coming together to seize political power. However, Ramoji Rao's support came only after the party was formed. If caste were the only guiding factor, Ramoji could have easily stood behind Nadendla during the 1984 crisis.

As pointed out earlier, the interests of several groups, one of them obviously being the Kammas, came together to throw up the new challenge in the form of NTR's TDP. These groups were for long disenchanted by the Congress's insensitivity to their rising aspirations for more access to the local political economy and saw a viable alternative in NTR.

Like in any major political upheaval, people across communities were sucked into NTR's brave new world. Analysts pointed out that though its detractors tried to paint the TDP as a Kamma party, NTR crossed the barriers of caste, creed and religion through his election campaign.

NTR enjoyed the advantage of being a well-known and much-loved film star, but his background in the cinema industry was widely used by the Congress to ridicule him. Even the media, except for *Eenadu*, was unsure about the impact that NTR would be able to create. Discussions were afoot on whether there was any space for a regional party, whether Telugus, known for their loyalty to national parties, would support a local party, whether NTR, a complete outsider to the political world, had what it took to lead a party, and whether his cinematic charisma was enough for his party to survive.

Doubts about NTR's ability to lead a political party were not entirely unfounded. Many of his colleagues and those who had observed him from close quarters for years in the film industry vouched that NTR was never interested in current affairs, either at the local or at the national level. Film journalist B.K. Eswar said that NTR was never seen reading anything—not even a newspaper—on the sets or in between shots.[50] He would not bother even to look up newspaper headlines. When occasionally he flipped through a Telugu newspaper, his attention was only on cinema news.

However, Eswar recalled NTR telling him that he read the popular south Indian English newspaper *The Hindu* every day at home and that it was more than enough to get a grip on worldly matters. While his grasp of Hindu Puranas and Telugu literature was widely acknowledged, NTR showed little interest in social issues. Even his films rarely touched upon contemporary social problems. *Yamagola* (1977) was a comic satire on Indira Gandhi's Emergency, but the movie was a lone exception. Some of his films dealt with social issues such as dowry, black market and corruption, but these were few. NTR was more focused on his craft than political matters. His views on some social issues were in fact reactionary. He produced and directed a film (*Tatamma Kala*, 1974) which opposed family planning as well as land reforms.

With such a reputation, NTR was perceived by many as unfit to be in politics. Soon after he announced his party, Chief Minister Bhavanam Venkataram, at whose swearing-in ceremony NTR was present, ridiculed him. 'NTR's entry into politics is like Duryodhana rushing into the Maya Sabha. Like the Kuru lord, he is dazzled by illusions. The real looks illusory and the illusions look real in Maya Sabha,' Bhavanam remarked, referring to the Mahabharata.[51] NTR was nicknamed 'Drama Rao' by his opponents for his political histrionics.

NTR's film background thus became a major poking point for his critics. The very first editorial on the TDP in *Andhra Patrika*, a couple of days after NTR announced his party, tried to lower the expectations. 'Both MGR and Ronald Reagan had political experience before they became CM and President. NTR doesn't have this advantage. TDP was just born on one fine morning—without history or political pedigree,' the paper said.[52] A cartoon in the same newspaper ridiculed the new party with this dig: 'If you want to join our party, remove that *topi* and wear a wig.'

Reams have been written about the support *Eenadu* extended to the new party. However, other Telugu newspapers, including *Andhra Patrika, Andhra Prabha, Andhra Bhoomi* and *Andhra Jyothy,* were not supporters of the new party.[53] *Visalandhra* and *Prajasakti,* the CPI and the CPI (M) mouthpieces respectively, were hostile to the TDP. *Zamin Ryot*, an influential local paper, was bitterly opposed to the TDP and editorially cautioned 'the politically aware people of AP against the shenanigans of the new party'.[54] The rest of the media was either indifferent or actively critical of the new party. The contribution of *Eenadu* was widely spoken about because of its subsequent emergence as a major media group in the country. The clout of publications such as *Andhra Patrika*, *Andhra Prabha*, *Andhra Bhoomi* and *Andhra Jyothy* got eroded drastically in the following decades.

Eenadu, established in Visakhapatnam in 1974 (the Hyderabad edition started in 1975), was the youngest but widely regarded at this time as the fastest-growing paper with better editorial, managerial and marketing capabilities. It was a conscious decision on the part of the paper's owner, Cherukuri Ramoji Rao, to take a stand in support of the new party. He was a witness to the continued deterioration of AP on all parameters under the iron grip of the Congress high command. For long, Ramoji was disappointed with the ragtag Opposition parties and their inability to take on Indira Gandhi. 'We backed the Opposition parties for a long time, but they were in no position to match her [Indira],' Ramoji told *India Today*.[55]

NTR did not know Ramoji Rao personally till he got into politics. According to Nadendla, Ramoji sent word through a senior journalist, S.N. Sastry, requesting a meeting with NTR soon after the actor announced his party. Nadendla claimed he had advised NTR to meet Ramoji as it would help the party's cause. Daggubati confirmed this meeting. The media baron invited NTR to his house for dinner. Daggubati accompanied NTR to Ramoji's residence at Begumpet, where after the meal, Ramoji and NTR withdrew to a room and spent an hour together.

The essence of the meeting was that Ramoji had once considered floating a regional party, but since NTR had already come up with one, the businessman-turned-media-baron decided to offer his unconditional support. 'I had several discussions with

NTR stretching over a month after he launched Telugu Desam. I was convinced that he was serious. We started backing him since then,' Ramoji said in the same interview. Ramoji Rao's intervention was interpreted by some analysts as the assertion of the local entrepreneurial class, which had come of age, for a say in local decision-making.

The support rendered by *Eenadu* was indeed significant. It helped the rookie party find its feet in the early days by providing extensive coverage to all its activities. The paper acted as a morale booster for the party. NTR was not used to criticism in all his years in the Telugu film industry, where he considered himself a supremo. 'People in the film industry would shudder in his presence. Even producers would not sit in his presence unless he specifically asked them to,' recalled Bhagiratha, a film journalist.[56] He would feel deeply offended when personally targeted.

Another film journalist, B.K. Eswar, reminisced how NTR was once offended by *Vijayachitra*, a respected film magazine from the Vijaya Pictures stable. When approached for an interview, NTR conveyed his displeasure. He was angry at not being referred to as '*garu*'—an expression that marked respect in Telugu—whenever his name was mentioned in its pages. Eswar explained that his fans affectionately called him just NTR, and the magazine was only reflecting this love. NTR was pleased with the explanation.[57]

The actor was thus both sensitive and credulous. Daggubati recalled that in the early days, he would show the positive reports that appeared in *Eenadu* to NTR in the morning so that he would not feel dejected after reading the negative stories that appeared in other publications. The job of *Eenadu* was easy since the paper was promoting an already charismatic and colourful personality who embodied an artistic urge to connect with the people.

Both NTR and Nadendla believed that *Eenadu* was as much a beneficiary of the coverage as the party. Indeed, the paper's popularity soared along with the fortunes of the TDP.

The circulation of the paper jumped from 2.3 lakh in June 1982 to 3.5 lakh by December 1982,[58] making it one of the most widely read newspapers in the state. This was a remarkable increase for a regional newspaper to achieve in six months—a period of high-voltage reporting on NTR's every move and act.

However, the contribution of *Eenadu* was more than just the coverage. The paper, through its vast network, gathered information on local issues and offered inputs to NTR before he visited a place.[59] A newspaper reporter and photographer always accompanied the actor on his campaign trail and provided colourful ground reports day after day. It was through *Eenadu* that pictures of NTR bathing and shaving in public spaces, sleeping outdoors and eating on the roadside became iconic. It was undoubtedly an all-out effort by *Eenadu* to get the man and his message to the last voter in the state.

The growth of media due to technological advancements and its expanding influence coincided with the TDP's mass approach to politics. NTR's entry into politics kindled a new-found interest in the middle class for information and, in a way, helped with the consolidation of *Eenadu* in the market. This was also the first time the relationship between politics and media underwent a dramatic change in AP. The changes that occurred in the media due to *Eenadu* during the emergence of the TDP were pioneering in regional media, according to political scientist G. Krishna Reddy.[60]

Both NTR and Ramoji Rao were from the Kamma caste, and both hailed from Krishna District. However, these two factors had little bearing on Ramoji's decision to unconditionally support NTR. But this rather obvious connection was made much of by some analysts. Political commentator Sambaiah Gundimeda made an elaborate effort to link 'the trajectory of *Eenadu* and its political manoeuvrings in favour of the Kamma-dominated Telugu Desam Party'.[61] But the premise appears overplayed because Ramoji and NTR were fiercely independent personalities with clear-cut objectives of their own, and caste camaraderie was not one of them. Ramoji was looking for an alternative to the Congress. The fact that even before the TDP was born, he 'attempted to convince Vengala Rao to start a new party' indicates that caste was not the guiding factor.[62] From a broader perspective, it could be said that the Kammas, representing the rising mercantile class, came together to resist the economic stagnation the state had suffered due to the Delhi-centric politics.

Ramoji and NTR were self-made men and highly egoistic individuals. They joined hands since their interests converged at this juncture. No conditionality existed between the two, as both wanted to keep their options open. Ramoji did not ask for favours in return for his service, nor did NTR promise anything.[63] NTR acknowledged much later that he had offered the position of chairman, State Planning Board, as well as a Rajya Sabha seat to Ramoji soon after the TDP was elected to power. But the newspaper baron had politely declined the offer.

That each maintained a certain distance even in the early days was clear from the experience narrated by Parvathaneni Upendra, who became a close confidant of NTR in the early years of the party. When Upendra, a public relations officer in Indian Railways, wanted to quit his job and work for the new party, he approached Ramoji for an introduction to NTR. By this time, NTR and Ramoji were in constant touch, exchanging notes on the shape that the party should take. However, Ramoji was reluctant to refer Upendra to NTR. 'He is very independent-minded. I suggest you meet him directly. But I don't think you will be able to stick with him for long,' Ramoji advised him.[64] Despite such a view, the media baron made a considerable contribution to the TDP's sustenance and growth. According to Upendra, most of the publicity material and party literature was also prepared in Ramoji Rao's offices and printed at his presses. Ramoji, however, was clear about his policy from day one. While he published a signed article a day before the election, calling the people of the state to vote for the TDP, he wrote another piece a day after, declaring that the paper had supported the TDP as a historical necessity. He said his newspaper would judge NTR's government, if it were to be elected, with the same standards as any other. Ramoji and *Eenadu* went on to play a crucial role in the subsequent ups and downs the party witnessed, but in a more complex way, unlike the full-throated support it had extended till then.

Colourful Campaign

NTR was far more than a media product. He could create enormous interest for himself and his party on the strength of his own personality. The election campaign in AP completely transformed after NTR's appearance on the political scene. Years of acting had taught him the art of effective communication. Add that to his extreme dedication in reaching out to every village and hamlet across the state. He believed in appealing to the people directly, instead of resorting to vote-gathering through local satraps and caste groups.

NTR abhorred any mediators between him and the common man. He was able to make even an illiterate woman in the far corner of the state believe that she could change her fate through the ballot. He took politics to the threshing points of hapless farmers, the machine wheels of disconsolate workers and the doorsteps of the despairing middle class.

From day one, NTR was meticulous in his plans to take the party forward. After the hugely successful Mahanadu (NTR brought into vogue this archaic Telugu expression which meant a 'great day' on which the general body of the party met) in Tirupati in May 1982,[65] NTR was ready to hit the road. Elections were far away, but he was focused on his goal—to tell people of his mission.

Daggubati recalled how NTR went about preparing for the trail. After the first round of campaigning in Telangana in June

1982, it was found that the open-top jeep was not a convenient
vehicle for a prolonged roadshow. NTR went to the garage at
Ramakrishna Studios and pointed at an old van—a Chevrolet of
1950s vintage. It was apparently one of the many items NTR had
bought when Gemini Studios in Madras had downed shutters.
The van looked like junk, but NTR sent for his mechanic, Allen
in Madras, and gave elaborate instructions on refurbishing it. The
engine and tyres were replaced, and new aluminium panelling was
installed inside. Seats were removed and replaced by bedding, an
aircraft-style chair, a table, and crates of soda and other knick-
knacks. A framed picture of Lord Venkateswara and his consort
Padmavati hung on one side. A sunroof was made so that he could
climb up with the help of a stepladder to the roof of the van during
the roadshows.

A permanent public address system was installed on top of the
van. Four speakers on the four corners of the camper van blared
specially composed as well as remixed old songs that were designed
to arouse nationalist feelings about the Telugu land, its people,
language and culture. Focus lights were installed on the van to
enable NTR to speak even during late evenings. In his theatrical
style, NTR called it Chaitanya Ratham. It became so popular on
the Indian election scene that many other leaders adopted the
mode. Upendra, who accompanied him throughout the campaign,
recalled the first day, when he had to face a tongue-lashing from
NTR for not reporting promptly at 5 a.m. NTR asked Nadendla
to campaign separately. The former Congressman's roadshows
gained little traction though.

It was on Chaitanya Ratham that NTR, attired in khaki pants
and a bush shirt, traversed across the state. The van became his
home during his extensive tours. He never stayed in guest houses
and refused to be entertained in the luxurious homes of fans or
well-wishers. He chose to carry out all his activities—eating,
sleeping or consultations with advisers—on the Ratham. His
morning ablutions were performed in the open, surrounded by

curious onlookers. Food consisted of simple fare, at times only roti and milk, prepared on the roadside by an assistant.

As surging crowds demanded all his time, he often went without food. He slept little and spent all his waking hours giving speeches. His voice became hoarse; his complexion turned dark. From his attire to his demeanour, the blaring songs from his Ratham to his outdoor bathing, the theatrical aspect was obvious. But people saw it differently. No one except NTR, they felt, could have chosen to go through such a rigmarole without any creature comforts. The rather simple mode of transport also enabled him to establish direct contact with people. His experiment saved both time and money. There were no expensive travel arrangements, no entourage, no elaborate lunches and dinners, and no guest houses.

As the booming speakers heralded the imminent arrival of the Ratham into a village or a town, people would run behind the van. Wherever a good number gathered, NTR would emerge out of his van and address them. NTR exhibited the same passion, same histrionics and same intensity for an audience of twenty or two hundred thousand.

NTR had almost no police security during his long and arduous campaign. He had a few people guarding him, most of them drawn from the film world. It was tough for them to control the frenzied crowds pushing towards NTR. Often, it looked like the van would turn turtle as the unruly crowds swarmed to see their matinee idol. He would address on an average fifty meetings in a day. The Chaitanya Ratham would stop for the night only around 1 a.m.

Zealous villagers would put up blockades at several places demanding that NTR address them, even when there was no scheduled stop. 'One wouldn't know whether he was leading the people, or people were leading him,' reminisced Upendra. The schedule always went haywire, as people insisted that NTR visit their village or hamlet. NTR had the habit of straining his vocal cords while speaking even when the gatherings were small.

He would get exhausted after a few speeches but would not rest. 'I would feel bad when I had to wake him from his quick nap to address the next gathering,' Upendra recalled.

Before he kicked off his campaign, NTR came up with the idea to use songs to popularize the cause of the party. He used some popular lyrics and got many new ones written to advance the party's ideology. Lyric writer Kosaraju Raghavaiah Chowdary, music director Chakravarthy and singer S.P. Balasubrahmanyam were involved in the exercise. These culturally evocative songs were specially recorded by NTR in Madras. 'Maa Telugu Talliki Mallepoodanda [A garland of jasmines to Mother Telugu]' was already known but made popular by NTR. 'Cheyyetti Jai Kottu Telugoda [Raise your hands O Telugu, and hail victory]' was originally written by Vemulapalli Srikrishna, an activist-writer of the communist party. The TDP's cassettes, introduced for the first time in a political campaign, became all the rage, with every roadside shop and eatery playing the stirring lyrics on a loop. This was, in fact, the first time in the state that cassettes and tape recorders played an important part in a political campaign. Enthusiastic fans recorded a couple of NTR's speeches during his roadshows, and copies of these cassettes later became much sought after across the state.

NTR introduced his own idiom into the political speeches that delighted the general public. His forte was combining classical Sanskrit expressions with colloquial, idiomatic Telugu phrases. 'Has the sky leaked, or the earth opened up!' he would exclaim at the teeming crowds. 'Aaru kotla andhrulu atma gouravam [The self-respect of six-crore Telugus]' was by now the most familiar of his phrases. His favourite was 'Samajame devalayam, prajale devullu [The society is the temple, and the public is the god]'.

NTR's campaign is considered phenomenal to this day because of the unprecedented euphoria it triggered among the people. His electioneering was exhaustive in terms of the kilometres logged,

NTR was the first politician in AP to have traversed the length and breadth of the state without the usual paraphernalia that accompanied political campaigns. He washed, bathed and shaved on the roadside during his roadshows.

Photographs courtesy of C. Kesavulu, *Eenadu*

the number of speeches delivered, and the massive response it generated everywhere. The campaign was carried out in several phases in June–July, August–September and October–November 1982, and from 16 December to 3 January 1983. It was a single-minded pursuit, with NTR barely sleeping three–four hours a day, especially during the last phase.

His Chaitanya Ratham trundled along the lush green fields of coastal Andhra, the rocky terrain of Rayalaseema and the dry landscape of Telangana, covering a massive 35,000 km. At a time when there were no mobile phones or televisions, let alone social media, NTR's message reached the remotest parts of AP. NTR would run hours and even days behind schedule, but people would wait patiently. They could be seen inquiring from occupants of passing vehicles about the status of the Ratham. The silhouette of NTR standing atop the moving Ratham, waving to the people, would send the crowds into a frenzy. Suman Dubey, the journalist who later became a press adviser to Prime Minister Rajiv Gandhi, wrote about NTR's roadshow:

> The effect is electric. From nowhere the crowds begin to pour on to the roads. Faces, of men, women and children of all ages, light up as recognition dawns. The coach keeps moving to the venue of the public meeting, and soon it is surrounded by a flowing river of people, running along pell-mell, stretching far behind and ahead of the coach.[66]

With his acerbic comments against the Congress misrule, his evocative call to restore the glory of Telugu language and culture, and his impassioned plea to give him a chance to transform the state's fortunes, NTR held sway over large swathes of the populace. Years of film acting have left an indelible mark on the man. In gesture or body language, NTR is an accomplished performer. Whether it is the flick of a hand or a turn of his shoulders to emphasise a point, the practised skill is evident,' described Suman Dubey in his first-hand account of the campaign.

NTR's dedication to his film craft was well known. He brought the same discipline and commitment to his political pursuit. The inclement weather, the potholed roads and the inconveniences of the rickety coach failed to dampen his spirits. NTR was so engrossed with party affairs that he missed the weddings of two of his sons, which were celebrated at the height of the campaign. His sons Balakrishna and Ramakrishna got married to Vasundhara and Jayasri, respectively, in Tirupati on 8 August 1982 in the absence of NTR.

Some used words such as 'performance' and 'cheap theatrics' to describe NTR's exaggerated gestures and dramatically delivered speeches, but they struck an emotional chord in the audience nevertheless. His unabashed indulgence of the masses was in sharp

Photograph courtesy of C. Kesavulu, Eenadu

This is an iconic image of NTR's historic campaign in 1982. The thespian visited every nook and corner of AP on his Chaitanya Ratham, a refurbished van of 1950s vintage, creating euphoria among the masses.

contrast with the regular politicians, who operated far from the madding crowds. His filmy persona was already known; he now conveyed his own distinct political persona.

The campaign turned out to be a people's revolution that swept away the Telugus. It was an edifying spectacle of democracy to watch a budding leader receive extraordinary warmth and love from the masses. *India Today* called NTR's campaign 'a one-man show'. It also noted his scintillating effect on the people: 'There is something powerfully dramatic about the way he is going about his quest for political power.' A host of local, national and international mediapersons intercepted the Ratham on the whirlwind tour to meet NTR and see for themselves the crazed following. Though they were not sure of the outcome, every reporter and observer could feel the political tremors being triggered by NTR's juggernaut.

There were no indications at this stage that NTR's two sons-in-law, Daggubati Venkateswara Rao and Nara Chandrababu Naidu, would go on to play a crucial role in the party's future course. Of these, Daggubati was with NTR from the start. But Chandrababu was already in politics and showed promise in his ability to manage the Congress group politics. Daggubati, married to NTR's daughter Purandeswari, had just completed his medical course in Madras. Chandrababu had already advanced in the Congress ranks to become a junior minister. Daggubati hailed from a wealthy agricultural family from the relatively prosperous coastal Andhra, unlike Chandrababu who began his career from humble origins in Chittoor District located in the arid Rayalaseema region. Daggubati was a politically naive idealist who was drawn to NTR's political foray more as personal help to his father-in-law. Jasti Chelameswar, then a young lawyer, who later rose to be a judge of the Supreme Court of India, was one of those attracted to the new party and worked alongside Daggubati from the early days. During the 1982 campaign, Chelameswar coordinated Maneka Gandhi's meetings in AP as the TDP's representative.[67]

He played a key role subsequently too when the party split in 1984 and later in 1995.

Daggubati was keenly involved in organizational matters, especially interacting with the innumerable people who started visiting Ramakrishna Studios. While he threw himself full-time into the party's work, NTR did not give him any special treatment. Daggubati would get easily offended and leave Hyderabad in a huff over minor disagreements. In one instance, he wanted the Congress MLAs who had joined the party along with Nadendla to be stripped of their positions because of their reported immoral activities. When NTR did not immediately respond, he left the campaign halfway, only to return much later.[68]

The case of Chandrababu Naidu was more complicated. His marriage into NTR's family was unexpected even for Chandrababu, given the disparity in the social and economic standing between the two families. The fact that he had become the minister of cinematography at a young age had impressed NTR's family. Chandrababu was elected to the AP assembly for the first time in 1978 from his native Chandragiri on a Congress (I) ticket. That was the time when seasoned Congress leaders everywhere had deserted Indira Gandhi. Nadendla, who was the Congress (I) general secretary, claimed he vetted the reference provided by P. Rajagopala Naidu, a senior political leader of Chittoor District, for Chandrababu's candidature. He won the seat and was able to make his way into the 'jumbo-jet' cabinet of T. Anjaiah. According to journalist I. Venkata Rao, NTR had used his good offices a couple of times to save his son-in-law from the Congress group politics. The young politician was just getting a hold in a party dominated by old war horses.

It was at this time, when Chandrababu was consolidating his place in the Congress (I), that NTR floated his party. There was no evidence that NTR had discussed his political plans with his son-in-law. Both seemed to have maintained a distance on this issue in the early days. This was apparently to avoid causing Chandrababu discomfiture in his own party. NTR was not willing to spoil his son-in-law's political career in the Congress (I) by getting him involved in his new experiment. Chandrababu too was unsure of NTR's ability to breach the Congress citadel and succeed in establishing a government. Venkata Rao claimed that Chandrababu was involved in the forming of the TDP though he was behind the scenes for obvious reasons. He even claimed that Chandrababu gave advice to NTR from time to time on various issues after the party was launched.[69] It was on Chandrababu's suggestion, according to Venkata Rao, that NTR agreed to give five seats to Sanjay Vichar Manch, a new outfit. However, Goné Prakash Rao, who subsequently got elected as MLA on a Manch ticket, recalled that it was mainly Nadendla's calculation and Ramoji's support to the tie-up that clinched the deal.

Daggubati had an entirely different story to tell about Chandrababu's attitude during this period. He went to Chandrababu's Banjara Hills residence immediately after the first public meeting of the party in Hyderabad. Daggubati says he wanted to convince his co-brother (*thodalludu* in Telugu) to join hands with NTR. He proposed that he should shoulder the responsibility of organizing the proposed Mahanadu, the party's first plenary, at Tirupati, which was in Chandrababu's native district. 'The party is going well. It has a great future. Now is the time for you to take over some of the organizational matters. Unlike us, you have experience in politics. The party needs experienced people like you. I am not very much interested in politics. You may have to sacrifice a little now, but you will be handsomely rewarded later if you take up reins now,' Daggubati reasoned with him.[70]

But an astute Chandrababu was not impressed. He took out a paper and scribbled some calculations. 'No, the party will not get more than 5 per cent votes. You know he [NTR] doesn't spend one rupee from his pocket. I don't think cine glamour will get him any votes. The party will disappear after the elections. I am now a minister in the Congress government. How can I leave all this and go with him?' Chandrababu retorted.

Left with no other alternative, Daggubati approached Veera Raghavulu Naidu in Tirupati, who was the chairman of the Rayalaseema Development Board in the Congress government. He responded positively, resigned from the Congress and joined hands with the TDP, helping with the arrangements for the meeting. Daggubati made another attempt to bring Chandrababu in after the Tirupati Mahanadu. He drove down to the minister's residence, and even as he was waiting for Chandrababu, the minister's personal assistant handed him the evening edition of *Andhra Patrika*.

The paper carried a statement that Chandrababu had made against his father-in-law. 'I am ready to contest against my father-in-law if the high command says so.' He had also dismissed, according to the report, NTR's party as a short-lived phenomenon, which would soon evaporate in the Indira wave. 'I saw that there was nothing I could do to prevail upon him and left without saying a word,' Daggubati recalled.[71]

Clearly, Chandrababu failed to see the impact that the new party would create at the ballot box. He was not willing to experiment with his political career. However, he had to face his share of hostility from his colleagues in the Congress because of his relationship with NTR. His loyalty became suspect; and to prove his credentials, the mild-mannered Chandrababu had to challenge his father-in-law to an electoral duel. But towards the fag end of the elections, he could sense that the public mood was clearly favourable to NTR. It was too late for the ambitious son-in-law to make amends. With his calculations gone awry, Chandrababu had to lie low for a while after the polls. Daggubati was on the right side at the moment. But not for very long, as things would take a favourable turn slowly but surely for the shrewd Chandrababu.

The Setting

NTR's quick upswing in AP politics was made possible by a variety of factors. Commissions and omissions of the Congress leadership

in Delhi were a significant part of them. NTR's foray came at a
time when the ruling Congress party and its government in the
state hit the nadir on every parameter. Groupism and infighting
were the order of the day. One group was always conspiring
against the other, feeding negative information to the back-room
operators in Delhi. At any given point of time, MLAs stationed
themselves in Delhi to lobby for or against a party leader. The
state Congress president had to issue a circular, asking the party
MLAs to not visit Delhi without the chief minister's knowledge.

The incumbent chief minister's primary job became to protect
his turf from the constant onslaught of the dissident activity.
Dissidence was actively encouraged by the party high command in
a bid to make sure that no single leader at the state level became
politically entrenched. In a messy attempt at placating the rival
camp, Anjaiah created the largest state cabinet ever, with sixty-
one ministers, which was humorously referred to as the 'jumbo-
jet' or 'airbus' cabinet. The joke was that when a legislator, Divi
Kondaiah Chowdary, met the chief minister on one occasion,
Anjaiah apologized to him for not being able to accommodate
him in the cabinet. 'But I am your minister, sir!' an embarrassed
Chowdary had to remind him.

There was no coherence either in the administration or in the
party. A cynical Indira Gandhi and her back-room boys in Delhi
played around nonchalantly with AP. The standard operating
procedure for the high command was to see that every state leader
was dispensable. Not one chief minister could consolidate his
position, even as the party leadership actively encouraged groups.
For example, Anjaiah was replaced, according to M.L. Fotedar,
the political adviser to Indira Gandhi, because P.V. Narasimha
Rao did not like him.[72]

Four chief ministers in less than five years turned the state
into a stage for a political circus. During 1980–82 alone, three
chief ministers—T. Anjaiah, Bhavanam Venkataram and
K. Vijayabhaskara Reddy—were installed in a cynical display

of brute power by the Congress leadership. In Telugu Puranic stage plays, a single character was played by more than one actor. Likewise, the chief ministers, who came and went in succession, came to be satirically called *Rendo Krishnudu, Moodo Krishnudu* (the second Krishna and the third Krishna). The state Congress leadership was in abject surrender to the high command. The state administration, as well as the party, was in a shambles. As a result, the economic and social indicators of AP lagged in every aspect. The state fell sharply on the development index by national standards. The growth of the state stagnated at an annual rate of 2.11 and 3.01 per cent in the 1960s and 1970s, slower than the national average. The literacy rate was a low 30 per cent. The per capita income was below the national average.[73]

The decadence was visible all around, but Indira's poverty alleviation measures, especially for SCs and STs, would probably have sustained her political grist a little longer. An emotive issue was required to kindle a spark against the existing set-up.

A most telling episode occurred during Anjaiah's period. This incident, otherwise an innocent goof-up, helped expose the haughtiness of the Delhi dynasty and rubbed salt in the public wound.

Rajiv Gandhi, the All India Congress Committee (AICC) (I) general secretary, was visiting Hyderabad. The chief minister was Anjaiah, whose elevation in place of the strongman Marri Channa Reddy had seemed mysterious to the party members. Since the rather unsophisticated and guileless Anjaiah owed his luck to the dynasty, he wanted to give a typical Congress welcome to the heir. Rajiv was officially an MP. Congress activists turned up in large numbers with garlands, banners, drums and other usual paraphernalia at Begumpet Airport. The chief minister himself was leading the rather unwieldy troupe, consisting of boisterous party workers, folk dancers and singers. They were all over the tarmac where the plane was to halt. There was also a big police contingent in tow. As Rajiv stepped out, he was aghast at the noisy and rambunctious welcome. Congress workers milled around him, raising slogans of *zindabad* even as they pushed one another to garland him.

Rajiv's face turned red at the cacophony. 'What is this nonsense? Is somebody's wedding happening here? This is unbecoming, I am going back to Delhi,' Rajiv, unable to control his anger, screamed at Anjaiah. The petrified chief minister was apologetic and, along with Union Minister P. Shiv Shankar, tried to pacify him. After much pleading, Rajiv accepted the garland but refused to formally release the caged doves into the sky to symbolize Indira's twenty-point programme. He took his special flight to Tirupati but told Anjaiah to not accompany him. But the prince-in-waiting allowed Shiv Shankar and other ministers to go with him on the flight.

Anjaiah was a staunch loyalist and timid chief minister, but even he could not stomach the public humiliation. He was almost in tears at the public shame. When the incident was widely reported in the media, the public were aghast at the temerity of the Delhi leader.[74] Anjaiah was subsequently removed as chief minister by the high command, further illustrating the *durbari* (court) culture.[75] This incident was fresh in the minds of the public when NTR, barely forty days later, spoke of 'Telugu self-respect' being trampled upon by Delhi.

One cannot blame Rajiv or Anjaiah for the farcical incident. It was the result of years of servility encouraged within the Congress ecosystem. Rajiv was still an outsider to the Congress political culture. For someone who was a professional pilot for a long time, the sight of unruly crowds dancing on the airport tarmac irritated him. He was not yet used to the crude displays of loyalty and devotion embedded in the Congress culture. Rajiv's exasperation could have been unfathomable for Anjaiah. The unfortunate incident was perceived by the already piqued public as a reflection of the Congress's deep disdain for the people of the state.

Meanwhile, Bhavanam Venkataram, installed in Anjaiah's place, was replaced after barely six months in office as he was considered feeble in containing NTR's onslaught. Veteran Congressman Kotla Vijayabhaskara Reddy, who was an MP and Central minister at this time, was brought in to retrieve lost ground.

This was the third time that a chief minister was not a member of the State Assembly. With his experience and political background, the blue-blooded Congressman was expected to take on the looming threat posed by the TDP. He had less than four months to do the job.[76] Kotla tried to dilute NTR's impact by implementing the TDP's scheme of providing rice at Rs 2 per kg.[77] The scheme was hurriedly rolled out in a few parts of the state. This was after Finance Minister Kona Prabhakara Rao released a white paper, arguing that it was impossible to do so. Despite such measures, the wind was blowing in the opposite direction. Less than five months after NTR launched his campaign, journalist S. Venkat Narayan, who covered NTR's roadshows, could feel the impact. 'Barring a miracle, in the next five months, AP appears set to become the second state in India after Tamil Nadu to vote a film star to power,' he declared.[78]

Even as Kotla was trying to get his act together, the party high command got nervous with the rising profile of the TDP. Against the advice of her own chief minister, Indira Gandhi chose to advance the date for the AP State Assembly elections, along with those for Karnataka and Tripura, to 5 January 1983, at least two months ahead of the regular schedule. The Congress leadership assessed that if given more time, the new party could spread its influence in the state. Early polls were expected to throw the TDP into confusion.

But it was the Congress that was not ready for the election. On hearing the announcement of polls, NTR, who was on tour in Adilabad, rushed back to Hyderabad and began the exercise for selection of candidates, along with Upendra and Ramoji. Candidates were selected by merit and character. There were many fresh faces with no political connections. Educated young professionals got preference. Gali Muddu Krishnama Naidu, who was a lecturer in a college, got a ticket based on his application. An educated Backward Caste youth, Chimata Sambu, was nominated likewise. K. Pratibha Bharati, daughter of a high court judge, was picked up after she actively participated in NTR's campaign in Srikakulam. P. Indra Reddy was selected for his role as a student leader at Osmania University. G.M.C. Balayogi, a Scheduled Caste youth (who later became the Lok Sabha speaker), was picked up as he was a law student.

The selection of candidates was not the only concern before him. Among the many challenges thrown at the party was a petition in the AP High Court opposing allotment of an election symbol to the TDP. The petitioner, V.R. Sreerama Rao, who called himself the president of the Sarvodaya Congress Party, argued that the new party should be denied an election symbol because of its 'promotion of chauvinism, propagation of sectarian ideas'. The petitioner claimed that 'granting of an election symbol to the Telugu Desam would be contrary to the letter and spirit of the sixteenth constitutional amendment act'.[79] In this regard, he referred to NTR's very first public speech 'appealing to the majority linguistic group of the state'. P.A. Chowdary was the judge before whom the case came up. He was well known among the legal fraternity for his judicial activism. Before concluding that 'the petitioner's opposition to the grant of an election symbol to the Telugu Desam cannot be supported on principle or authority or history', Justice Chowdary launched into a harangue on Telugu history and culture:

> Their [Telugus] history of sacrifice in the cause of the country's freedom is not easily excelled in this country. Their language is one of the treasures of the Indian literary history preaching patriotism and social responsibility. The praise of such settled and ancient institutions is not likely to lead the Telugus astray, nor to any disturbance of an ancient nation's basic equilibrium.[80]

The judge unequivocally rejected the contention that appealing to Telugu culture and identity was tantamount to sectarianism.

'Any movement, even a political movement for the revival of love for such an ancient and hallowed language cannot, even applying the narrowest of standards of a bigoted vision, be adjudged as sectarian or secessionist,' he said. He then dealt with the issue of making election appeals based on language. The judge ruled that the clause, however, could not be an impediment to the right to conserve language. The provision applied only to 'such language appeals that endanger the integrity of the nation'. In the judgment, Justice Chowdary, giving great latitude for political parties in the course of their work for social and political change, declared:

> It must therefore follow that Telugu Desam cannot be denied an election symbol by the election commission even if the aims and objectives of the Telugu Desam are in conflict with any existing part of the Constitution or the existing law because any political party should have a legitimate right and chance to appeal to the voters to vote to amend or even to abrogate those parts of the laws and the Constitution.[81]

The judgment remains a great validation of the constitutional as well as the political justification of regional political parties in India.

The legal hurdle was removed quickly. But the charge that NTR's evocation of linguistic identity and pledge for the restoration of the glorious past—imagined or real—of the Telugus amounted to secession was raised many a time by political adversaries, especially the Congress (I). However, such an attack failed to elicit any response from the public as NTR himself was clear about his views. While he promised to bring glory to Telugu language and culture, he never spoke ill of other languages and cultures. He was very open to other communities and affirmed that the culture and lifestyle of minorities would be protected and respected.

As an actor much removed from the gritty realities around him, NTR attracted ridicule for his lack of knowledge about the world of politics. Nadendla claimed that he was aghast at times at NTR's ignorance of political affairs. NTR did not even know what the Left or the Right meant in political terms, and took these words literally, said Nadendla. However, NTR turned out to be a quick learner. He displayed an instinctive understanding of the politics on the ground. During an informal interaction with the media in Krishna District, as part of his campaign, NTR analysed the attitudes of the different sections of the electorate as he understood them:

> The rich extend its support to whoever is in power. The upper middle class, though not happy with the dispensation, does not come out openly because it must get going. Hence, this class will be friendly with TDP too. The middle class is looking for a change and is solidly behind TDP. The poor are desperate for a new beginning and pinning all their hopes on TDP. The students, along with women, have become emotionally connected to the party. The young children are so taken up with TDP, I don't know why . . .[82]

NTR's understanding of the political situation was not far off the mark. Though the Opposition parties in AP never made it in the elections, they always commanded a sizeable vote bank. It was the communists who challenged the Congress party's claim to power in the early decades. The Janata, Lok Dal and even the old Congress, then called Congress (R), attracted respectable support in consecutive elections. In the 1978 assembly polls, the Janata Party won a tidy sixty seats, while the old Congress managed to secure thirty. Before that, in the 1977 Lok Sabha polls, the Janata Party garnered 35 per cent of the votes polled, though it could manage to win only the Nandyal seat.

The non-Congress vote, which was substantial, was waiting to be consolidated in AP. With the credible challenge offered by

NTR, most of these sections turned to the TDP as a real alternative. NTR could sense this shift during his campaign, and this was the reason he was hesitant to give away the lion's share of the seats to these parties under the alliance. NTR's recent political acumen was also evident in his assessment of the relative strengths of the other parties. His reading was that the support base of non-Congress parties such as the Janata, Lok Dal and the former Swatantra Party had shifted in favour of the TDP. But the communist pockets of influence were intact. This was why he was prepared to negotiate with the Left even at the last moment. However, when the communists unilaterally declared their candidates for seventy seats even before the alliance was finalized, NTR decided to do it alone.

NTR was also intuitive in projecting himself as a leader with a difference. At a time when promises were not taken seriously by politicians, and cynical pursuit of power was the order of the day, he was able to convey that he was a man of his word. The first test to his credibility came over defections. Three MLAs, M. Adaiah, G.V. Rathaiah and C. Narayana, had joined hands with NTR along with Nadendla. The three continued to hold their positions despite the party's stand that they should leave their seats in the assembly. They failed to honour the party's principle, and, as a result, NTR expelled them. Later, senior politicians like Nallapareddy Srinivasulu Reddy and Ashok Gajapathi Raju resigned as MLAs before joining the TDP. NTR's stance cemented his image as a stickler for norms.

NTR did not have any bookish knowledge of politics. But the way he hit upon the plank of Telugu self-respect and articulated it was undoubtedly a stroke of native genius. 'Atma Gouravam' was not a mere slogan for NTR. He was able to expound it with an emotional fervour and linguistic felicity. This was rare in AP political campaigns. The Telugu diction that he employed to demonstrate the concept of self-respect also played a significant part in taking his message effectively to the masses. He adopted a pseudo-classical style of language for conveying the sense of hurt caused to Telugus because of the Centre's inept handling of local affairs.

Even while making evocative speeches about Telugu cultural nationalism, NTR came up with a string of promises that strengthened the party's image as a 'party of the poor'. The most important of these was the 'Rs 2 per kg' rice scheme. 'When NT Rama Rao promised rice at Rs 2 per kg in 1982, it was greeted with derision by the Congress party,' recalled K.R. Venugopal, a respected civil servant, who successfully implemented the scheme later as the commissioner of civil supplies.[83]

The TDP manifesto was not a hotchpotch document pandering to the regional sentiments, but rather a well-thought-out charter of serious intent on a range of issues. The very first sentence reflected the party's ambition to emerge as a real alternative to the status quo: 'Telugu Desam, if voted to power, will remove lock, stock and barrel, the discredited culture created by the Congress (I) and provide a clean and efficient administration.'[84]

The party's manifesto had several important policy initiatives, including remunerative prices for farmers' produce, minimum wages for agricultural labour and industrial workers, more powers to panchayats (village bodies), priority to housing, a midday meal scheme in primary schools, streamlining of law and order, fast completion of irrigation projects, no political interference in day-to-day administration and stringent action against corrupt practices.

Women were particularly attracted by the TDP's promise of equal rights for them in ancestral property and the establishment of a women's university. Freedom of the press, autonomy for radio and television, and judicial independence were announced as its principles. Electoral reforms, including a ban on defections, were demanded. The manifesto also proposed that the Election Commission bear all the expenses of conducting elections, including those of political parties. Another significant promise was to observe secularism in letter and spirit and make sure minority rights were protected. On Centre–state relations, the TDP manifesto was more radical:

> Telugu Desam will work according to the spirit of the federal character of the Constitution which ensures greater autonomy to the States. Only defence, foreign affairs, currency and communications should be under the purview of the Central Government.

Underlining its belief that Centre–state relations were interdependent and that a strong Centre emerged only when states enjoyed more powers, the TDP manifesto proposed a relook at the federal structure. 'TDP, after coming to power, would set up a high-powered committee to go into the question of Centre–State relations, including clear demarcation of powers and to suggest necessary constitutional amendments, if necessary,' it said. While demanding more autonomy for the states, the TDP was strongly in favour of national unity. 'Even while opposing the dictatorial tendencies of Congress (I), the TDP, if voted to power, will work in coordination with any party in power at the Centre,' NTR announced.

Despite the outcry raised against the TDP's allegedly provocative Telugu nationalism, the party manifesto contained only two references to regional aspirations. Under 'Pride of Place to the Telugu Language', the manifesto promised to make it the official language right up to secretariat level and medium of instruction at the university level. While promising to work for the enrichment of the Telugu language, the party manifesto mentioned that the TDP would encourage and protect the language and culture of people from other states as well. The only other reference to Telugu culture was this:

> It [the party] is determined to uphold the honour and prestige of the Telugu people and to revive the glory of their proud heritage.

Despite such political content in NTR's campaign, many commentators still belittled the TDP's political programme, giving more emphasis to the emotive nature of his speeches. Juergen Neuss, for example, concluded that 'Telugu Desham (sic) hardly had any political programme worth mentioning'.[85]

Reel or Real God?

Any reference to NTR's astonishing foray into politics is always followed by the observation that his entry was made easier because the masses regarded him as a god as he had played those characters on the screen. Such characterization is belittling to both NTR's illustrious career and the audience that patronized him for decades.

NTR's long film career certainly gave him a head start in the political battlefield.[86] But to attribute his victorious entry into politics to his filmi aura would be an overstatement. That the masses voted for him because he played god in his films and hence they regarded him as Lord Krishna's avatar is the most banal understanding of a prominent political event that changed the course of history in AP. NTR was undoubtedly the most known face to Telugus and enjoyed a cultural and linguistic bond with the people over an extended period. But it was not merely cinema that defined his political character.

It is true that NTR excelled in playing a host of godly characters from the Hindu pantheon such as Lord Krishna and Lord Rama, and heroic personalities such as Arjuna, Bhishma and Bhima. But it is important to mention that he also played with artistry a number of negative characters in the Hindu epics, including Ravana, Duryodhana, Kichaka and Karna. In fact, NTR, inspired by the Dravidian philosophy of questioning existing narratives, made several films that portrayed Ravana, Duryodhana and Karna in a positive light.[87] *Daana Veera Soora Karna* (1977), the most successful mythological film produced and directed by NTR, portrayed Duryodhana as a radical who questioned the caste structure. The film even showed Lord Krishna in a negative shade through his attitude towards Karna. All three characters were incidentally played by NTR.

Generations of Telugu audiences indeed were mesmerized by the way NTR perfected the role of Krishna, showing the god as human and divine simultaneously.[88] NTR's Krishna was mystical but playful, romantic now, esoteric the next, earthy and angelic alternatively. Unflappable always, he maintained a beautiful poise that was both charming and celestial. NTR combined the masculine and the feminine of the character in an endearing way. He was probably the most handsome Krishna ever seen on-screen, who also had the right amount of gravitas to give the character depth. His utterances as a divine being were measured but spoken with warmth and grace. There was a certain amount of stylization in his depiction of Krishna. It was understated, restrained and conveyed a transcendental experience.

Whether he was romancing Satyabhama, teasing the Pandavas or censuring the Kauravas, NTR's Krishna retained the divine aura. The best of directors, writers, cinematographers and supporting cast helped NTR 'kill' the role in film after film. His own discipline and dedication when playing these roles were legendary. Though a foodie, he did not touch meat during the shooting of such films.[89] He slept on the floor and rarely indulged in small talk. His costumes and jewellery, many of which he would help design, weighed many kilos during the prolonged shoots.[90] He would patiently sit through hours of make-up to get the right look.[91] He was also an amateur sketch artist, and came up with the look of many of the Puranic characters. Egged on by eminent directors like K.V. Reddy and Kamalakara Kameswara Rao, he practised every move, every gesture, every expression and every turn of phrase for hours. Such devotion helped him confer these mythological characters with a recognizable persona.[92]

NTR carved a niche for himself as Lord Krishna in *Maya Bazaar* (1957); Ravana in *Bhookailas* (1958); Lord Venkateswara in

Sri Venkateswara Mahatyam (1960); Bhishma in *Bhishma* (1962); Rama in *Lava Kusa* (1963); Valmiki in *Valmiki* (1963); Arjuna/ Brihannala in *Narthanasala* (1963); Bhima in *Pandava Vanavasam* (1965); and Duryodhana in *Sri Krishna Pandaveeyam* (1966). His versatility became especially evident in essaying diametrically opposite characters such as Rama and Ravana, or Krishna and Duryodhana, sometimes in the same film. As he gained the confidence of the audience, NTR went on to play two, three, four and even five Puranic roles in the same film.[93]

His ability to define each Puranic character distinctly and elevate them to a level unseen on the Telugu screen was widely recognized and appreciated even by the unlettered viewer. He had a talent for memorizing long-winded, alliterative and declamatory monologues, and modulating them with excellent voice control and pitch. While earlier actors continued with the stage performance style of the portrayal of gods and mythical personalities in motion pictures, NTR came up with more refined and nuanced presentation. He experimented with storytelling, characterization, the idiom of language and the technique of presentation in his films. He produced, directed and wrote some of his mythological movies. He would get greatly excited by any new perspective on mythological stories and continuously update himself on the nuances of these tales. Over time, his expertise in interpreting mythological stories and characters on-screen was acknowledged.

Every one of his movies on Lord Krishna remains a classic in Telugu cinema. The much-acclaimed *Maya Bazaar* was his first full-length portrayal of Lord Krishna. After that, he essayed the role seventeen times, leaving a lasting impression on the viewers.[94] Calendar art of NTR as Lord Krishna was much sought after from the 1960s in AP.[95] If Ravi Varma's art gave the Hindu gods their most recognizable form, NTR's rendering of these avatars—mainly Krishna and Rama—appealed to the Telugu sensibility. As a result, NTR's interpretation of divine beings became the gold standard of Telugu mythological films.

But the man himself was not worshipped as a god. It is true that the Telugu pilgrims to Tirupati made a detour to Madras to meet and greet NTR. This was especially after he played the role of Lord Venkateswara, an avatar of Vishnu in the film *Sri Venkateswara Mahatyam* (1960).

But to conclude that the credulous audience regarded him as the very god would be a stretch. Film critic Chidananda Das Gupta was convinced that the unlettered people of AP mistook NTR for his screen roles. 'Early in the morning, a crowd would assemble before his house every day, crying, 'Devudu! Devudu!' [God! God!] when he appeared on the balcony,' he wrote rather incredulously.[96] Das Gupta also affirmed that when NTR stood for elections, women washed the roads along which he travelled. Such a thing was never reported in the media. Based on such

NTR's portrayal of Lord Krishna left a deep impact on generations of Telugu audiences. The picture above is a popular artistic impression created by film artist Eswar.

faulty assumptions, the film critic said that the illiterate people of AP were hoodwinked by his screen renditions.

According to him, only in states like Kerala and West Bengal 'does the cinema audience have a ready ability to separate myth from fact'.[97] Nothing could be more condescending because in Indian democratic experience, voting patterns time and again proved that the rural masses were more clued into political realities than the urban citizenry. The NTR phenomenon—as far as his mythological films were concerned—was like fans considering Sachin Tendulkar a cricketing god. The audience bowed to NTR's genius. There was absolutely no evidence that he was considered divine by even the most illiterate of his fans.

Besides, the mythological characters, divine or otherwise, have had nothing to do with Telugu nationalism per se. In fact, they are all pan-Indian stories with little local bearing. Then how did the mythological movies help NTR in establishing the political connection so quickly?

It was partly due to 'the genius of Telugu mythological films' that embodied Telugu culture by drawing heavily from the state's social and cultural milieu. These films recreated the Puranic world in a formal and ceremonial language that made them a quintessential Telugu experience. According to researcher T. Vishnu Vardhan, after *Maya Bazaar*, the films started using high-sounding Telugu—*grandhika bhasha*—which became the hallmark of the genre.[98] NTR displayed mastery over such Telugu, which was 'both timeless and distinctive, facilitating the identification between the genre and classical Telugu'. It is this mastery, according to Vishnu Vardhan, that allowed NTR 'to stake a unique claim over embodying Teluguness'. So, NTR carried over the linguistic identity of these films into his political campaign, and not his divinity. It was the literary, formal and slightly archaic nature of his political speeches that prompted critics to dub him 'Drama Rao'.

The mythological films offered a certain linguistic pleasure to the Telugu audience through their carefully constructed artifice woven around the dialogues and monologues that became popular in their own right. S.V. Srinivas, in his scholarly work *Politics as Performance*, says, 'The voice modulations, rhythms, and cadences of the utterance, the awesome ability of the actor to fluently speak interminable lines and impossibly difficult words are sources of spectatorial pleasure.'[99] It is through the use of this distinctive Telugu—replicated from the movies to the political arena—that the electorate was reminded of NTR's association with the cinema, according to Srinivas. Besides, mythological cinema had pride of place as a cultural achievement for the Telugu viewer. And by association, NTR's role in this achievement made him a saviour of the Telugu nation.

But NTR was not known only for his mythological films. From 1949 to 1993, he acted in only about forty films that were based on Hindu mythology. His repertoire was larger. He acted in fifty-two folk films, starting with the iconic *Pathala Bhairavi* in 1951. Many of the folk films showcased him as the swashbuckling knight in armour. His 'social' movies—a body of work larger than his mythological films—cemented virtue signalling in his character. Because of his portrayal as a rebel in folk films and his characterization as a simple, rustic but righteous protagonist in many of the social films, NTR emerged as the first mass hero of Telugu cinema. His filmi persona was unlike that of his counterpart ANR, who enjoyed an urban and female following due to his sensitive, educated lover-boy image in films. With cinema being the only popular means of entertainment, NTR's film persona became a part of the Telugu cultural consciousness. NTR was so popular by the 1960s that in one year, as many as sixteen of his films were released, which meant he was never out of public memory. Besides the Padma Shri, several pompous-sounding titles were bestowed on him by fawning cultural associations, such as 'Nata Ratna', 'Kala Prapoorna' and the mouthful 'Viswa Vikhyatha Nata Sarvabhowma'.

From the late 1970s onwards, Telugu films became formula-driven and more geared towards the frontbenchers, even as

Image courtesy of K. Eswar

Contrary to the myth that NTR was popular for playing godly characters, the actor was equally famous for essaying negative roles like those of Duryodhana and Ravana. The picture above is artist Eswar's rendering of NTR's Duryodhana.

the calibre of the technicians, especially directors and writers, witnessed a steep fall. NTR too fell into the trap. He, along with ANR, wore outlandish costumes and wigs and resorted to 'dance steps' with heroines half his age. Such films, though, were panned by the critics for being outrageously puerile. 'Rama Rao garu, stop making such horrible films,' screamed a review of *Rowdy Ramudu, Konte Krishnudu* (1980) in *Zamin Ryot*.[100]

NTR, however, was happy being commercially relevant in the industry, charging Rs 10–15 lakh per film.[101] He gradually turned into an over-the-top, highly strung hero with exaggerated gestures fighting societal ills. These stentorian characters, played with melodramatic bluster by an ageing NTR, did command a considerable following among the masses. During this time, he was playing dual roles in such movies. The other character usually was a young man with heavy greasepaint, prancing around youthful heroines like Sridevi. Just seven years earlier, she had acted as his granddaughter.

NTR was aware of the absurdity of such films but justified them by saying he was a commercial artiste and had to go by the taste of the new generation. Despite the box office success, there was crudity about these films. After 1975, directors such as Raghavendra Rao and Dasari Narayana Rao made films with NTR that were loud, cheesy and raunchy on every parameter. Many of them, such as *Sardar Papa Rayudu* (1980), *Kondaveeti Simham* (1981), *Justice Chowdhary* (1982) and *Bobbili Puli* (1982), were melodramatic attempts at evoking the legacy of the star that NTR was. These films used this star power to further glorify him as a figure of authority as he fought against the system. But the order that the hero fought against was not located in specific Telugu social, cultural or political context. If anything, more than the people, NTR himself was influenced by his own characters. 'The patriotic flavour in *Sardar Papa Rayudu* set me thinking about politics,' NTR said in an interview to *Andhra Prabha*.[102]

In an interesting analysis, S.V. Srinivas elaborated how NTR's films during the late 1970s, which he called 'campaign' films since they carried a certain amount of political messaging, did not actually have any affinity with either 'Teluguness' or the Telugu language. These films were not particularly located in an identifiable regional setting, or dealt with issues that were local in nature. Srinivas referred to 'the absence of overt reference to language and linguistic identity in NTR's career' and underlined the lack of 'historical link between language politics and fandom' in AP unlike in Tamil and Kannada cinema.[103] NTR's semi-historical films, such as *Chanakya-Chandragupta* (1977), *Akbar-Salim-Anarkali* (1978) and *Samrat Ashoka* (1992), for example, were not even remotely connected to Telugu geographical or linguistic nationalism.

The only exception to this was the film *Talla Pellama?* (1970) which had an anecdotal reference to the need for Telugu unity against the backdrop of the ongoing agitation for a separate Telangana state. The song 'Telugu jaathi manadi, ninduga velugu jaathi manadi' talked about the greatness of Telugu nationalism and the need to keep it intact. Two films that NTR made after his political entry, *Sri Madvirat Pothuluri Veera Brahmendra Swamy Charitra* (1984) and *Srinatha Kavi Sarvabhowmudu* (1993), were about Telugu personalities. But they had little political relevance.

Then how do we relate NTR's political slogan of Telugu self-respect and Telugu nationalism to his decades-long film career that had no overt linguistic chauvinism? According to Srinivas, 'Cinematic pleasures were potentially identifiable as sources of linguistic identity because the Telugu cinema had, after all, emerged as the one cultural form that Telugus across Andhra Pradesh had in common.'[104] The fans were invested in the star as a member of the Telugu nation, and it was this underlying relationship that helped NTR.

The role of films in NTR's political career thus was way different from that of Tamil stars. His movies were never a direct vehicle of propaganda. Even the last few films that NTR made after he announced his political entry offered little by way of his political philosophy. As many as eight of his movies were released between 1982 and 1983—the period in which he established the TDP and captured power.[105] All these films were formula-driven, melodramatic and over the top. Terrible direction, loud music and exaggerated acting were their hallmarks. Some of them were box office hits, but none even remotely had any political message to convey. 'Will real N.T. Rama Rao, please stand up?' screamed an *India Today* review of *Chanda Sasanudu*. It was the last film (released in May 1983) he acted in before becoming the chief minister.[106] The film—made during the height of the campaign—was nothing more than 'a sloppy patchwork quilt of stunts and sentiment'.[107] There was a lumpen quality about these films. If anything, they eroded NTR's credibility as an actor, though his stardom remained untouched.

NTR's film career was certainly not at its peak by the time he started dabbling in politics, though he liked to believe otherwise. At this time, he looked more like a fading star who was desperately trying to stay in the limelight. But his body of work was such that his fan following remained mostly intact. What made him stand out in this long career was his emergence as a Telugu cultural symbol, however indirect it was. The social capital NTR accumulated over more than three decades as an actor helped cement his political appeal.[108] NTR was aware of this all through his campaign. He rebutted the suggestion time and again that his movie stardom was the sole reason for the people's support to his politics.

Besides, cinema glamour by itself rarely worked. Turlapati Satyanarayana, one of the first general secretaries of the TDP, recalled how NTR's cine glamour had failed to work in the past.[109] NTR had sought a ticket for one of his producer-friends in the 1978 assembly elections from the Congress and Janata parties. After failing in his efforts, he asked his friend Yeleswaram Nageswara Rao to contest from Prathipadu in East Godavari District as an independent candidate. As promised, NTR camped in the constituency and campaigned for his friend for fifteen days, but he lost the election.

In 1983, with a combination of factors helping him, NTR quickly emerged as a legitimate political player. While every Opposition party wanted a poll alliance with NTR's new outfit, all of them fought shy of being seen soliciting a political novice like the TDP. Instead, they kept on making prickly statements against the party. While the CPI alleged that the TDP was in cahoots with the BJP, the saffron party charged that the communists were running after NTR for a tie-up. The CPI national general secretary Chandra Rajeswara Rao was particularly upset at the TDP for not responding to his rhetorical questions. He demanded to know NTR's stand on American military presence in Diego Garcia and how the party planned to do away with the capitalist system.[110] Even at the last minute, NTR offered sixty seats to the communist parties, but they insisted on ninety-four seats. By this time, NTR saw no merit in giving away large chunks of seats to parties which were fast ceding their space to the TDP.

Maneka Gandhi flew to Hyderabad and met NTR for an alliance in the Telangana region. She wanted Sanjay Vichar Manch candidates in ten seats, but finally agreed to the five offered by the TDP. These were Karimnagar, Manthani, Peddapalli, Kamareddy and Chennur. It was not as though Maneka or her party had a following in AP. The idea was to embarrass Indira and give voice to Maneka to vent her ire against her mother-in-law. Even Jagjivan Ram of the Congress (J) wanted a tie-up with the TDP, and Jagjivan's son Suresh Ram called on NTR and sought forty seats. NTR was told that the veteran leader was keen to campaign in AP along with the actor. When the tie-up did not materialize, Suresh Ram blamed it on NTR's arrogance. Even Salahuddin Owaisi of Majlis-e-Ittehadul Muslimeen (MIM) approached for an alliance with the TDP but in vain. The TDP fielded candidates in all seats minus the five given to Maneka's party.

The TDP did not receive large-scale funding. Upendra recalled how the candidates were disappointed when they were given only publicity material and no cash or vehicles. Later, the Scheduled Caste (SC), Scheduled Tribe (ST) and women candidates were given Rs 10,000 each in two instalments. The Congress candidates, on the other hand, were financially sound; and the party took care of those with limited funds. But the TDP had an advantage with its election symbol: Bicycle.[111] It was the most common means of transport and had high visibility. During the campaign, the party's fans would put up actual cycles atop buildings and trees, and at public meetings. In his younger days, when the family fell on hard times, NTR would sell milk on his bicycle. In Madras, he used it for some time to run around studios before he could afford a car. That sentiment seemed to have played in his decision to select the common man's transport as the party symbol.

It was truly a multi-cornered contest in this election. Besides the Congress and the TDP, the Progressive Democratic Front consisting of the Janata, Lok Dal, and Congress (J), the CPI and the CPI (M), as well as the BJP, were in the race. The Congress hoped this would split the Opposition vote and benefit the ruling party. The mother–son duo campaigned extensively, with Indira covering at least two-thirds of the 294 constituencies. She addressed a dozen meetings a day.[112]

The prime minister targeted NTR as a painted face who daydreamed of becoming the chief minister. She also mounted an attack against narrow regionalism and regional parties, which were a threat to the nation and its integrity. Another recurrent strain in her speeches was how the various poverty-alleviation programmes being implemented by her government were in danger of getting derailed due to Opposition politics:

> Besides the right-wing extremists, here [in Andhra Pradesh] we also have drama artistes in the field. I like dramas. You also probably like them. But one requires a lot of understanding to appreciate the complexity of the issues staring at us.[113]

Indira Gandhi, however, could see the change of the mood on the ground. 'Log the, jaan nahi thi [the people were there, but no enthusiasm],' she told her adviser M.L. Fotedar during the campaign.[114]

Interestingly, Maneka attracted more curious crowds to her election meetings than any other national leader. While she spent four days in coastal Andhra, Maneka campaigned extensively in Telangana, where her party candidates were in the fray. NTR also addressed a few meetings together with Maneka, and they were smash hits.

Once the selection of candidates was completed, NTR began his final campaign from 16 December 1982. He had already gone around the state on his Chaitanya Ratham a couple of times in the preceding months. But still, people did not seem to have had enough of him. The last nineteen days of this campaign were the most intense of all his roadshows. As his Ratham rode into constituency after constituency, it left an electoral twister. The NTR wave was manifest even to his bitterest critics. *Zamin Ryot*, one of the oldest local papers published from AP and an unabashed critic of NTR, bemoaned thus after the whirlwind tour of the TDP chief in Nellore two weeks before the polling:

> This is really beyond our comprehension. Who are these people? Where are they coming from? The masses are crazy about film stars, we know. But why are they swarming around him like flies? These indeed are not just cinema fans. There is clearly a political attraction. How come so many of them waited without complaining, even though he was late by at least two days![115]

The local media was polarized and presented an incongruous picture. With the sole exception of *Eenadu*, which acted as the TDP's mouthpiece, the rest came across as defenders of the Congress's interests. They were either hostile or apathetic to NTR and his party. The traditionally pro-Congress Telugu newspapers—most notably *Andhra Patrika*, *Andhra Jyothy* and *Andhra Bhoomi*—were downright hostile. 'Telugu Desam is more an optical illusion than a reality,' declared the *Deccan Chronicle* in its editorial ten days before the polls.[116] However, even the unfriendly media had to acknowledge towards the end that the bitter fight was down to 'Congress vs TDP'.

The national media seemed mostly disinterested in NTR's challenge to Indira Gandhi till the last lap of the campaign. *India Today* was an exception and reported on the eve of the polls that the new party posed 'the most serious threat to the Congress'.[117] The magazine carried two consecutive cover stories 'A Battle Royal' and 'The Conquering Hero' on NTR and his victory. *India Today's* forecast conducted by well-known pollster Prannoy Roy and the Indian Market Research Bureau, however, failed to get the outcome right. The poll gave the ruling Congress 'an absolute,

though greatly reduced, majority with an estimated 156 seats',
while the TDP was to get a 'very creditable 102 seats'.

Historic Victory

The most awaited election results poured in with a dramatic twist.
In a classic case of misdirection, the first result came out in favour
of the Congress (I). The party candidate, P. Shankar Rao, won
against the TDP candidate, P. Radhakrishna, with a margin of
3003 votes from the Shadnagar (Mahabubnagar District) reserved
constituency. This result was out early as the electronic voting

NTR spent little money for election campaigns. This was one of the very few
newspaper advertisements issued by the TDP in the 1983 elections two days
before the day of the polling.

machine (EVM) was deployed in this constituency for the first time.

But NTR, who was confidence personified, was not unduly perturbed. True to his belief, TDP candidates were soon on a winning spree. The party made a clean sweep in the coastal Andhra and Rayalaseema regions, while making significant inroads in Telangana. It secured more than 46 per cent of votes, setting a record in the electoral history of India. While it needed 148 seats to form the government, the party secured 198 seats in its debut election. Sanjay Vichar Manch, supported by the TDP, got four seats.[118] The Congress, for the first time since AP's formation, had to be content with sixty seats after managing 33 per cent of the votes.

It was an electoral tsunami as Indira's iron grip on her pocket borough was literally washed away under NTR's mighty spell. The oldest party got decimated by an amateur outfit that was formed just nine months ago. 'This was arguably the most spectacular defeat the Congress had suffered,' historian Ramachandra Guha said, 'for its previous conquerors, such as the communists, the DMK and the Janata Party, were all led by experienced politicians who had a solid cadre of co-workers to organize their campaigns.'[119] *India Today* exclaimed, 'The film star-turned-politician's fantastic victory over a formidable leader with an international reputation like Mrs Gandhi has no precedent in world history.'[120]

Senior Congress leaders, including several ministers, were left licking their wounds in the aftermath. Some of the stalwarts who lost included fifteen members of the outgoing cabinet, such as N. Janardhana Reddy, Kona Prabhakara Rao and M.A. Aziz, and Assembly Speaker Agarala Eswara Reddy.

The 'national' Opposition parties were on the receiving end in these elections because of the TDP sweep. The Janata Party, which had won sixty seats in 1978, was dismally reduced to one MLA. The Lok Dal was wiped out. The strength of the communists in the assembly got reduced to nine with the CPI (M) securing five and the CPI four seats. It was an even more sobering experience for the Left as the CPI and the CPI (M) had a seat adjustment for the first time after 1964. The BJP, which fielded eighty candidates, managed to keep its three seats. The Congress (J), which contested for eighty seats, got one. The Congress (S) drew a blank. The MIM was the only party which increased its strength from three to five seats, predominantly from the old city of Hyderabad. The honourable exceptions who withstood the NTR onslaught included the Janata Party's S. Jaipal Reddy and the BJP's M. Venkaiah Naidu.

The impressive victory of four of the five candidates fielded by Sanjay Vichar Manch was entirely due to the TDP's support. This was the largest number of MLAs Maneka's party, which was soon rebranded as Rashtriya Sanjay Manch (RSM), had ever managed to win in any election.

There have been a plethora of analyses and commentaries on how and why the historic win happened. The victory is significant because NTR's feat of capturing power within nine months of founding a political party remains unassailable to this day.[121] No single factor can be attributed to the spectacular change of regime. The man and the moment coalesced to bring about a dramatic shift in the course of AP's history.

NTR's ability to project himself as a viable alternative to the Congress (I) was a major reason. The anti-Congress vote was out there for the asking. What was needed was a credible choice. Where all the other Opposition outfits failed, the TDP succeeded because it could mirror people's aspirations more accurately. The *Indian Express* in its editorial, while describing 'the emergence of the Telugu Desam as an avenging fury', said that NTR 'captured a mood' even as his pledge to restore the Telugu 'self-respect' struck a responsive chord.[122] The way NTR fine-tuned his 'self-respect slogan' without elements of bigotry was surprisingly in tandem with Telugu nationalism historically. As K.C. Suri points out, 'The Telugu people have exhibited this tendency since the beginning of the twentieth century of finely mixing the Telugu national pride with that of Indian nationalism.'[123]

NTR's native imagery and localized idiom, drawn heavily from the traditional and cultural repertoire of Telugus, produced an instant connection for the common man. He time and again referred to *atma gouravam* (self-respect), *jati gouravam* (honour of the Telugu race), *dharma yuddham* (the fight for justice) and *kurukshetram* (the epic war in Mahabharata). All of these were expressions that appealed to people's cultural instincts. Sociologist Ratna Naidu explained how the TDP's campaign material that included a booklet consisting of seven pictures of NTR in various mythological and historical roles—such as Lord Krishna, Lord Rama, emperor Krishnadevaraya, mystic Veerabhrahmendra Swamy and medieval minister Brahma Naidu—conveyed 'leftist and radical principles through home-grown imageries and idioms available in the backyard of the nation'.[124]

NTR's dramatic speeches in idiomatic Telugu captured the voters' imagination. For example, on the issue of corruption in the Congress party, he would rhetorically question, 'Whose father's money is this?' To underline the point that the Congress was no longer an honourable party, he would say it was 'selling rotten fruits in the name of the tree'. Also, the attempt to portray NTR and his party as narrowly regional or separatist did not really gel with people for the same reason. NTR was not a secessionist, and actually used pan-Indian symbolism such as Rama Rajya, the Hindu concept of ideal governance, which was culturally an integral part of the national imagination. As sociologist Ratna Naidu pointed out, the TDP campaign was very different from that of the DMK of Tamil Nadu in its content and tone. NTR's appeal to Telugu nationalism all through was never antithetical to the idea of national identity.

The no-holds-barred coverage in *Eenadu* was widely seen as a major factor in NTR's debut victory. 'Who says NTR has won? It is Ramoji Rao who has won,' Indira Gandhi reportedly said.[125]

Analysts pointed out the significant change in the social background of the TDP legislators, suggesting it contributed to the party's astounding victory. The TDP brought about an alliance between dominant caste groups and Backward Castes (BCs).[126] This contrasted with the Congress (I)'s combination of the upper-caste groups and the Scheduled Castes and Tribes. The BCs have since been the backbone of TDP's electoral support.

It may be interesting to note that the number of Reddy MLAs in the 1983 assembly was still dominant at sixty-eight, while that of Kammas was fifty-two in the 294-strong House. As many as forty-five Reddy MLAs were elected on the TDP ticket. The number of Kamma MLAs elected on the TDP ticket was marginally higher at forty-eight, while only three Kammas made it on the symbol of other parties.[127] On the face of it, more Kammas seem to have found their way to the assembly through the TDP. But even in 1967, as many as forty-four Kamma legislators were returned to the assembly when there was no TDP around.[128]

The victory of the TDP as a triumph of regional assertion has also been widely discussed. The argument goes that since Independence, the emerging regional capitalist class was increasingly finding it difficult to defend and promote its interests in the Delhi-centric world of politics. This assertive class, as exemplified by businessman and media baron Ramoji Rao, contributed to the rise of regional parties such as the TDP. Significantly, since the 1980s, the states, especially those ruled by non-Congress parties, began demanding a more meaningful share in the power structure.

The fact that NTR's political success was markedly different from that of MGR in Tamil Nadu was noted by several commentators. MGR had a long history of working in politics before he floated his own party and staked a claim to power. NTR's foray was sudden and without a shred of past political involvement. NTR was acutely aware of his own phenomenal success. 'Comparing what I have achieved this time with the others is not a fair proposition. They have been in politics long before they achieved success. I have done it in nine months,' NTR protested in an interview to *India Today*.[129]

The emergence of the TDP, in a way, put paid to any possibility of a 'national' party, including the resurgent BJP, being able to rise to power in the state in the foreseeable future. Even after the bifurcation of the state in 2014, two regional parties, the TDP and the Telangana Rashtra Samithi (TRS), captured power in AP and Telangana, respectively. In 2019, again the regional parties, the TRS and the YSR Congress, stormed to power in the two Telugu states. The BJP and the Congress remained weak Opposition parties. Inspired by the success of the TDP, several regional outfits sprouted subsequently, with some degree of achievement, but none with the same dramatic impact.[130] Likewise, among all regional parties in the country ranging from the AIADMK (founded in 1972) to the AAP (formed in 2012), NTR's TDP performed the best among the first-timers in the country.[131]

Clearly, NTR and his party did not ride to power just on his film glamour. His success was accompanied by a new native ideology and political culture. The moment was right for a viable political alternative, and the man rose to fill the void. How this significant political development was more than a filmi affair became evident decades later when another bid was made by another film star, Chiranjeevi, on the same lines, but not with the same result.

Thanks to the NTR phenomenon which resulted in victory against Indira Gandhi and the well-entrenched Congress, the Telugus certainly gained new-found recognition in the eyes of the rest of the country. One of the perennial complaints of the Telugu people was that they had been subsumed under the 'Madrasi' tag in the north Indian consciousness even after the linguistic state was formed. NTR's arrival on the scene brought about a definite change in the way AP was looked at by politicians and media in Delhi. B.P.R. Vithal, a distinguished civil servant, was serving the African country Sudan as a budget adviser during the dramatic political developments in his home state. Vithal, who later worked as deputy chairman, planning board, in NTR's government, recalled:

> I saw the swearing in of Sri NT Rama Rao, as the chief minister of Andhra Pradesh, in a public ceremony at the Lal Bahadur Stadium in January 1983, live on the Sudanese TV in Khartoum, Sudan. It was the first time that the entire Arab world came to know that an important part of India was Telugu country. Till then, even North Indians knew us as only 'Madrasis'. What we wanted to achieve by having a separate linguistic State was emotionally achieved only then and entirely due to NTR.[132]

NTR was indeed able to arouse such tremendous curiosity through his historic win in the media that three European television crews—the British, West German and Italian—visited Hyderabad to film him in action. Delhi-based journalists, for the first time in recent years, descended upon Hyderabad to see what was so special about the film actor who trounced Indira Gandhi.

A Failed Reprisal

A quarter century after NTR launched his party and smashed the polls in record time, another equally, if not more, popular hero sought a repeat of this phenomenon in AP.

It was a pleasant Sunday morning on 18 August 2008 in Hyderabad. A press meet had been organized by the reigning star of the Telugu screen, Chiranjeevi, who had been described by an English weekly during the peak of his career as 'bigger than Bachchan'.[133] Unlike NTR, the hero image of Chiranjeevi, known as Chiru to fans, was carefully nurtured and promoted by his brother-in-law Allu Aravind, a leading producer and distributor. Every single move of Chiranjeevi, whose real name is Konidela Siva Sankara Prasad, in both films and politics was conceived and executed by a band of close-knit supporters led by Aravind. Now, the stage was set for a repeat of this performance in politics.

The venue for the announcement was a spacious and recently renovated building in the upmarket Jubilee Hills. For at least six months, there had been intense speculation in the media that Chiranjeevi was going to make a grand political entry. The actor had a large fan base and was called a megastar. It was a period when the Telugu television media, especially its news version, was making its first aggressive strides in pursuit of eyeballs. The expanding media was hungry for the tantalizing proposition of a film hero breaking into politics. The Chiru brigade led by Aravind, an expert in film marketing and branding, used the new opportunity to the hilt. 'We are all waiting on the platform for Chiru's train,' was Aravind's cryptic statement during this time. His words provided the grist for columns in the papers and hours of prime time on television channels.

Having extracted the maximum pre-release publicity, the trailer now seemed set for release. Despite the prior knowledge of the actor's intentions, there was much anticipation and excitement before the press conference. 'It appeared as if the media bosses wanted to make up for the opportunity missed in the early 1980s to cover the original story of N.T. Rama Rao's political entry,' remarked K. Rama Rayalu, an analyst.[134]

The event was well choreographed. The news channels vied for a live telecast of the dramatic political moment. The noisy room was bursting with the press corps, as the TV crews pushed one another for space. A grinning Chiranjeevi entered the hall that was decorated with a flex poster featuring pictures of Mahatma Gandhi, B.R. Ambedkar, Mother Teresa and Jyotirao Phule. The huge banner gave a political touch to the otherwise filmi atmosphere. Confidence oozing from his every pore, Chiranjeevi made the grand announcement of his political entry, enacting his practised moves to perfection. *The Hindu* reported the electrifying gush in the room:

Elaborate arrangements inside the new party office were simply inadequate to accommodate the 200-strong media contingent. The result was that every question had to be shouted out to the star-actor who walked back and forth on the stage and bent over the podium, straining to hear.[135]

The timing of the announcement was impeccable. The Opposition TDP was still on the defensive, unable to counter Chief Minister Y.S. Rajasekhara Reddy's aggressive politics. The public was discontented with the corrupt governance of YSR, as Rajasekhara Reddy was known. The Telangana sentiment was strong at this point of time, and the existing parties were unable to come to terms with the issue. Demand for social justice—an aspiration of the intermediate castes, along with the Dalits, for a major share in the power structure—was being articulated by various sections of the people, even as they were looking for an alternative. The Kapus, an umbrella term for a string of middle castes, had already found in Chiranjeevi an icon for their community to make a serious bid for power.

Thus, Chiranjeevi's Praja Rajyam Party (PRP) met most of the requirements to attempt a repeat of the TDP's success. The party was equipped to do it better than NTR in terms of stardom, planning and resources. The glamour was in abundance and a loyal fan following was in place. The caste configurations were favourable and the media's new avatar, the television, was handy. The undercurrent of support was strong among sections of the public and the promise of social justice as a political goal was alluring. Nothing seemed to be lacking in this perfect script.

So self-assured—or presumptuous, depending on the point of view—was the new party that its leadership consciously chose to break the record set by NTR in achieving political power in nine months flat. So, the PRP was formally announced on 26 August 2008, with a view to capture power in less than eight months as State Assembly elections were due in April 2009. The campaign

was on the same lines as that of NTR in 1982. Chiranjeevi, as
expected, generated frenzy among the crowds across the state. His
entire family of actors, including the charismatic Pawan Kalyan,
campaigned for the party. A confident Aravind was reported by
the press as stating that the party was winning in 292 out of 294
seats, apparently saving YSR and Opposition leader Chandrababu
Naidu from ignominy.

But all that euphoria ended in anticlimax. The well-honed
script failed to work its magic on the voters. When the results
started pouring in, in May 2009, the PRP and Chiranjeevi were
in for a shock. Out of the 288 seats it contested, the party just
scraped in by eighteen. The contender stood third in terms of vote
percentage, managing 16.72 per cent of the votes polled, behind
the TDP, which emerged as the largest Opposition party with
ninety-two MLAs. The ruling Congress managed to keep power
with a reduced margin of 156 seats. Chiranjeevi, who contested
from two seats, lost in his native Palakollu constituency in West
Godavari District. The possibility of a hung assembly because of
the Chiranjeevi factor remained a damp squib.[136]

The only accomplishment of the PRP was that it contributed to
the split in the Opposition vote and helped the YSR-led Congress
party retain the government with a wafer-thin majority. Post
elections, Chiranjeevi was unable to sustain the party for long. His
interest in politics diminished rapidly without power. The party
ignominiously folded less than three years after he floated it. The
party was merged 'unconditionally' with the Congress. Chiranjeevi
unabashedly declared that the decision was taken keeping in mind
the 'best interests' of the people as both the PRP and the Congress
stood for social justice.[137]

In return, he was amply rewarded by the Congress which
made the actor a Rajya Sabha member and later a junior minister
in the Union cabinet. However, despite the Congress's best hopes,
the megastar-turned-politician failed to turn the tide in the next
elections in 2014. Chiru's political visibility greatly diminished

after the Congress lost badly in parliamentary as well as assembly elections in Telangana and AP in 2014. Many of his political colleagues soon left the Congress and joined one of the regional parties, the TDP or YSR Congress Party. Chiranjeevi is now busy resurrecting his movie career.

The top star in Telugu was inspired by NTR in his quest for power and, in fact, was better placed to seek a replay. Due to the explosion in media and communication, his charisma as a star got amplified many times more than that of NTR. At fifty-three, he was younger at the time of his political entry and much followed by the youth. Many TDP leaders joined the PRP and strengthened its base on the eve of the 2009 polls. Between the Reddy-dominated Congress and the Kamma-controlled TDP, Chiranjeevi's party appeared to enjoy the goodwill of the rest of the social groupings.

Despite all these advantages, why couldn't Chiranjeevi repeat NTR's success? In the answer to this query lies the real reason for NTR's accomplishment. NTR's film glamour, his charisma, the political bankruptcy of the ruling Congress, the disillusionment of the public in the establishment, surely provided the background for the TDP's show. But what really made the difference was NTR's ability to convince the voting public that he was the real deal in terms of an alternative to the Congress. His own conviction in what he had set out to do was apparent in all his actions.

Chiranjeevi tried to bring together all these elements but at a superficial level. His campaign began with an assumption that he was the chief-minister-in-waiting and that he had to just walk through the elections to occupy the chair. His managers took his supporters for granted and did not bother to go the extra mile. NTR never allowed such smugness to taint his cause.

While NTR used his celluloid image to reach out to the public, he never relied on his glamour alone. The political content of NTR's campaign was much more focused and serious, while Chiranjeevi's was more style than substance. NTR himself remarked on his success thus, '. . . a mere good leader is not enough. He must take up the burning issues in the state and articulate people's grievances and expectations.'[138]

Both NTR and Chiranjeevi began with a lack of understanding of the world of politics. But the former was quick to master the nuances behind various intractable issues. Chiranjeevi, on the other hand, was expected to have a better grip of the problems, considering he came on the political scene much later than NTR, but failed in getting that image across.

The contrasting outcomes help us understand as much about NTR's successful political transformation as they throw light on the reasons behind Chiranjeevi's debacle. The takeaway? Being famous may be the first easy step up the political ladder, but reaching the top is an entirely different game. One must accurately reflect the public mood, articulate their concerns and hopes, and earn their trust before one can make a mark. NTR overcame every one of these challenges with flying colours. The rest, as they say, was history.

~

Act II

A New Beginning, Interrupted

It had been exactly a month since the winds of change had started blowing in AP. There was a freshness in the corridors of power with a brand-new chief minister and a crisp and raw government in the secretariat. The imposing figure of N.T. Rama Rao walked in for a press briefing after a marathon cabinet session that had extended for nearly four hours. By this time, 8 February 1983, mediapersons were used to dramatic announcements by the new dispensation. However, even the most seasoned reporters were not ready for the drastic decisions that were to follow this day. A few minutes into the presser, the mediapersons were already getting overwhelmed by the slew of momentous announcements by the actor-turned-chief minister.

Each one was of far-reaching impact. NTR began by declaring the government's intention to abolish the Upper House of the assembly, the Legislative Council. He announced that a bill would soon be introduced to ban defections of elected representatives from one party to another. Donations to secure a seat in educational institutions, especially professional colleges, was proscribed. The cabinet proposed to introduce a radical legislation to give equal rights to women in ancestral property.

It decided to establish a women's university to empower girls through higher education.

The most sensational of the announcements was reserved for the last: reduction of the age of retirement from fifty-eight to fifty-five years for state government employees.[1] Suddenly, there was a commotion in the hall. Few were prepared for such a drastic announcement. All the other decisions, however significant, were already floating around in the columns of newspapers. The reporters, rattled by the radical move, posed a barrage of questions, but NTR seemed little perturbed by the far-reaching consequences of his controversial call.

Indeed, the first few months of NTR's administration were characterized by a politically tense atmosphere. The chief minister went about translating his ideas and plans with no regard to their explosive impact. Few newly elected chief ministers would have taken such politically and administratively huge steps as NTR did in his first hundred days. He was confident of the mandate given by the people and went about his mission with great passion, unmindful of the fact that he was ruffling many an entrenched interest in the process. His non-political background helped him to go about his task without care for vote banks, constituencies or media backlash.

NTR had kicked off his new role on 9 January 1983, his swearing-in a spectacle conducted in the presence of a hundred thousand people at Lal Bahadur Stadium. Traditionally, the venue for the oath-taking was the dreary confines of Raj Bhavan. Barely forty-eight hours after the results were out, NTR formed a full-fledged ministry. This itself was a remarkable feat, considering the legacy of the Congress during the previous three decades. Till then, the ministry formation was characterized by back-room politicking, chaos, mutual recriminations and ferocious shuttling between Hyderabad and Delhi. The ministry itself was a great relief, being the most compact for a long time. Hand-picked by NTR, it had twelve new faces out of a total of fifteen. Except for three, Nadendla, Nallapareddy Srinivasulu Reddy and Puttapaga Mahendranath, the rest were debutantes. The ministry settled in no time, marking a complete break from the Congress culture.

NTR was an outsider to governance, but he quickly developed a unique approach. His working style was a departure from the laid-back manner of the Congress regimes. He was an early riser and started work before dawn. He preferred to see his senior officers, aides and visitors from 5 a.m. onwards. NTR was punctual with his appointments and disposed of matters and files quickly. He was focused and insisted on getting results quickly. He appeared to be a man in a hurry.

NTR's government rolled out radical steps one after another. Government corporations, which had become political rehabilitation centres, were rationalized, and forty-eight such entities were merged to make a lean thirty-four. Telugu was made the language of correspondence at all levels of administration from the Telugu new year, Ugadi. Padmavati Mahila Visvavidyalayam (a women's university), the first such initiative in south India, was inaugurated in Tirupati on the same day. The restructured and subsidized rice scheme was launched across the state. Pension payment for former legislators was discontinued. Private practice of government doctors was prohibited. Government teachers were banned from giving private tuitions.

Another major move, pompously named in NTR's inimitable style as Telugu Ganga, was an agreement for the supply of drinking water to Madras. NTR and the Tamil Nadu chief minister, M.G. Ramachandran, signed a deal in Hyderabad on 26 April 1983 to provide the water of Krishna River to Madras.

This had been on the cards for some time. But it was NTR's gratitude to Madras, where he had lived for thirty-five years of his most productive life, which ensured the quick resolution of some minor irritants.

During his election campaign, NTR spoke about changing the name of the state. In an interview to the news agency UNI

NTR with Prime Minister Indira Gandhi and Tamil Nadu CM MGR in 1983,
formalizing the Telugu Ganga agreement to supply drinking water to Madras.

immediately after winning the elections, NTR said that his
party had decided to change the name of the state from Andhra
Pradesh to Telugu Nadu.[2] The idea was to remove the Andhra–
Telangana regional feelings that had caused two big agitations
in the past. NTR also wanted to give a Telugu nomenclature to
the state. However, he later announced that the idea had been
shelved.[3] He was apparently dissuaded by his advisers. The state
would have lost the advantage in alphabetical listings with a
change of name.

Battling against Bureaucracy

One of NTR's first priorities was to curtail red tape and tighten
the administration. A man of strict discipline and a hard
taskmaster, he wanted the government staff to follow suit. It was
in this effort that he ended up making the government employees
his enemies, and it was this hostility that would cost him dearly
later. Ten days after he was sworn in, NTR issued orders that
included a series of dos and don'ts to curtail the whiling away

of time in offices. The directive asked the secretariat staff to not move out of their seats during the stipulated timings. They had to sign a register to leave their chairs. Attendance registers were removed after 10.30 a.m. and only a grace period of ten minutes was allowed for latecomers. Lunchtime was cut by half an hour. Canteens opened only during lunch hour. Demonstrations within secretariat precincts were banned. Security was beefed up, and hangers-on were not allowed inside. Entry passes were mandatory. Legislators were asked to not bring in followers without reason.

'Indeed, a visit to the secretariat in Hyderabad is a pleasant experience. Perhaps no other secretariat in a state capital looks so clean. Admission is strictly controlled. Employees are served tea at their desks, and the cups and saucers are promptly cleared away. Senior officials have enough time to work in peace,' stated Bhabani Sen Gupta of *India Today* who visited the secretariat in 1983.[4] He also noted the crackdown on corruption. 'No hush-hush transactions can take place between petty officials and seekers of licenses or permits over cups of tea in the canteens,' he wrote.

All these measures helped restore a semblance of order and streamlined the administration in the secretariat. With requests for transfers and promotions by MLAs expressly prohibited by NTR, the senior officers worked without interference. The staff too seemed to cooperate. But not for long. They felt stifled by the new rules. Soon, they demonstrated against what they dubbed as a 'mini Emergency'. NTR came forward to pacify them. His charm worked a couple of times. 'The 3,000-odd government employees in the secretariat smarting under the new restrictions . . . were superbly mollified by a non-stop half-an-hour Telugu rhetoric let loose by the chief minister,' a report in the *Indian Express* said.[5] But the situation deteriorated again. The reduction in retirement age and the ordinance issued subsequently to save the government from legal scrutiny of the controversial decision further alienated the government staff.

Over 18,000 government staff and 10,000 public-sector employees were superannuated as a result of the order. The government argued that the decision was imperative to solve the unemployment problem that had gone up to 17 million by the end of 1982.

It was the last straw for the government employees who had been chafing at their treatment by the TDP government. The action committee of employees and workers called for a strike, which soon became a tug of war between the government and the staff. Government employees going on strike was not new in AP. But this time, the NTR government decided to take the issue to the public and put nearly six hundred thousand employees on the defensive. A belligerent NTR accused the government employees of regarding themselves as being above the law. 'The poor villagers may be without work or enough food, but the NGOs [non-gazetted officers] must have their pound of flesh,' he alleged. The chief minister tried to mobilize public opinion against their 'unjust' demands. 'I am a trustee of the government funds. The people must judge the demands of the employees', he said.[6]

The TDP organized bandhs against the demands of the staff. Soon the row turned into an all-out battle, provoking *India Today* to call it an 'uncivil war'. The Congress, along with other Opposition parties, stood behind the employees. The government's tough stance helped bring together even warring factions—such as the Andhra and Telangana unions of the employees. Finally, the newly appointed chief secretary, G.V. Ramakrishna, was able to open negotiations, and the strike was called off after nineteen unsettling days.[7]

This was one of the angriest confrontations in the history of the state's administration. 'I would never think of causing any harm to government employees who are the wheels of the administration,' NTR reassuringly said.[8] But the bad blood that flowed during the bitter days of the strike put a strain on relations between NTR and government employees for a long time to come. Faced with a series of actions that directly or indirectly affected them, the staff became hostile towards the TDP regime.

NTR had a healthy contempt for corruption. An episode from his early life illustrated this visceral hatred.[9] Soon after his graduation, NTR got selected by the Madras Service Commission in 1947 as a sub-registrar and was posted in Mangalagiri in Guntur District. He was getting a princely sum of Rs 190 a month. Within the first few days, he found out that his coat pocket, hung to the back of his chair during the day, would be filled with money by evening. It was his share of the underhand money. NTR was furious and decided he would not continue in such a job. He quit in less than three weeks.

The incident stayed with NTR, even three and a half decades later when he came into the government. He was determined to root out corruption from the administration. 'I will chase the corrupt officials like Yama [the god of death],' he warned the bureaucracy in the first district collectors' meeting. Immediately after coming to power, the chief minister created a new office, Dharma Maha Matra (DMM).[10] NTR's pick for the post, E.V. Rami Reddy, a retired IAS officer, displayed a lot of zeal and struck terror among the officials. Senior officers expressed objections to his way of working, which they considered intrusive and beyond his purview. He was bestowed with powers to call for files, inquire into public grievances and refer cases to the Anti-Corruption Bureau (ACB). In a short time, the DMM received about 7300 complaints against officials from the public. About 250 officials were placed under suspension for possession of disproportionate assets. Raids were conducted on the premises of an inspector general of police (IG), six IAS officers and several other senior officers. Rami Reddy recommended retiring two IAS officers, B.R.K. Sastry and L. Malakondaiah, who chose to voluntarily quit.[11] Reddy was increasingly seen as NTR's weapon to get at recalcitrant officers. Adding more teeth to the anti-corruption drive, NTR brought in the Lokayukta Act in the very first year of his administration, which started functioning from November 1983.

NTR's campaign against corruption unleashed terror among senior officers. Even as the tiff with NGOs continued, the upper echelons of the bureaucracy, especially the IAS and the IPS, felt shaken by his aggressive approach to complaints of corruption. Besides shuffling scores of them in the first three months, NTR also suspended several senior All India Services officers. The action against bureaucrats such as K. Santhanam, N.K. Muralidhara Rao, H.K. Babu, M.V.S. Prasada Rau and P.V. Pavithran created dread in the officialdom.[12]

NTR was impatient when it came to rooting out suspected malfeasance. He was credulous, and this trait was apparently manipulated by those close to him against select targets. Once he was convinced in such matters, he was unmindful of the fall-out. He was impervious to the consequences either to him or to the officer concerned. The ACB, which had been toothless since the 1970s, was vested with extensive powers to raid and file cases against state government employees. Former IPS officer V. Appa Rao, who was brought into the ACB, recalled that NTR personally monitored investigations into charges of corruption.

NTR took his war on corruption to the extreme in some instances, wherein he did not hesitate to subject officers to humiliation. P.V.R.K. Prasad, the IAS officer who went on to become media adviser to Prime Minister P.V. Narasimha Rao, recounted his own ordeal.[13] Prasad returned to the state from his UK stint when the TDP government took over. He was waiting for a posting when he found out that the new regime was out to deal sternly with officials suspected of corruption. Prasad heard that his name too figured in the list of corrupt officials prepared for suspension by the DMM. Prasad was depressed, having failed to fathom what the allegations against him were. Finally, unable to wait any longer, he decided to give the joining report. Immediately, he received a call, saying that the chief minister wanted to see him.

Prasad met NTR with trepidation. As expected, NTR did not mince words. He said he had three complaints against the officer. These were related to his stint as executive officer of Tirumala Tirupati Devasthanam (TTD), which ran Tirumala, the pilgrim centre. He began with the first charge: 'Did you dole out lakhs of rupees of the TTD to thousands of Brahmins?' Prasad explained that the government had launched a scheme under which *kramapatis* and *ghanapatis* who studied Vedas for sixteen years and recited them in the nearest temple would be paid Rs 600 and Rs 800 respectively. These were only 370, and the government had entrusted this responsibility to the TTD, and he had only implemented the decision. Then NTR referred to the allegation that Prasad had received a huge bribe during the construction of the Papavinasanam dam in Tirumala. Prasad gave a detailed explanation of how he not only expedited the dam construction despite hurdles but also never paid a rupee extra to the contractor. An unrelenting NTR hurled another accusation which sounded more serious. 'What about the misappropriation of diamonds during the making of the diamond-studded crown for Lord Venkateswara?' he questioned. Again, Prasad explained in detail how he was not even involved in the purchase of diamonds since he had already been transferred by then.

This episode shows how caustic NTR could be about corruption in the administration. In the first five years of his government, as many as thirty-nine officers of the All India Services and about 600 from the state services were suspended on one charge or another.[14] But NTR was not always high-handed. As Prasad broke down at the undeserving accusations thrown at him, NTR clasped his hand and cooled him down. 'Don't think we believe all these allegations. We decided to speak to you and get our misgivings dispelled,' he said warmly. Within one hour of this meeting, Prasad received posting orders.

While he was fastidious in choosing his civil servants, NTR was not always overbearing. He was courteous to the ones he believed were competent and honest. K.R. Venugopal, a respected IAS officer who successfully implemented the subsidized rice scheme, spoke highly of his association with NTR: 'While civil servants of those days held varying opinions about him, I had the highest respect and regard for him, especially because he wanted the poor to be free from hunger. At a personal level, he was impeccably courteous towards me. I had complete freedom of speech with him as with any other leader, though some officers did feel constrained by his style.'[15] Y.V. Reddy, the former RBI governor who was the planning secretary in his government, agreed: 'With me, NTR was almost always respectful and warm.'[16]

NTR was strict even with his own ministers whom he suspected of political corruption. In an unprecedented episode in the annals of Indian politics, NTR resorted to an elaborate drama to expose corruption in his cabinet. A year after taking office, in February 1984, NTR laid a trap to catch his own minister for labour, M. Ramachandra Rao, red-handed while accepting a bribe in his office. NTR himself signed on the currency wad that was offered to the minister. A disgraced but protesting Rao, who was a first-time legislator from Khairatabad, was dismissed even as NTR announced the dramatic development in the budget session of the assembly.[17] The Opposition Congress predictably called the episode an attempt to revive the sagging image of NTR, aimed at diverting attention from the allegations of corruption against him and his government. Some questioned the legality behind the ACB laying the trap when only the Lokayukta had the power to investigate charges of fraud against ministers and legislators.

But soon NTR realized that his measures to rein in corruption were not going the way he had expected. E.V. Rami Reddy, NTR's favourite, was able to send shivers across the babudom through his unconventional methods. But a problem arose when the Lokayukta Act was passed, and Justice Avula Sambasiva Rao was appointed to the post. Lokayukta's functions were listed out in the act and covered most of the officers being investigated by the DMM for the preceding nine months. Senior officials saw DMM as an instrument of tyranny and maintained that the office became superfluous after the Lokayukta was instituted. It was finally decided that the DMM would henceforth cover employees not falling within the purview of the Lokayukta Act—officials whose pay was less than Rs 1150 per month. The DMM resented its jurisdiction over 'peons and clerks' and expressed disinterest in the job. The office of the DMM was subsequently scrapped by the Nadendla government. But the Lokayukta under Justice Avula Sambasiva Rao did a commendable job in dealing with corruption in the government.

While NTR undoubtedly could send chills across the bureaucracy and political class through such measures, he was not able to tackle the problem effectively as the malaise was deep-rooted and his move was strongly resisted by bureaucracy. He was also constrained by the complicated procedures that provided a protective shield to the corrupt. According to Y.V. Reddy, NTR's 'erratic enforcement of disciplinary actions increased the distance between NTR and the senior bureaucracy, and this discord was strengthened by a hostile union government'. A year after his sincere efforts, NTR admitted his failure thus:

I have failed in rooting out corruption. I do want to create a society that's free of corruption. But it is not entirely in my hands. Procedures have to be followed to punish the corrupt. It takes time. But I'm not giving up my fight against corruption. I'll fight it till the last day of my life. Whether I'll succeed or not, I don't know. Only time will tell.[18]

While NTR's sincerity towards rooting out corruption was admired at least in some quarters, his attitude when it came to cultural affairs left the observers dumbfounded. Since he was an icon of performing arts, there was high expectation that fine arts would be a priority for his government. NTR indeed was keen to streamline the culture department in the government, but what he set out to do became controversial.

During the Congress regime, a number of state laureates had been appointed in the culture department. When T. Anjaiah was at the helm as chief minister, he had as many as eleven laureates named. These were Dasarathi Krishnamacharyulu (poet), Emani Sankara Sastry (veena player), Mangalampalli Balamuralikrishna (classical singer), M.S. Subbulakshmi (classical singer), Syed Abdul Kareem Yakubi (poet), Aziz Ahmed Warsi (qawwali artiste), Nataraja Ramakrishna (dance guru), Peesapati Narasimha Murthy (stage actor), Yella Venkateswara Rao (mridangam player), P.T. Reddy (artist) and V. Ganapati Sastry (Vedic scholar). Some of these laureates, such as Dasarathi, were given lifelong appointments by government order. They each drew an annual honorarium of Rs 12,000 and were entitled to a car, telephone and office help.

Most of the laureates were indeed eminent in their respective fields. But the practice of state patronage was decried by many as feudal and anti-democratic. The TDP government decided to stop the practice. It considered such appointments as 'constitutionally bad, economically undesirable and morally indefensible'.[19] Following this thinking, the minister for education, P. Ananda Gajapathi Raju, wrote to the laureates, inviting them to relinquish their appointments and the perquisites attached to them. One such letter to poet Dasarathi read thus:

My dear Dasarathi,

Ever since we have assumed responsibility of Government, we have, through our decisions and actions, conveyed to the people, who have reposed such great confidence in us, that we are determined to maintain austerity and economy in expenditure, respect high ethical values and build an egalitarian society.

While it is a matter of pleasure to all of us that you have attained excellence in your field, you will agree that State's recognition of it through a title like 'Poet Laureate in Telugu' [Asthana Kavi] is of little additional consequence. On the other hand, such sanctions take away much of the dignity and evoke uncalled for comments and comparisons in view of certain perquisites being given. We feel that in our endeavour to encourage talent and pursuit of various arts by a large number of citizens of our State and country, the present practice of grant of distinctions and perquisites to few persons is incorrect and we must need, therefore, to discontinue it.[20]

The minister's letter ended with the following appeal to the poet:

I trust, as an eminent person in your field but interested in encouraging a large number of aspirants, you will also have no hesitation in relinquishing both the distinction of 'Poet Laureate' in Telugu and the perquisites that go with it and also help us in evolving a new cultural policy for the State Government.

With kind regards, Yours sincerely, P. Ananda Gajapathi Raju, Minister for Education.

While all except one relinquished their posts, many of the laureates were naturally miffed with the NTR government. A few, like Mangalampalli Balamuralikrishna, accused NTR of killing the culture and fine arts in the state. Dasarathi refused to resign and was terminated by government order. He went to the court against the decision. The case, however, was dismissed with the judge ruling that 'the institution of Poet Laureateship cannot be regarded as consistent either with the nature of poetry or with the democratic polity'.[21]

NTR went about implementing more radical changes in the sphere of culture. There were as many as ten academies for fields such as music, drama, literature and dance, besides a World Telugu Institute. The first thing NTR did was to appoint Narla Venkateswara Rao, an eminent journalist and scholar, to submit a report on the restructuring of the culture department. Based on the report, the academies, including the Telugu Sahitya Academy, were terminated. The film development corporation too was wound up as a separate entity, and its activities were entrusted to the information and public relations department. Many officials of the department of cultural affairs (DCA), who were on deputation from other departments, were shunted out. J.V. Somayajulu, the director of DCA and a well-known Telugu stage and film actor, was also transferred to the parent department.

Sensing NTR's determination to recast the culture department, the nominated heads of different academies such as actress Jamuna (Nataka Academy) and Balamuralikrishna (Music Academy) resigned in a huff. They attacked the government as being anti-culture. An upset Balamuralikrishna vowed to not hold a concert in AP till the academies were revived.[22] The minister for education and culture, P. Ananda Gajapathi Raju, did not help matters when he dubbed the cultural czars dominating the academies as 'dead wood'. He also said that the government would save money by reconstituting the multiple academies into just two, one for literature and another for performing arts.[23]

All those heading the academies, such as Nataraja Ramakrishna, Balamuralikrishna and Peesapati, were indeed stalwarts in their respective fields. However, it was widely felt that these academies did not come up with much creative output. The way NTR went about the changes did not bring about improvement in the situation. Instead, he attracted much criticism for dismantling the set-up without a well-thought-out replacement. The TDP government thus earned the ire of the cultural establishment in the state, which in any case had strong Congress links.

As the government mulled over giving some funds after restructuring, the art and culture personalities boiled with rage. Theatre legend A.R. Krishna, opposing the proposal for clubbing music, dance and drama together, mockingly asked NTR to allocate Rs 300 crore 'in compensation for each Rama Rao film that has distorted and lowered the cultural tastes of the Telugu people'.[24] Narla felt terrible at the way things turned out. Neither he nor NTR had given any thought to alternatives before doing away with the existing arrangement. There was great disappointment in the Telugu literary and artistic world that someone like NTR, who hailed from the world of cinema, had treated the arts so shabbily. P.V.R.K. Prasad oversaw the cultural affairs during this period. He made efforts to pacify the writers and artistes by proposing a Kala Peetham (academy of arts) to replace the dislodged set-up.[25] Narla threw his weight behind the idea, and NTR gave a green signal.

Telugu Vignana Peetham, with chairs in Nritya (dance), Sangeetha (music), Vangmaya (literature) and Janapada (folk arts), was started with Telugu scholar Thumati Donappa as a special officer. In December 1985, Telugu Vignana Peetham was converted into Telugu University, later named after Potti Sriramulu, with the object of functioning as a high-level research centre for the Telugu language, literature and culture. One of the few language universities in India, it made a significant contribution to Telugu language studies. The establishment of Telugu University, later recognized by University Grants Commission (UGC), was an important contribution of NTR's administration. At the time, though, he was denounced by many cultural personalities for rattling the status quo.

National Recognition

After upsetting the apple cart in AP, NTR turned his attention to Delhi. The 1983 elections in AP projected NTR across the nation as a credible—albeit a regional—foil to Indira at a time when

the national Opposition parties were in disarray. He received a
hero's welcome in the nation's capital during his five-day visit in
February 1983. He, the first non-Congress AP chief minister, was
extensively profiled by national newspapers. He called on President
Zail Singh, greeting him in traditional Sikh style with 'Sat Sri Akal'.
He had discussions with Prime Minister Indira Gandhi and other
Union ministers on pending issues. The PM found NTR cordial
and non-confrontational. He also addressed the Press Club
of India, which was brimming with inquisitive journalists. He
famously told them he preferred to be Lord Krishna in politics,
though he liked to play Lord Rama in movies. The celebrity
chief minister attended a gathering of adoring Telugus living in
the capital. He visited Rajghat and Shantivan, the resting places
of Gandhi and Nehru, to pay his respects. He offered prayers at
Birla Mandir, Nizamuddin Dargah and Gurudwara Bangla Sahib,
houses of Hindu, Muslim and Sikh worship. He looked like a
visiting foreign dignitary during his elaborate itinerary.

Journalist Venkat Narayan recalled that editors of all leading
papers attended the lunch hosted by NTR at Andhra Pradesh
Bhavan. M. Chalapathi Rau, editor of *National Herald*, G.K.
Reddy, the New Delhi bureau chief of *The Hindu*, and Girilal Jain,
the editor of *Times of India*, were among those who interacted with
NTR. The chief minister occasionally exchanged a few words in
Telugu with veteran journalist Chalapathi Rau, who was a native
of AP. When one of the editors complained that the Telugus were
monopolizing the show, Rau quipped, 'For once, I am proud of
being a Telugu man!' An impressed Girilal Jain also remarked,
'Mr Rama Rao, it is refreshing to hear you talking. If you are able
to achieve even half of what you have set out to do, Hyderabad is
not the place for you. Delhi will be wanting you.' Coming from
Jain that was no mean compliment, Narayan said.[26]

Later, NTR met up with a group of fifteen Delhi intellectuals
over tea. Impressed by his humility, leading minds such as
M.L. Sondhi, a professor at Jawaharlal Nehru University (JNU);

V.A. Pai Panandiker, director, Centre for Policy Research; Romesh Thapar, editor, *Seminar*; Raja Chelliah, vice chairman, National Institute for Public Finance and Policy; and Pran Chopra, columnist, offered their detailed suggestions and advice to NTR, who dutifully noted them down. 'This volcano of sympathy, admiration and goodwill for him among a bunch of highly respected people whom he had never met before moved Rama Rao,' Venkat Narayan said.[27]

NTR stepped up his profile as a giant-killer by continuously harping on Indira's alleged transgressions in conceding the rights of the states. But he was careful to not be unnecessarily belligerent. 'The fight is only for securing the rights of the states, but not to weaken the Centre,' he said.[28]

The party's philosophy on the issue of more autonomy to the states was articulated in the governor's address to the assembly held barely a week after the government took over. NTR followed up his stance as an active participant in the Bangalore conference of the southern chief ministers held on 20 March 1983, which was attended by the chief ministers of Tamil Nadu (M.G. Ramachandran), Karnataka (Ramakrishna Hegde) and Pondicherry (P. Ramachandran). Their primary demand was that the provisions in the Constitution should change to accommodate and give full play to the new definition of the Centre–state relationship.

An immediate outcome of the Bangalore meeting was the appointment of the Sarkaria Commission by the Indira government. The Centre appointed Ranjit Singh Sarkaria, a retired Supreme Court judge, to 'examine the working of the arrangements between the Centre and the States and recommend such changes in these arrangements as may be appropriate within the present constitutional framework'. This was a good augury for the southern chief ministers' effort.

Soon NTR was on to bigger things. His first major effort to bring together the disparate Opposition parties was undertaken

at the May 1983 Mahanadu. The conference was followed with
great interest by the media as well as the Congress. The conclave
signalled NTR's increasing ambition in and involvement with
national politics. NTR's personal charisma certainly played
a part in bringing together, for the first time after the failed
Janata experiment, the leading lights in the Opposition camp to
Vijayawada. A few of them had never agreed to appear together
on a common political platform until that point. The leaders who
attended the conclave included L.K. Advani (BJP), S.S. Barnala
(Akali Dal), Chief Minister of Tamil Nadu MGR (AIADMK),
Chief Minister of Karnataka Ramakrishna Hegde (Janata), J&K
Chief Minister Farooq Abdullah (National Conference), Ravindra
Varma (Janata Party general secretary), A.S. Mishra (Lok Dal),
Sharad Pawar (Congress [S]), H.N. Bahuguna (Democratic
Socialist Party), Maneka Gandhi (Rashtriya Vichar Manch),
Jagjivan Ram (Congress [J]), Makineni Basavapunnaiah (CPI
[M]) and Chandra Rajeswara Rao (CPI).

'In those days, it was indeed an incredible spectacle to behold
leaders of the BJP at one end; the left communist parties at the other
end and leaders of other parties in the middle, converging together
under his aegis, to discuss anti-Congress strategy,' remarked P.S.
Ramamohan Rao, who was director general of police in the NTR
government and later the governor of Tamil Nadu.[29]

The meeting was held at the peak of the blazing summer at the
hilltop guest house of the state electricity board in Ibrahimpatnam.
The conclave issued a joint statement. The real threat to national
unity and integrity, it said, emanated primarily from the failure
of the ruling party at the Centre to find timely and acceptable
solutions to urgent issues of the people, and of different areas.
The conclave also endorsed the call for a review of Centre–state
relations. It also asked for an enlargement of the terms of reference
of the Sarkaria Commission.

'The significance of the Vijayawada conclave lay in the fact
that, for the first time in the history of independent India, 14

disparate non-Congress political parties got together at one place and were able to issue a joint statement, howsoever bland it may be,' Sumit Mitra of *India Today* commented.[30] Girilal Jain, the editor of the *Times of India*, found that NTR 'has taken to politics as fish do to water', and also remarked that 'there is little doubt that he wants to play a major role on the national scene'.[31]

The historic meeting indeed catapulted NTR to the national scene. In subsequent meetings in New Delhi in June 1983, Srinagar in October 1983 and Calcutta in January 1984, NTR emerged as one of the leading lights in the Opposition camp at the national level.

Starting at the 1983 Mahanadu, TDP made the right noises on the autonomy of states and federal principles. In the very first convention after the party captured power, the TDP spoke about the issue. 'In a country which is diverse in all respects, it is not appropriate to bring in forced unity. It is important to strengthen nationalism by protecting the rights of all regions. In this backdrop, regional parties are a historical necessity,' the 1983

Photograph courtesy of C. Kesavulu, *Eenadu*

Soon after he became CM, NTR focused his efforts on bringing together the national Opposition parties to build an alternative to the Congress. He gathered the who's who of Opposition leaders at the Mahanadu meeting in Vijayawada in 1983.

resolution declared. NTR's increasing confidence in his national role was evident.

NTR's was probably the first consistent, credible and theoretically sound voice in the country against the Centre's increasing accumulation of powers at the expense of the states. His crisp enunciation that 'Centre is a myth' caused much furore in Delhi. NTR explained that the words Centre and Central government, however common under a unitary constitution, 'are alien to us'. He emphasized that India was a union of states, and pointed out that centralized control and concentration of power in any single entity was not contemplated by the Constitution. 'Ours is a cooperative federation, with the Union on the one hand and the States on the other, each independent in its own sphere and at the same time working hand-in-hand for the good of the people,' he maintained.

The Congress (I) found his unrelenting stance an annoyance to its government at the Centre. Interestingly, in the neighbouring Tamil Nadu, MGR maintained cosy relations with Indira. 'My personal friendship with MGR in no way can influence my stand against the Congress Party. My political ideas are not borrowed ones. There is no question of getting close to Indira Congress,' NTR said on the eve of the first anniversary of his government.[32] It is this consistency and clarity that made NTR, in the words of Bhabani Sen Gupta, 'a more ardent advocate of a more equal relationship between the Centre and the States than the chief ministers of Tamil Nadu and Karnataka'.[33] His efforts to form a national alliance against the Congress, however, received a temporary setback following the August 1984 crisis, when he was toppled through a constitutional coup.

Costume Drama

Standing up to Prime Minister Indira Gandhi was not the only feat that popularized NTR. The costume drama that he enacted in his political debut was indeed an attention grabber. One of the features of NTR's movies was his character appearing in various disguises for comic relief. This routine from his cinema days seems to have had some influence on his penchant for the strange sartorial selections in his political avatar.

NTR wore khaki trousers and shirt for his campaign but reverted to Telugu-style dhoti and loose kurta on becoming the chief minister. He appeared in the saffron attire of a Hindu sannyasi on Ugadi, 15 April 1983, four months after he took office. 'I changed into these clothes after reading about the rape of a young girl, which disturbed me,' he claimed.[34] Upendra and others confirmed the story of the rape news being the reason for NTR's sartorial transition, which soon became his trademark and a butt of jokes. The chief minister claimed that the costume was a symbol of the purity of his intent and incorruptibility. Later, he sported a single earring on the left lobe, along with a string of beads around his neck. Towards the middle of his reign, NTR started wearing a turban to complete the look. This Vivekananda get-up was greeted with derision in the Opposition camp and bewilderment among onlookers.

The assembly saw all kinds of developments that were unheard of in the first year of the TDP rule in the wake of NTR's peculiar dress sense. Baggidi Gopal, an MLA from Punganur (Chittoor District), who fell out with the ruling party, appeared in the House sporting saffron clothes. He wore a *rudraksha* with *vibhuti* smeared on his forehead à la NTR. His dramatic entry caused a commotion in the treasury benches.

NTR was subjected to extreme ridicule because of his attire. Many members had a field day in the assembly and the council, making sneering comments on NTR's theatrical appearance. The Janata Party legislator, S. Jaipal Reddy, quipped that the people were not taken in by the khadi of the Congress, nor would they be deceived by the saffron of NTR. Boyi Bheemanna, a writer and nominated member, gave a sarcastic explanation as to why NTR wore a lone earring. 'Half the population in the state are women; he intends to represent them,' he said tongue in cheek.[35]

S. Basavapunnaiah, a Congress member in the Legislative Council, raised a point of order. He wanted to know whether a sannyasi could run a government and whether the budget passed by a sannyasi government would have any validity. He referred to Hindu traditions as propounded by Vashishta, Narada and Yajnavalkya that a sannyasi was as good as dead to the secular world. He said Islam and Christianity also followed this tradition wherein fakirs and saints never ruled over people.[36] Mukassir Shah, the council chair, sought an explanation of what it meant to be a sannyasi in Hindu tradition. He wanted to give a ruling on the Congress member's point of order based on the definition. NTR bravely explained that he was not a sannyasi but a *rajarshi*.

The difference, he said, was that the former completely gave up secular life in search of spiritual solitude, while the latter functioned within the temporal fold but sought to work for the welfare of the people. Unlike a sannyasi, a rajarshi might not give up the good things of life such as jewellery and costumes, he said. NTR went on to explain that a rajarshi worked for the betterment of the world while being part of the social and political fabric. He quoted the names of Viswamitra, Janaka, Ambarisha and Nahasha as examples of rajarshis. He also showed for the benefit of the members the different ways in which a sannyasi and a rajarshi wore their traditional dhoti, by folding and unfolding the raiment in the august House. But his rather lofty elucidation did not impress the sharp-tongued Opposition members who continued to taunt the professed symbolism of his flashy attire.

K. Rosaiah was the Congress leader in the Legislative Council. Known for his stinging wit, he regularly poked fun at NTR. 'Not every left-handed person is a leftist, NTR should know that,' he would say to the chief minister, who insisted that he was a leftist.[37] The well-known civil rights lawyer K.G. Kannabiran dubbed the costume conundrum as a 'one-man fancy-dress competition'.[38]

Despite all this jeering, NTR remained unruffled. 'I will not be insulted for my appearance,' he insisted. During Queen Elizabeth's visit to Hyderabad in November 1983, though, NTR removed his lone earring on the advice that he might come across as a punk to the visiting royalty.

Trust was not NTR's strong point. He always suspected that all those surrounding him might exploit the proximity to resort to unethical practices. Both Nadendla and Upendra, two of the key players in the TDP in the early stages, attested to this fact. It could be one of the reasons why he looked for support from his family. In any case, he had a weakness for family, especially his sons-in-law. His wife and sons were neither keen nor ambitious about a career in politics. So, they always kept away from the public gaze. But his sons-in-law had his tacit support to steadily increase their footprint in the party.

The elder son-in-law, Daggubati Venkateswara Rao, had disappeared halfway through the election campaign. He made a comeback from Madras soon after the TDP was elected to power. He started working in the party and was made convener of Telugu Yuvatha, the party's newly formed youth wing. There were murmurs of protest. But since Daggubati had been associated with the party from the beginning, the issue did not escalate. Soon after, the way was paved for him to become an MLA in the by-election for the Martur constituency. The doctor-turned-politician clearly enjoyed NTR's blessings.

The younger son-in-law's case was different. As a Congress minister, he had challenged NTR to an electoral duel. But after losing the election, Chandrababu Naidu could not keep away from the seat of power, now controlled by his father-in-law. NTR harboured a soft corner for Chandrababu. Nadendla alleged that NTR chose to field a weak candidate against his son-in-law in Chandragiri to ensure Chandrababu's victory.[39] However, in the TDP wave, the party candidate, Venkatarama Naidu, won with a good margin. Veeraraghavulu Naidu, a senior leader from Chittoor

District, had contributed to the strengthening of the party in the district in the early days. He was denied a ticket on Chandrababu's intervention, claimed both Nadendla and Daggubati. It was because Veeraraghavulu Naidu had every chance of becoming a minister in NTR's cabinet if he were elected.

Once Chandrababu made overtures, NTR showed undue haste to create the right conditions for his arrival. Two weeks after the election results, Chandrababu announced his resignation from the Congress (I). He also announced his intention to join the TDP, along with many leaders from Chittoor District. NTR was all set to provide him with a smooth ride into the party.

But something unexpected happened. The party supremo was taken aback at the strong resistance shown by party legislators when he brought up the matter at the TDP's state-level meeting. Some of the legislators, including Venkatarama Naidu, questioned the move. NTR tried to pacify them, saying that a committee would filter all such requests. However, many MLAs reiterated their stiff opposition to opening the doors to defectors from the Congress (I). NTR left the meeting midway in a huff. He was rattled by the defiance of party members.

Meanwhile, NTR was growing impatient. Nadendla claimed in his autobiography that NTR had told him that his daughter Bhuvaneswari was pressuring him to admit Chandrababu into the party. He appeared emotionally disturbed, caught between his family and the party. He kept bursting out in private talks at the intransigence of the legislators. A suggestion came that it was better to leave the decision to a committee. The five-member committee was initially unwilling to give a royal welcome to NTR's family member, considering the wrong message it could send to the people. An impatient NTR gave the task to Upendra, who by now was his confidant. He met with each member of the committee separately, conveyed NTR's wish and made them sign on the dotted line. Nadendla, however, was a tough nut to crack. When Upendra finally approached him, Nadendla, who called himself the co-pilot in the government, was furious. 'What are you people planning to do with this party? Are you intent on destroying it?' he shouted. But he relented finally, and after signing the resolution to admit Chandrababu into the party, literally threw the paper at Upendra.

The overwhelming sentiment among the party cadre was against Chandrababu's admission, fearing the TDP would soon turn into a private limited company of NTR. A senior leader, Bezawada Papi Reddy, did not mince words, saying the party was turning into a 'Kamma *rajyam* [Kamma bastion]'. Even some of NTR's family members, including Daggubati, were not favourably disposed to Chandrababu's entry. The media too was critical of the development.

To his credit, Chandrababu kept a low profile after joining the party. Even though he threw himself deep into party work, he did not seek a party post or position in the government for quite some time. However, he enjoyed a say in party matters. He tried to impress everybody within the party with his managerial and political skills. He gave inputs on the party's strategy during assembly sessions. But NTR was a hard taskmaster. He did not give too much leeway to Chandrababu till the latter proved his political worth. This came into full play during the 1984 August crisis.

It was, however, clear in the first year of the government that NTR's sons-in-law were destined to play an influential role in the party, despite NTR's half-hearted protestations.

Upendra, who emerged as another key player, was an outsider in many ways. Parvathaneni Upendra Chandra Chowdary was not a regular politician, though he harboured political ambition. At the time of the TDP's formation, he was joint director, public relations, in Indian Railways and was posted as the editor of their in-house magazine, *Indian Railways*, in Delhi. After having spent most of his career in Kolkata, Upendra had an opportunity to work as special assistant to Madhu Dandavate, who was the railway minister in the Janata government. After the fall of the Janata government, he was back in the department. But he was averse to continuing in the job. As a young man in AP, Upendra had rubbed shoulders with socialists and entertained thoughts of a career in politics during his student days. But his circumstances had not allowed him to follow that path earlier. Now, tired of the long service in railways, Upendra was keen on pursuing a political career. Having heard of NTR's political initiative, Upendra, who had excellent people skills, met him in Hyderabad through some acquaintances.

NTR agreed after much persuasion to allow Upendra to resign from his job with thirteen years of service still left and accompany him on his Chaitanya Ratham. NTR, a workaholic, was very demanding of his colleagues, and Upendra survived his expectations. He grew closer to NTR during the campaign and gradually had his eyes and ears. His brief stint as a journalist in the past and his exposure to north India, especially Delhi, stood him in good stead in his new role. He was one of the few confidants whose inputs were taken into consideration during the selection of candidates for the election. He was considered a member of the inner coterie after NTR became the chief minister.

Nadendla was suspicious of Upendra from day one. Nadendla thought of Upendra as an agent of Ramoji Rao with whom he had a cold relationship. Such was the animosity of Nadendla for Upendra that he referred to the latter in his autobiography by the epithet 'Delhi stranger'. Nadendla was of the firm opinion that Ramoji had airdropped Upendra into NTR's coterie to ensure that he was kept at bay. However, Upendra claimed that NTR wanted him to be part of the cabinet without portfolio so that he could help him in day-to-day matters. An alarmed Nadendla immediately tried to put a brake on the proposal, saying that having a non-MLA in the cabinet would send wrong signals to the public, besides causing heartburn among the legislators. Upendra said that though NTR initially insisted on having his way, he later yielded to the pressure put by Nadendla, who also provoked NTR's family members against Upendra's elevation. During this period, Upendra accompanied NTR to the secretariat and helped him in both administrative and party matters. Soon, he earned the tag of 'extra-constitutional authority'.

Meanwhile, NTR wanted Upendra to contest the election, which was the ambition of the bureaucrat-turned-political aide. Upendra claimed that NTR had promised during the cabinet episode that he would vacate the Tirupati assembly seat from where Upendra could get elected. Again, things didn't turn out the way Upendra had expected. Chandrababu Naidu joined the TDP and influenced the decision-making process. NTR looked for ways to restore Chandrababu's political career and entertained the idea of fielding him from Tirupati. However, Chandrababu was not willing to be in the fray as a TDP candidate, having been defeated only recently. Even NTR must have felt that such a decision might not be appreciated by the party workers. So, on his son-in-law's recommendation, the ticket was given to a local doctor in Tirupati. Upendra was left with no choice but to contest from Himayat Nagar, the urban constituency in Hyderabad, which fell vacant following the sudden death of Narayana Goud, a TDP MLA.

The election, however, proved to be a disaster for the TDP and particularly for Upendra's ambitions. The urban constituency had a history of little loyalty to any one party. Besides, the recent outrage among the government staff had put a strain on the party's winning chances. The defeat in Himayat Nagar was the first, though a minor, setback for the TDP.

Though disheartened by the defeat, Upendra continued to play an important role in the party's affairs. He had an opportunity to show his networking skills during the national Opposition conclave held in Vijayawada. A fluent speaker in Hindi and Bengali, besides Telugu and English, he was entrusted with the task of inviting all the major non-Congress figures to the meet. It was during this time that he began cultivating contacts in Delhi. The conclave's success boosted his image within the party. He appeared to be riding high as NTR made him the general secretary in the same Mahanadu. It looked like Upendra was unstoppable in the party.

But there lay the rub. He started encountering hostility from those around NTR. Upendra said when the decision to appoint him general secretary became known, family members poisoned NTR's mind against him. Since he had already disappointed Upendra several times in the past, NTR went ahead with his decision. But the fluster in NTR's mind as a result of these forces working in opposite directions was visible on his face. 'When he announced my elevation in the Mahanadu, there was no excitement or cheer in NTR's visage,' Upendra recalled.[40]

Despite his position, Upendra had little say in any matter. A think tank consisting of Bhujanga Rao, Tummala Chowdary, Minte Padmanabham and Prof C. Lakshmanna, known for their socialist inclinations, advised NTR. Chandrababu's graph was rising. Though he held no official position either in the government or in the party, he was able to project himself as a power centre. Daggubati, too, cultivated his own group within the party. He was already the convener of Telugu Yuvatha, and later an MLA through a by-election. Upendra managed to survive through sheer tenacity. From being an influential adviser, he turned into one of the many aides to the party's president. NTR had a habit of consulting many people before any decision, but no single person was able to influence him entirely. NTR's fondness for his sons-in-law, however, was becoming evident in his decision-making process.

Upendra sensed that the environment in the party office—which had moved from Ramakrishna Studios to Himayat Nagar—was not conducive for his growth. When offered a Rajya Sabha seat, he jumped at the opportunity. Upendra alleged that the family members conspired to send him out of Hyderabad. He also wanted the same as he thought he could create more impact in Delhi. Upendra was one of the five members who formed the first batch of TDP representatives elected to the Rajya Sabha. The others were B. Satyanarayana Reddy,[41] Y. Sasibhushana Rao, P. Radhakrishna and Prof Lakshmanna. Upendra was named TDP parliamentary party leader. For a railway employee, whose career best was working as a special assistant to a Union minister, this elevation in less than a year of his political entry was rather dramatic and indeed fulfilling.

Congress Convulsions

The deep-rooted Congress establishment in the state found it difficult to face the new regime and the new actors that emerged on the political firmament. They were shell-shocked by the sudden loss of power. It took some time for them to gather themselves. It was not easy in the earlier days. The anti-Congress sentiment was still strong. However, with sixty MLAs in the assembly, the Congress was able to gradually make its voice heard. A youthful Y.S. Rajasekhara Reddy got recognition within the Congress (I) for standing up to the government on many issues. Indira was impressed with YSR's fight against NTR. She made him the state Congress president at the young age of thirty-four, against the wishes of many senior leaders.

Several measures of the TDP government in the early phase were aimed at further weakening the Congress's hold on the political and administrative structures. The move to abolish the Legislative Council, entirely dominated by the Congress, was clearly for political purposes. The ruling party, having come into existence recently, had no representation in the Upper House. With the council acting as a stumbling block for all the TDP government's decisions, NTR decided to go ahead with the abolition.

The Indira government in Delhi, however, sat for a long time on the assembly resolution passed in March 1983. 'It's a politically motivated decision. Why should the Centre pass the resolution when it is not convinced with the reasons?' the then Union law minister Jagannath Kaushal said in Parliament a year after the AP legislature passed it. It was only when Rajiv Gandhi took over that the state government's resolution was passed.

The council, before it wound up, caused much trouble to the ruling party. Led by veteran Congressman K. Rosaiah, the council members of the Opposition needled NTR daily. The Congress members, aided by the chair, Mukassir Shah, another Congressman, always had their say because they had a majority. The council held up important bills by sending them to select committees and formed House committees on every issue. The Upper House generally stonewalled the government business. It was one of the reasons why the TDP government, despite its substantial majority in the assembly, had to often resort to issuing ordinances to implement major decisions.

The council tried to take on *Eenadu* and its chairman, which further hastened the process for the abolition of the council. A House committee was constituted by the Legislative Council to go into the affairs of chit fund companies in the state.[42] Ramoji was known to draw his financial power from his chit fund company, Margadarsi Chit Fund.[43] The finance minister, Nadendla Bhaskara Rao, not a fan of Ramoji Rao, played along with the Opposition to constitute the committee. Only one belonged to the TDP in the seven-member committee. This decision to put Ramoji in the dock was disconcerting to NTR. But more serious was the privilege motion moved by the Legislative Council against *Eenadu* and its editor, Ramoji Rao. This was in reaction to a headline in the newspaper for a report on the pandemonium in the House. 'Peddala Galabha [Ruckus by Elders]' was not a particularly derogatory headline.[44] But the House, dominated by Congress members, took serious objection to it. Ramoji Rao editorially supported the move of the NTR government to abolish the council, and hence even non-Congress Opposition members, particularly those from the BJP, were not happy with him.

The privilege committee of the House, after dragging the issue for over a year, found the headline mischievous and summoned Ramoji to appear before it in March 1984 to receive admonition. Ramoji wrote back, questioning the lack of fair procedure and implied the action was politically motivated. The council considered Ramoji's response as attributing motives to the House and asked the police commissioner to produce him before it. Ramoji turned to the Supreme Court, which granted a stay. The council took umbrage at what it regarded as the court stepping into the legislative domain and asked the police to ignore the judicial intervention. The apex court stepped in once again and asked the police to not arrest Ramoji. When the police commissioner, K. Vijayarama Rao, who later headed the Central Bureau of Investigation (CBI), went to the *Eenadu* office at Somajiguda to take the portly businessman into custody, a smiling Ramoji handed over the court order.

What began as a political tug of war between the TDP and the Congress now turned into a full-scale confrontation between the legislature and the judiciary. NTR was clearly unhappy with the proceedings in the council and wrote to President Zail Singh to resolve the situation—which threatened to blow up into a constitutional crisis—by referring the issue to the Supreme Court. In retaliation, the Legislative Council adopted a resolution requesting the president to ignore the chief minister's letter. The Legislative Assembly immediately passed another resolution urging the president to disregard the council's recommendation. Before the clash could get ugly, NTR chose to avert a crisis by getting the Upper House prorogued. The council was done away with, and the Ramoji issue automatically died down.

The chief minister celebrated the TDP government's first anniversary at the crowded Lal Bahadur Stadium with the same dramatic flourish as the swearing-in. NTR firmly cemented his populist image with a series of announcements. However, the anniversary celebrations, which were held in January 1984, witnessed a bizarre incident that raised many eyebrows. There was

an alleged attempt on NTR's life by an unemployed youth.
After his address to the sea of people gathered at the elaborately
decorated stadium, NTR, along with several other ministers, sat
down to enjoy a mridangam performance by Yella Venkateswara
Rao. Suddenly, a youth attacked him with a knife. NTR's quick
reaction and defensive move saved him from fatal injuries, though
his left thumb got a nick in the attack. Blood spilled on to his
saffron clothes, even as the dignitaries on the stage were shocked
at the unexpected incident. Ganga Bhavani, a party leader, tore
off her saree pallu (loose end) and bandaged NTR's wound.
The youth was immediately surrounded and taken away. NTR,
however, was unperturbed and asked the agitated crowd to quieten
down. He even shook hands later with the artistes, appreciating
their performances. He stayed put for some time on the stage
before being persuaded to go to a hospital.

A youth from Guntur named Mallela Babji had carried out the
attack. Some reports said that he shouted 'NTR down' and 'Indira
Gandhi zindabad' while pouncing on NTR. The Opposition
leaders were quick to condemn the 'dastardly incident'. Several
political leaders from all over the country sent their best wishes.
Fans swarmed the chief minister's residence. NTR played lofty,
asking people to not get agitated by the attack and assuring them
that nothing would happen to him as long as his well-wishers
stood by him. He also addressed the people through Doordarshan
showing his bandaged finger prominently.

Doubts were, however, expressed at the way the incident played
out. Some media reports even suggested it was all orchestrated to
draw sympathy. The allegation was that the ruling party resorted
to the gimmick due to the government's sagging image. The
controversy refused to die down and threw up more revelations
a few years later. But, at this point of time, NTR's charisma was
still intact.

By the end of the first year in governance, NTR became
known across the country for both his sartorial quirks and populist

schemes. Within AP, he was regarded as a maverick messiah who was determined to make a difference, though he was prone to commit mistakes in the process. He was self-righteous and considered himself incorruptible. But he was far from inured to personality cult and consciously nurtured the image of the saviour on the lines of Indira Gandhi. In the process, his authoritarian streak was becoming evident. Despite such aberrations, he was mainly guided by his sense of public good, however lopsided it was. Since he was dismantling the established political set-up, there was, not unexpectedly, high resistance to his decisions from powerful sections.

But still, NTR was able to push through many of his radical measures because of the unstinted public support. 'I am swimming against many odds,' he admitted in an interview to *India Today* on his government's first anniversary.[45] But he was undaunted by the pitfalls and ready to plough ahead, unaware that forces inimical to his kind of politics had begun to plot his overthrow.

As he stepped into his second year of administration, NTR went on to bring fundamental changes in the social and political structure in the countryside. This constituted a radical transformation of the panchayat raj system, the rural administrative apparatus. The first step was to abolish part-time hereditary village officers who had wielded an enormous amount of power and clout.[46] Known as *karanam* and *munasabu* (munsif) in Andhra, and patel and patwari in Telangana, these traditional village officials were mostly upper-caste landholders. They had a reputation for being manipulative and biased in the village's revenue matters and enjoyed considerable hold—despite their apparently insignificant jobs—on the government. The NTR government considered the system of part-time village officers outmoded.

According to former RBI governor Y.V. Reddy, NTR believed that feudal relations, as well as corruption, could be eliminated by selecting village-level officers on merit. The Andhra Pradesh Abolition of Part-time Village Officers Ordinance resulted in an estimated 37,000 village officers losing their employment from 6 January 1984.[47] After that, the government ordered the creation of 4800 posts of village assistants in the revenue department, heralding a new era in village administration.

The move affected many people who had a stranglehold on the village administration. But the dismantling of the old structure was perceived, not incorrectly, as eliminating the Congress patronage system and replacing it with that of the TDP. The move was so disruptive that it forced the Congress to sit up and take note. It organized a state panchayat conference in Vijayawada to protest the decision. The who's who of the state Congress, including P.V. (as P.V. Narasimha Rao was known), Kotla Vijayabhaskara Reddy and P. Shiv Shankar participated in the event. But an unfazed NTR went ahead. The reason for the Congress's trepidation was the 'threat the reform posed to its social base'. But the people, particularly the marginal sections in the hinterland, widely welcomed the change because it ended an autocratic institution. The measure would also weaken pro-Congress caste groups like the Reddys by eroding their rural stranglehold. The move was particularly welcomed in Telangana where rural oppression was associated with the patel–patwari system.

The Game Begins

The Congress suffered a sense of deep unease about the TDP's growing political clout. Indira was annoyed at NTR's attempts to float a national alternative to the Congress party. 'Why does he run around with all these [Opposition] persons? We could cooperate with him like in Tamil Nadu if he concerned himself with his state,' she told Upendra, the TDP group leader in Parliament.[48] Things, however, took an unexpected turn when cracks opened up in the ruling TDP government, sooner than anyone had expected. The Congress wanted to seize the opportunity when Nadendla got in touch with party leaders in Delhi.

Nadendla, who was steadily being pushed into a corner, finally decided to strike. He had all along been valiantly trying to assert his position as number two in the government, but apparently with little success. Nadendla was more experienced as an administrator and seemed to have genuinely tried to get along with the oddball chief minister. But NTR's personalized style of functioning meant that there was only one leading man in his political script. NTR believed that people had voted TDP on the strength of his character and promises, so he alone was accountable to them. In this scenario, there was little place for others, including the ministers and MLAs. Nadendla found himself outside the charmed circle of NTR too soon. Several of the government's announcements came as a surprise to him. Nadendla was stripped of his general secretary position in the party immediately after being made a minister. It was on the principle that every party leader should hold only one post. However, NTR exempted himself from this rule and continued as party president.

NTR and Nadendla were from two different worlds. NTR was idealistic, emotional, fancied himself as a do-gooder and was out to make a dramatic impact on the state. Nadendla was from the cantankerous world of politics, where balancing power and political compulsions were of utmost importance, and administration needed to be tempered with ground reality. Nadendla could not share NTR's enthusiasm for leaping into the unknown through his extravagant decisions. He claimed that NTR had little understanding of the nuances of administration and revelled in his own naivety.

As an example, he quoted how NTR responded when he expressed doubts about the Telugu Ganga project. 'Don't worry, brother. If I give a call to my fans, each one of them would come forward with a trowel and basket, and complete the project in no time,' NTR apparently declared in all sincerity.[49] Nadendla also claimed that he had a falling-out with NTR on the issue of lowering the age of retirement, because his elder brother was one of the victims of the decision. The decision caused much resentment among the employees, which led to Nadendla's own discomfiture as finance minister and one of the top party leaders. Nadendla was also opposed to the decision to do away with the patel–patwari institution, another of NTR's bold decisions which unsettled the administration.

In his second year in power, NTR became more self-absorbed and aggressive in his decision-making process. His directions were government orders, and his utterances were party policies, Nadendla recalled. NTR was least concerned with the consequences of his audacious moves. Nadendla considered himself a victim of NTR's follies. NTR, for him, was becoming a cunning and dictatorial personality behind a facade of righteousness. He thought NTR's only ambition was to alternately shock and gratify the ordinary people with his crazy ideas and project himself as their guardian angel. Nadendla was not involved in organizing the Opposition conclave in Vijayawada on Mahanadu. He opposed such meetings, arguing against taking a provocative stand on Indira Gandhi. He thought NTR's ego was being massaged by those close to him to stake a claim for a role at the national level.

Eenadu, by now considered a confirmed TDP supporter and a significant influence on NTR politically, was uncharitable towards Nadendla, suggesting he had been a corrupt minister in his stint in the Congress government.[50] It was never clear what exactly caused the hostility between the two. His Congress background was a sore point with *Eenadu*, which in recent years had emerged as a robust anti-Congress voice. Nadendla claimed that Ramoji Rao had suspected him when the previous Congress government had ordered an inquiry into Margadarsi, the latter's chit fund. Nadendla recollected that he had no axe to grind against Ramoji. It was on the order of the then chief minister, M. Channa Reddy, that he had instituted the inquiry. Though nothing came of it, Nadendla got into the bad books of Ramoji.

As the TDP government entered its second year of rule, Nadendla felt more and more humiliated, both at the personal and political levels. The growing distance between the two was evident by May 1984, when the party's annual conference was held in Visakhapatnam. Nadendla's presence in this Mahanadu was minimal. During this time, he began tapping into the resentment which was brewing among many party leaders, ministers and legislators against the increasing hold of NTR's family, especially his sons-in-law.

NTR's refusal to entrust governance to him as a senior minister during his month-long absence caused much heartburn for Nadendla.[51] During NTR's bypass heart surgery in the US in July–August 1984, the government had no political authority at the helm. NTR, allegedly on Chandrababu's advice, had not named an in-charge during his absence.[52] Adding insult to injury, a circular was issued that district collectors would hoist the flags for Independence Day in their respective districts rather than the ministers, which was the regular practice.

Nadendla had already received feelers from the Congress during his recent meetings with Prime Minister Indira Gandhi and Union Finance Minister Pranab Mukherjee. A couple of months before the August 1984 coup, Nadendla met Indira to seek assistance for drought relief. Indira conveyed her displeasure over NTR hobnobbing with the Opposition leaders. She also hinted that Nadendla was welcome back in the party. She asked him to keep in touch with the AICC general secretary G.K. Moopanar. Nadendla also claimed that Pranab Mukherjee met him in Hyderabad at the house of a Congress leader and apparently pumped him up, saying, 'Bhaskara Raoji, it seems only you have the majority following among legislators.'

Nadendla decided to quickly make his move for the takeover of the party even as NTR was returning home from the US. The coup had all the elements of a cloak-and-dagger thriller: Ageing, fragile and unsuspecting patriarch returns to the kingdom, after recovering from a major illness, only to find that he was being betrayed.

During his first trip to the US in June 1984, NTR had undergone a medical check-up. He was diagnosed with coronary artery disease. NTR did not initially take the problem seriously, but realized the need for treatment after his return to India. NTR once again left for the US on 15 July and returned on 14 August after the bypass surgery, which was performed by world-renowned surgeon Dr Denton Cooley. The triple bypass coronary operation was conducted on 18 July at Houston with Dr B. Soma Raju, a well-known cardiologist from Nizam's Orthopaedic Institute in Hyderabad, by his side. NTR recovered faster than any younger patient, Dr Kakarla Subba Rao, a distinguished radiologist in the US of Andhra origin, recalled. Doctors advised rest for eight weeks and asked NTR to not strain himself for more than three to four hours a day.

By the time he returned, the political colours were changing in Hyderabad. NTR received inputs about something fishy going on back home. He flew from New York to Bombay in the early hours of 14 August and took a connecting flight to Hyderabad. Ministers, party leaders and many film industry personalities welcomed him. It took him half an hour to come out of the jam-packed airport where he was mobbed by thousands who had gathered to greet him. Among those who shook hands with him and embraced him at the airport was Nadendla. 'Anna, why did you return in such a hurry? You should have taken rest for a few more days,' Nadendla showed his concern.

However, within a few hours, the co-pilot caused turbulence in the political firmament. He had already prepared the ground for an uprising by mobilizing signatures of legislators. Nadendla was gathering supporters on the plea that the Centre was set to overthrow the TDP government.

A series of dramatic developments started to unfold in quick succession. Having got wind of Nadendla's plan to break away,

NTR lost no time in recommending his ouster from the ministry to the governor. After hearing of this, Nadendla immediately sent in his resignation. This was followed by three other ministers— S. Ramamuni Reddy, T. Jeevan Reddy and S. Satyanarayana— announcing their departures from the cabinet. The unexpected turn of events created tremors in the ruling party. The TDP leaders charged that Nadendla was hand in glove with the Congress in this operation. Congress leaders feigned ignorance and maintained that the development was an internal affair of the TDP. As the political temperature began to rise, NTR loyalists were summoned to Ramakrishna Studios, which was to become their hideout for a long time to come.

Coup on I-Day

Independence Day of 1984 was a day of political intrigue in Hyderabad. As news of the split in the TDP spread, Raj Bhavan turned into a stage for political chicanery of the worst kind. Both factions of the TDP got ready to fight it out in the presence of Governor Ram Lal.

Had the governor been remotely concerned with the majority support for NTR, the story would have ended with a floor test. NTR clearly enjoyed a comfortable majority in the 294-member-strong House at this time. Ram Lal had other plans. He parlayed with not only Nadendla twice but also with Madan Mohan, the Congress legislature party leader. Nadendla was trying to prevail upon the governor that NTR had lost the majority in the House. He claimed many TDP MLAs were ready to sail with him. He came up with a list of ninety-one TDP legislators, fifty-one Congress MLAs, six independents, five from the AIMIM and two from Sanjay Vichar Manch, totalling 161.

He also claimed ownership of the TDP. He founded the party, and NTR was merely an invitee, he told the reporters.

He blamed NTR for turning the party into a family fiefdom, alleging his relatives were calling the shots. NTR's dynastic politics was exactly what he had accused Indira of. Despite his strong objections and advice, NTR had been quarrelsome with the Centre, unnecessarily getting involved in national Opposition politics. NTR's whimsical decisions had caused much harm to the state's interests. The actor-politician's dictatorial manners had alienated the legislators, who now found a saviour in him, Nadendla declared.[53]

Most of what Nadendla said in the press conference had some truth. Except that he did not have the support of the majority of TDP MLAs, which he hoped he would be able to muster soon if everything went according to the plan. The governor's confabulations with Nadendla and Madan Mohan and his lukewarm attitude towards the NTR group betrayed where his sympathies lay. The TDP sent minister N. Srinivasulu Reddy and the TDP legislature party secretary Tripurana Venkataratnam to hand over a letter to the governor with signatures of 168 MLAs. But that did not break the ice with Ram Lal who was all set for a constitutional coup, even as NTR received the official salute at the parade of the thirty-eighth Independence Day celebrations in Secunderabad.

The NTR camp was quick to react, and in a hurriedly called-for cabinet meeting, announced the convening of the assembly session on 18 August for a show of strength on the floor of the House. If NTR had hoped that everything would get sorted out in seventy-two hours with this move, he was mistaken. The ordeal was long and tortuous, and his famed determination and stamina was put to test. NTR attended the at-home hosted by the governor at Raj Bhavan that evening, unaware of the plans being formulated in the very same hallowed precincts.

Nearly twenty-four hours after he precipitated the plot to overthrow NTR, Nadendla was still short of the simple majority. But Governor Ram Lal moved fast, unfolding a series of bizarre developments for a single day. He sent a missive in the morning of 16 August, stating he was convinced that NTR had lost his majority in the House and sought his resignation. At the time, NTR was conferring with 149 TDP and nineteen non-Congress MLAs in the presence of Opposition leaders, including S. Jaipal Reddy and M. Venkaiah Naidu, at Ramakrishna Studios. The chief minister immediately dashed off a letter to the governor, asserting, 'I am ready to produce before you, now itself, the majority of MLAs.'

However, the governor moved with alacrity to dismiss the NTR government, sending shock waves across the political spectrum. Without further ado, he followed this up with another devious move—the swearing-in of Nadendla as the state's twelfth chief minister.[54] NTR was replaced overnight 'with a rival politician who pledged cooperation with the Government of Prime Minister Indira Gandhi', the *New York Times* reported the next day.[55] Nadendla, however, later lamented that Ram Lal had delayed his induction by a day, which made the would-be defectors diffident. 'Things would have been different had the governor acted immediately on our representation and handed the government to us,' he said.

The NTR camp, though jittery, was determined to not let the governor get away with what they felt was the murder of all democratic norms. The Opposition parties, including the Janata Party, the BJP and the communists, joined hands with NTR to fiercely oppose the governor's move.[56] The MLAs, including those from the Opposition ranks, trooped to Raj Bhavan. But they were stopped at Lakeview guest house, a few hundred yards before the governor's residence where Nadendla was to be sworn in shortly. As NTR's supporters refused to leave, Ram Lal agreed to meet NTR and a small group of his MLAs in his chambers.

A drooping NTR, leaning on a walking stick, handed over a letter to the governor, insisting he still commanded a majority and requested the governor to call for a session of the assembly for a floor test. He demanded that the governor recall his ouster order, and refused to leave till he was restored as the chief minister. Still recuperating from the heart surgery, NTR lay on the sofa in the room, while the MLAs surrounded the governor, obstructing him from leaving the study. Ram Lal got restive as it was getting late for the Nadendla swearing-in. Finally, he ordered the police chief Mahender Reddy to take NTR and the MLAs into custody, which was promptly attended to. The governor was already delayed and swore Nadendla in at 2.45 p.m., at least half an hour behind the auspicious mahurat. Nadendla rued years later that it was this lousy timing that got him undone. The governor administered the oath during the inauspicious *Rahu Kalam*, which spelt doom to his government, Nadendla bemoaned.

This clandestine act—barely a dozen people, including Nadendla's family members, were present at the ceremony that contrasted NTR's spectacular public swearing-in—exposed the insidiousness of the operation. The governor was obviously prevailed upon to go for the kill, in the firm hope that this action would turn the tables against NTR, as the legislators would take the hint and queue up in Raj Bhavan to support Nadendla. The governor, who was not ready to give three days to NTR to prove his majority in the House, offered a generous thirty days to Nadendla to show his support in the assembly.

Meanwhile, the police took all the MLAs away from Raj Bhavan in a police van. They requested NTR, the chief minister till a few moments ago, to come along with the police van in a separate car. But he refused and climbed into the police truck with difficulty and sat along with the other MLAs. The picture of a crestfallen, sick NTR sitting at the back of the police van, holding himself together with the support of the walking stick, appeared in next day's papers and earned him instant sympathy. 'NTR Surgery—Successful Abroad, Fatal at Home,' summed up a witty banner put up at Marine Drive by Nana Chudasama, the former Bombay Sheriff.

Soon after the oath, Nadendla made all the right noises. He addressed a press conference, pledging cooperation and support to the Centre. He claimed that his was the real TDP government and that he would follow all the founding principles of the party. He alleged that NTR was holding many TDP MLAs to ransom at Ramakrishna Studios and that he would initiate action against this 'abduction'.[57] The series of developments left the people as well as the Opposition parties stunned. Protests and demonstrations erupted across the state spontaneously, even as three battalions of CRPF were rushed to the capital. The Opposition parties in Parliament cried murder of democracy. In the Lok Sabha, all except for the AIADMK and Muslim League walked out to protest the governor's action.

Ram Lal's letter earlier asking NTR to resign had reached him at around 12.30 p.m. when he, along with Opposition leaders, was addressing 168 MLAs at Ramakrishna Studios. In his response to the governor, NTR had stated the same and said that he would present each one of them physically at Raj Bhavan to satisfy his concern. 'I will be the last person to continue as chief minister, even for a day, if I do not enjoy the majority support in the assembly,' NTR had affirmed in his missive. Even the media was witness to the 168 MLAs present with him earlier at Ramakrishna Studios and later at Raj Bhavan.

The calculations of the Congress high command had clearly gone south. Indira was possibly misguided by the likes of Arun Nehru.[58] The PM's managers believed Nadendla's claims of brewing discontent in the TDP and his capacity to draw a sizeable number of TDP MLAs to his side. But it did not take long for the Congress high command to realize their folly. It was, however, too late in the day to go back. So, a long-drawn political tug of war was chalked out to weaken NTR's sway over the legislators and give more breathing time to Nadendla.

For the next thirty days, the state witnessed unprecedented civil unrest and political turbulence as Delhi forced its choice of chief minister on the people of AP. On the day NTR was dethroned, as many as eleven persons were killed in police firing during a protest in Rayalaseema.

Meanwhile, Nadendla gave the image of being busy in the business of governance. He got three ministers—S. Ramamuni Reddy, T. Jeevan Reddy and S. Satyanarayana—sworn in. All three were ministers in the NTR cabinet, having resigned to join hands with Nadendla. He kept on repeating that TDP MLAs were being held against their will in Ramakrishna Studios. He sent the police to the studio to 'free' the abducted legislators based on a complaint in the Chikkadpally police station. Opposition leaders, including A.B. Vajpayee, Farooq Abdullah and Venkaiah Naidu, were present at the time. The police gave a report, saying the MLAs were voluntarily staying there. However, attempts were made again and again to wean away legislators of the NTR camp by hook or by crook.

In a bid to turn the tide, Nadendla announced a series of decisions to undo NTR's actions. He began with the abolition of Dharma Maha Matra and issued orders to withdraw all cases under investigation by the ombudsman, a move that gratified the government employees' associations. The decision to lower the age of retirement was reversed amid cheers by the employees. Rules were amended to restore pensions to former legislators. House sites for all accredited journalists in districts were announced. Mess charges in hostels for students of Backward Castes were hiked. The Congress appointees were reinstated in the various academies. The new chief minister was cheered and felicitated heartily by the old culture establishment of the state. However, the public was not fooled by his generosity. People came out in large numbers to demonstrate in the streets.

If Nadendla and the Congress were counting on NTR's poor health to pave the way for their smooth takeover, they were mistaken. Indeed, NTR had been told by doctors to not strain himself, but he refused to take the humiliation lying down.

Physically weak and against doctors' advice, NTR embarked on a difficult and protracted struggle to claim his right, belying the expectations of his detractors.

NTR attended a public meeting at the Nizam College grounds. The huge gathering was addressed by leaders of the Opposition, including Charan Singh, Sharad Pawar, Neelam Rajasekhara Reddy, Farooq Abdullah, Samar Mukherjee, H.N. Bahuguna and Era Sezhiyan. When NTR stood up to speak, there was an uninterrupted round of applause for five long minutes. He waited for it to die down and then conveyed his anguish at the way the people's mandate was sabotaged. He was able to rouse the anger of a hundred and fifty thousand people at the patent injustice. As a humped NTR gulped medicines handed over by his brother Trivikrama Rao midway through his speech, he symbolized victimhood.

The NTR camp, led by Upendra from the front and Chandrababu from behind the scenes, was quick to realize that the fight was going to be long and hard. They would have to keep up the momentum if they were to get back their due. They hit upon the plan to shift the scene to Delhi to create heat in the political corridors of the capital. The decision to move the legislators who were supporting them all the way to Delhi and parade them before the president of India was a master stroke. The legislators were to travel by AP Express, and NTR, along with some Opposition leaders, was to take a flight. However, the railways provided only one bogie though three were requisitioned for carrying more than 160 MLAs. The legislators were packed like sardines in the general compartment, but the train reached the destination ten hours late. The appointment with the president was at 6:30 p.m. but the train reached Nizamuddin Station at 6 p.m. NTR was scheduled to join the Opposition leaders for a press meet in Delhi. He could not because the flight was delayed due to a bomb threat and reached Palam Airport four hours late.

With both the train and the flight delayed, it became impossible for the MLAs to reach Rashtrapati Bhavan for the proposed parade before the president. NTR was taken to a clinic after disembarking from the flight due to his fragile health. The MLAs were given a rousing welcome at the railway station. They had to be accommodated at Hotel Surya Sofitel under the guise of a wedding party, apparently to evade the prying eyes of the Intelligence Bureau (IB). Opposition leaders Chandra Shekhar and Biju Patnaik met the president and alleged the government's role in the undue delay of the journey of the TDP leaders and legislators. President Zail Singh had already been intimated about the hold-up. He graciously offered to see the delegation any time. The time was fixed for 11.45 a.m. the next day, 21 August.

The optics of the day were glaringly in favour of a wheelchair-bound NTR, as he paraded 161 legislators in the historic corridors of Rashtrapati Bhavan. President Zail Singh received NTR and his MLAs with warmth. Though he politely refused to take a count of the MLAs, the president was convinced that NTR commanded a majority. So was the media—national and international—that had assembled to report the event. Zail Singh's decision to meet NTR and the MLAs was a slap in the face of the Central government.

The photos of the MLAs being paraded before the president were flashed widely, providing concrete evidence to the nation. Emerging from Rashtrapati Bhawan, where he had gone in an ambulance, NTR addressed a press meet in which he warned of a long-drawn struggle against his removal. He also opposed any move to impose President's Rule in the state to save face from the ignominy of restoring his government. Mounting pressure on Delhi, the national Opposition leaders, including Charan Singh, met the president, demanding that NTR's government be restored at once. They also demanded the recall of Governor Ram Lal. Zail Singh did his bit, conveying to the government his unhappiness over the AP episode.

The sacked chief minister, who emerged as a regional strongman, taking his fight to Delhi to restore democracy, was swamped by national and foreign correspondents and television crews in the capital. The public meeting the same evening in support of NTR saw one of the biggest crowds in the capital. It was described as the largest rally in Delhi since the one Lok Nayak Jayaprakash Narayan had addressed in early 1977 to launch the Janata Party. It was also the most emotionally charged public meeting in a long time.

Indira Gandhi tried to put the blame on Governor Ram Lal. Claiming that she was not aware of the change in AP, Indira said that at no stage did the governor consult the Centre. She also claimed that even her own party's support to Nadendla's breakaway group was not known to her. 'The conclusion which the governor had arrived at that Shri NTR had lost the majority in the legislative assembly was based entirely on his own judgment and was not in any way influenced by me, by the government in the Centre or by my party at the Centre,' the prime minister declared in Parliament on 21 August.[59]

But there was intense speculation that the overthrow was meticulously planned and executed. It was alleged that M.K. Narayanan, the joint director (operations) of the IB, had a key role in the coup.[60] His deputy director, P.S.V. Prasad, was in Hyderabad for about a month before the crisis. The four-hour delay in the Indian Airlines flight due to an alleged bomb scare and the ten-hour delay of AP Express were considered strange coincidences.[61]

Another incident that occurred in Delhi at the same time led to further speculation about the role of the intelligence. NTR's fight against his overthrow was widely covered by the foreign press. Film clips of NTR parading his MLAs in Rashtrapati Bhavan and his press conference in Delhi were shot by news agencies, Visnews and UPITN, and sent by Air India for use in various international networks. However, both the packets were tampered with during the transit. When they reached their respective destinations, one of the packets contained dummy cassettes, while another was filled with animal excreta.[62]

Informed of the same, the news agencies in Delhi sent some more clips by Lufthansa Airways, but they reached the destination after several days. The role of government agencies was suspected. *India Today* reported that the European Broadcasting Union in Geneva discussed the issue of the missing films. The foreign press became more obsessed with the NTR case, even as the credibility of Indira Gandhi suffered another blow. 'Originally, NTR was not a hot subject for foreign markets. But thanks to the action at the airport, there is a great demand for these films,' said *India Today*.[63] Indira became jittery over the fallout of NTR's Delhi sojourn.

While NTR's cause was well recognized in the capital, it was not enough to restore the status quo ante. The Delhi trip was a morale booster for the NTR camp, but there was no change in the brass tacks. 'Even the apex constitutional authority of the country could not do justice to me,' a disappointed NTR rued. The challenge was now to protect his flock. It was with great difficulty that the managers of the NTR camp had guarded the legislators against the constant attempts at poaching by the Nadendla camp. The journey to Delhi proved perilous as Nadendla's supporters sought to intercept them.

Because of such a threat, the NTR camp had to come up with an alternative to secure the legislators. They found a haven in Karnataka. Several ministers of fellow non-Congress chief minister Ramakrishna Hegde's cabinet took it upon themselves to provide refuge to the TDP legislators. Even as the MLAs shuttled between Nandi Hills, Bangalore and finally Mysore, NTR and Upendra coordinated the party's moves in Hyderabad and Delhi. For the nearly 160 MLAs staying at the Dasaprakash Paradise Hotel in Mysore, the forced hibernation was painful but appeared worthwhile given the overwhelming support they received back home.

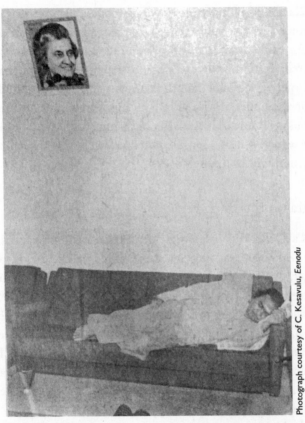

A sick and exhausted NTR resting on a sofa at Begumpet Airport in Hyderabad in 1984, before embarking on the plane to go to New Delhi to parade his MLAs before the president of India.

Despite its best efforts, the Nadendla camp was outwitted in public relations by the NTR group. The plot against NTR was rolled out when he was the most vulnerable, following his cardiac surgery. He was ferried around in an ambulance, moved about in a wheelchair and could barely walk without a walking stick. The symbolism of a sick and fragile patriarch backstabbed by the vile courtier triggered a wave of sympathy for NTR. The thespian used it to the hilt.

Nadendla's image as a back-room operator was further reinforced in the public mind. Though many disgruntled TDP MLAs would have crossed the floor if they were left free, Nadendla suffered from the disadvantage of being cast in the mould of a usurper. His major failure lay in his inability to mobilize the required number of MLAs to back him before he embarked upon his misadventure. This misstep cost him much, and, as a result, there were few takers for his protestations, however genuine some of them might be.

Indira on the Back Foot

NTR's Delhi trip created ripples in the national capital. With media interest reaching its crescendo over the NTR political thriller, Indira's men found themselves on the back foot. The Centre was clearly disturbed by the theatrical way NTR made an issue of his dismissal. 'Sack the Governor', the *Times of India* editorial screamed. The *Hindustan Times* called the entire episode 'Shameful'. Indira's aides had no explanation as to how NTR was still able to manage the support of so many MLAs, making a mockery of the governor's action. The NTR issue threatened to become a focal point of the Opposition efforts for unity.

Unable to carry on the farce any longer, Indira blinked first, making Governor Ram Lal resign from his post a week after he dismissed NTR. He promptly obliged. 'Ram Lal's resignation as the governor "to uphold the dignity of the office" shows that whatever faculties he might have lost, he has not lost his sense of humour,' said an acerbic Nani Palkhivala, the well-known jurist.[64] The first wicket fell even as NTR was getting ready to take out his Chaitanya Ratham. It was the first smell of victory for NTR's camp and gave the exasperated leader new strength.

A disgraced Ram Lal, who took the next available flight to Delhi, was in Hyderabad for precisely a year and two weeks as governor. A six-time MLA and twice chief minister of Himachal

Pradesh, Ram Lal was a loyal Congressman. He was brought in as governor of AP after he had been asked to step down as chief minister of Himachal Pradesh in April 1983. Interestingly, he was not particularly disliked by NTR till the 15 August developments. In fact, NTR had earlier clarified that his comments against the office of the governor during the Calcutta conclave of the Opposition were made as part of the party's stand on this issue and they were not targeted at Ram Lal. 'We have no issue with him. We get along well with him,' he had said. Compared to the later governor, Kumudben Joshi, who played politics from day one of her appointment, Ram Lal had been largely noncontroversial in his role till he triggered the infamous coup. His short stint in AP earned him notoriety that lived long even after he left the state.[65]

'Our first demand has been fulfilled,' a jubilant NTR said on Ram Lal's ouster. However, the war was not yet over. The Congress leadership did not give up on the possibility of making NTR's downfall a reality. Neither was NTR ready to rest till his campaign succeeded. He, along with major Opposition figures such as A.B. Vajpayee, went on a whirlwind tour of coastal AP, explaining the Delhi drama. Against the advice of his doctors, NTR went ahead with his campaign on his Chaitanya Ratham across the three regions of the state. He drew one of the largest crowds in the non-election period. BJP leader M. Venkaiah Naidu accompanied NTR throughout and protected him from overexertion. Still, NTR would get emotional and strain his vocal cords, even as the assembled crowds would plead with him to rest.

Meanwhile, Shankar Dayal Sharma, a mild-mannered and seasoned Congress veteran, was sent as the new governor. Sharma, a legal luminary himself, took some time to study the situation. NTR lost no time in sending representation to the new governor for convening the House for a floor test at the earliest. Nadendla was not willing to call for a session before the deadline, arguing that the MLAs were being held against their will. Both the Congress and Nadendla camps tried every trick in the trade to somehow make the MLAs secured in Bangalore and Mysore leave the camp. They kept harping on how the freedom of these MLAs was curtailed and how they were not able to attend even family emergencies.

A few hours after taking over as governor, Sharma, in a surprise move, swore in seventeen new ministers in the Nadendla cabinet, making it twenty-one-strong. The list included Speaker Tangi Satyanarayana and Deputy Speaker A. Bheem Reddy, who had played hide and seek with both the camps. Satyanarayana was the one who had provided temporary assembly ID cards to the NTR camp MLAs, accompanied them to Delhi and personally presented them to the president. On his return to Hyderabad, however, he joined Nadendla. Tripurana Venkataratnam, the young MLA who went to Raj Bhavan on the first day of crisis in support of NTR, changed sides the next day. She was rewarded with a junior minister portfolio.

A distressed NTR alleged the Centre's complicity in ministry expansion when the floor test was yet to be conducted. M. Baga Reddy, a senior Congress member, was inducted as a pro tem speaker by Nadendla. The governor's move appeared to bolster Nadendla's prospects with the MLAs. This was what the NTR camp had feared all along. Sharma refused to give clarity on when the assembly session might be convened, putting NTR in a tight spot. His MLAs were still confined in Karnataka. Without a definite date for the floor test, it became difficult to hold the legislators away from their families and constituencies. The families of the MLAs were ferried to Bangalore and Mysore to spend time with them. NTR kept shuttling between Karnataka and AP.

NTR's undemocratic dismissal was denounced by civil liberties organizations. The People's Union of Civil Liberties (PUCL) condemned how democratic principles were given a go-by in the hands of the governor. Leading intellectuals and civil rights activists Nani Palkhivala, V.M. Tarkunde and Arun Shourie addressed meetings in Hyderabad, condemning the Centre's role in the AP episode. Meanwhile, the new government was trying to wear NTR thin. He was vilified by his own MLAs who were now in the Nadendla camp. Taking a leaf out of Indira's book, Nadendla alleged that NTR was in collusion with some foreign countries to undermine India.

NTR was not facing a mere political turmoil, he was also experiencing a personal tragedy. Basavatarakam, his wife of nearly forty years, mother of his eleven children and a companion through thick and thin, had been diagnosed with life-threatening cancer and was fighting for survival at Adyar Cancer Institute in Madras. While NTR had been undergoing a heart operation at Texas Medical Center at Houston in the US, his wife was receiving treatment for pelvic cancer in the same country. She was staying with renowned American radiologist Dr Kakarla Subba Rao's family in New York. NTR would call her every night from Houston and spend quite some time inquiring about her health, Dr Kakarla recalled. She was later brought to Madras for continued treatment. NTR was so preoccupied with his political fight that he could not even visit his sick wife often in Madras. She died less than a month later, on 1 October 1984. Her early death would have repercussions on NTR's life that few could anticipate when it happened, but at the time he was focused on the immediate task of reclaiming his throne.

As Nadendla failed to make Governor Sharma 'free' legislators from NTR's 'clutches', he had no other option but to call for the session. Sharma was also putting pressure on Nadendla to prove his majority as quickly as possible. The assembly was finally convened to meet on 11 September, four days before the deadline given by the previous governor. The NTR camp felt relieved; the sooner the floor test, the easier for NTR to secure his MLAs' support. However, the Nadendla camp did not give any indication that the House would take up the floor test as soon as it was convened. They had plans to take as long as it was convenient for them to win over MLAs to their side. Suspecting their plans, NTR came up with the idea of inviting observers, such as Arun Shourie and V.M. Tarkunde from PUCL and journalists such as Kuldip Nayar and S. Sahay.

NTR also invited national Opposition leaders to be present in Hyderabad during the floor test, as an insurance against the suspected ploys by the Congress and Nadendla. The steering committee for 'Save Democracy' in the state called for vigilance by the people during the floor test. This committee, consisting of the non-Congress Opposition leaders in the state, including Venkaiah Naidu and Jaipal Reddy, had been spearheading the agitation across AP to bring NTR back to power.

The atmosphere in Hyderabad was already tense as the Ganesh festival and Muharram were to fall around the same time with their attendant security issues. These two religious events had become a nightmare for the law-and-order machinery, as processions had become a show of strength for the BJP and MIM. The old city had been wrecked by communal incidents a few days earlier, and a curfew was still in force across many parts of the city. The air was thick with rumours that the fragile communal situation might flare up once again with the active connivance of vested political interests.

On the governor's instructions, the administration took every precaution to ensure that all entry points to Hyderabad were sealed. Several battalions of central reserve forces took control of the main streets. Horse-mounted police formed a ring around the assembly building, and only those with ID cards were allowed inside the premises. With empty roads and shuttered shops, Hyderabad turned into a ghost city. The air was tense, and the atmosphere disquieting. The capital convulsed at the political uncertainties that lay ahead.

A day before the session, the NTR camp legislators started their journey in specially chartered Karnataka RTC buses. NTR received them at the state border. They were stopped on the outskirts of Hyderabad by the police, who claimed the group could not be let in as the curfew was in force. They were asked to proceed to the police control room first and obtain passes. The civil rights activists and leaders accompanying them protested the police move. Karnataka minister M. Raghupathy too was at the front of this convoy, travelling in his official vehicle. Considering their presence, the police could not hold the caravan for long, and the MLAs were safely brought to Ramakrishna Studios. Meanwhile, the Congress announced its unconditional support to Nadendla ahead of the floor test.

The assembly premises turned into an impregnable fortress. The security cover extended to over a kilometre around the legislature building. However, that did not stop the ugly drama from unfolding. Unprecedented developments ensued on the eve of the long-awaited session on 11 September. As a result of the curfew, people from across the state could not come to Hyderabad. The communal conflagration in the city had always been political. But this time it was premeditated and executed surgically with the help of those running the government.[66] Shops owned by Muslims in Abids were selectively targeted and set ablaze. Communal violence flared up twice in a matter of one month. The situation was so bad that the Union home secretary, M.M. Wali, had to rush to Hyderabad to take stock of the situation. The Nadendla camp, as well as the Congress leadership, wanted a sense of uncertainty to prevail during the floor test so that they could make use of this breathing space to swing a tidy number of MLAs in their favour.

On the other hand, the session itself was not allowed to function by fomenting disorder. Despite the NTR camp's repeated request to call for the session for the express purpose of testing the majority support of the Nadendla government, Speaker Baga Reddy convened the House for regular business. As a result, the Nadendla camp got the opportunity to postpone the floor test by filibustering, Indian style.

The session was to start at 11 a.m., but the legislators began arriving from 9 a.m. While NTR came in riding his Chaitanya

Ratham, his MLAs arrived in four tourist buses, which were well-guarded by party managers. But the first day of the session was a washout even before it commenced. As the speaker started to read a condolence message for a member who had passed away recently, N. Srinivasulu Reddy of the NTR camp rose to raise a point of order. Even before he could be heard, some members belonging to the Nadendla camp started creating bedlam. Barely a couple of minutes after the House assembled, the speaker adjourned for the day amid din and cacophony.

The same farce was enacted on the second day. Salahuddin Owaisi and Baqar Agha of the MIM, followed by Thomas Chowdary of the Nadendla camp, started gesticulating wildly and talking loudly, drowning the speaker's voice. Meanwhile, Minister Jeevan Reddy got up, showing a copy of the *Deccan Chronicle* and shouting at the NTR camp. The paper, owned by Congress MP T. Chandrasekhara Reddy, published conspiracy stories about the NTR camp regularly. Nadendla's supporters started chanting 'shame, shame' at NTR. They pulled out the mics and banged them on the table. All through this clamour, NTR and the legislators of his camp sat quietly, even as the speaker adjourned the House.[67]

The third day was a repeat of the previous two days but with a twist. Apparently, unable to handle the wild behaviour of some of the members, Baga Reddy threw up his hands and left the House in a huff less than ten minutes after the members assembled. He complained of illness in his chambers and sent in his resignation before being taken to a hospital in an ambulance.[68] The situation deteriorated from bad to worse for the NTR camp with the day's developments. They felt Baga Reddy's resignation was a ruse to further delay the floor test. Owaisi, the floor leader of the MIM, replaced Reddy, causing further unease in the NTR camp. Owaisi's appointment was unacceptable to them as he had been actively disrupting the proceedings all through. NTR dashed off a letter to the governor, which detailed his objections to the elevation of Owaisi as the pro tem speaker. Owaisi did not speak Telugu or English. Very few MLAs understood Urdu, in which Owaisi could converse.

A delegation of Opposition leaders in Delhi led by Charan Singh met with President Zail Singh to immediately appoint NTR as the chief minister and allow him to prove his majority within twenty-four hours. The Opposition leaders, some of whom were in Hyderabad during these astonishing developments, told the president that the assembly proceedings were being deliberately stalled to avoid the floor test.

During the three days of assembly proceedings that were a no-show, NTR and his camp MLAs displayed exemplary patience in the face of grave provocation. Most of the time, the target was NTR at whom the opponents hurled the most obnoxious invectives to rattle him. 'His [NTR's] demeanour did not change even as pro-Bhaskara Rao MLAs like Baggidi Gopal and M. Kesava Reddy came up menacingly, as though to physically attack him, or MLAs like Edara Deviah and Allam Sailu stood just one foot away showering abuse,' recalled R.J. Rajendra Prasad, *The Hindu* correspondent who was a witness to the proceedings.[69] A faint-hearted person would have given up his political career. But not NTR, who stood like a rock even when he was heckled by legislators, many of whom had cut their teeth in politics because of him. NTR stoically faced these excruciating moments, though he was physically and mentally worn out due to the machinations of the coup.

Hyderabad became the focus of the national as well as international media. The foreign correspondents who descended on Hyderabad—more than seventy, according to one report—were not provided entry passes for covering the proceedings. The Editors Guild of India condemned the government action. William K. Stevens of the *New York Times* was present in Hyderabad during these strange times. 'Has Mrs Gandhi now taken a step too far?' he wrote.[70]

Following the resignation of the speaker, the Congress high command had breathing time to think over the developments. The unrest across the country continued unabated. Bandhs and protest demonstrations were the order of the day in the state. The Opposition parties in Delhi gave a call for Bharat Bandh. Indira was agitated at the unseemly developments which were damaging the ruling party's reputation. She must have by now understood that Nadendla had misled her into believing the extent of his support base. The rising profile of NTR in the media became a thorn in her side. 'An influential foe of Mrs Gandhi,' was how the *New York Times* described NTR.[71] An exasperated prime minister could not fathom why such a big deal was being made of the AP imbroglio. 'At least the heads are being counted now. It wasn't so then,' a bemused Indira Gandhi said, referring to the dismissal of several state governments during the Janata regime.[72] Now she was looking at an honourable way out. Imposing President's Rule was an option, but wise counsel prevailed on Indira. Governor Shankar Dayal Sharma received appropriate instructions for an exit strategy.

The next day, 16 September, exactly a month after he was toppled, NTR received an invitation from the governor to take over the reins of the government. It was an unexpected but pleasant surprise for the beleaguered NTR and his party. The assembly was earlier scheduled to meet on 20 September following Baga Reddy's resignation and Owaisi's appointment to the post. But before that, the status quo ante was restored. Nadendla's game was clearly up, and the governor was not willing to prolong the drama.

A beaming NTR, along with eight other ministers, was sworn in at the Darbar Hall of the Raj Bhavan—the only occasion when NTR did not take his oath in public. Even the sound system was not in place for the impromptu installation ceremony. Still, within no time, crowds gathered around Khairatabad junction to catch a glimpse of NTR coming out of Raj Bhavan. 'It is a victory of not just the people of Andhra, but the entire country,' an elated NTR declared.

'*Lok shakti* won over Rajya *sakthi*,' A.B. Vajpayee remarked in his poetic style.

Feather in NTR's Cap

The reinstatement was one more feather in NTR's political cap. No other chief minister in independent India had been able to wrest back power after being thrown out in a well-coordinated coup. Just a month before the die was cast in Hyderabad, a similar experiment in J&K, where Chief Minister Farooq Abdullah was stripped of his position and replaced by his estranged brother-in-law, was a grand success. Farooq, who later actively participated in the 'Save Democracy' movement for reinstalling NTR, could not fight back in his own case. In NTR, Indira found an unconventional politician who refused to take the humiliation lying down. The national Opposition leaders, though pleased at the outcome, were themselves bewildered at how Indira had uncharacteristically retracted.

For the second time in his short political career, NTR scored a victory that very few considered possible. His comeback was mainly due to his capacity to move large sections of people to his cause and his unflinching faith in the power of communication. He was also able to influence public opinion across the country by making his dismissal a national issue. The Opposition parties found in him a worthy candidate to fight for in this battle. As veteran journalist Girilal Jain wrote, 'No other issue since the Emergency had stirred the Indian people as the wholly illegal dismissal of the NTR ministry.'[73]

With this stupendous feat, NTR's name spread far and wide. The heart surgeon who had operated on NTR, the legendary Dr Denton Cooley, was so enthused by the news of the TDP's return that he wrote a congratulatory note to NTR, saying he

considered him to be the right person to succeed Indira Gandhi
herself in Indian politics.

Nadendla cried foul at the governor's action and questioned
the propriety of reinstating a dismissed chief minister. The proper
procedure, he asserted, would be to call Madan Mohan, the
Congress legislature party leader, to form the government. But
Nadendla had already turned into persona non grata in AP politics.
He was swiftly pushed into the margins of history because of the
failed coup, and permanently tarred as a disgraced politician. In
hindsight, Nadendla was far from the villain he came to be painted
in the media and etched in public memory. He was, in fact, a
balancing factor in the otherwise volatile TDP government as it
took baby steps in the administration. Acting as a foil to NTR's
eccentricities that threatened to rock the boat every once in a
while, he was a stabilizing force in matters of governance.

But he committed the mistake of moving before the time was
ripe. There was certainly widespread disillusionment among the
party leaders, especially the ministers and MLAs, because of the
way NTR was pushing his pet schemes and treating everyone as
dispensable. NTR's hold on the people appeared to be showing
cracks, but it was yet to reach a critical stage where he was
replaceable. While the political class as well as many sections
of the population were tired of his antics, the masses were still
prepared to give him time.

Nadendla was not unaware of this situation. His increasing
frustration, along with the tantalizing proposition from some
Congress leaders, helped seal his determination to dislodge NTR.
Once he fell for the bait, Nadendla had no alternative but to resort
to every trick in the game to stay afloat. He certainly appeared
brazen in his attempt to hold on to power. The fact that he joined
hands with the Congress robbed him of the moral high ground.
His subsequent desperate machinations to steal the flock received
deserving condemnation. But the reality was that he acted out
the wishes of a good section of the legislators. If it were not for

the moral outrage of the public, which did not approve of the way NTR was ambushed, the revolt would not have caused such revulsion. Nadendla also unwittingly became the poster boy of all that was wrong with Congress politics at the national level, where the Opposition parties were desperately looking for a unifying factor to take on Indira Gandhi.

Nadendla was afterwards reduced to political insignificance. NTR instituted an inquiry by former Supreme Court Justice V.R. Krishna Iyer into the controversial decisions of the month-old Nadendla government. These were the exemptions extended to Chiran Palace lands, Vinedale Distilleries, Ramakrishna Wines, McDowell's and Rayalaseema Mills.[74] Nadendla later floated the Democratic (Prajaswamya) Telugu Desam Party, which did not last long. Many of the TDP MLAs such as T. Jeevan Reddy chose to join the Congress.[75] His group contested the 1985 assembly elections with zero results. After being treated as a pariah even by the Congress for another four years, Nadendla was finally admitted into the party by Rajiv Gandhi in May 1989. He successfully contested for Tenali on a Congress ticket to the assembly in the November 1989 polls and later won as MP from Khammam in the 1998 Parliament polls.

Another critical factor in the August coup was that the masses were organized systematically by the TDP leaders to force their MLAs to take a stand in the ongoing crisis. For the first time in the country, in a situation like this, the MLAs had to yield to the wishes of their local constituents. In a rare show of solidarity, most of the media, regional and national, and most Opposition parties and civil society organizations, threw their weight behind NTR during the crisis, providing him with the oxygen to continue his month-long fight.

As for the Congress, the party tried to salvage its image by saying that the return of NTR had proved its democratic credentials. 'Would NTR have come back if Mrs Gandhi did not believe in the highest principles of democracy?' asked the party general secretary, A.K. Antony. NTR's image further soared in Delhi with many non-Congress parties looking up to him for inspiration and leadership. 'NTR should get ready to rid Delhi of Kauravas,' Bhim Singh, a veteran J&K leader, said.

NTR's return to power was one of the rarest cases where Indira had to eat humble pie. P.C. Alexander, Indira's trusted aide, insisted that NTR's dismissal in 1984 was done without the knowledge of Indira Gandhi or anyone else in the PMO:

> Indira Gandhi has been most unfairly criticised by some people for her alleged involvement in the dismissal of N.T. Rama Rao's government in August 1984. The truth is that she came to know of Governor Ramlal's action, for the first time, when I got the news from the Intelligence Bureau and brought it to her notice. She was quite upset and annoyed at the action taken and even took it as part of a move on the part of some interested groups close to her to malign her and to weaken her authority.[76]

But few believed that Indira was not involved in the NTR episode. The brazen operation could not have been initiated without her tacit approval. 'Hardly anyone believed her [protestations],' Inder Malhotra, a senior journalist remarked.[77] The account of former intelligence operative R.N. Kulkarni, in which he narrated how the IB was given the brief by the Congress leadership to 'permanently secure' Nadendla's position, sealed any doubt about the PM's role in the ouster episode. IB's resources were put to full use by Nadendla to win over NTR's MLAs who were taking shelter. But, according to Kulkarni, without any success:

> IB infiltrated the Hotel Dasaprakash Paradise where the MLAs were staying despite the dragnet of state Special Branch of Police. The waiters, sweepers, cooks, managers, telephone operators were tapped and used, and yet the number of MLAs and their identities could not be ascertained. This left the

Congress (I) leadership—Arun Nehru (Minister of State for
Security), Rajiv Gandhi (General Secretary, AICC) and Indira
Gandhi (Prime Minister)—in the lurch.[78]

The former operative also revealed that the IB's failed efforts to
dislodge NTR cost the organization a huge amount of money.

The response of the then president, Zail Singh, on the
other hand, was remarkable. He showed some spine to meet
NTR and his retinue of MLAs in Rashtrapati Bhavan, causing
much embarrassment to Indira. NTR's well-wishers, MGR and
Y. Nayudamma, the former director general of Council of
Scientific and Industrial Research (CSIR), also played a role in
mellowing Indira's approach to the crisis.

The governor gave thirty days to NTR, as he had done
with Nadendla, to prove his majority in the assembly. However,
NTR chose to take up the vote of confidence on the first day of
the next session, which was 20 September. But NTR was now
dependent on the MLAs of the communist parties, the BJP and
the Janata Party for his government to survive. NTR, at this time,
had the backing of 143 TDP MLAs, along with five independent
legislators who had joined the party. He was supported by another
fifteen legislators belonging to various Opposition parties. The
Nadendla group was left with fifty-five MLAs, though many of
them ended up supporting NTR.

NTR was so grateful for the unstinted support extended by
the non-Congress Opposition parties that he invited them to
join the government. However, knowing fully well that such a
proposition would be untenable, the Janata Party, the BJP and
the communist parties politely declined the offer. Venkaiah
Naidu, who played a highly visible role in the fight for NTR's
restoration, recalled that even Ramoji Rao had advised him to be
part of the government.

NTR's reinstatement was greeted with jubilation across the
country. Sikhs in Delhi and elsewhere who considered NTR a

friend after his condemnation of the army raid on the Golden Temple celebrated his comeback.

Though Maneka Gandhi stood by NTR during the agitation for his reinstatement, RSM MLAs sided with Nadendla during the August 1984 crisis. As a result, NTR refused to have any electoral tie-up with the party later. Maneka and NTR apparently had a falling-out during the 1982 campaign. According to Goné Prakash Rao, a former MLA, who played a key role in Maneka's political foray in Telangana, she felt offended during the joint campaign in Telangana with NTR. Prakash Rao recalled that NTR made Maneka wait at the Manthani (Karimnagar) guest house till midnight as he got delayed. Later, at Peddapalli, when the crowd clamoured for NTR to speak first, he snatched the mic from her. These episodes resulted in cold relations between the two.[79] Without an alliance with the TDP, Maneka's party soon lost its footing in AP.

Following his political resurrection, NTR was expected to be less temperamental and more circumspect. Indeed, he seemed to have slowed down. Some decisions of the Nadendla government, such as restoring the retirement age to fifty-eight, were untouched. But NTR was clearly unhappy being a dummy chief minister.

Trial by Fire

Immediately after the restoration, there was speculation that NTR was likely to dissolve the assembly and call for early elections. The reason was not difficult to fathom. His government was now compromised. He did not command the overwhelming majority in the House that he had once enjoyed. Many of the MLAs who were with him had tainted backgrounds since they had hobnobbed with the Nadendla group during the August crisis. There were rumours that even those who had sailed with him had accepted money from the other side. Many legislators were now openly demanding favours. Besides, NTR could not take decisions with the same free will as he had done in the past, since he was dependent on the non-Congress Opposition support to stay in power.

NTR, during this period, was withdrawn and sullen, mainly because of the betrayal of his own MLAs. NTR was taciturn on the subject, because he knew the MLAs might not like the proposition to dissolve the assembly when they were clearly entitled to another three years of their term. NTR was also not confident the governor would go by his recommendation for the same.

Meanwhile, the assassination of Prime Minister Indira Gandhi on 31 October 1984, followed by her son Rajiv Gandhi taking up the mantle, brought about a sudden change in the political equation in the country. NTR was moved by the news, though she was his political foe. He had called on her less than a month earlier, on 4 October. Indira's personal secretary, P.C. Alexander, recalled that the meeting was held in a cordial atmosphere. 'Indira Gandhi herself was extraordinarily courteous and friendly to him. NTR repeatedly thanked her for her message of condolences on the demise of his wife, addressing her very warmly as our beloved prime minister,' he wrote.[80]

On learning about Indira's death, NTR wanted to immediately go to Delhi. In those days there weren't frequent flights from Hyderabad to Delhi. An Avro flight of the Navy which was in Hyderabad at the time was organized for NTR, Governor Shankar Dayal Sharma and former President Neelam Sanjiva Reddy. Delhi was in turmoil. The body of the slain leader was brought from the All India Institute of Medical Sciences (AIIMS) to her residence at around 9 p.m. NTR paid his heartfelt respects. He also paid homage at the Teen Murti Bhavan where her body was kept. As he was a harsh critic of the former prime minister, NTR had to be escorted back to the airport after the riots broke out in Delhi.

The groundswell of sympathy in the wake of the dastardly killing of Indira was overwhelming. Lok Sabha elections were announced for the last week of December 1984. NTR mulled over whether going for simultaneous polls would be wise given the prevailing favourable atmosphere for the Congress in the country. More worrisome was whether the Centre would allow him to have his way on midterm polls to the assembly. If they chose, the Congress could give him trouble. NTR asked H.J. Dora, his Intelligence DIG, who had accompanied him to Delhi after Indira's demise, to stay put and secure a positive response from the capital. Dora met M.K. Narayanan, who was the special director of IB, and conveyed NTR's wish. Rajiv Gandhi later gave a green signal on the condition that NTR would not campaign outside his state.[81]

On 22 November 1984, exactly five weeks after he returned as chief minister, NTR's cabinet recommended dissolving the House to Governor Shankar Dayal Sharma. The latter accepted the advice and asked NTR to continue as the caretaker chief minister. 'The developments during the August crisis corrupted the political atmosphere in the state. We need to bring back the principled approach to our politics. Hence, we recommend dissolving the House and holding fresh polls,' the resolution by the cabinet stated. Both the Congress and the Nadendla group criticized the move as diluting the verdict given by the people for five years.

A man of deep mythological sensibility, NTR was enacting the trial by fire, on the lines of Sita in Ramayana. But the Congress and the TDP splinter group leaders dubbed the move derisively as one more self-inflicted addition to NTR's long list of abolitions, annulments and dissolutions.

The immediate acceptance by Governor Sharma of NTR's proposal for midterm polls surprised both the state Congress leaders and the Nadendla group. The Congress suspected, not incorrectly, that the new leadership under Rajiv Gandhi and NTR had an understanding over early polls to the state. However, it was not immediately clear that simultaneous elections would be held as there was barely a month left for Lok Sabha elections. Finally,

NTR's cabinet recommended polls for the state legislature on 3 March 1985, a couple of months after the general elections. His request to the Election Commission came as a surprise as NTR had seemed to be in a hurry for fresh polls. But now he was going to continue as caretaker chief minister for more than three months. NTR wanted to assess the impact of Indira's death on Lok Sabha elections and be prepared accordingly for assembly polls.

As per his understanding with Rajiv, NTR did not campaign in other states, but went ahead with his efforts to present a united front of various Opposition parties against the Congress across the country. However, he could do little given the raucous relations among the Opposition leaders, who failed to forge an alternative against the Congress. In AP, he successfully stitched together a coalition by offering seat adjustments to non-Congress Opposition parties.

NTR's Chaitanya Ratham rolled out once again but in a different set of circumstances.[82] He was now facing Rajiv instead of Indira in the campaign. Sporting a saffron dhoti and kurta (sometimes, he wore saffron trousers and shirt) instead of khaki, NTR was as emotional in his appeal as he was a couple of years back. The changed political scenario in the country did not dampen his aggressive campaign. However, Rajiv was not yet part of the political establishment of Delhi that NTR was so fond of attacking. In the wake of the ultimate sacrifice made by his mother for the country, Rajiv attracted a lot of sympathy in AP too. His public meetings in the state were well attended. Given his unsoiled and youthful political background, the Nehru–Gandhi scion offered freshness and hope, just as NTR had done a couple of years ago. NTR was fighting against such formidable optics. The earlier perception of his being wrongfully dethroned in the conspiracy hatched in Delhi now appeared to have faded.

NTR's criticism of Operation Bluestar was projected by the Congress as being anti-national. 'Would you choose Telugu Desam or Bharata Desam?' Rajiv dramatically asked the voters.

It appeared that the fight was essentially between sympathy for NTR for the way he was ousted, and the wave of empathy felt for Indira at her untimely death.

Rajiv's Congress looked for some of its own star power to win the elections. Actors Amitabh Bachchan and Sunil Dutt jumped into the election fray elsewhere in support of Rajiv. In AP, actor Krishna, whose brothers were closely associated with the Congress party, finally took the bait and formally joined in. He made a twenty-minute-long film, directed by his actor-director wife Vijaya Nirmala, on Indira's ultimate sacrifice. Actors Vijayachander, Prabhakar Reddy and Jamuna also joined the Congress and campaigned for the party. Krishna, launching his campaign in Tirupati, castigated NTR as a power-hungry person who loved only his money. The actor, accompanied by his wife, elicited an excellent response. He conducted a week-long campaign for the Congress. Enthused by the crowds attending his meetings, the Congress thought he was the foil to NTR that the party badly needed. Still licking its wounds following the 1983 debacle inflicted by NTR, the party seemed to have sensed the prospect of making a comeback in AP in the Lok Sabha elections to be held on 27 December 1984.

But all those signs turned out to be false. Once again, NTR proved the political pundits wrong by swinging a difficult election in his favour even as the whole country rooted for the Rajiv-led Congress. The election results showed that the Congress was flying high across the states. The party received the most comprehensive victory ever with 404 seats in the Lok Sabha, the largest ever for a single party since Independence. But that did not give much solace to the AP Congress, which was met with the most ignominious defeat ever, having been reduced to just six out of forty-two seats.

The TDP registered its first stunning victory in the national elections, securing thirty of the thirty-three seats it contested.[83] The regional party emerged as the single largest Opposition party in its debut in Parliament—another record for a party that was less than three years old. The Opposition parties supported by NTR—the BJP (Chandupatla Janga Reddy famously defeated P.V. in Hanamkonda), CPI (Sode Ramaiah in Bhadrachalam), CPI (M) (Bhimreddy Narasimha Reddy in Miryalaguda), Congress (S) (Kishore Chandra Deo, Parvathipuram) and Janata Party (S. Jaipal Reddy made his debut in the Lok Sabha from Mahbubnagar)—had a smooth sail.[84]

But for the communists, the Congress would have got one seat less.[85] The Left parties failed to reach an understanding in Khammam and allowed Jalagam Vengala Rao, the former chief minister, to walk away with the victory. The MIM made its debut in the Lok Sabha with the win of its president Salahuddin Owaisi from Hyderabad.

All six Central ministers—P.V. Narasimha Rao, Kotla Vijayabhaskara Reddy, Pendekanti Venkata Subbaiah, P. Shiv Shankar, M.S. Sanjiva Rao and P. Mallikarjun—and seventeen other sitting Congress (I) members fell by the wayside in the NTR tsunami. Shiv Shankar lost from Medak, which had sent Indira Gandhi to Parliament in the 1980 election. Kasu Brahmananda Reddy, the former chief minister, received a drubbing. The Congress was crestfallen because the result was the lowest figure for it in any Lok Sabha election since Independence. In the last election in 1980, the party had swept forty-one out of the forty-two seats in the state. In Hyderabad, the TDP gave a scare to the MIM's Owaisi, losing the seat by less than 4000 votes and pushing the Congress to third position.

The stupendous victory was another major political accomplishment of NTR. At a time when the Opposition stalwarts failed to enthuse the people across the country to support their respective parties, NTR, an emerging regional leader who came into the game rather late in his life, was able to buck the trend. The TDP's achievement presented a stark contrast to the so-called national parties. The BJP contested 226 seats and won two, one of them because of NTR's support.

Vajpayee himself bit the dust from Indore. The Dalit Mazdoor Kisan Party (DMKP) of Charan Singh, who harboured hopes of becoming the prime minister, contested 168 seats and won three. The Janata Party fought 207 seats and won ten, with its leader Chandra Shekhar losing in Ballia. And the Congress (S) got four (again one of them from AP with the TDP's support) seats. Between them, the four national Opposition parties managed to secure nineteen seats, compared to the TDP's thirty. Close to two-thirds of the total opposition was from two states, AP and West Bengal—with the former leading by thirty members to the Left Front's twenty-six. It appeared NTR had finally made his mark at the national level. *India Today* noted that the TDP was no flash in the pan:

> The Telugu Desam sweep across the board to win in all parts of the State has also debunked the theory about it being a one-man, one-election party propped up by a section of the mercantile Kamma community in the deltaic districts of the State.[86]

In tune with his newly acquired national stature, NTR sounded patriotic in his first address to the newly elected MPs of his party. 'We are first Indians, then citizens of this state. The unity and integrity of the nation are paramount for our party.' He offered constructive cooperation to the new prime minister. On the opening day of the eighth Lok Sabha, a proud NTR watched from the VIP gallery the induction of TDP MPs—all awash in yellow, the party colour—taking their oaths in Telugu. Upendra was appointed the TDP parliamentary party secretary while C. Madhava Reddy was made the party leader in the Lok Sabha. The TDP was recognized as the largest Opposition 'group' since no single party had the necessary 10 per cent strength in the House to claim the status. The party extended wholehearted support to the anti-defection bill proposed by the Rajiv government.

Third Coming

The success of the allies in AP was primarily due to NTR's ability to forge unity. The experiment gave confidence to NTR that a coalition of Opposition parties was needed to take on the Congress. Enthused by the success in the state, he once again wanted to make a concerted effort at a national alternative to the Congress. The idea of floating a Bharata Desam Party, with which he had toyed briefly during the height of Opposition conclaves in 1983, once again surfaced in NTR's mind. But that would have to wait till he successfully faced the midterm polls to the assembly.

NTR decided to contest from three constituencies in the three regions of the state—Gudivada, Nalgonda and Hindupur. NTR justified his action saying he wanted to represent all regions of the state. Nadendla fielded his party's candidates in 222 seats, though many of his former TDP colleagues deserted him soon after the failed rebellion. He allied with the MIM, which had recently emerged as a force to be reckoned with in the old city of Hyderabad. Nadendla himself was in the fray from Malakpet in Hyderabad.

The Congress, which fielded candidates for all 294 seats, inducted 150 new faces, including actor Jamuna from Mangalagiri in Guntur District. Maneka's RSM also contested from several Telangana districts and Guntur District in the coastal region. Following the TDP's disinterest in a tie-up, the party contested independently.

The campaigns by both the Congress and the TDP were as aggressive as in the earlier elections, though these polls lacked the same euphoria and enthusiasm. There was a sense of fatigue as the polls came in quick succession. For Rajiv, this was the third time he was campaigning for his party in the state, with the last two having ended in losses. For NTR, going to the people came naturally. The crowds were always overflowing at his meetings. The Congress's confidence primarily rested on the fact that in the recent general elections, it had increased its voting by 9 per cent, though it got a smaller number of seats. Besides, Rajiv's leadership was expected to positively influence voting behaviour.

But the poll results showed NTR's hold on the state remained unchallenged. The outcome was one-sided in the TDP's favour, leading to a landslide victory. The party bagged 202 out of the 250 seats it contested, bettering its own performance of the 1983 polls. NTR picked all the three seats that he fought from. The Congress got less than it managed in the 1983 elections—sliding from sixty to fifty seats.

The non-Congress parties rode on the crest of the TDP wave, registering their best show in recent times. With eleven MLAs each in their kitty, the communist parties dramatically improved their strength in the assembly. The BJP had its best performance ever in the state, winning eight seats out of the ten it contested. The Janata Party increased its tally from a lone member to three. As against the forty-two seats that were in the race, the TDP allies got thirty-three seats. Their combined strength was thirteen in the last assembly.

The last word was pronounced on Nadendla's pretensions to project himself as an alternative to NTR. His party was comprehensively routed; except for two candidates, including Nadendla, all his contestants lost deposits. Upendra took a dig, 'Their contribution to Andhra politics is Rs 500 each to the state exchequer,' referring to the election deposit at the time. This election also saw the last of Maneka and her party in the state; the RSM candidates were a washout.

'We have got the people's mandate once again to complete the unfinished tasks,' said a jubilant NTR. The 1985 assembly elections catapulted NTR to a position of political invincibility. In a matter of two years, his party contested three elections and won every one of them hands down. It looked like it was impossible to break the spell cast by NTR on the people of the state. For the third time in a row, he was sworn in as chief minister at a spectacular public ceremony; this time at Parade Grounds in

Secunderabad. *India Today* called NTR's impressive win 'the third coming'. NTR quickly formed his ministry and went about his task with more zeal.

The next five years were a political roller-coaster, as the state embraced the full impact of NTR's tumultuous rule and his increasingly personalized style of functioning. AP also witnessed a desperate Congress resorting to every trick in the trade to put spokes in the TDP juggernaut.

~

Act III

Stirring Things Up

'Reddy garu, I can face the consequences of my decisions. I am like Lord Shiva. I can swallow poison and hold it in my throat.' NTR was talking to Y. Venugopala Reddy (later the governor of the Reserve Bank of India), who was the planning secretary in his government.[1] They were discussing the proposals for radical reorganization of administrative units. It was proposed that the earlier talukas and blocks would be turned into smaller units called *mandals*. The chief minister wanted the planning secretary to go for a geographical approach to the reorganization. Reddy told him that such an approach, if implemented keeping in view the political interests of the TDP, might come under judicial scrutiny. If it were done objectively, NTR's party might be at a political disadvantage. The chief minister was quick to dispel any misgivings on this score. It did not matter even if the new system did not serve the interests of his party. 'I want to go ahead because I want to change the old order,' NTR firmly told Reddy.[2]

This was how NTR kicked off a series of 'institutional changes that would fundamentally alter existing economic and social structures',[3] fully aware of the resistance from entrenched interests and the likely adverse political consequences. Many of the changes indeed faced considerable political opposition and bureaucratic resistance. But an undeterred NTR went ahead, though he did not succeed in all of his initiatives.

As an outsider to the political system, NTR's focus was on the basic needs of the people. His primary concern soon after coming to power was alleviating starvation. The popular subsidized rice scheme was implemented despite many challenges. It was an election promise that NTR was committed to fulfilling, though the task entailed a heavy burden on the exchequer. When his efforts came to fruition, nearly 1 crore families received 25 kg of rice at Rs 2 per kg every month through a well-networked public distribution system (PDS).

The PDS was not robust before 1983 and was limited to urban areas. Besides, rice was hardly distributed through the PDS. Sugar and kerosene were the only items that were distributed. The ration shops thus had little relevance to rural AP for food supplies. K.R. Venugopal, an IAS officer, was tasked with the implementation of the new programme. Venugopal, who was later secretary to Prime Minister P.V. Narasimha Rao, described the beneficial effects of the rice scheme:

> For the first time, as many as 27,221 villages saw the actual arrival of rice into their fair price shops, for distribution to the poor at near-affordable prices. The village fair price shops, which hitherto were essentially sugar or kerosene shops, could now hope to operate as viable small businesses because of increased turnover and margins. Rice began reaching the remotest corners of the State, previously not served by the PDS.[4]

Around the time, nearly 43 per cent of the rural and urban population was estimated to be living below the poverty line in AP. Based on the planning commission criterion, an income of Rs 3600 per annum was calculated as below the poverty level for rural families. But the data obtained later showed that the incidence of poverty in the state was higher. Because of this, NTR raised the income level from Rs 3600 per annum to Rs 6000 per annum. The number of beneficiary families, as a result, rose to 1.43 crore, which was nearly 86 per cent of the total households in AP at the time. Also, while initially it was decided to supply 10 kg of rice per family, later it was proposed to raise the entitlement to 25 kg per household per month.

C.D. Arha, an IAS officer, who succeeded Venugopal as commissioner of civil supplies, was all praise for NTR's commitment. One could not have had a better chief minister to implement an ambitious programme like the subsidized rice scheme, he said. Though rice millers were an influential lobby, they could not put pressure on NTR. The procurement of rice for a large number of people through an expanded PDS was a significant challenge. But the state administration rose to the task. 'The CM gave us a lot of confidence to do our job,' Arha said.[5] A staggering quantity of 15 lakh tonnes was made available through the PDS in 1983 as against 41,000 tonnes distributed in 1982. By 1985, it rose to 18 lakh tonnes.

According to Venugopal, such large-scale procurement was made possible because of 'the uncompromising commitment to the programme of making rice available at Rs 2 per kg to the poor on the part of the state's political leadership at the highest level'.[6] The total subsidy for the scheme was a huge Rs 1626 crore by 1988–89, half of which was borne by the state.

The government, over time, needed more than 20 lakh tonnes of rice to meet the annual demand. NTR found himself in trouble whenever drought conditions affected production. He would complain that the state was not getting its due share of rice from the central pool. Despite such issues, the scheme was a roaring success in AP, helping diminish hunger and prevent starvation deaths. NTR was so committed to the scheme that he refused to entertain suggestions by several officials to dilute the subsidized rice programme to lessen the burden on the exchequer.

There were, of course, a few shortcomings in its implementation but the benefits outnumbered them. According to Venugopal, the programme led to the weakening of the age-old *paleru* (an agricultural labourer who attaches to a landlord for a yearly wage) system, helped reduce indebtedness among the agricultural labour class and checked the price rise in the open market for rice, among others. The most important benefit of the scheme was that the poor enjoyed food security. No wonder, NTR and his welfare approach became synonymous with the subsidized rice scheme across the country.

Though the image of a populist stuck with him, NTR was against giving doles indiscriminately. While meeting the basic needs of the people was a priority, he also showed keen interest in the industrialization of the state. Prathipati Abraham, who was the commissioner of industries in the AP government, recalled that NTR 'believed in the rapid industrialisation of the State so that it would provide much-needed employment to the rural youth'.[7] NTR retained the industries portfolio with him, and 'spared no efforts in promoting industrial development'.

NTR took a business delegation with him during his first US trip in 1984 and sought investments from Telugu NRIs. Then industry secretary T.L. Sankar also accompanied him. NTR gave rousing speeches and called on the Telugu professionals settled in the US to serve the homeland. Dr Kakarla Subba Rao was one of those who responded to the call and came back home.

AP had 390 large and medium industries in 1982–83. During NTR's tenure, another 216 units were established, recording a growth of 55 per cent.[8] Small-scale units increased from 37,813 to 58,263 by 1989. The NTR regime pulled the state public undertakings out of perennial losses. While all state public enterprises put together incurred a loss of Rs 47 crore in 1984–85, in 1985–86, they made a profit of Rs 74.43 crore. The loss-making enterprises came down from twenty-four to seventeen. The power sector also witnessed growth. The installed capacity increased from 2606 megawatts to 3604 megawatts by 1987.

AP's state financial corporation (SFC) was number one in disbursing loans among all SFCs in the country for four consecutive years during NTR's period. This was a remarkable achievement for AP, considering the high level of industrial development in some other states, according to Abraham. The road transport corporation (RTC) incurred a loss of Rs 26 crore in 1980–81 but made a profit of Rs 7 crore by 1986–87. Incidentally, the two major bus stations in AP, the Mahatma Gandhi Bus Station in Hyderabad and the Pandit Nehru Bus Station in Vijayawada, were built by his government.[9] The handloom industry, which is a large employer in the state after agriculture, received NTR's special attention through his Janata cloth scheme, which improved employment.

Overall, though, AP did not make substantial progress in the industrial sector during NTR's regime. 'During NTR's tenure, the anti-Centre politics and populist policies and uneven thrust on agriculture in their combined effect led to the neglect of the industry,' stated a study by the Centre for Economic and Social Studies (CESS).[10] The average annual growth rates of the state domestic product from the manufacturing sector in AP from 1980–81 to 1982–83 was 5.97 per cent, while in the period between 1984–85 and 1987–88 it was 4.70 per cent. But the growth rate in the next three years (by 1992–93) during the Congress regime fell to 2.88 per cent. Clearly, NTR did not do too badly on the industrial front.

Altering Status Quo

NTR had announced his intention to bring in fundamental changes in the panchayat raj (system of local governance) set up in the early part of 1984. But he had to wait three years before he could come up with the much talked about 'mandal' revenue system. A 'mandal' is an administrative division. In a shake-up of the rural power structure, the government created 1104 revenue mandals in place of the 305 talukas. NTR's idea was to decentralize the administration to make it more efficient. The move was intended to curtail the domination of the upper castes in local bodies. NTR was of course also creating a solid base for the TDP.

Despite stiff resistance from Opposition parties, especially the Congress (I), the new legislation, known as the Andhra Pradesh Mandal Praja Parishads, Zilla Praja Parishads and Zilla Abhivrudhi Sameeksha Mandals Act, was brought into force with effect from 15 January 1987.

As the earlier talukas were larger units, it was not easy for far-flung villages to access government services. The new system of local government was introduced by constituting a lower tier, a middle tier and an upper tier—panchayats, mandal praja parishads and zilla praja parishads. Every revenue mandal, which replaced the talukas, was designed to have twelve to twenty villages covering between 35,000 and 55,000 people. The idea was to take the administration to the doorsteps of the people and empower them to solve local issues. Another goal was to ensure that the benefits of government welfare schemes reached the remotest parts of the state. Accordingly, the government proposed to provide each mandal with a primary health centre, a school, junior and degree colleges, a police station, a market, an agro-service centre and a veterinary hospital.

For the first time in the country, direct elections were envisaged for all tiers, including for mandal and zilla parishad (ZP) chairpersons. In a progressive step, seats were reserved for the underprivileged sections. A total of 50 per cent of political executive positions was set aside, including 15 per cent for SCs, 6 per cent for STs, 20 per cent for BCs and 9 per cent for women. Elections were held on a party basis. This was the first instance in the country when elections were fought with political party symbols in the panchayat raj system.

The mandal system introduced by NTR proved revolutionary in many ways. The direct elections and the quota for various communities increased political participation among sections that were hitherto denied access to rural power structures. Due to the reservation policy, BCs and women came to occupy political positions such as ZP chairpersons and mandal presidents. Direct elections to the local bodies also contributed to increased political awareness in rural AP. The move indirectly helped the TDP build its own rural political base. In the elections held in March 1987, the TDP romped home in the majority of the mandals. The party grabbed a significant share of ZP chairperson posts. The ruling party bagged eighteen out of the twenty-one ZPs and 632 out of the 1058 mandal parishads.

The mandal system was widely welcomed in rural AP, and, as a result, attempts by the later Congress government to scrap the model did not succeed. In many ways, it was a political master stroke as it helped entrench the TDP in every nook and corner of the state, while strengthening democracy at the grassroots. Political considerations certainly played a part in creating the mandal system, but the restructure effectively decentralized administration and strengthened local panchayat institutions. As reservations opened new avenues for BCs and rural women to empower themselves, many first-generation leaders emerged from these politically under-represented sections. The significant presence of BCs and women in local politics in Andhra and Telangana today is largely due to the recasting of the panchayat raj and provision of reservations by NTR's government.

NTR had a special attachment to women, whom he always addressed as 'aada paduchulu [sisters]'. From the day he entered politics, women of all ages became a great source of strength to his party. They sometimes outnumbered men in his election campaigns. NTR put special emphasis on women-centric initiatives in the government. As promised in the TDP manifesto, he took up the establishment of an exclusive women's university in Tirupati as soon as he came to power. The Sri Padmavati Mahila Visvavidyalayam, set up in 1983, has grown and has a student population of nearly 4000, imparting about fifty-nine courses at the undergraduate and postgraduate levels.

In 1984, the NTR government passed another significant order to reserve 30 per cent of all government jobs for women. According to the new policy, in the matter of direct recruitment to posts for which women were better suited than men, preference would be given to the former.

Another radical initiative by NTR to empower women was to give equal rights to daughters in inheritance. The bill was first introduced in the assembly in March 1983. A select committee of the state legislature gave its approval to the bill in 1984. But the Legislative Council dominated by the Congress stalled it, and the NTR government was removed from power soon after. A tenacious NTR took up the bill once again in September 1985 after he returned to office.

The bill, which became an act on 10 October 1985, sought to give daughters, who were majors but unmarried, a share in the Hindu joint family property. Daughters were to be treated as coparceners (joint heirs) from birth. Earlier, in the Hindu joint family governed by the Mitakshara law, a woman acquired the right to ancestral property only on the death of a parent, while the son acquired it at birth. AP was the first state which passed a law to provide equal rights to women by amending the Hindu Succession Act. It took nearly two more decades for the Centre to bring in a similar act. The 2005 amendment to the Hindu Succession Act by the Centre was in line with the 1986 amendment introduced by AP. When the bill was introduced in the Lok Sabha, NTR's daughter, D. Purandeswari, who was by this time an MP from the Congress, recalled her father's contribution in this regard.

NTR also began the practice of registering house site pattas in the name of women. Special courts to try crimes against women were also introduced. In his third term, NTR earned the gratitude of rural womenfolk when he banned alcohol sales in the state and enforced the law strictly.

Reformist Zeal

NTR brought about several innovative changes in the education sector, besides starting institutions of higher learning in the state. Three universities—the Padmavati Women's University, the University of Health Sciences and the Telugu University—took shape under his personal initiative. Andhra Pradesh Open University, though formally launched earlier, materialized during the TDP regime. According to Prof G. Ram Reddy, the first vice chancellor of Andhra Pradesh Open University, NTR's support to the new institution was 'a turning point in the development of the university'.[11] The establishment of a council for higher education was also the result of NTR's initiative. The Andhra Pradesh State Council for Higher Education (APSCHE), the first of its kind in the country, came into existence on 20 May 1988. Its mandate was to advise the government in matters relating to higher education.

NTR's principal adviser on education, Koneru Ramakrishna Rao, was its first chairman. 'With my over sixty years of experience as an academician, I can confidently say that no chief minister in the State paid as much attention to education as NTR did,' Rao said.[12] In a radical move, NTR banned the payment of donations for admission to professional institutions. The Andhra Pradesh Educational Institutions (Regulation of Admissions and Prohibition of Capitation Fee) Act, 1983, prescribed that access to educational institutions should be based on merit. What is known as EAMCET (Engineering Agriculture and Medical Common Entrance Test) in AP and Telangana was introduced by NTR's government. The government also regulated the fee to be collected by the educational institutions.

A research paper of the National Institute of Educational Planning and Administration stated that the NTR government successfully foiled the efforts by the private managements to dilute the ban on capitation fees.[13] When the Congress government came to power in 1989, it was quick to seek an amendment to the Education Act, 1983, to relax the ban on capitation fees.

Though residential schools in *gurukul* style were first started when Narasimha Rao was the chief minister, during 1971–73, it was NTR who sanctioned a school for every district after he came to power in 1983. Such was the popularity of these schools that the system was adopted nationwide when Rajiv Gandhi became the prime minister, leading to the establishment of Jawahar Navodaya Vidyalayas.

NTR was disappointed with the state of affairs in the field of education, which he often expressed publicly. He felt the existing system was producing clerks and not self-reliant individuals. He believed an effective education curriculum should have six months of classroom teaching and six months of practical work. 'I don't want students to become slaves through employment, I want them to become independent persons,' he said.[14] NTR advocated individual enterprise as the most effective way to achieve anything in life. He firmly believed that the dysfunctional education system should be rejuvenated by imparting job skills. As a result, NTR took the lead in introducing vocational training courses in 345 high schools.

NTR had a dream of creating a huge, self-contained residential campus for education which would provide teaching and research facilities from kindergarten to PhD. The school was envisaged as an exclusive educational retreat far away from the bustling crowds. NTR wanted to have a gurukul system where students would be brought in at an early age and leave only after they were equipped with all the existing knowledge. He wanted it to be a model for all educational institutions. Venkata Ramana Reddy, an architect, even drew the blueprints for his dream campus, and NTR held several meetings with officials to make it a reality. But the idea did not take shape.

However, he was able to carry out his vision for imparting education to young students through novel and engaging methods. His government was the first in the country to introduce audio-visual aids for teaching in schools. During 1986–88, the celebrated artist and film director Bapu (Sattiraju Lakshmi Narayana) and his close buddy, writer Mullapudi Venkata Ramana, were engaged by NTR. They were requested to design and produce audio and video lessons for classes I to V. NTR brought in his old associate from the film world, Vallabhajosyula Sivaram, as director of the State Institute of Education Technology (SIET) to make better use of the production facilities.

Given the Centre's hold on electronic media, NTR also wanted televisions and video cassette player sets to be provided to every school. They were to serve as a network through which the state government could send its message across. Music maestro A.R. Rahman, then an upcoming young artiste, composed the jingles for the lessons. The programme was initially launched in 600 schools in 1986–87, and by 1989 was rolled out in 11,000 schools. NTR's personal interest ensured that the project progressed without any hitches. Bapu and Ramana also designed pilot lessons for adult literacy programmes. The duo refused remuneration for their work which was spread over nearly three years. A grateful NTR honoured them with the Raghupathi Venkaiah Award, Telugu cinema's highest recognition.

However, the audiovisual education programme did not continue under the Congress government later. The project never took off on the scale NTR had envisaged because of the change of guard. The hard work put in by Bapu and Ramana, and NTR's desire for a cultural education was lost due to political and bureaucratic apathy.

Concerned at the way the children were losing their cultural moorings, NTR constituted a committee to prepare the syllabus for Telugu textbooks for classes I to V. Titled *Telugu Bharathi* by NTR himself, the textbooks focused on teaching young minds Telugu traditions, conventions and culture.[15] The trigger for NTR's initiative was a letter written by a boy related to him with the wrong salutation. Traditionally, elders addressed the young as 'Chiranjeevi [the one assured of long life]', but the young man greeted his uncle as 'Chiranjeevi'.

'What was remarkable about NTR was his willingness to embrace new ideas,' recalled R.V. Vaidyanatha Ayyar, who worked with NTR as state education secretary.[16] In the 1960s, school textbooks were nationalized, disabling their private production and distribution. As a result, by the 1980s, it became difficult for government printing presses to organize centralized production and distribution. Ayyar decided to try the idea of allowing private printers, along with the government presses, to print the textbooks prescribed by the government and market them through private channels. 'It was not difficult to convince NTR to approve the proposal,' he said. As a result, the shortage of books vanished overnight. For its time, the proposal was extraordinarily innovative, as privatization was anathema in the corridors of the government. The move was reversed by the Congress government later.

NTR had plans to establish a rural university, an institute of professional studies to foster linkages between classroom and industry and workshops in every mandal headquarters as part of the vocationalization of education.

He was criticized for interfering with the autonomy of institutions of higher learning. The TDP government not only had done away with elections to university syndicates but also introduced the system of nominating members to them. However, NTR stopped nominating MLAs, MPs and party workers to academic bodies like the executive council or academic senate of universities. He aimed to choose the best talent to head these universities. 'Since this government came to power, we have not appointed a single person from outside the academic world as a vice-chancellor,' NTR said in 1988 at the conference of vice chancellors.[17]

The chief minister had a tiff with the governor over appointments of vice chancellors to universities. He decided to appoint himself as the chancellor of universities in a bid to circumvent the governor's interference. He became the chancellor of the newly created University of Health Sciences and later the Telugu University—a position usually reserved for the governor. These were subsequently reversed by the Congress regime.

NTR wanted to reform school education in a big way. He appointed a committee with Koneru Ramakrishna Rao as chairman in 1994 to provide a blueprint for the task. 'To my great admiration, I found that he had very specific ideas and the general direction in which we should go in order to bring out comprehensive reforms,' Ramakrishna Rao said.[18] The report was ready in a short period, and a bill was drafted to be introduced in the assembly. But NTR was deposed from power before he could see this through. Though NTR was not an educationalist by training or practice, Prof Ramakrishna Rao was 'amazed at the depth of his thought, his commitment to action and his restless search for ways to translate his ideas into action'.[19]

The chief minister's penchant for fresh ideas extended even to the religious institutions which were under government control. Despite his public image as a deeply religious person, NTR displayed a secular zeal for pushing reforms in the endowments department. Few political leaders would have dared to intervene in Hindu religious matters the way NTR did. He moved to bring about a series of reforms in the temple administration, focusing on the TTD which administered Tirumala, the popular pilgrim destination and abode of Lord Venkateswara. Some of these decisions turned out to be controversial, and many angered the priestly class which had enjoyed the unquestioned acceptance of their control of these matters, especially during the Congress regime.

NTR's first salvo was the controversial fiat to the TTD to transfer all surplus funds held in commercial banks to the government treasury. Given the ambitious schemes of the TDP government, the state's financial position was under pressure. The government was forced to take an overdraft. Always looking for ingenious ways, NTR hit upon the idea of making use of the surplus TTD funds. He promised that the government would pay the same amount of interest. As expected, there was severe backlash from the vocal sections.

Kanchi Sankaracharya Jayendra Saraswati criticized the government's move. M. Venkaiah Naidu, the BJP legislator, called the decision 'encroachment into the affairs of a Hindu religious endowment'. Janata legislator S. Jaipal Reddy insisted that the 'government should not tamper with the funds of religious organizations'. However, NTR stood his ground. 'God does not take exception to his treasure being utilized to provide drinking water to the thirsty or to feed his starving children,' he said.[20] The TTD board had no option but to approve the transfer of Rs 33 crore to the state's account. The move was reversed by Nadendla's short-lived government in August 1984, and NTR left it at that.

NTR's second term saw more of his reformist zeal in Hindu endowments. In 1985, he appointed a commission by Challa Kondaiah, the former chief justice of AP High Court, to recommend measures for adequate maintenance of temples in the state. Based on its recommendations, the government enacted the Andhra Pradesh Charitable and Hindu Religious Institutions and Endowments Act, 1987. The radical law recommended, among others, the abolition of hereditary priesthood and trusteeship in Hindu temples, heralding a new chapter in the Hindu temple management practices.

According to the act, all hereditary rights of persons holding the office of *Pedda Jeeyangar, Chinna Jeeyangar, mirasidar* or *archaka* or *pujari* in any religious institution or endowment stood abolished. And all powers and emoluments that accrued as a result of such hereditary rights were revoked. The temple functionaries, including archakas (temple priests), were to be recruited through a well-laid-out process and paid regular salaries.

At the time, there were about 32,201 temples in AP, out of which 7761 were assessable institutions, and 582 had each an income of more than Rs 10,000 per annum. Around eight temples had an income of more than Rs 20 lakh per annum each. Of these, the Tirumala Tirupati Venkateswara temple was the largest and the richest.

The Challa Kondaiah Commission report was attacked by several associations of priests and religious heads. They organized protest meetings and warned against its implementation. Religious leaders characterized the report as interfering with the Hindu religious beliefs and traditions. Unfazed by the opposition, NTR went ahead with the new law. Like many of NTR's decisions, the act was challenged in court. The case went on for nearly ten years, and the Supreme Court finally upheld the act in 1996.

The petitioners argued that a temple priest inherited his office from his ancestors, following the Vaikhanasa Agama Shastra rules. These rules governed the Tirumala Temple on the principles of 'heirs in the line of succession' among four families—Paidapally, Gollapalli, Pethainti and Thirupathannagaru. All of them traditionally enjoyed certain rights known as 'mirasi' (hereditary rights and responsibilities). They earned their livelihood through these rights, which included lands given by the temple for the performance of services. Besides, archakas got a share of the offerings made to the temple, while persons in charge of preparing the prasad (offerings to God), known as *gamekars*, got a percentage of share out of their sale. The money earned through these rights ran into crores of rupees. For example, emoluments paid by the TTD in cash and kind to the archakas and gamekars of the temple were worth about Rs 27 crore from June 1987 to January 1996,

when the case was still pending in the court.[21] In the preparation
of laddus alone, the mirasis, archakas and gamekars were paid
Rs 3 crore a year as their share.

K. Parasaran, an eminent lawyer, argued on behalf of the priests
in the Supreme Court. He contended that abolition of hereditary
rights was interference with religious practices and customs. The
act conferred power on the secular state to decide who should be
appointed as archaka, mirasidar and other office holders. The state
government contended that the act established a clear distinction
between matters of religion and secular activities of a religious
institution. The act sought to regulate only the administration and
maintenance of the secular part of the religious institutions, the
government argued.

The court, while upholding the new act, noted that the
hereditary mirasis were not offering services personally but
through their agents. The mirasis lived in cities like Madras and
Bombay and appointed agents to carry out their responsibilities.
'The *Archakas* and *Gamekars* have not been rendering any service
personally but only through their deputies working for and on
behalf of head priests for consideration. The hereditary nature
of the right, therefore, became irrelevant,' the court said.[22] The
court also declared that the hereditary rights that governed the
appointment of archakas was a secular usage which could be
regulated by law. As a corollary to the abolition, the legislature was
competent to prescribe qualifications for archakas, the judgment
delivered by the bench, consisting of Justices K. Ramaswamy and
B.L. Hansaria, stated.

The endowments act further estranged Brahmins from the
TDP. They were already affected by the government's decisions
on retirement and abolition of the office of hereditary village
officers. The community which formed the cream of the state's
bureaucracy felt persecuted.

NTR, even while regulating temples and their administration,
helped the propagation of the Hindu faith abroad. His government

facilitated allocation of funds from the TTD's coffers to Hindu
temples in foreign lands, mainly the US, where a good number
of Telugus and Indians from other states lived. This was the first
time in India that such grants and loans were provided through a
government-controlled body. In 1984, during his visit to the US,
NTR laid the foundation stone for Sri Rama Temple in Greater
Chicago. Also, representations were made to him for financial
help. After his return, NTR came up with the TTD Overseas
Temples Construction Financial Aid Scheme. Accordingly,
loans to the tune of Rs 48 lakh were approved to seven temples
in foreign lands—Hindu Community and Cultural Centre,
Walnut Creek, US; New England Hindu Temple, Wellesley
Hills, Massachusetts; Hindu Temple of Greater Chicago,
Lemont, Illinois; Sri Venkateswara Temple, Greater Chicago,
Palos Park; Hindu Temple Society of South California, Glendale;
Sri Venkateswara Temple Association, Jackson, Mississippi; and
Temple Association, Rama Gate, Sydney, Australia. An amount
of Rs 5 lakh was granted on loan to Vishnu Mandir, Hindu
Dharma Sabha, Bangkok.

NTR had dreams of transforming Tirumala into a holy
city with special status on the lines of the Vatican in Rome. He
mooted the idea in 1984, but the August crisis in the same year
put paid to his plans. After coming to power in 1994, NTR
revived his plans to bestow special status on Tirumala, calling it
'Balaji Divya Kshetram'. He wanted Tirumala to be free of any
private property, and planned to transform it into a truly sacred
place with its own administration. Inaugurating the golden jubilee
celebrations of the Tirumala-Tirupati Devasthanams (TTD)
in April 1995, NTR proclaimed, 'If the Vatican is the religious
centre for Christians, Tirupati should be the same for the Hindus
all over the world.'[23]

The draft bill prepared by his adviser Devanathan envisaged
a supreme council with Lord Venkateswara as the chairman and
NTR himself as the vice chairman and chief executive. However,

several legal pundits said such an arrangement would not stand the test of law. Shankar Dayal Sharma, who was the president of India at the time and himself a staunch devotee of Lord Venkateswara, dismissed the proposal during one of his visits as 'unnecessary'. NTR's idea of creating an exclusive spiritual enclave was clearly inspired by his cinematic vision. However, unlike in the past, NTR was more circumspect about his pet projects in his third term and gave up the proposal.

It was during NTR's time that Tirumala developed into a well-administered pilgrim centre. He contributed to the increase in the greenery of the hills and built several new facilities such as an ultra-modern queue complex. He also tightened the administration of the hills. The restrictions his government imposed on temple entry through the *mahadwaram*, the main entrance, caused a rift between him and the former president of India, N. Sanjiva Reddy. The former president got offended when his family was not allowed to accompany him according to the new protocol.[24]

NTR took care to appoint persons with integrity as the board members of TTD. In 1995, he chose film actors Rajinikanth and Raj Kumar as board members to represent Tamil Nadu and Karnataka, respectively, as many devotees to Tirumala hailed from these states. NTR was also responsible for the introduction of the 'Anna Prasadam' scheme in 1985, for providing free meals to every pilgrim visiting Tirumala. On an auspicious day, about two hundred thousand devotees are served free food at Tirumala.

Tirumala was the only temple that NTR visited each time he launched and concluded his election process. He tonsured his head at Tirumala—as per religious practice—after every electoral victory. He also had framed pictures of the lord and his consort prominently hung behind his desk at home and in the office. The popular 'Venkateswara Suprabhatam' (Hymn of Morning Salutation to Lord Venkateswara rendered by the legendary M.S. Subbulakshmi) played at NTR's residence early morning.

Telugu Cultural Rejuvenation

In his first year in governance, NTR tried to recast the state's culture scenario by pulling down the various academies that he considered merely Congress interest groups. In his second term, he proactively implemented major initiatives that helped transform Hyderabad into a distinctly Telugu city. The Tank Bund project and the Hussain Sagar Buddha project were his two major contributions that imparted Telugu flavour to the city. NTR's cinematic sensibilities came into full play in executing these two projects.

The Tank Bund project, constructed in 1986, was NTR's way of paying tribute to several personalities who played a significant role in shaping the culture of Telugu-speaking people. Statues of thirty-three luminaries associated with the Telugu language, culture and land had pride of place on Tank Bund abutting Hussain Sagar lake in the heart of Hyderabad. NTR called the project in his verbose, Sanskritized style Telugu Velugula Murthi Nikshiptha Kala Pranganam (artistic gallery of the Telugu luminaries). The tall, dark-bronze statues were visualized by NTR as an embodiment of Telugu identity. A long-time resident of Madras, NTR was clearly influenced by the DMK's installation of Dravidian cult figures on Marina Beach during the late 1960s to reinforce Tamil pride in regional culture and history.

NTR undertook an elaborate exercise before implementing the project that cost Rs 2.29 crore. The 2.5-km-long bund on Hussain Sagar that connected Hyderabad and Secunderabad was already choking with traffic. NTR's first move was to widen it, as well as construct a retaining stone wall behind the bund. A hue and cry was raised, claiming any tinkering with the bund would submerge the city. However, a determined NTR went ahead with the help of senior officials led by the then municipal commissioner C. Arjuna Rao, and the task was completed faster than anyone expected.

Meanwhile, the making of statues in Madras and Hyderabad involved his personal attention. NTR visited Madras several times. In Hyderabad, the workshop was located near the secretariat, and NTR would often stop by to check the progress and give suggestions. Sattanatha Muthaiya Ganapathi, popularly known as Ganapathi Sthapathi, the chief architect and sculptor of the endowments department, coordinated the project. Under his supervision, a team of sculptors chiselled the statues for months.

A controversy was kicked up during the 'separate Telangana' agitation on the choice of the historical figures for the project. Against this backdrop, it is interesting to note that initially the number of personalities listed was much more than the thirty-three that finally adorned Tank Bund. Some of the other illustrious names that were under consideration included Sarojini Naidu, Salar Jung, Chittoor Nagaiah, Durgabai Deshmukh, C.P. Brown, Srinadhudu, Adibhatla Narayana Dasu, Ghantasala, etc. However, since the area available on Tank Bund even after the widening was not spacious enough to accommodate so many statues, it was decided to narrow down the list from around sixty to thirty-three. The idea was to have another project for the other icons, but it never materialized. Historical figures from the first century CE to the modern time made it to the final list.

NTR's active involvement was visible at every stage of the project. He took a keen interest in the design of each statue in terms of their physical and aesthetic appearance. He also played a role in deciding the order in which they would be placed on the bund. While the Carnatic musical genius Tyagayya was placed at the centre, the modern figures were on the Secunderabad side, and towards Hyderabad were the pre-modern statues.

However, this order had a slight deviation, with Rani Rudrama Devi at the entrance from the Secunderabad side. This was because NTR visualized that the two historical figures of Salivahana and Rudrama Devi should welcome visitors as they entered from either side of the bund. The line-up of imposing statues on either side was flanked by two traditionally built *thoranams* (gateways), the southern gate replicating elements of Vijayanagara architecture, and the northern entrance resembling the famous Kakatiya arch in Warangal.

NTR inaugurated the refurbished boulevard on Tank Bund with its awe-inspiring iconography with fanfare on 1 November 1986, the formation day of the linguistic state. He delivered an inspiring speech, detailing the great qualities of the stalwarts standing on Tank Bund. Each one of the statues was unveiled by a prominent personality invited for the occasion. For example, the statue of Rani Rudrama Devi was formally unveiled by writer Illendula Saraswathi Devi. Sir Arthur Cotton's statue was unveiled by Rev. Bishop B.G. Prasada Rao and that of Sri Sri (Srirangam Srinivasa Rao) by Justice K. Punnaiah, while Pothana's statue was uncovered by Prof Biruduraju Ramaraju.

NTR had roped in the services of film cameramen in Madras such as Marcus Bartley and Jaihind Satyam to help give shape to some of the personalities of the distant past. The historical iconographies created in films through photography in the past were used as the visual reference. An example was Tyagayya, portrayed by Chittoor Nagaiah in a film of the same name from the 1940s. As NTR had, in his films, played historical personalities, such as Sri Krishnadevaraya and Pothuluri Veerabrahmendra Swamy, they were modelled on his portrayal. For others like Nannaya and Tikkana, literary references were used as clues. There was obviously less of a problem with twentieth-century figures. NTR had requested his long-standing writer-friend Jnanpith awardee C. Narayana Reddy to come up with pithy couplets in lilting Telugu. The verses captured the valuable contributions made by these eminent personalities. These were inscribed on the six-feet-high pedestal of each nine-feet-tall statue. For example, the write-up on Pothuluri Veerabrahmendra Swamy read thus: 'Aagami kalagnana karta, purogrami samaaja samskartha [Foreteller of times ahead, forward-thinking reformer].'

Evidently, a lot of thought and effort went into the project. An analysis of the figures would show the liberal and democratic spirit behind the selection. The eclectic list included: the early literary trinity Nannaya, Tikkana and Yerrapragada; followed by Pothana of *Bhagavatham* fame; modern literary and reformist figures like Gurajada Appa Rao, Gurram Jashuva, Veeresalingam Pantulu and Srirangam Srinivasa Rao (Sri Sri); cultural icons who contributed to Telugu devotional poetry such as Annamacharya, Kshetrayya, Ramadasu and Tyagayya; the first Telugu emperor of yore, Salivahana; the founder of modern Kuchipudi, Siddhendra Yogi; progressive medieval writer Vemana; accomplished woman poet Kummari Molla; the celebrated king who presided over the golden period of Telugu literary history, Krishnadevaraya; social reformer Raghupati Venkataratnam Naidu; editor-journalist Mutnuri Krishna Rao; historian Suravaram Pratapa Reddy; national flag designer Pingali Venkayya; Hindu mystic Pothuluri Veerabrahmendra Swamy; philosopher and statesman Sarvepalli Radhakrishnan; rationalist playwright and reformer Tripuraneni Ramaswamy; educationist and scholar C.R. Reddy; iconic revolutionary Alluri Sitarama Raju; modern theatre personality Bellary Raghava; broad-minded medieval minister Brahmanaidu; liberal Muslim ruler of Hyderabad Abul Hasan Tana Shah; the enlightened sixth Nizam Mir Mahabub Ali Khan; the builder of a gigantic irrigation development work in the Godavari Delta, Sir Arthur Cotton; progressive Urdu poet Maqdoom Mohiuddin; and the valorous queen of Kakatiya Dynasty, Rani Rudrama Devi. It showed the heterogeneous, non-sectarian and broad-based approach adopted by NTR to represent the glorious achievements of Telugus.

However, several pro-Telangana commentators, during the peak of the separatist agitation, saw in the Tank Bund statues 'regional hegemony', a thinly veiled expression for alleged Andhra domination. One objection was that the Telangana region did not get adequate representation. Though proportional regional representation was not the goal, out of the thirty-three personalities, seven were from the Telangana region, sixteen from coastal Andhra, six from the Rayalaseema region, and four were born outside the erstwhile united AP.

Another criticism was that the project helped mainly to consolidate the TDP's identity and inscribe NTR's image within it. Critics said the facial features of some of the statues looked suspiciously like NTR's.[25] Santosh Kumar Sakhinala, an art researcher, alleged that the visual symbolism of the Tank Bund statues involved 'a form of occupationist intervention in the city', by suppressing 'the syncretic Islamic historical identity of Hyderabad by projecting a new hegemonic Telugu history'.[26]

The argument of these scholars appears to be that the 'Islamic historical identity' of Hyderabad should be frozen for all times to come despite the city having emerged as the capital of Telugu-speaking people, with their distinct culture and long history. The subsequent destruction of several of these statues on Tank Bund by highly charged Telangana activists[27] was certainly not an effort to restore this 'Islamic historical identity'. It was more an assertion of the Telangana ownership of Hyderabad. The act of defilement, however, was explained away by the apologists as a legitimate expression of the long-suppressed anger of the people at the continuing injustice done to the region.

None of the stalwarts on the Tank Bund at the receiving end of the separatist ire would have had any inkling of these latter-day rumblings. Nor could they, by any stretch of the imagination, be accused of partaking in the alleged discrimination since regional identities were not formed in the way they came to be perceived in modern times. In any case, NTR took his mission as one of bringing a sense of community among the Telugu-speaking people. He wanted the Tank Bund iconography to serve as a reminder of past glory and its continuity in the present. 'There is no future for people who forget their past,' NTR said on unveiling the statues. He called the icons 'inspiring symbols' that showed the way for a 'society devoid of caste, class and religious discrimination'.[28]

In conceiving the project, NTR directed his efforts towards broader cultural nationalism and not the narrow confines of linguistic chauvinism. He wanted to draw inspiration not merely from Telugu-speaking people but anyone who was related to Telugu or contributed to its glory. That was the reason non-residents and even non-Telugu speakers found a place on Tank Bund. But ironically an affirmation of regional identity was later subverted by a counter-assertion of subregional identity.

NTR's project of a Telugu cultural renaissance continued with the ambitious installation of a Buddha statue in the middle of Hussain Sagar Lake. NTR was inspired by the Statue of Liberty during his visit to the US in 1984. The idea of a Buddha statue was mooted by the earlier Congress regime near Nagarjuna Sagar, a predominantly Buddhist area since ancient times. However, nothing came of it till NTR assumed power and finalized the location in the middle of Hussain Sagar.

NTR formally inaugurated the sculptural work in October 1985 and closely supervised the complex project. A replica of the Buddha statue in standing posture from the relics of Nagarjunakonda in Guntur District, once a centre of Buddhism in Andhra, was chosen to serve as the model. The quarry near Raigiri in Nalgonda District on the Hyderabad–Hanamkonda road was identified as the most suitable for carving the statue out of a single monolithic stone block. Ultrasonic tests were conducted on the rock for detecting cavities, cracks, fissures, etc. The rock in its rough form was hewn out of the mother rock at Raigiri and transported to the *Shilpashram* adjacent to the AP secretariat.

Once a major part of the work was finished, transporting the gigantic statue from the remote Raigiri Hills to the bustling city of Hyderabad, a 64-km journey, was a task. It weighed about 450 tonnes in its semi-finished form. The contractors for the work, Assam and Bengal Carriers (India) Ltd, known as ABC (India), undertook the arduous journey, and the giant rock statue reached its destination in November 1988. The expedition made news for the elaborate exercise conducted by the government for its smooth transport. The administration had to widen roads, clear overhead obstacles, remove electricity lines and build bypasses. T.R. Seshadri, an engineer who was intimately involved with the project, wrote on how the colossal statue was transported:

> A special 24 axle, hydraulically operated trailer of 192 wheels with a carrying capacity of 720 tons was brought from Germany by the company for the purpose. As the existing bridges and culverts en route were not capable of carrying the heavy load, diversion roads were formed, culverts strengthened. The loading of the statue on the trailer at the hill slope was a herculean task which could be tackled by the company with their foreign consultants by using sophisticated equipment and high technology.[29]

NTR was present to receive the convoy at the Buddha Purnima site near the secretariat. He climbed aboard the trailer, walked solemnly around the rough-hewn Buddha and offered prayers. Speaking on the occasion, NTR said that the Buddha statue was being installed not to preach a religion, but as a mark of love and respect to the great social reformer.[30]

It was under the watchful eye of Ganapathi Sthapathi, who had supervised the Tank Bund statues, that the Buddha statue was carved. About forty sculptors and workers chipped and hammered the rock into its final shape. The gigantic monolithic statue, weighing 320 tonnes and standing 17 metres tall, was given final touches on the shores of Hussain Sagar before it was ferried to the Rock of Gibraltar, the man-made island in the middle of the lake. The statue was ready in its finished form by the end of August 1989. But before NTR could see the completion of the project, he was voted out of power.

The work on ferrying the statue into the middle of the lake began in March 1990 under the Congress government. However, tragedy struck when the barge lost balance as soon as it started moving towards the Rock of Gibraltar. Having travelled hardly 60 metres from the shore, the statue slipped into the waters, killing eleven workers, including ABC's (India) project manager, S.K. Mundra. NTR, now in the Opposition, was upset. 'I am sorry. The great saint is lost in the waters of the Hussain Sagar,' he said.

The salvage operation took a long time, given the challenge of lifting the statue that was lying face down on the lake bed. In an intricate, complicated but successful operation, the Buddha was rescued, and, finally, in December 1992, it was hoisted on a 24-by-24-metre concrete platform. The entire cost of the project was Rs 9.63 crore. In its final avatar, the statue, with its right hand raised in *abhaya* mudra, gazed towards the Tank Bund. The imposing Buddha statue, visible prominently from all sides of Hussain Sagar Lake, is an engineering marvel as well as an artistic achievement. But more importantly, the serene Buddha remains a testament to NTR's zeal and passion for celebrating the Telugu cultural past and its historical association with Buddhism.

The choice of Buddha for the large Hussain Sagar statue throws light on a facet of NTR that is at odds with his perceived image as a quintessential Hindu. NTR referred to the humanitarian aspect of Buddha's life and teachings as being his inspiration for installing the statue. 'Buddhism is the base for socialism and communism and other such theories. Buddha is not a god; he is a social reformer, a holy force,' NTR said.[31]

Either consciously or subconsciously, NTR was drawing from the remarkable wealth of Buddhist heritage and sculptural remains that Andhra was known for.[32] Researcher Catherine Becker in her book on Buddhist sculptures in AP pointed out that the Hussain Sagar Buddha adopted the pose and attire associated with numerous Buddha images from ancient Andhra. According to her, the Andhra-type standing Buddha of the first millennium, with its distinct robe and hand gesture, was popular across South East Asia. 'The Hussain Sagar Buddha's visual citation of this particular type of standing Buddha evokes the State's contribution to a global Buddhist visual culture,' she said.[33] NTR considered the Buddha statue 'a non-religious emblem of regional-cum-national pride'.[34] NTR's inclusive approach to religion and culture was unmistakable. In the current scenario of erecting giant statues with narrow political agendas aimed at vote banks, NTR's initiative comes across as all-embracing.

The status of Telugu as the state's official language was firmly established during NTR's tenure. Telugu had always been the language of the people, but it received primacy in the administration after NTR took over the reins. Thereafter, the use of Telugu became widespread in all government functions and official events. NTR himself was a brand ambassador for the language. NTR's identification with the native tongue elevated it to prominence in the administration.

His party had every document, statement and press note, including the party manifesto, released in flowery Telugu. The ruling party's annual conventions were awash with Telugu historical and cultural ethos, and all its declarations and resolutions were invariably put out in the same language as well.

C. Narayana Reddy claimed that when he had told NTR in 1982 about Sri Krishnadevaraya's famous poem on the prominence of Telugu language, the latter was not aware of it. Thrilled by the verse, 'Desa Bhashalandu Telugu Lessa [Of all the languages of the country, Telugu is the best]', NTR got it on a piece of paper and immediately memorized it.[35] He would often recite the poem with great feeling to express his love for Telugu in public meetings.

NTR had a distinctly formal way of speaking Telugu with alliterative wordings. His Telugu was idiomatic but also Sanskritized. He had also a literary way of speaking. His poetic composition of dry sentences, reminiscent of dialogues in his mythological films, invested him with a Teluguness that people were familiar with. His public speeches, especially in meetings related to education and culture, were full of Telugu cultural motifs with quotes from well-known writers like Gurajada and Rayaprolu. No other politician of AP delivered such ornamental speeches, not even the more scholarly and erudite Narasimha Rao.

One of NTR's real-life performances was as a priest, presiding over a wedding ritual in the Telugu tradition while he was the chief minister. NTR officiated a marriage in 1988 in the family of Telugu writer Nagabhairava Koteswara Rao, who had written dialogues for his film *Brahmarshi Viswamitra*. NTR was following the tradition of 'Kamma Brahmins' prevalent in the 1940s when some Kammas learnt the relevant mantras and officiated at weddings in their community. Effortlessly slipping into the role, NTR guided the ritual, explaining the meaning of the proceedings and elucidating the connotation behind each custom such as *jeelakarra-bellam* which is specific to Telugu marriages. Through such acts, NTR epitomized Teluguness.

But he was not content in merely providing a psychological fillip to the status of the language. He went about systemically promoting the use of Telugu in governance. For the first time, orders were issued for implementing Telugu at all levels of administration from 1 November 1988, the State Formation Day. Training programmes were conducted for principal secretaries and below for making 'file notings' in Telugu under the aegis of the Official Language Commission headed by Narayana Reddy. The chief minister wanted all communication to the Centre to be carried out in Telugu, along with an English copy.

The Official Language Commission made a significant contribution during NTR's tenure. Besides conducting training programmes, the commission prepared glossaries for thirty-four departments and a pocket-size dictionary, titled *Karyalaya Padaavali*, for general use with 1000 words and phrases. The commission, during the chairmanship of Nanduri Ramakrishna Acharya, ensured that 11,000 typists were trained in Telugu typing. The government set up Telugu *vignana samachara kendralu* (libraries) in all the districts. 'We have to recognise the basic fact that the student can always learn in his own mother tongue more efficiently,' NTR told a meeting of vice chancellors, suggesting to the universities to introduce Telugu as the medium of instruction even at the postgraduate level.[36]

NTR imprinted every government scheme with a 'Telugu' tag, starting from Telugu Ganga. He called, for example, distribution of land to the landless poor Telugu Maganam Samaradhana, scholarships for meritorious school students Telugu Vignana Parithoshakam, and an afforestation programme Telugu Vriksha Sankshema Pathakam. Financial help to build movie theatres was called Telugu Chalanachitra Kala Vikasam, and the scheme to create assets in rural areas was referred to as Telugu Grameena Kranthi Patham. Supply of dhotis and sarees at cheaper prices was referred to as Telugu Vastra Pradana Vidhanam; pension scheme for poor widows was termed Telugu Vitantu Upadhi Kalpanam; help to poor pregnant women was Telugu Matrudevatha Samadaram; and a health scheme for schoolchildren was called Telugu Chiranjeeva Sukheebhavam.

NTR's penchant for naming all government schemes and policies in highly Sanskritized Telugu sometimes verged on being funny. A plan to provide public toilets for women was rather a mouthful: Telugu Mahila Bahirbhumi Pathakam. NTR, who extensively used pure Telugu words with Dravidian origins in his films, surprisingly chose pretentiously high-flown Sanskrit in government.

The famous Telugu Talli (Mother Telugu) statue near the secretariat was installed by his government. The 10.5-feet-tall bronze statue weighing 800 kg was sculpted by Devu Shankar at a cost of Rs 90,000 in 1986. NTR also took an interest in building Telugu architectural-style edifices in the secretariat as well as in the Telugu University campus, including Telugu Lalitha Kala Thoranam, an open-air theatre in Public Gardens.

The annual Mahanadu events of the TDP, coinciding with his birthday, overflowed with Telugu cultural traditions. Every Mahanadu had a 'mela'-like atmosphere. A few hundred artists and performers participated in the cultural events, entertaining a sea of people who thronged the temporary venue throughout the week. Huge cut-outs, elaborately decorated venues, a big stage, engaging cultural shows, displays of traditional arts and crafts, and a rich variety of Andhra cuisine featured in these annual events. The who's who of the Opposition graced these occasions. A stall on NTR's film career was always a part of the event. The 1988 Mahanadu, which marked the completion of five years in power for the TDP, was a spectacular affair. Held in Vijayawada in a 100-acre area, it was as much a Telugu cultural extravaganza as it was a political meeting. Bullock cart races, kabaddi, wrestling and other rural sports entertained audiences at Satavahanapuri.[37] The entry points, reflecting Telugu history, were called Dharanikota and Nagarjuna gateways. Telugu folk art forms such as Veedhi Bhagavatam, Tappeta Gullu, Kolatam, Harikatha, Burrakatha, Pagati Veshalu and Puli Veshalu were performed every evening. A mini zoo with a lion, a tiger, an elephant, deer and birds was set up as a special attraction. The stage, designed by film set designer Ketha, was called 'Samyamanam [Fortitude]'. NTR liked to dazzle the who's who of the national Opposition with such cultural and visual spectacles.

Though a Telugu lover, NTR was far from a linguistic fanatic. In one of the meetings of the Official Language Commission, many participants argued that all hearings in courts should be compulsorily in Telugu. NTR asked in which language the law course was being taught. 'English,' came the answer. 'Then how can we insist them to argue court cases in Telugu, when we are not teaching law in Telugu? First, prepare all law textbooks in Telugu,' he instructed.[38]

The credit for infusing Telugu language and culture into the ethos of Hyderabad mainly goes to NTR. Before him, the

Deccani culture of the city reflected few traces of Telugu or
Telangana. Even decades after the formation of AP with the
merger of Andhra and Telangana regions, Hyderabad continued
to be a Nawabi city, dominated by an Urdu and Nizami cultural
milieu. Telugu had a lower standing among the languages spoken
in the state capital for many historical reasons, though numerically
the speakers were always in the majority. The elite of Telangana
preferred to speak in Urdu to be counted among the aristocracy of
the erstwhile princely state.

In Hyderabad, the elite would take pride in Deccani *tehzeeb*,
which was considered a confluence of various cultures. But the
reality was that Telugu, and its speakers, who constituted the
majority in the Nizam kingdom (Hyderabad state), were looked
down upon. Urdu was the official language, Farsi, Persian and
Arabic had a pride of place, and even Marathi enjoyed a better
status. In fact, a Lucknowi or a Punjabi would have felt more at
home in Hyderabad than a Telugu from coastal Andhra or interior
Telangana. 'It was amusing to note that in the heart of the capital
of a Telugu-speaking State, Telugu didn't always work,' recalled
Narendra Luther, a former civil servant who authored several
books on Hyderabad.[39] While Telangana festivals like Bonalu or
Bathukamma were celebrated in the city, they were looked down
upon as working-class carnivals. As for people from coastal Andhra
and Rayalaseema, they did not exactly feel at home in the capital
of their own state due to the cultural and linguistic alienation.

It was against this backdrop that NTR's arrival on the scene
made a significant difference to Hyderabad's cultural landscape.
For the first time since Hyderabad became their capital in 1956,
the middle classes from coastal Andhra and Rayalaseema regions
felt an emotional connection to the city. This was a direct outcome
of NTR's linguistic nationalism. The population of Hyderabad
began swelling from the 1980s as people from Andhra swarmed
to the city in search of opportunities under a regime where Telugu
had pride of place. Once linguistic affinity was established with

the rest of Andhra, Hyderabad, a sleepy city till the 1970s, grew as a bustling metropolis. The city's highest growth was recorded between 1981 and 1991, when the population expanded from 25 lakh to 43 lakh, registering a yearly increase of 5.3 per cent.

New colonies around the city came up. Ubiquitous tea shops and food joints (called Andhra messes and curry points in local parlance) replaced Irani cafes. Movie theatres playing Telugu films sprang up. Hyderabad became the hub for the Telugu cinema industry. Telugu newspapers, which were based in Vijayawada for a long time, made Hyderabad their headquarters.[40] Telugu cultural events became prominent in the city. Telugu writers, artists, publishers, traders, professionals, business persons and everyone looking for opportunities made Hyderabad their new home. The migration of people from Telangana also accelerated. The Tank Bund statuary and structures like Lalitha Kala Thoranam imbued the city with a new Teluguness. Hyderabad began redefining its character as a Telugu city with a Deccani past. 'Hyderabad is now the centre of a dynamic modern Telugu culture, one that will receive attention from other researchers in the future as the transformations underway gain still more momentum,' acknowledged historian Karen Isaksen Leonard in her book on Hyderabad.[41]

There has been criticism in some sections, primarily among the Telangana elite, against the loss of the city's 'Deccani character'. The alleged colonization of Hyderabad by Andhra settlers, especially after the turn of the millennium, became a leading cause for the last leg of the 'separate Telangana' agitation. From a different perspective, this disapproval underlined NTR's contribution to Hyderabad's newly acquired personality as a Telugu metropolis. The various strands of Telugu culture, subdued for long, are now conspicuous in the Deccani legacy. Hyderabad's identity as a predominantly Telugu-speaking city has endured in its new avatar as the capital of Telangana.[42] In fact, even after bifurcation, Hyderabad remains the only Telugu metropolis for both Telangana and AP. Significantly, a large chunk of Andhra and Rayalaseema people living in the city chose to stay back even post-division.[43]

Conservative Backlash

NTR's style of politics was such that conflicts cropped up soon enough. The chief minister's actions unsettled many interest groups. The non-gazetted officers (NGO) in the government were one such. The bad blood created during NTR's first stint with the NGOs continued into his second term as well. Differences arose over the recommendations of the pay revision commission (PRC). The government accepted the report, but the NGOs argued there were many anomalies and put forward new demands. NTR refused to yield. The NGOs went on strike, which continued for fifty-three days, causing a severe rupture in the administration.

As NTR played hardball, the NGOs also went overboard, personally targeting him. One of the NGO leaders even demanded President's Rule in the state. The government responded by dismissing several NGO leaders and even arresting them. 'People and their welfare are more important than NGOs and their demands,' NTR said. He refused to personally invite them for talks. 'Why do they need an invitation? Is it about any wedding in my family? If they have issues, they should come. I will not stand mute if the striking employees talk about pulling down the government. They will be dealt with under the law,' he thundered.[44]

The average person on the street did not show much concern for the NGOs given their reputation for harassing the public. 'For the first time in four years, Andhra Pradesh Chief Minister N.T. Rama Rao was sticking to his guns—and gaining in public esteem as a result,' *India Today* remarked.[45] The Opposition parties sided with the NGOs and fired at the government from their shoulders. NTR continued to be on the offensive, announcing 'no work, no pay' and dies non, a service break for the striking employees.

Finally, beaten at their own game, the NGOs had to give in, and a settlement was arrived at.

The employees might have compromised, but their dislike for NTR became palpable. Their seething discontent against the chief minister found expression in an ugly and unprecedented incident during the anti-reservation agitation a year later.

Meanwhile, the decision to reduce the age of retirement in February 1983 continued to make news even though the short-lived Nadendla government had restored the age of retirement to fifty-eight in August 1984. The apex court upheld the government's power to make changes to the age of superannuation. But the court restored all those who had lost their jobs during the interregnum, between February 1983 and 23 August 1984, after having completed fifty-five years of age. 'They have become the helpless victims of certain swift moves on the political chessboard. Justice demands that the petitioners should be saved of their predicament,' the Supreme Court bench headed by Justice O. Chinnappa Reddy said.[46] The government, on court orders, had to pay the full amount of the salaries to the retired employees for the remainder of their service. An approximate 18,000 such employees were paid a staggering Rs 86 crore. All through this prolonged spat, the NTR government came across as being stubborn and unsympathetic towards the employees.

While the decision on early retirement was taken in good faith, the move to do away with the Legislative Council, the Upper House in the state, had political overtones. The NTR government passed the bill with a two-thirds majority for the abolition of the Legislative Council in March 1983. The then prime minister, Indira Gandhi, refused to get it passed in Parliament. Following an understanding with Rajiv, NTR took up the issue once again.[47] A similar resolution was passed in April 1985, as there were apprehensions that the earlier resolution passed by the seventh assembly might not hold. While the CPI, CPI (M), Janata and MIM supported the bill, the Congress and BJP opposed it and walked out. The resolution was sent to Parliament, which passed it without a fuss. Following the assent given by the president, the Andhra Pradesh Legislative Council, constituted on 7 July 1958 and inaugurated by the then president, Rajendra Prasad, ceased to exist.[48]

The Congress and its MLCs were greatly pained by the willingness shown by Delhi to abolish the council. The party had many stalwarts in the Upper House like K. Rosaiah, who were disappointed at the action. They could not understand how Rajiv Gandhi had given into NTR's wishes, as it went against the Congress party's interests. According to several sources, Rajiv and NTR came to an understanding before the Lok Sabha polls to cease hostilities for their mutual benefit. NTR's proposed national party Bharata Desam was a non-starter, and the chief minister was thought to be gradually withdrawing from his proposal. Rajiv was also told by his advisers that NTR would eventually fall in line to cooperate with the Centre like MGR had in Tamil Nadu. Rajiv's approval for council abolition was thus, according to these reports, part of this pact.[49]

Though he claimed the council was a wasteful expenditure and had turned into a political rehabilitation centre, the provocation for NTR was that it had become a bugbear for him and his government. Interestingly, the TDP was all set to gain a majority in the council by June 1985. But having decided once, NTR was adamant that the council should go.

Puvvada Nageswara Rao, a senior CPI leader, later said three 'R's were responsible for the abolition of the Legislative Council in 1985: Rama Rao, the chief minister; Rosaiah, the then leader of the Congress in the Legislative Council who constantly irritated NTR; and Ramoji Rao, who was summoned by the council for a news report.

Another of NTR's bold decisions was to increase the quota in government jobs and college admissions for the BCs from 25 to 44 per cent. The well-meaning initiative, instead of bringing laurels as NTR had expected, ended up being a political albatross around his neck. The violent reaction of upper castes and the judicial rejection to what he thought was a radical step caused him much anguish and anger.

The BCs in AP, neglected by the Congress in the past, were drawn to the TDP from the beginning, and NTR for long wanted to come up with a radical step to better their lot. In July 1986, he decided to put his thoughts into effect. Following a special cabinet meeting, at Jubilee Hall in Public Gardens, he dramatically announced the acceptance of the N.K. Muralidhara Rao (MR) commission report on BCs. He issued government orders (GOs) to implement the recommendations even before the report was discussed in the assembly. According to these orders, the government accepted the following recommendations of the MR Commission: to enhance the reservation for BCs from 25 to 44 per cent; to have five subgroups among the BCs and ensure distribution of quota among them; to have no interchange among the different groups of BCs; to carry forward any unfilled vacancies in any of the groups to the same group for three years; and to restrict the benefits of reservation for BCs to those belonging to families whose income did not exceed Rs 12,000 per annum.

The decision meant that NTR had increased reservations from 49 per cent to a staggering 71 per cent—44 per cent for BCs, 15 for SCs, 6 for STs and 6 for special groups like handicapped persons. Besides, NTR also announced political reservations to BCs by allocating 20 per cent quota in elections for the newly created mandals.

The forward castes, as was expected, were up in arms against the decision. Resentment was already brewing against the TDP government in some sections, and the latest decision came in handy for them to whip up passions. The Opposition parties were on the defensive since they could oppose BC reservations at their own political peril. But that did not stop them from surreptitiously provoking the upper-caste students into agitation. Some prominent BC leaders with Congress affiliations too joined the chorus of protest. Popular BC leader Konda Lakshman Bapuji and others dubbed NTR's move as politically motivated and aimed at causing differences among the BCs. Their objection was against the exclusion of the creamy layer. The Kapus—along with other sub-castes such as Balija, Telaga and Ontari—also jumped into the fray, demanding BC status. Forward-caste students formed the Andhra Pradesh Nava Sangharshana Samithi (APNSS) and kicked up an agitation.

NTR stood his ground. He considered himself a saviour whose noble intentions were misinterpreted. He underwent another sartorial change, sporting a brand-new saffron turban, saffron-hued footwear and a sceptre-like baton, completing the Swami Vivekananda look. He went around the state addressing public meetings about his revolutionary step. But the realpolitik was way more complicated than NTR's make-believe world. The Congress (I) indirectly and the BJP openly helped upper-caste students to sustain their protests. The BC students also formed an outfit in favour of reservations, called the Andhra Pradesh Sama Sangrama Parishad (APSSP). But they were not as vocal and vociferous as the APNSS was. Gujarat had already seen an anti-reservation agitation. The move was successfully scuttled there by forward-class students. The Andhra counterparts took a leaf out of the Gujarat agitational methods, and some more.

The protracted agitation by the anti-reservationists in 1986 was one of the most well-managed, creatively choreographed and widely reported protest movements. For nearly two months, the protests received extensive coverage in the press. The students resorted to every known form of protest such as rallies, 'rail roko', 'rasta roko', strikes and bandhs. They also came up with novel methods such as cleaning up roads and polishing boots. From day one, it was clear where the sympathies of the media lay in this battle of uneven forces. All through, the visibility of the anti-reservation stir was more pronounced than that of pro-reservationists, given the superior socio-economic status of the former.

Meanwhile, the AP High Court stayed the GOs, but the anti-reservationists became more aggressive, mocking the very concept of reservation. The anger of the forward castes was too much to handle for NTR, who sued for peace by announcing 20 per cent extra seats for meritorious students. But the agitators refused to back down and further intensified their protests. So shaken was the government that senior state intelligence officials were deployed to act as mediators between the student leaders and the administration to see that the agitation did not spiral out of control.

In a scathing article, political analyst K. Balagopal pointed out how the establishment—the bureaucracy, the police and the media—showed bias towards the prolonged agitation by upper-caste students. They were handled with uncharacteristic sensitivity, as their stance touched an emotional chord among the dominant sections. 'Not one agitation since NTR came to power has been tolerated so benignly; and never have the Andhra police smiled so much at agitators,' wrote Balagopal wryly.[50]

NTR's police might have treated the forward-caste students with kid gloves, but the chief minister himself was targeted by many sections for his radical move. Government employees, especially those working in the secretariat, were one such aggrieved section. Mostly belonging to upper castes, they had been at loggerheads with NTR since he took over as the chief minister. Now the hike in reservations further riled them. Their pent-up anger burst out in the open when an unruly group among them raided NTR's chamber and nearly roughed him up in the secretariat precincts. The incident occurred when the anti-reservationist students called for a 'Chalo Secretariat' programme on 3 September 1986. Many secretariat employees, some of them parents of the agitating students, gathered at the gates in support. After a while, the police decided the time was up and asked the students to leave. When there was no response, the cops started to forcibly disperse them.

The employees became restive watching the police hurling lathis at the boys and girls and started throwing stones at the cops, injuring the city police commissioner T.S. Rao. The angry cops hit back with stones and chased the staff back into the secretariat office buildings. The irate employees ran straight to the chambers of the chief minister, breaking flowerpots and damaging furniture on their way. They stormed into NTR's office and launched into a diatribe, spewing unprintable abuses against him. NTR was taken aback by the vituperative shouting. He sat through the unpleasant episode expressionlessly. The few aides who were present at the time immediately formed a protective ring around him and saved him from further humiliation.

As some semblance of normality returned, more secretariat staff gathered at the chief minister's chamber. They demanded an apology for allowing cops inside the secretariat. But when NTR came out of his office with folded hands, he was not allowed to speak. Even as the staff continued to shout 'shame, shame', NTR's eyes appeared to swell with tears. Finally, he left the secretariat without saying anything.[51] It remains the most disgraceful incident ever to happen in the annals of the AP secretariat and shows the extent to which the staff harboured animosity against the chief minister. It was evident to NTR as well as his advisers that the situation was getting out of hand. But NTR would not go back on his decision. Even if he did, the BC backlash would be too hot to handle in such an event. It was at this juncture that the high court came to the government's rescue.

A writ petition had already been filed in the AP High Court against the increased reservations, and a single judge had stayed the GOs. The government appealed and about a month later, on 5 September 1986, two days after the secretariat incident, a three-judge bench of Justices B.P. Jeevan Reddy, K. Ramaswamy and Y.V. Anjaneyulu struck down the increased quota in reservations for BCs as unconstitutional. The petitions were filed by both OCs (Other Castes) as well as BCs, the latter questioning the creamy layer conditions in the orders. The main contention of the OCs was that the population figures, on which the orders were based, were wrong. The bench in its judgment accepted the argument and said that given the decisions of the Supreme Court in several cases, the total reservations could not generally exceed 50 per cent.

While the verdict gave NTR the much-needed political relief, the anti-reservationists did not rest until the government assured them that it would not appeal against the verdict. NTR wised up after the experience and chose to appoint another commission to go into the population figures of BCs, allowing the issue to die down.

The reservation issue was one of the low points for NTR. It was the first major decision that NTR could not push through. Though the courts did save him from further ignominy, NTR felt the judicial system was coming in the way of his radical reforms.[52] More humbling was the fact that instead of appreciation from the public for his move, all he got was brickbats. The BCs, led by leaders with vested interests, did not come out in full support of the government. He was pounded even by the pro-reservationists. BC organizations led by ageing leaders of various political parties and organizations, such as Bala Goud, Konda Laxman Bapuji and Gouthu Latchanna, had their own axe to grind against NTR. They latched on to the income ceiling provision and did their best to discredit him. In one of the large public meetings held in Hyderabad by BCs, a lone young man who wanted to thank NTR for the decision was thrashed by the organizers.

NTR's move on reservations was much resented by the assertive middle classes, who considered him as increasingly posing a threat to their interests. Unsurprisingly, the prolonged agitation led by Nava Sangharshana Samithi had a Kamma and a Reddy— Dr Sai Kishore Chowdary and Ravinder Reddy respectively—at the helm. Politics and class interests got mixed up in this unrest. Once class interests were served, narrow politics surfaced, leading to a split in both the APNSS and APSSP, one faction accusing the other of acting at the behest of a political party.

Face-off with Naxalites

A notable feature of NTR's rule, especially from 1985 to 1989, was the increased clout of the police and the resulting high-handedness in dealing with dissenting voices. This was also a period when Naxalites—ultra-communist armed groups, also referred to as Maoists—resorted to extreme violence. It led to a surprising transformation for NTR who during his first campaign had declared Naxalites 'true patriots'.

In the early period of his government, NTR was indulgent in dealing with Naxalites, enabling them to bolster their cadres and enlarge their presence in the state. The People's War Group (PWG) of Kondapalli Seetharamaiah was formed in 1980, and it actively sought to expand its clout by violent means. Of the ten groups of extremists functioning in the state, the Seetharamaiah group was the most militant, the state government had declared at the time.

In a major incident, Seetharamaiah made a dramatic escape from Osmania General Hospital in Hyderabad, where he was earlier admitted following a heart complaint. The PWG founder had been in jail since 1982 when he was caught at Begumpet Railway Station. The daring escape in which six armed Naxalites killed the police constable on guard caused consternation among the public. The cop, a young Mohammad Ibrahim, was shot point-blank when he took the Naxal leader to the hospital bathroom in the early hours of 4 January 1984.

'The gain in strength till the mid-1980s was spectacular,' said security analyst Ajay Sahni about the Naxalite footprint in AP.[53] Their increasing presence and ferocity was causing alarm, so the cops had to take note and rein in the violence. 'By 1985, after a series of ambushes of police parties and the increasing use of landmines to blow up official and police convoys, even the grateful NTR could no longer ignore the menace,' Sahni remarked.[54] PWG collections from beedi leaf and arrack contractors amounted to roughly Rs 3 crore a year.[55] Senior cops, such as K. Vijayarama Rao and H.J. Dora, who wielded clout over the chief minister, prevailed upon NTR on the need to tackle the violence with force.

Dora described how he changed NTR's perspective on Naxalites. As DIG in Warangal, he was determined to put down the Naxal activity in north Telangana districts. He, along with the then Warangal superintendent of police, Ramavtar Yadav, sought an appointment with NTR and explained that Naxals were feared, not loved by people. They said that armed rebels needed to be dealt with firmly for the government to function effectively in rural areas. NTR asked them what was expected of him. They gave him a long list of pending demands of the local law-and-order machinery. These included a police station in Kakatiya University, a special sub-court, adding new cells to the jail and provision of more staff. Within no time, GOs were issued to make these a reality. 'We never expected the chief minister to respond so positively and so quickly,' Dora recalled.[56]

NTR also immediately gave approval for another proposal—to have government-sponsored folk cultural troupes for staging plays. The cops wanted to 'educate' the masses about Naxalite violence and their anti-development stance through song and dance. Soon, Dora claimed, the police had the upper hand in controlling extremist activities. But civil rights activists were aghast. 'The absolute freedom given to the police by NTR's government is beyond all comprehension,' Balagopal, who was with the Andhra Pradesh Civil Liberties Committee (APCLC) then, wrote.[57]

It was during NTR's regime that a special task force was established to take on Naxalites. Many armed outposts were created in the seven worst-affected districts of Adilabad, Nizamabad, Karimnagar, Warangal, Khammam, East Godavari and Visakhapatnam. In Hyderabad, as part of Operation Red Rose, a crack team busted a shelter of extremists. The cops caught Nalla Adi Reddy, the secretary of the PWG, along with six of his associates and a cache of documents, dealing a fatal blow to the Naxalite campaign. The expression 'encounter'—widely regarded as a euphemism for the point-blank killing of captured Naxalites—became popular in the Telugu media. According to Balagopal, Kota Srinivasa Vyas, popularly known as K.S. Vyas, 'a trigger-happy police officer', revived 'encounter' killings in 1981 as the police superintendent of Nalgonda. Such police encounters, he noted, had become routine by NTR's time.[58]

According to the account of civil liberties organizations, within ten months, from January to October 1985, forty-two alleged Naxalites and sympathizers were killed by the police in 'encounters'.[59] APCLC, which was actively exposing human rights violations at this time and was seen by the police as an extension of the Naxalite groups, found itself at the receiving end of the NTR regime. The police excesses continued unchecked even after the daylight murder of Dr A. Ramanatham, a senior APCLC activist. He was allegedly killed in his Warangal clinic in September 1985 by the cops.[60] The liquidation was apparently an act of revenge for the murder of a sub-inspector, Yadagiri Reddy, by the Naxalites.

The brazen act was committed even as the funeral procession of the slain police officer was moving through the lane where the good doctor's clinic was located. 'NTR has become a pawn in the hands of the police establishment,' Rajni Kothari, the well-known political scientist who was associated with People's Union for Civil Liberties (PUCL), stated.[61] Balagopal, the APCLC general secretary, was often entangled in false cases, including those of sedition, and put in jail innumerable times. He was even kidnapped in August 1989 in Khammam, with demands made for the release of two constables abducted by the PWG.[62]

Along with the National Security Act (NSA), the Terrorist and Disruptive Activities (Prevention) Act (TADA), passed recently by Rajiv Gandhi's government, was put to liberal use in the state, with an estimated 1500 persons behind bars under the draconian law. The government armed the police with more and more powers to tackle the increasing violence of the left-wing extremists. A proposal was made, though not pursued, by the NTR government to bring out its own version of the anti-terrorist bill, targeted at Maoist radicals. Officers involved in anti-insurgency operations were provided with incentives and rewards. According to a pamphlet brought out by the People's Union for Democratic Rights (PUDR), the TDP government's unflattering civil rights record was stained by 185 encounter deaths, 112 custodial deaths, ninety-eight deaths in police firing, besides twenty-seven cases of missing people from 1983 to 1989.[63]

The increasing acts of violence, destruction of public and private property and the newly adopted kidnapping strategy of Naxalites provided justification for the police to counter them with the same brutality. The kidnapping of seven IAS officials in December 1987 in Gurtedu of East Godavari District was the high point in the face-off between the government and the Naxalites. NTR had to concede the demand to release jailed Naxalites.[64] The first abduction by Naxalites in AP had occurred in September 1984, but the kidnapping of IAS officers was sensational news, putting the government on the defensive. The officers kidnapped— S.R. Sankaran, secretary, social welfare department, M.V.P.C. Sastry, collector, East Godavari District, V.M. Manohar Prasad, officer on special duty, Girijan Coffee Development Corporation, among others—were all highly respected civil servants known for their commitment to improve the lot of the tribal populations (Girijans). The government could not have remained lenient following this loss of face. The PWG and other Naxalite groups were banned, and combing operations intensified.

Unable to deal with the increasing cases of murders and kidnappings, the NTR government even approved a policy for arming villagers to take on the extremists. Orders were issued for the setting up of village self-protection committees (Grama Swayam Samrakshana Samiti). These committees were to be armed with weapons to 'ensure that individuals defend themselves, their families and their villages' from antisocial elements, which meant Naxalites. NTR said he would liberalize arms licences and give bank loans for those who wanted to own revolvers. The move was condemned by the Opposition parties as 'hasty and dangerous'.

In June 1989, Malhar Rao, a mandal parishad president in Karimnagar, was abducted and shot dead when the government failed to produce two missing Naxalites, Gopagani Ilaiah and Burra Ramulu. These acts enabled the cops to convince NTR to further harden the stand against armed squads. NTR did try to broker peace, but these measures were rebuffed by the ultra-left groups. In fact, he extended the deadline for surrender from one month to three months, but without much success. He also announced the policy of presenting cash rewards to Naxalites who surrendered.

The Maoists continued with the kidnapping strategy to dilute the impact of the government's surrender call. This was also an attempt to show that their writ ran in the interiors despite the publicized surrender of several Naxalites.

One after another, they kidnapped six mandal presidents belonging to the ruling party. A panicked NTR conceded their demand for reconstructing Naxalite martyrs' memorials which had earlier been destroyed by the police. This was used against NTR and his government by the Congress. Rajiv Gandhi, in a meeting at Nalgonda, mocked NTR for his 'abject surrender' to Naxalites. Jalagam Vengala Rao, a Central minister and Congress leader, alleged that the ultras were running a parallel government in AP. Chief ministers of three Congress-ruled states—J.B. Patnaik of Orissa, Motilal Vohra of Madhya Pradesh and Sharad Pawar of Maharashtra—and the governor of Karnataka, Pendekanti Venkata Subbaiah, apparently at the behest of the Centre, issued a joint statement, asking NTR to stop restoring Naxal memorials, as the action amounted to 'bestowing respect on their ideology and activities'.[65]

NTR refused to take back the decision and said it was wrong to pull down the memorials in the first place, and hence the government had considered it right to restore them. He blamed the Centre for non-cooperation in providing men and material to the state to tackle the issue. 'We have been asking for 12 companies of CRPF battalions, training for State police and provision of weapons to tackle the Naxalite issue. But there has been no response from the Centre,' he said.[66] Meanwhile, Naxalite violence worsened. Naxals blasted a landmine in Bheerpur village of Karimnagar District, killing twelve civilians, including five women and two children, travelling in a jeep. Apparently, they were mistaken for police personnel. As the Naxalite attacks continued unabated, the Congress slammed the helplessness of the NTR government.

The TDP government suspected that the Centre was deliberately holding up men and material, while the Congress in the state appeared hand in glove with the Naxalites. The CPI (M) also stated that Naxalites appeared to be acting as tools in the hands of the Congress (I) to topple the TDP government.[67] Despite NTR's tentative overtures to Naxalites, the carnage did not stop. When they kidnapped another mandal president, Nalla Sanjiva Reddy, in Jafargad in Warangal District, a flustered NTR blurted out, 'When I talked about giving weapons and gunmen, I was ridiculed. If one can't even stand up against one woman and two men toting guns, what can we do?'[68]

As part of the efforts to contain the increasing violence, the government created a special operations group within the AP police called 'Greyhounds' under the leadership of the tough cop K.S. Vyas in June 1989. The determination to create Greyhounds was cited by some security experts as a reason for the Maoists' murder of Daggubati Chenchuramaiah, the father of one of NTR's sons-in-law.[69] Many of the sustained security operations that more or less flushed the Maoists out of AP in later years are credited to Greyhounds.[70]

The violence perpetrated by the Naxalite groups, however, provided perfect cover for the police and the administration to unleash an oppressive regime on the civil unrest too. The protest movement launched by the Dalit Mahasabha in the wake of the Karamchedu killings was one of the long-drawn agitations sought to be muzzled by a hardened police regime. Ordinary people were picked up for petty crimes and treated to third-degree methods, resulting in custodial deaths. With more and more sweeping powers, the police became a law unto themselves and made the force indispensable to the government in quelling popular dissent. Naxal violence became a convenient stick for the cops to beat anyone with for questioning their brazen acts.[71]

Civil rights groups said that as many as 107 persons who were killed in custody during this period had no Maoist connections even by official records.[72] In one case in February 1986, the cops arrested four sex workers in Vijayawada and got their heads shaved, a barbaric act symptomatic of the increasing police arrogance.[73] This incident resulted in public outcry. In one of the custodial deaths the same year, the Vijayawada police deliberately misidentified a dead person, which was exposed only when the body was exhumed on a court order. Such excesses by the police during NTR's rule became worryingly routine.[74]

As a result of such draconian measures, NTR steadily became a symbol of a repressive regime for civil rights groups, including the APCLC, which had ironically protested his dismissal in 1984. In a congratulatory letter written after NTR was restored in September 1984, the president of the Association for Protection of Democratic Rights (APDR) saw a champion of democracy in NTR. 'Being once a victim of authoritarianism, you will, no doubt, appreciate the role of civil rights organisations in mobilising public opinion against repression and undemocratic practice,' he wrote.[75] However, their hopes were belied.

At the peak of Naxalite violence, NTR did try to defuse the situation by meeting up with civil liberties leaders, including K.G. Kannabiran, K. Balagopal and G. Haragopal, to discuss the issue. But the situation did not change on the ground. The paradox was that NTR emerged as a champion of democracy in Parliament, where his party was the main Opposition. But he was being dubbed a fascist in his state by human rights activists. Despite the frequent protests by civil rights groups against NTR's attitude, his reputation remained undented. In 1989, the leaflet brought out by the PUDR on NTR's civil rights record began with these lines penned by Avtar Singh Sandhu, alias Paash, a poet of the Naxalite movement in Punjab:

> *I have bought a ticket*
> *and seen the drama of your democracy*
> *I have earned the right now*
> *to hoot and shout at your theatrics*

That sums up how the civil rights groups viewed NTR. But the radical groups contributed no less to the police repression during this period. The continued violence perpetrated by armed groups provided NTR little legroom to negotiate a middle path. There were allegations of some understanding between the Naxalites and the Congress. And that the insurgents created mayhem in the state with the sole aim of cornering the TDP government.[76] On the one hand, the Naxalites rebuffed the peace overtures of the NTR government, while on the other the Centre refused to provide forces or equipment to tackle the issue. The CPI (M) suspected collusion between the Congress and the Naxalites, and, interestingly, the Congress government under Channa Reddy, which came to power in 1989, gave free rein to the extremists for a time, giving credence to the nexus.[77]

During the campaign for the 1994 polls, NTR reiterated his old stand that Naxalites were not criminals and that he shared their concern for the poor. On his return to power in December 1994, NTR tried a more rational and restrained approach, asking the police to not resort to fake encounters. His government also released 216 jailed Naxalites. The administration decided to treat the Naxalites as political detainees. However, he was not in power long enough to see his new approach through.

Activist-educationist Prof G. Haragopal met NTR a few times when he was in power along with K. Balagopal and K.G. Kannabiran to discuss the issue. He recalled that NTR was always responsive to the arguments of civil rights activists. 'You are running a butcher's shop,' an emotional Kannabiran burst out during one of the meetings, but NTR didn't lose his cool. Instead, he sought their suggestions on how to address the problem.[78] In 1995, NTR, to the surprise of the activists, readily agreed to lift the ban on the PWG. 'Even Balagopal didn't expect that NTR would agree to the demand so easily,' Haragopal told the author in an interview. However, NTR's legitimacy as a mass leader was used by the police to unleash repression during his tenure, according to Haragopal.

NTR's instinct was to work out the tensions with Naxalites, but the militancy of the extremist groups and the Congress party's political stratagem left little space for the chief minister to meet their demands halfway. Interestingly, while civil rights activists alleged that NTR was giving a free run to the police to repress Maoist activities, the cops considered the chief minister as being soft on the extremists.

NTR and the Media

NTR was the toast of the media at the time of his political debut. Being a colourful personality with unrivalled charisma in the state, NTR offered much grist to the media. Some like *Eenadu* painted him as a messiah of the masses; many others like *Andhra Bhoomi* barely disguised their anathema for him. But whatever their political stance, no media house could ignore NTR. Given his total departure from the Congress culture, his personalized style of functioning, his antics from time to time and his propensity to come up with unpredictable decisions, NTR's period in politics was marked by a heightened interest in newspapers, especially in AP.

NTR also grabbed the attention of the national media as the challenger of Indira Gandhi and the Congress. A host of senior journalists from Delhi visited Hyderabad soon after the change of regime to get a sense of the phenomenon he was. All of them without exception were floored by the new political and administrative culture that NTR was trying to bring in the early days. Inder Jit, editor of India News and Feature Alliance (INFA), found Hyderabad 'buzzing with excitement as it seldom did before'.[79] He wrote how NTR was clearing files at a fast pace and fairly. He quoted a senior officer as having told him, 'We never thought that we would ever live to see the day when the Registrar's office would register land and property without taking money.' Veteran journalist Kuldip Nayar wrote about 'a new enthusiasm' that had seized the people under NTR. S. Sahay of the *Statesman* was struck by the 'utter sincerity' in NTR's voice. 'If he is play-acting, then he does it to perfection,' he said.[80]

The Congress politics till NTR's time were mainly concentrated in Delhi. The formation of a regional party changed the way political news was generated and consumed, as the corridors of power became more accessible to local newspapers. NTR's regional plank helped boost readers' interest in local news. A year after NTR came to power, *India Today* carried a report titled '1984 to Be a Boom Time for Telugu Press', indicating the growing circulation of papers.[81]

The extensive coverage that he received in newspapers during the 1982 election campaign made NTR beholden to the press. He felt further indebted to the media for its decisive role during the TDP government's dismissal. For these reasons, NTR had a positive attitude towards the press. It was not as though the papers were always singing paeans to him. A section of the media that was obligated to the Congress establishment was highly critical of him from day one. Besides, NTR was not given to cultivating the press, like his predecessors. A year after he came to power, *India*

Today wrote, 'Since he sees no virtue in cultivating the press, he gets a bad one. Most newspapers in the State are critical of him, but then they are owned by Congress (I) supporters.'[82]

But overall, the TDP was on good terms with the media in the early days. That was till NTR returned to power after the 1985 assembly elections. In the next four years, the mainstream media was stinging in its criticism of the government and NTR. Almost all newspapers, including *Eenadu* and the newly launched *Udayam*, never missed an opportunity to caricature NTR and his whims and fancies. *Andhra Bhoomi* and the *Deccan Chronicle*, belonging to the Congress MP T. Chandrasekhara Reddy, were particularly vicious in targeting NTR personally.

One example of motivated writings against NTR was related to the proposal to give land to Maharishi Mahesh Yogi. NTR in 1984 considered allotting land in Vijayapuri South in Guntur District to Maharshi Veda Vignana Vishwa Vidya Peetham. The *Deccan Chronicle* published reports alleging that thousands of dollars were deposited in Swiss bank accounts belonging to NTR's relatives for giving away 1110 acres at Rs 500 per acre to Mahesh Yogi. NTR appointed Justice M. Krishna Rao to look into the case under a commission of inquiry. 'It is seen from a perusal of the evidence that there is no iota of evidence in support of the allegation,' the commission said in the report.[83] The judge even suggested to the state government to 'send this report and relevant papers and the evidence to the Press Council of India for taking appropriate action, if necessary, against the *Deccan Chronicle*'.[84]

Given his unusual personality, NTR lent himself to sarcastic commentary in the media. *Zamin Ryot*, a long-standing weekly from Nellore, was always dripping with sarcasm in its writing about NTR and his government. This was how the paper lambasted NTR on his newly acquired sartorial accessory, the turban, in 1986:

NTR is known to stick *topi* on the pate of the ordinary people (*an idiomatic expression in Telugu to describe a charlatan*). Now he has gone a step ahead and put one on his own head. Like all else, the new avatar is also political. He is of late worried about his fading image. He went into a huddle with astrologers and make-up artists, experimented with various get-ups and finally zeroed in on the Vivekananda look. Additionally, he procured a baton used in his film *Chanda Sasanudu*. His tactic did work wonders, what with people who came to his meeting at Maheshwaram in Ranga Reddy district staring at his latest sartorial transformation in amazement. They must have seen him as Rama, Ravana, Duryodhana, Karna, Krishna, Kichaka etc. but not certainly in this all-new look. That's precisely what he wanted. One last worry, though. If people get bored with his Vivekananda look by the next assembly elections, would he opt for the Vemana attire (*Vemana, a radical Telugu poet, wore nothing but a loincloth*)?![85]

NTR was a cartoonist's delight, given his marked physical attributes, his sartorial choices, his affected style of speaking and his larger-than-life personality. Cartoonists Papa and later Sridhar in *Eenadu* and Mohan in *Udayam* excelled in highlighting his oddities. Sridhar's comic strips on NTR, which ran into thousands, were a big hit in the 1980s. Sridhar, who called NTR a 'cartoonists' politician', told this author that he drew hundreds of sketches before he could get his lines right for NTR. 'He was a good-looking politician, and it was not easy for a cartoonist to caricature him,' he pointed out.[86] Given NTR's propensity for dramatics, Sridhar and the other cartoonists had a field day. One cartoon in *Eenadu*, for example, depicted NTR flagellating himself in the manner of a ritual lashing in some communities, after the chief minister, in a fit of anger, called himself a crazy person. 'But he never seemed to have gotten offended with many outlandish cartoons that we did on him. I met him a couple of times, and NTR was very respectful,' recalled Sridhar.

Despite the unflattering reportage about his government and the lampooning of his policies and personality traits, NTR never seemed to be unduly bothered with the media coverage. For one, he never had the habit of going through the daily newspapers. He did not know too many reporters by name—local or national.[87] But NTR was on friendly terms with leading journalists Kuldip Nayar and Arun Shourie, following his emergence as the unifying force behind non-Congress Opposition parties. They extended moral support to him in the 1984 crisis. This association prompted NTR to oppose Rajiv Gandhi's infamous Defamation Bill in 1988. Otherwise, he reacted to the media only when attention was brought to his notice about damaging reports. He always believed that so long as he commanded the following of the people, the media and its message would have little impact on his politics.

However, by 1985, a new crop of yellow magazines became the rage in the state. They offered titillating stories about politicians. The 'scoops' were presented in a language that was obscene and derogatory. With crazy titles like *Encounter*, *Commando*, *Caligula*, *Bloodhound*, *Nuisance*, etc., these journals had a no-holds-barred policy, coming up with the most sensational scandals and conspiracy theories. Their credibility was low, but that never came in the way of their popularity. 'Their contents, needless to add, are offensive in every sense of the term: in bad taste, obscene, untruthful at least by half, and full of vulgar innuendo and suggestive phrases,' said Balagopal, providing the following example of their style of writing:

> For instance, a news item about a Congress leader trying to get a Telugu Desam ticket would run somewhat like this: 'That well-known eunuch who pimped faithfully for the Nehru family all these years now wants to get into the brothel house at Hyderabad by licking NTR's behind'.[88]

Such coarse writings, however, were lapped up by a section of the neo-literate readers, mainly in coastal districts, who derived vicarious pleasure in this unbridled calumny against the powerful and the mighty. These journals, for which Vijayawada was the leading publication centre, were generally one-man shows—led by the owner-editor—and became a thorn in the flesh for many influential politicians and bureaucrats. Pingali Dasaratharam, a hot-blooded young rebel with confused causes, was one such editor-owner who ran the much-sought-after rag by the name *Encounter*. The weekly, launched in 1979, was a trendsetter for such scandal sheets, covering sensational scoops about alleged sexual escapades and corrupt deals of politicians. As can be expected, these reports were far from investigative and mostly based on hearsay and rumours. While there might have been rare nuggets of truth in these tabloids, the exposés were mainly concerned with serving up salacious but unverified accounts.[89]

NTR and his sons-in-law, among others, were the targets of many of these offensive reports. It was against this backdrop that a deeply upset NTR wanted to bring out a press bill against such scurrilous writings. The proposed legislation was based on the notorious Bihar Press Bill that had been withdrawn recently following media furore. NTR was naive in thinking that such a bill was necessary since 'it would be used against only yellow journals'.[90] Since he had only recently emerged as the defender of democratic principles, the proposed press bill did not go down well even with the 'friendly' Opposition parties. Facing stiff resistance from media organizations and journalist associations, NTR chose to not go ahead with the bill.

Meanwhile, at the height of the protests over the press bill, Pingali Dasaratharam was stabbed to death in Vijayawada on 21 October 1985, while he was travelling in a rickshaw in Satyanarayanapuram. The killing of the twenty-nine-year-old quirky journalist immediately cast doubts on the role of the government. TDP critics alleged that NTR and the then home minister, Vasantha Nageswara Rao, were behind the murder, though there was no evidence unearthed to link them to the crime.[91] Vasantha's family was the target of several vulgar stories in *Encounter*. Civil rights groups hinted at the role of the TDP government in the murder.

Subsequently, the police arrested two of Dasaratharam's former associates, holding them responsible for the killing. The accused, Banerjee Nath and Thota Ramu, had broken away from Dasaratharam and launched their own yellow journal, *Political Encounter*. The case was dismissed for lack of evidence.[92] Apart from this episode, the NTR government was mostly tolerant of the mainstream media's criticism.

NTR's political tenure was undoubtedly an exciting time for the media, though his full potential as a telegenic politician remained untapped as he lived in the pre-television era. One of the few TV interviews he gave in the early days was to Doordarshan during his first Delhi visit. The interview, conducted by journalist and NTR's biographer S. Venkat Narayan in January 1983, was telecast allegedly after being delayed by a week. NTR did quite well in his debut TV appearance, according to well-known media critic Amita Malik. She wrote in the *Indian Express*:

> Rama Rao, for an actor, was an unexpectedly relaxed TV personality... NTR's smile and laugh—which were frequent—made him seem more human too.[93]

NTR wanted to bring out a publication on behalf of his party to reach out to people. One of the reasons he offered for acting in *Brahmarshi Viswamitra* was to raise funds for the proposed *Naa Desam* paper. While the paper did not materialize, he made another effort to publish his ideas and thoughts through a fortnightly magazine. Called *Naa Desam* once again, the magazine was all set for publication in 1989. Lakshmi Parvathi, who later became NTR's second wife, also contributed articles for the magazine, but the project was shelved before seeing the light of day.

In his third term, NTR faced a hostile media that caused him much distress. He often expressed his disapproval of the tendentious writings about his second wife. The role of a significant section of local Telugu and English media in scuttling NTR's political career during the internal rebellion within the TDP in 1995 remains controversial.

NTR has the curious distinction of being the only politician in AP who was lampooned in films.[94] Movies with an overtly political tone were a rarity in Telugu, but NTR was an exception. His politics was the subject matter of several films. They were made specifically to ridicule NTR, his policies and personal idiosyncrasies. He was parodied and mocked in these coarse films, but NTR or his government never put any hurdles to prevent their release. The producers and actors of these films were either opposed to NTR or were Congress activists.

Ghattamaneni Krishna, his bête noire from filmdom, was behind at least three such films. The others engaged in this enterprise to defame NTR included dialogue writer Tripuraneni Maharadhi, actors M. Prabhakar Reddy, Kota Srinivasa Rao (the latter joined the BJP and became an MLA) and Vijay Chander, the grandson of Tanguturi Prakasam. At least five films were rolled out coinciding with the period when NTR was the chief minister, with a couple of them aiming to discredit him just before the 1989 elections.

As early as in 1986, Krishna made a film, *Naa Pilupe Prabhanjanam*, lampooning NTR's rule. Besides the chief minister himself, his sons-in-law, especially Chandrababu Naidu, were caricatured in the movie. Veteran actor Kota Srinivasa Rao essayed the role of NTR. A crude political spoof on NTR's autocratic style, the film fared averagely at the box office. The next year, another film, *Mandaladheesudu*, a frontal attack on NTR and his politics, was funded by Krishna, though he did not act in the movie. Kota Srinivasa Rao, who reprised his role as NTR, faced some animosity from the movie industry. But the film did not have any problems in its screening. It was released on the eve of mandal and ZP elections in the state but had little impact on the TDP's victory.

Sahasame Naa Oopiri was another Krishna film, directed by his second wife, Vijaya Nirmala. The film referred to several incidents and allegations during NTR's rule. Made in 1989 at the fag end of NTR's term, the movie had one Nellore Jagga Rao in the lead role. An NTR lookalike, he played the chief minister's character in the latter's trademark saffron attire and mimicked his dialogue delivery. The film showed NTR's alleged involvement in Vangaveeti Ranga's murder and had references to Dasaratharam's killing. It also had several scenes caricaturing real-life incidents such as NTR's sit-in at the secretariat gate. The hilarious scene from *The Great Dictator*, where Charlie Chaplin as Hitler plays around with an inflatable globe, was replicated with NTR's character in this film. It did not set the box office on fire.

Gandipeta Rahasyam (1989) was another satire released on the eve of the 1989 elections. The title was a play on NTR's residence at Gandipet as well as his earlier film *Gandikota Rahasyam*. Actor Krishna, who produced the film, appeared as himself at the beginning of the film to call upon the people to bring NTR down. The film used noted cartoonist Mohan's grotesque caricatures of NTR during the credits. Comedy artiste Prudhvi Raj played NTR's character. Several incidents during NTR's regime, such as the chief minister acting in *Brahmarshi Viswamitra*, and a host of allegations of corruption against him found a place in the movie. On the eve of the general elections in 1989, *Kaliyuga Viswamitra*, another political film, was made. Vijay Chander, who had campaigned for the Congress (I), essayed the role of NTR. Again, the film made fun of NTR and his obsession with *Brahmarshi Viswamitra*. These last two films, which showed NTR and the political developments during his rule in a farcical style, did their bit in the undoing of the TDP in the 1989 elections.

All these were mostly low-quality, B-grade films that sought to project NTR as a buffoon. They were without exception intended to target NTR's image and, in the process, benefit the Congress.

Except for *Naa Pilupe Prabhanjanam* and *Mandaladheesudu*, which did reasonably well, the other films had little box office success. The movies clearly had the blessings of the Congress, though the party was not directly in the picture.[95] Such films, if made today, would create a lot of problems for the makers for their controversial content, but NTR did not bother to come in their way. Nagabhairava Koteswara Rao, the writer of his film *Viswamitra*, recalled how NTR remained cool even though some of his close aides tried to provoke him. 'Let the viewers decide. Why to get worked up,' an unruffled NTR said.[96]

Interestingly, NTR made a couple of films to get across his own message. *Sri Madvirat Veerabrahmendra Swamy Charitra*, which was shot in 1981 before his political entry, was released only in November 1984 due to censor issues. The film on the medieval saint and oracle Pothuluri Veerabrahmam contained several conservative ideas that condemned feminism, family planning and land reforms. The movie, a commercial hit, also attacked the Brahminical dominance of Hindu religion. NTR was the producer, director and writer of the film. It was striking that NTR partook in the conservative and orthodox values of the society, even while advocating anti-Brahminism that had roots in Tripuraneni

Available in the public domain

No politician in AP was lampooned in as many films as NTR was during his tenure as chief minister. A still from *Gandipeta Rahasyam* (1989).

Ramaswamy's radical ideology. *Brahmarshi Viswamitra* (1991) also revealed an evident anti-Brahminism strain, besides hyping up the protagonist's character beyond recognition.

Apparently, NTR wanted to make a film on the Bofors scandal titled *Mr Clean* targeting Rajiv Gandhi in the late 1980s. The project was to be handled by veteran producer D.V.S. Raju, and the story was prepared by writer Mullapudi Venkata Ramana. Raj Babbar and Mohan Babu were to play the lead characters in Hindi and Telugu versions. However, the movie did not make it to the sets, because NTR was fully immersed in national and state politics at the time.

Nearly a quarter century after his death, NTR was once again the subject of a few Telugu films in the run-up to the 2019 elections to the Parliament and AP assembly. Probably for the first time, NTR was seen in glowing terms on-screen in the two-part series, *NTR-Kathanayakudu* and *NTR-Mahanayakudu,* made by his son and TDP MLA Balakrishna. NTR was also shown in a positive light in director Ram Gopal Varma's *Lakshmi's NTR,* though it was primarily aimed at vilifying Chandrababu Naidu on the eve of the 2019 elections. Like the earlier spoofs on NTR, these hagiographies, made with political intent, failed to capture NTR's complex personality.

Karamchedu Carnage

The ugly portrayals in films did cause some damage to NTR's reputation, but what eroded his government's image were issues of a more serious nature. The Karamchedu killings were the first major setback to NTR's rising stardom. The TDP and NTR had failed to gain the confidence of Dalits or those belonging to the SCs—traditionally Congress supporters—from the early days. Three infamous incidents—in Padirikuppam, Karamchedu and Neerukonda—that occurred during NTR's rule further alienated Dalits from the TDP. The Karamchedu killings were widely acknowledged as having marked a new Dalit consciousness against the prevailing social, economic and political inequity in the country.

When NTR had burst on the political scene, he had offered fresh hope, and Harijans, as Dalits were referred to back then, had also looked at the new development positively. By this time, the Dalits were consolidated as a vote bank by the Congress party. Indira Gandhi had emerged as their champion. Despite this, a significant section of Dalits chose to try the new party. The Congress, however, fought back to retrieve their total support by successfully instilling a sense of suspicion among them about the TDP. The TDP's perceived pro-BC tilt was also a cause for misgivings among Dalits over the party's political philosophy. The government's handling of the Karamchedu and Neerukonda incidents later did not exactly inspire confidence among the new crop of Dalit leaders. They viewed the TDP and its leadership as being feudal and inimical to their interests. This perception was further accentuated by the Congress, which harped on the alleged anti-Harijan character of the TDP government.[97]

The Padirikuppam incident happened on 5 January 1983 even before NTR took over. But the killings of one Harijan and three unknown persons said to be non-Dalits occurred during a clash between the group supporting TDP MLA candidate E.V. Gopala Raju and the Harijans. The Congress was quick to apportion the blame to the new party. An inquiry commission, headed by Y. Venkateswara Rao, a retired judge, confirmed that one person, named Tingamma, a Harijan, was torched to death, while three other persons, non-Harijans, also perished in the fire. The other three persons 'died not on account of the fire mishap but by reason of their having been burnt alive in the raging flames of a burning house', the report said.[98] The government ordered prosecution of all those responsible for the deaths in the incident.

But by the time of the shameful Karamchedu killings in July 1985, the NTR government found itself on the defensive. The perpetrators this time were Kammas, the caste to which NTR belonged. Karamchedu was the village from which NTR's son-in-law Daggubati Venkateswara Rao hailed. His father, Daggubati Chenchuramaiah, was one of the landlords with influence and wealth in this coastal village. Six Dalits (Madigas in this case) were brutally attacked and killed. The carnage became a watershed moment in the radicalization of Dalits against caste atrocities.

The Harijans in the village were allegedly Congress (I) supporters, and the Kammas were said to be TDP supporters, but tension between the two communities was apparently unknown in the past. It was instead a small incident that set off the explosion. According to reports, a Kamma youth, Pothina Srinivasa Rao, was feeding bran to his buffalo near the Harijans' tank. Some of the bran dribbled down into the tank, and a Madiga woman, Munnangi Suvarta, who had come to fetch water objected to it. A scuffle ensued, but the quarrel was settled after the elders intervened. That night, the Kamma youth allegedly planned to attack the Madigas and gathered fellow caste men from neighbouring villages. A mob of reportedly hundreds on tractors and motorcycles surrounded the Madiga houses. Rights activist Balagopal who visited the village a week after the incident described the gory details:

> The way the 70-year-old Moshe was killed is illustrative of the massacre that took place that day. He first begged with them to spare him, for he was an old man. When they started beating him, he ran into the fields. They caught up with him, hacked him with an axe, and as he fell on his back, they dug a spear into his groin and twisted it.[99]

The brutality of the attack shocked the conscience of the state. In a first-of-its-kind initiative, the victims organized themselves into a Dalit Mahasabha under the leadership of Dalit activist Katti Padmarao and carried out a sustained protest movement, regarded as an important milestone in Dalit resistance. The Mahasabha set up a camp for the Karamchedu Madigas in the nearby town of Chirala. It did not allow political parties to take over their agitation. But the Congress, eagerly waiting in the wings, pounced at this opportunity to paint Kammas as the oppressive ruling caste and NTR as their patron saint. 'Neither he [the then Congress State president Vengala Rao] nor his party is doing anything to help the refugees who have camped in the church at Chirala, but they are out to pull down the State government if they can,' Balagopal wrote.[100]

Karamchedu became a political pilgrimage centre for politicians of all hues who were eager to score brownie points. According to one report, at least a hundred political leaders, including ministers, legislators, both present and former, made a beeline for Chirala, where the victims and their families were camping. NTR visited the victims the day after the attack and expressed regret that such a despicable incident happened during his regime. 'I consider this [incident] as a personal tragedy,' he said. The chief minister responded to the carnage by ordering arrests of all suspects and agreeing to demands of relief such as building houses for the Dalits and providing them jobs.[101] But the blot remained. NTR fell short of the expectations of an emerging and assertive Dalit leadership. And with the active abetment of the Congress, the wedge between the Dalits and the TDP deepened further in the years to come. Justice was served in the case but after a long-drawn fight. The trial court at Guntur convicted and sentenced the five accused in the case to life imprisonment in 1994. Another forty-six accused persons were sentenced to rigorous imprisonment for three years.[102] A bench of Supreme Court justices, B.N. Agrawal and G.S. Singhvi, upheld the trial court judgment in 2008.

The inquiry commission headed by Justice D.P. Desai, a retired judge of the Gujarat High Court, gave an inconclusive report. It said that 'there was some exciting cause or factor which had been kept back from the Commission' for the attack.[103] But the impact of the incident was widely felt. The Karamchedu case is cited as having become the impetus for the 1989 SC/ST (Prevention of Atrocities) Act, which provides special protection to Dalits against caste atrocities.

The Karamchedu massacre was particularly damaging to NTR's standing because of the alleged involvement of Daggubati Chenchuramaiah. He was made the prime accused in the private case filed by the Dalit Mahasabha. This was an important reason the carnage received such wide publicity. Chenchuramaiah was later murdered by Naxalites at his residence on 6 April 1989, in apparent retaliation for the Karamchedu killings four years earlier. The sensational killing was believed to be a tactical decision by the PWG to gain Dalit support. However, Chenchuramaiah's role in the Karamchedu carnage was never established. The judgment in the Chenchuramaiah murder case was also delayed for twenty-six years, and the accused Naxalites were exonerated due to lack of evidence. Before the trial court delivered its judgment, Daggubati Venkateswara Rao, Chenchuramaiah's son and NTR's son-in-law, had moved a clemency petition in favour of K. Vijaya Kumar, one of the accused.

The narrative in the Karamchedu incident has been tendentious, even as it evolved as a landmark reference point in Dalit studies at the national and international level. While the Kamma villagers who killed the Madigas were the culprits without a doubt of a dastardly act, the portrayal of the unfortunate episode acquired dimensions that went beyond the pale. While many testimonies are available from the victims' point of view, documented extensively by Dalit activists and scholars, there is little reported from the other side. An *Andhra Patrika* report quoted Karamchedu Sangheebhava Samithi (Solidarity Committee) secretary K. Venkateswarlu, which was at variance with the established narrative.[104] According to him, there was no untouchability practised in the village, and there was no long-standing rivalry between the two castes.

Neither the Madigas nor the Kammas cooperated with the Justice D.P. Desai commission of inquiry. 'The non-cooperation of concerned Madigas with the work of the Commission appears to be planned and organised,' Justice Desai commented.[105] Despite this, two Madigas, Tella Lebon and Tella Satyavardhana Rao, came before the commission and gave their account of the incidents. The commission found that there were no ill feelings between Kammas and Madigas before the incident. 'Their relations were normal.' The records in Parchur Police Station, under which the law-and-order jurisdiction of Karamchedu village fell, were also perused by the commission. They revealed that no cases of incidents of violence between Madigas and Kammas were registered from January 1981 to the day of the murders in July 1985.

The village had no history of untouchability, Noothalapati Nageswara Rao, a Harijan member of the panchayat, told the commission. Others said that all communities got drinking water from the same tank in the village. Many Madigas worked as agricultural labourers in Kamma households, and food was also shared between them, the commission found. K. Balagopal, who filed an affidavit before the commission, said that agrarian tensions prevailing in the village between landed farmers and Harijans, most of whom were labourers, were the principal reason behind the incident. However, the commission found no evidence of agrarian tension prevailing in the village.

The attempt to drag Chenchuramaiah into the incident and portray him as the kingpin behind the attack because of his relation to NTR lacked any factual basis and appeared to be an exercise in sensationalism. The intended suggestion obviously was that the killers were not only from NTR's caste but also linked closely to his family. The optics provided by such a narrative were devastating to NTR and the TDP. Chenchuramaiah was named as the accused in the private case filed by the Dalit Mahasabha. But in every retelling of the Karamchedu incident, Chenchuramaiah as NTR's relative figures definitively as the 'main accused'.[106]

Daggubati Venkateswara Rao claimed that his father was originally a Congressman and always kept away from violence. On the day of the incident, his father was in Madras. Some of the accused Naxalites in the Chenchuramaiah killing later met Daggubati and told him that the murder was a calculated move by their leadership to create a sensation and gain a following among the Dalits.[107] Security experts shared the view.

The 'Kamma-dominance' account also got oversimplified. For example, Patricia Gossman of Human Rights Watch made a factually incorrect observation. 'At the time, the Kamma caste enjoyed a disproportionately high number of cabinet positions in the government of the then Chief Minister N.T. Rama Rao.'[108] However, besides NTR, there were only three Kamma ministers in a cabinet of twenty-three in 1985. Balagopal gave a more nuanced commentary on the terrible episode. 'And just in case somebody thinks it is only the Kamma gentry that has gained moral strength from the accession of NTR to power, let it be recorded that at Padirikuppam the arsonists were Naidus, and in the Rangareddy villages they were Reddys—which happen to be the dominant landed castes of the respective areas.'[109] However, the characterization of the Karamchedu incident as being a result of the Kamma political arrogance borne out of the rise of NTR and the TDP to the corridors of power remained strong in all writings on this carnage.

The killing of another Harijan, Mannem Seshaiah in Neerukonda (near Mangalagiri in Guntur District), in July 1987 further eroded the TDP government's credibility regarding the safety of Dalits. The Congress once again tried to score political brownie points by bringing Prime Minister Rajiv Gandhi to visit Neerukonda victims. As the affected Dalits, egged on by the Congress leaders, complained against the unresponsive police to Rajiv, the chief minister was left red-faced.

Part of the reason for the alienation of Dalits from the TDP could be, as many alleged, the Kamma assertion in villages of their newly acquired power against the backdrop of a Kamma-led government. The Congress helped to widen this wedge by provoking Dalits against the TDP at every available opportunity. It was a period of Dalit rising, and NTR failed to reach out to Dalit angst.

Meanwhile, allegations of nepotism began undermining NTR's integrity. After the August 1984 crisis, NTR became more dependent on his family. That was when Chandrababu Naidu got an opportunity to show his commitment and capability. His managerial skills were in full play during this difficult time. Since he joined the TDP in 1983 against the wishes of many in the party, Chandrababu showed patience and fortitude in keeping himself out of the limelight for long. This did not prevent his detractors from accusing him of being an extra-constitutional authority. Unmindful of the criticism, Chandrababu concentrated on party work without angling for any position either in the TDP or in the government. But the role he played following NTR's dismissal and the subsequent developments brought him closer to his father-in-law. NTR always had a soft corner for his sons-in-law, but now he found a worthy, capable and reliable hand in Chandrababu. Though Daggubati had been with NTR since the party's inception, he was already lagging behind Chandrababu in his ability to get a grip on the party and government affairs.

The younger son-in-law (he was, however, older to Daggubati in age by three years) lived and breathed politics. He had already shown that he was temperamentally more suited to the grind of politics than Daggubati, who came across as an ineffective idealist. A workaholic, Chandrababu kept himself busy building the party and cultivating relationships at all levels. Chandrababu strengthened the party's organizational base as well as his own place by organizing training camps for the party cadre, including legislators, at the new party headquarters, Telugu Vijayam at Gandipet, on the outskirts of Hyderabad. Nearly one hundred thousand members were provided orientation programmes on the party's policies across the state in these camps. He was already thinking ahead when in 1985 he talked about 'a computer system which will have data on the membership profile available to the chief minister at the touch of a button'.[110]

NTR began relying more and more on Chandrababu in running the party's day-to-day affairs. The elder son-in-law felt his position was being threatened. He took barbs in the press against the importance being given to those who had defected from the Congress. Daggubati was an MLA besides the head of Telugu Yuvatha, but still could not outshine Chandrababu. A covert war between the two sons-in-law broke out in right earnest.

Chandrababu's grind at Telugu Vijayam finally got him the coveted position in the party in the January 1986 Mahanadu.[111] His anointment as general secretary was a milestone for the party as well as his career. At the same time, Daggubati was removed as Telugu Yuvatha president since he became a legislator, on the principle of one person, one post. Chandrababu waited for a long time to come out of his self-imposed hibernation, but the wait was worth his political future. Once he took over the reins as general secretary, Chandrababu became more active. Every day he travelled to Gandipet and devoted himself to managing party affairs. Having realized his growing importance, ministers and prominent party leaders started queuing up at Gandipet. In fact, Chandrababu Naidu had become so inseparable from the party and the government that after NTR, he turned out to be the most natural target for the Opposition barbs.

Interestingly, Daggubati was rarely criticized by the TDP opponents and detractors. The reason was that even though Daggubati was equally embedded in the TDP, he was widely regarded as a dreamer who chose to keep himself away from controversies. Chandrababu, on the other hand, was managing the affairs of both the government and the party and was not afraid of getting his hands dirty.

The race for getting a grip over the party was intense between the sons-in-law, but still, they were not a patch on NTR in popularity. The TDP owed its very existence to NTR. The party's successive and impressive electoral wins in assembly and parliamentary polls were widely acknowledged to be the result of NTR's personal charisma and hard work. Within three years of establishing the party, NTR acquired a formidable stature even outside the state. Understandably, he was the top gun in the party, and there was nobody who could come close to him in commanding the TDP. The entire machinery, both the government and the party, had to run according to his wishes.

From the beginning, the TDP was less of an institution and more of an instrument for NTR to realize his own political goals, however lofty they might be. Nadendla was not off the mark when he accused NTR of running the TDP as his personal property. NTR's grip on the party became firmer subsequently. Telugu Vijayam, the party headquarters since 1985, was built in the premises of his ashram at Gandipet. The party plenary, Mahanadu, was held every year to coincide with the party founder's birthday. The party constitution was changed in 1985, authorizing NTR to hand-pick a twenty-six-member executive committee and choose party office-bearers from among them. The centralization of authority in NTR's person was formalized with this step.

By the 1986 Mahanadu, the TDP had arrived as a political party with a strong organizational structure but with a supreme leader at the helm. The Mahanadu, held in January in Hyderabad, was a show of strength. The party displayed its political muscle, with hundreds of thousands of people converging at its meet. NTR had always been the prime attraction at the party's meetings in the past. This time, his indispensability to the party was consciously underscored. By 1988, Upendra declared that the partymen were not ashamed of the personality cult around NTR, as the TDP had survived and thrived only because of its leader. NTR was the source of all power. It became all too important to be in his good books to survive on the frontlines of TDP.

NTR's fondness for spectacle turned the rather bland affair of politics into a colourful and fun-filled pageant. He was influenced by the elements of carnival in Dravidian political gatherings. Apart from the yearly Mahanadu, this was also evident in the grand manner in which he organized the Filmotsav in 1986. NTR bestowed personal attention on this film event for which he built a tastefully designed open-air auditorium, Telugu Lalitha Kala Thoranam, at Public Gardens in Hyderabad. Completed in record time, the architecture of the auditorium reflected Telugu culture. The who's who of the Indian film industry, including Raj Kapoor, Ashok Kumar, Raj Kumar, Dilip Kumar, Randhir Kapoor, Saira Banu, Babitha, Hrishikesh Mukherjee and Prem Nazir, was present. He was on his feet all through the inauguration, inviting and bringing up each guest on to the stage. Hyderabad sported a festive atmosphere that January. Addressing around 1800 delegates, veteran actor Ashok Kumar said NTR looked tough from outside, but he was a very gentle person with great determination.

Akkineni Nageswara Rao (ANR), the senior-most actor from the Telugu film industry, did not attend his own retrospective at Filmotsav. Relations between him and NTR had soured by this time. The NTR government had issued notices to ANR and another actor, Krishna, over their film studio lands. Annapurna and Padmalaya Studios of ANR and Krishna, respectively, were built on land earlier given at concessional rates by the Congress governments to encourage the film industry in Hyderabad. The notices by the NTR government had threatened to confiscate unused land parcels from the actors. NTR had also instituted an inquiry into the alleged irregularities in the allotment of house plots in the Film Nagar Cooperative Society. NTR's reputation among his associates from the film industry as petty-minded was reinforced by this action. 'Government did not put any conditions on the time frame for building a studio at Annapurna. I will not join politics for seven acres, nor will I meet NTR on this issue,' an angry ANR said.[112] Film industry colleagues grumbled that NTR never liked others to be more successful than him. But NTR believed that he was protecting government interests.

Many of his party colleagues advised NTR against issuing notices to the actors, as the act could be viewed as vengeful. But NTR told them that rules were for everybody. ANR and Krishna obtained stay orders from the courts. But they never forgave NTR for what they considered his vindictive action.

NTR had his foibles, but he was not, as the media instigated, an eccentric and abnormal person. From early on, he was portrayed by a section of the Telugu press, which was sympathetic to the Congress, as an outlandish, even weird, personality. The national media too bought into these clichéd images which were bereft of the nuances in NTR's complex character. Many innuendos were in circulation over his alleged peculiarities. Some of NTR's actions, including his sartorial quirks and a few behavioural oddities, appeared to lend credence to these rumours, however incredulous.

One such story that started floating around soon after he took over for the third time in 1985 was about his necromancy, the practice of communicating with the dead. NTR would allegedly practise black magic in the wee hours at his newly constructed Gandipet Ashram, which he called Santhi Kuteeram. Located some 20 km away from the secretariat on the banks of Himayat Sagar Lake, the *kuteeram* was a traditional hermitage-style structure with all modern facilities. This was where NTR retired for the night in those days. Rumours spread that he was indulging in occult practices, and dead bodies were being ferried to the kuteeram for a ritual called Shava Puja. NTR reportedly slept with a saree wrapped around him—to simulate the *ardhanareeshwara* (half male, half female) form in Hindu mythology—on the recommendation of his astrologer to ward off evil.

Except for *Andhra Bhoomi* and the *Deccan Chronicle*, the
pro-Congress media outlets, no mainstream Telugu or English
newspaper in Hyderabad carried these sensational but unverified
reports. The gossip seemed to have originated in the notorious
columns of scandal sheets like Pingali Dasaratharam's *Encounter*.
Whether people believed such fantastic stories or not, these
became the subject of animated conversations in political circles.
Surprisingly, the hearsay became an established fact over time as
it got repeated ad nauseam by ill-informed commentators in the
national media. So much so that the *Times of India* editor Girilal
Jain wrote that it was common knowledge that NTR 'had behaved
oddly as, for example, when he had worn a saree'.[113] Even Indira
Gandhi was 'aware' of NTR's 'cross-dressing', as was evident when
she made a mention of it in an interview with journalist-writer
Tariq Ali.

Some people were inclined to believe these stories because
NTR himself provided the grist to such talk. He triggered
rumours about his astrological beliefs in late 1983 by sporting
a glittering emerald on his left earlobe, soon after adopting his
saffron costume. It was a strange look for a chief minister, but
NTR seemed thoroughly comfortable. When asked about it,
NTR said the stone was gifted to him for its auspicious qualities.
After announcing reservations for BCs, he made another addition
to his sartorial innovations—a turban. There was drama in the
way the headgear took shape. Initially, the turban's tail fell over
the chief minister's right shoulder. Later, it veered over to his left.
A photographer was apparently commissioned to take pictures of
the turban on NTR's head from different angles, which were sent
to Madras for designing the final look.

NTR tended to ignore the ridicule poured on his idiosyncrasies
in the media. However, perturbed by the freaky tales being spread
about his nocturnal activities, NTR extended an invitation to
reporters to visit his Gandipet kuteeram, which was otherwise out
of bounds to the media. After being taken around the ashram,

a reporter quipped, 'We were expecting to see creepy things but disappointingly nothing of the sort!'[114] After showing them around the place, NTR clarified that he did not believe in 'tantras and mantras'. He had a puja room where he offered worship. He said he did not believe in gurus and babas. 'I believe in the god that resides within me,' he said. He expressed deep displeasure at the baseless gossip being spread about his tantric practices. 'I started this [the construction of the kuteeram] when my wife Basavatarakam was alive. I thought we would have a peaceful time here, especially after my heart surgery. Unfortunately, she is no more. But it is in her memory that I have built it. I consider this a sacred place,' he told reporters.[115]

NTR's ochre robes and his Hindu spiritual outlook led to an impression that he was very religious, even orthodox. Commented *India Today* in 1986, 'If Tamil Nadu's M.G. Ramachandran introduced the combination of cinema and politics, the saffron-clad NTR has gone a step further, patenting a heady mix that has not just cinema and politics but religion as well.'[116] But the reality of his personality was quite different. NTR was not an atheist, but he was certainly not an obscurantist either. Senior cop H.J. Dora, who moved closely with NTR as his key intelligence aide, vouched that NTR, contrary to the popular image, cared little for gods and religious rituals. 'He did not put much faith in gods or in daily worship. I have not seen any *vratam* [pious religious observance] or ritual being performed in his home. Except for a photo frame of Lord Venkateswara, I did not see pictures of any other gods in his office or residence. He rarely visited temples except for Tirumala,' Dora recalled.[117]

Even when his party legislators invited him to have a darshan of some local temple during his tours, NTR would show little interest. 'You perform the puja and get me some *prasadam* [devotional offering to god],' he would tell them.[118] NTR was known to offer prayers every day at 3.30 a.m. in his home, but after that, he did not like to participate in any religious programmes.

Religion was intensely personal for NTR, and he did not believe in imposing his views on others. Asked about his attire, NTR clarified in an interview, 'These are my personal predilections. I should be judged by my actions,' suggesting his overt religious appearance had no bearing on his governance. Despite such protestations, for NTR, his dress was also a political message. Soon after he started wearing the turban, NTR said his clothing indicated lack of want and lust. 'Some people might think I am an ordinary person and try to lure me. I feel they will back out once they see my outfit. The way people see danger board and avoid the move, they would look at my attire and would regard me as somebody above the worldly pulls,' he declared.[119]

This confusing mix of secular and spiritual, political and practicable, costume and conviction was a defining trait of NTR's personality. And despite his vehemence that he had finally settled on his attire, NTR's passion for sartorial experiments continued. He wore earrings once again in 1989 at the peak of the Naxalite violence, apparently on the advice of astrologers. And then, he switched back to traditional Telugu-style white dhoti and kurta with a *kanduva* (a piece of an upper garment), following his new avatar as a *grihastha* (family man).

Probably at the behest of his second wife, Lakshmi Parvathi, NTR in his later life participated in yagnas and visited the Shirdi Sai Baba temple a couple of times on actor Mohan Babu's invitation. But at no point did NTR exhibit religious fanaticism.

Secular Swamiji

Despite his avatar as a Hindu holy man, NTR exhibited a strong secular streak in his public life. The communal riots that had become a regular feature of Hyderabad under the Congress regime were put down with an iron hand. Assured of no political interference, the cops tackled the recurrent problem effectively. This was a departure from the earlier situation when politicians from different parties, including the BJP, MIM and the ruling Congress made political capital out of engineered riots.[120] During the next five years of NTR's rule, Hyderabad remained peaceful. NTR's contribution to containing communal tension in Hyderabad, while known in the state, did not get deserving acknowledgement from researchers.[121]

From early on, NTR took care to make sure that his party and government did not give any wrong signals to the minorities. Nadendla recalled that during the early days of the TDP, NTR met Muslim leaders from the old city of Hyderabad to assure them of the party's secular credentials. During civic polls in Hyderabad, NTR wore a fez cap, spoke in Urdu and sang 'Sare Jahan Se Acha', the Urdu patriotic song, to please his audience. Of course, this act was ridiculed as part of NTR's repertoire of dramatics, but he had a genuine desire to convey that he belonged to everybody. Dr Kakarla Subba Rao, who is credited with establishing the first super speciality government hospital in Hyderabad, recalled that NTR insisted on retaining the name of the newly established super speciality hospital after the Muslim ruler Nizam despite resistance from many of his advisers. The former Nizam Orthopaedic Hospital became Nizam's Institute of Medical Sciences (NIMS).

Another notable example of NTR's secular instinct was his immediate condemnation of the army operation on the Golden Temple. NTR was one of the few political leaders who expressed opposition to the move instantly. He also ensured the safety of the Sikhs living in the twin cities of Hyderabad and Secunderabad in the aftermath of Indira Gandhi's assassination. No wonder, the local Sikhs considered NTR a friend. In an article in the Chandigarh-based *Tribune*, journalist Brijender Singh Panwar said:

> The Sikhs, according to the senior citizens in the twin cities, were traditional Congress voters. But all this changed with Operation Bluestar in 1984. There was a complete shift in the voting pattern towards the Telugu Desam of N.T. Rama

Rao, mainly because of post-Operation Bluestar. While the whole country saw violence against Sikhs, in Andhra Pradesh, N.T. Rama Rao ensured their safety.[122]

NTR's choice to leave a mark of his own on Hyderabad did not come from the pantheon of gods, Lord Krishna or Lord Rama, he had played all his life. The giant statue in the middle of Hussain Sagar Lake was not of a Hindu god, but Lord Buddha's. He told the *Washington Post* that he had chosen to depict Buddha because 'he was a humanitarian who told the whole truth to the people. It is our pride. He was born in our country.'[123] NTR's selection of Buddha as Hyderabad's Statue of Liberty pointed to his idealism as well as his non-religious perspective.

We have already seen how NTR wanted to make use of the cash deposits of TTD for secular purposes. The move was later given up, but it showed NTR was not shy of offending conservative Hindu groups. In his second term, NTR went ahead with more drastic decisions to clean up temple administration, attracting the ire of the priestly class and its supporters. But he did not budge an inch and proceeded with the abolition of hereditary rights of temple priests. This is further proof of NTR's unique character vis-à-vis his approach to and understanding of Hindu religious matters. The communists in Bengal and Kerala or the Dravidian parties in Tamil Nadu did not dare to ruffle the feathers of Hindu interest groups who were involved in the management of temples the way NTR did.

However, the symbolism surrounding NTR as a person and as an actor perpetuated the myth of NTR's religiosity in politics. Posters depicting NTR as Lord Krishna, blowing a conch shell, were used during election campaigns by many TDP candidates. Many cases were filed in courts against victorious TDP candidates for using religious symbols to exhort voters to defeat the Congress. In two such cases, the AP High Court set aside the election of TDP candidates in the 1989 polls. But the Supreme Court reversed the decision on the ground that there was no evidence that the offending posters had been used in the election by the TDP candidates themselves.[124]

Fans and party activists were known for putting up such posters and hoardings with NTR's tacit approval. But NTR used references from Hindu mythology to effectively convey his political message, rather than to derive advantage through religious divide. He was firmly against resorting to communal politics for political benefit. During the peak of his National Front days, NTR was perturbed by the attempts of the BJP to derive communal advantage by raking up the Ram Janmabhoomi issue. He later cut off ties with the BJP for its stand on the Ayodhya issue. He remained committed to his position till the end.

But like most Indian politicians, NTR had a weakness for Vastu, numerology and astrological advice. Few were aware of what exactly motivated him to follow his several quirks. Many believed that these were inspired by his weakness for astrology.

Photograph courtesy of Department of Information and Public Relations, Government of Andhra Pradesh

His saffron attire notwithstanding, NTR was secular to the core in his public life. Here, NTR is seen participating in Islamic prayer.

His frequent change of residence from Abids to Nacharam to Gandipet, his move from the new office to the old one in the secretariat, and his sartorial transformations undoubtedly pointed to his superstitions borne out of Vastu.

NTR enthusiastically introduced Hindu astrology as a subject of study at Telugu University. 'There is a need to study astrology in-depth. Because of western influence, we have ignored our own science like astrology,' he said in a conference.[125] While no evidence was available for his rumoured cross-dressing, he did wear rings with all kinds of precious stones, recommended for their astrological benefits.

But NTR was a pragmatic believer. When he complained of a nagging pain in his neck, doctors advised him to remove his Vivekananda-style headgear. He promptly followed their instruction.

NTR almost never visited any swami or baba, either during his film career or as a politician. In fact, his award-winning film *Kodalu Diddina Kapuram* (1970), a home production, made fun of Puttaparthi Sathya Sai Baba, the most popular spiritual leader in the state at the time. What NTR thought of babas was evident in the spoof which revolved around the shady character of Swami Satchidananda, a Sathya Sai lookalike.[126] The film was refused censor clearance in Madras but was later approved by the Bombay certification board. Since then, it was widely held that NTR had a low opinion of Sathya Sai Baba, though the latter wielded considerable influence among politicians, bureaucrats, businessmen and celebrities across the country. According to journalist Narisetti Innaiah, a peeved Sai Baba did not even visit Hyderabad as long as NTR was the chief minister.

Dora was a staunch follower of the baba. According to him, NTR never expressed any animosity towards him. He initially refused to give government land to build a stadium in Puttaparthi. Dora prevailed upon him, explaining that it was a public service initiative. Later, in his third term, NTR provided government support when the Sathya Sai Trust undertook an ambitious scheme to provide drinking water to the parched villages of Anantapur. While NTR appreciated the social service being rendered by the baba, he did not regard him as Bhagwan (god). This exception was notable since every prominent politician from Narasimha Rao to Chandrababu Naidu paid obeisance to him.

Dora once wanted to send a few trucks of levy rice to the ashram of Sai Baba in Puttaparthi to feed the visitors that thronged the place in hundreds daily. He approached the civil supplies commissioner C.D. Arha for the favour. Arha wanted NTR's permission, but the chief minister vetoed the proposal. 'They are rich. They can buy rice in the open market,' he said without mincing words.[127]

NTR had a complicated outlook on religion and religious practices. He was steeped in ancient Indian culture and spirituality but was not a blind follower. He described his spiritual orientation as *harihara tatvam*,[128] as exemplified in the way he named his children. All his boys had Vaishnava names, while all the girls were named in the Shivaite tradition.[129] His long career in the film industry was spent studying the Itihasas and Puranas. While he greatly appreciated ancient Indian lore, NTR tried to give a new spin to many of the Puranic characters in his movies in the light of rationalist interpretations. Such commentary was offered especially by Tripuraneni Ramaswamy, a poet, rationalist and reformer of the early twentieth century from coastal Andhra. The dialogues penned by another rationalist, Kondaveeti Venkata Kavi, for one of his home productions, *Daana Veera Soora Karna* (1977), questioned the obsession with caste and presented Duryodhana in a positive light. Films such as these and their alternative treatment reflected NTR's non-conforming attitude towards the traditional narrative of ancient texts. NTR was more a cultural and spiritual Hindu than a religious zealot. But his appearance was mistaken by many as a reflection of a conservative religious outlook. President Giani

Zail Singh always referred to NTR as Swamiji, convinced that the chief minister was a holy man.[130]

NTR's love for ochre robes and penchant for spiritual accessories can be explained by two of his personality traits. The performance was an essential part of his messaging. He did not merely want to be a selfless politician but rather to be seen and understood as such through his costume. It was not accidental that he started sporting the Vivekananda-style saffron turban soon after he announced a steep hike in reservations to the BCs.[131] The costume was the medium through which he chose to convey the message. 'I want to be a saint in politics,' he said smugly in an *India Today* interview. How would he communicate this to the people? Not through press statements but through his appearance, literally. He explained:

> My aim is not only to make myself pure but that my clothing, my appearance should be such that nothing corrupt can come near me.[132]

No wonder, he would take offence when compared to Swami Vivekananda. He would protest, 'I designed this turban myself; I can tie it myself. It is not copied from anyone.'[133] This dressing up to convey his intent was, of course, a legacy of his long career in films. However dubious it might look, NTR seriously entertained notions of embarking on a journey to sainthood. In his clumsy attempt at bringing together three unconnected fields— spirituality, cinema and politics—NTR conveyed confused signals of who he really was.

Fight for the States' Rights

The home-grown politician's proclivities might have come across as flippant, but he was unwavering when it came to matters of the 'state'. NTR was consistent in asserting the rights of the states throughout his political life. Autonomy to the states—financial and administrative—was one of the cardinal principles of the TDP's philosophy under his leadership. The August 1984 crisis further strengthened his resolve to fight against the preponderance of the Union government on the affairs of the states.

NTR first grabbed national attention when he walked out of a National Development Council (NDC) meeting, to protest the dismissal of the Farooq Abdullah government in J&K. The council meeting held on 12 July 1984 in Delhi was chaired by Prime Minister Indira Gandhi. Chief Ministers Jyoti Basu (West Bengal), Ramakrishna Hegde (Karnataka) and Nripen Chakraborty (Tripura) walked out of the meeting along with NTR in a coordinated action. The chief minister did not give any clue to his officials about his plan to deviate from the prepared draft and deliver a political speech at the meeting.

The Andhra officials were taken aback when NTR, instead of reading the prepared speech, denounced the action of the Centre in dismissing an elected government. Planning Secretary Y.V. Reddy recalled that he, along with other officials, was disconcerted at being kept in the dark over the matter.[134] The officers were later told that it was done to protect them from embarrassment.

NTR and Indira had sharp exchanges as the former began reading a statement on behalf of the four chief ministers. He was interrupted by the prime minister, but he and the other three chief ministers insisted that he be allowed to complete his statement. After the chief ministers walked out, a resolution adopted by the council condemned their action. The showdown certainly played a part in the decision of an irked Indira Gandhi to trigger the ouster of the TDP government barely a month later.

NTR's was one of the few state governments that took the Sarkaria Commission seriously. NTR met with Justice Sarkaria and submitted a fifteen-page memorandum to the commission, seeking to redefine the federal structure in the country. Stressing the need to give more autonomy and resources to the states, NTR also suggested an independent body of advisers to the president of India for deciding issues concerning the All India Services officers.[135] He opposed the transfer of items from the state list to the concurrent list[136] and demanded autonomy to Akashvani and Doordarshan, failing which the states should have a right to have their own radio and television channels. NTR was of the view that states had more responsibility in the welfare of the people and should undertake poverty reduction programmes. Hence, they should have more resources to generate revenue, NTR argued. He alleged that the states' rights were being chipped away with every constitutional amendment.

NTR expressed disappointment with the Sarkaria Commission Report when it came out in January 1988. 'Catching a rat after digging a mountain,' was how he characterized the report using a Telugu analogy.[137] He was unhappy that the Sarkaria Commission had failed to make any radical recommendations such as the removal of Article 356 (which empowered the Centre to impose President's Rule in states) from the Constitution.

In defending the primacy of the states, NTR famously came up with the concept that the Centre was *mithya* (non-existent, unreal). Pointing out that there was no mention of the Centre in the Constitution, NTR maintained that India was only a union of states. 'The Constitution says so,' he declared many times.[138]

He felt centralizing power was a legacy of the British. His grouse was that the Centre tried to restrict the resource base of the states. He argued that the Centre should have objective criteria to help all states in equal measure. NTR was annoyed by the Centre's big-brotherly attitude over various issues involving AP. Delhi's non-cooperation in granting approval for Telugu Ganga and other irrigation projects aggrieved him. He was unhappy with the little assistance offered by the Centre in times of droughts, floods and natural calamities. He was resentful that the Centre should hold the purse strings, while it was the states that contributed to the national coffers.

He was also one of the few chief ministers who fought tooth and nail against the Rajiv Gandhi government proposal in 1989 to funnel funds directly to the panchayats. He castigated the move as deliberate and motivated, which would erode the autonomy of states provided by the Constitution. He also took objection to Rajiv's proposal to address district collectors directly.

The role of Ram Lal in the 1984 coup had made NTR suspicious of governors. In fact, even before the coup, the Mahanadu resolution that year said that the office of the governor was a colonial remnant that served little purpose in the modern era. Time and again, NTR protested the fact that the governor acted as an agent of the Centre. The TDP was the only party in the country that advocated the abolition of the institution of the governor. NTR considered it anachronistic and a relic of the colonial era. The party fought long and hard on this score without much success. Ram Lal's unceremonious exit was a matter of satisfaction for him. While he got along with his replacement, Shankar Dayal Sharma, reasonably well, the same could not be said about his successor.

Kumudben Manishankar Joshi was a Gujarati politician who had no qualms in treating her position as an extension of her party affiliation. Constitutional expert A.G. Noorani called Kumudben Joshi's 'place in the annals of gubernatorial impropriety' as 'beyond challenge'.[139] Despite his insistence, the chief minister was not consulted on her appointment in November 1985. Soon, it was clear that Joshi was more interested in being an activist than a constitutional functionary. She openly entertained politicians from the Opposition at the official residence. State Congress leaders often shared the dais with her in official functions. In one such event, Uma Gajapathi Raju, wife of TDP MP Ananda Gajapati Raju, announced that she was joining the Congress (I). The governor also toured the districts without informing the government. She spent more time travelling various districts in the state than in Raj Bhavan, prompting the ruling party to suspect she was building a base for the Congress (I). She attended a thousand public events in her four-and-a-half-year tenure, outdoing the chief minister.

Joshi frequently called for files and summoned officials for clarifications in a manner that piqued the ruling party. She floated social organizations, the National Institute for Social Action (NISA) and Chetna, from Raj Bhavan and solicited public donations without the approval of the state government. Unable to tolerate her independent functioning, the TDP came out publicly against the governor and accused her of turning Raj Bhavan into the Congress office. The TDP government also made an issue of the mounting expenses of Raj Bhavan.

NTR dashed off letters to the president as well as the prime minister in 1987 and 1988, protesting against her 'conduct and attitude'.[140] In a six-page letter to the president, NTR accused Joshi of causing embarrassment to his government and 'carrying on a relentless campaign of calumny'. He charged the governor with 'using the State Red Cross as a sort of launching pad', and 'making excursions into the domain of normal developmental administration which is legitimately the sphere of elected governments in a parliamentary democracy'.[141]

But Joshi was unfazed. 'I am a citizen first and governor next,' she said nonchalantly. She clearly had the blessings of the leadership in Delhi. The state cabinet adopted a resolution criticizing the 'tenor and content' of her Republic Day parade speech in 1988. The governor highlighted the Centre's contribution while 'belittling the remarkable progress' made by the state. Joshi also wilfully delayed in giving assent to several bills such as the Karshaka Parishad Bill. She returned the file appointing Justice R.N. Agarwal as Lokayukta thrice, prompting irked cabinet ministers to complain to the president. Even though the state government fulfilled all obligations required for the appointment of Lokayukta, Joshi raised uncalled-for objections, they alleged.

NTR's nomination of Justice Agarwal as Lokayukta never materialized as Joshi sat on the file for more than a year, by which time the term of NTR's government came to an end. The chief minister dashed off another letter to the president, taking exception to the governor's behaviour. Acting on the complaint, President Zail Singh despatched an angry letter to Kumudben Joshi asking her to not get involved in state politics. 'Since a governor is to maintain a cordial Centre-State relationship, you should be careful in what you actually do,' the president even advised her.[142]

These experiences cemented NTR's resolve to fight for more constitutional equity to the states. He reiterated at the Bangalore conclave of Opposition leaders in 1987 that the office of the governor had become a political rehabilitation centre. 'Governors have become a menace to the country's polity,' he said in a scathing attack.[143] Ironically, the report of the Sarkaria Commission, which was formed four years earlier following the demands put forth by regional parties like the TDP, came out during this time. The report recommended that 'a politician from the ruling party at the Centre should not be appointed a governor of a State, run by another party'.[144] But the Centre did not honour the Sarkaria report. Ironically, Kumudben Joshi outlasted NTR in her position as governor. While NTR was voted out in December 1989, Joshi stayed on till February 1990.

Not surprisingly, the national alternative to the Congress that NTR had in mind was essentially a federal party that stood up for the rights of the states. This plank was the basis of his much-talked-about Bharata Desam Party. After settling into power following the March 1985 polls, the TDP passed a resolution for taking steps for the formation of Bharata Desam. However, NTR remained undecided on whether the proposed party would be a federation of existing regional parties or an

amalgam of regional outfits to be established under the banner
of Bharata Desam.

Meanwhile, NTR was invited by the newly formed Asom
Gana Parishad (AGP) leaders to campaign on behalf of their party
for the Assam assembly elections in December 1985. An obliging
NTR toured Assam extensively through tea-garden areas where
people of Telugu origin were in large numbers, 'tipping the scales
decisively' through his campaign. *India Today* reported that '. . . by
far the greatest contribution was made by Telugu Desam' in the
AGP victory.[145] According to the report, NTR drew huge crowds.
The TDP also extended logistical support by getting many AGP
posters printed at Rajahmundry at a nominal cost. It even held a
training camp for the party leaders deputed to spend a month in
Assam to help the AGP.

However, NTR could make little progress in his national
plans for a long time. He was preoccupied with the political
developments in the state. The ideological and personality clashes
among the non-Congress party leaders also meant NTR could
make little headway in forging a viable alternative. He also could
not come to an understanding of the shape and ideology of the
proposed national alternative. The Opposition parties were cold
to the idea, as a new party would not serve the purpose in their
view. NTR was not unaware of the futility of following up on an
unworkable idea and wisely chose to keep Bharata Desam in cold
storage.

NTR, however, did not give up on the idea of a non-Congress
front. In January 1986, he came up with the proposal of a national
forum of Opposition parties and organized a meeting in Hyderabad
to discuss coordination and joint action on issues to which they
had a common approach. The main objective of the forum was
to achieve a greater say in national affairs for the regional parties.
Thirteen parties participated in the meeting, including the Janata
and the Congress (S) and some of the smaller regional parties
like the All-Party Hill Leaders' Conference of Meghalaya, the

Manipur People's Party, the People's Conference of Mizoram, the Naga National Democratic Party, the People's Party of Arunachal Pradesh, the Rashtriya Congress of Gujarat, and the Panther's Party of J&K. The 'Hyderabad declaration' pledged to forge a common forum for discussion and action on various problems and issues. The communists and the BJP, who were left out, were critical of the meeting.

NTR's repeated attempts at forging a semblance of unity among the squabbling parties did not make much headway. But the TDP leader continued to test the waters in northern India. He campaigned vigorously in the Haryana assembly elections held in June 1987 with considerable success. He began his journey on the Chaitanya Ratham from Delhi in the sweltering heat of the north and addressed public meetings in around a dozen places in Haryana, including Gurgaon, Jhajjar, Bhiwani, Jhind, Charkhi Dadri, Hansi, Khainal, Kurukshetra, Karnal, Panipat and Sonepat. In preparation for his northern forays, he made conscious efforts to learn Hindi. To the utter delight of the large crowds, NTR delivered his practised speeches in idiomatic Hindi. Journalist Chidanand Rajghatta, writing for the *Telegraph*, noted that NTR 'drew the biggest crowd any leader had managed in Gurgaon and had them riveted with a crackling display of histrionics'. He described the euphoria created by NTR at Gurgaon (now Gurugram) thus:

> He began with a couple of opening lines in Telugu which had the Haryanvi audience tittering. But the chuckles soon died and in minutes the audience was enraptured by the most stunning speech they had heard. 'Guru Brahma, Guru Vishnu, Guru Devo Maheshwara . . .' he bellowed. 'Residents of Gurgaon, this place reminds me of Dronacharya, of Krishna, of the battle between the Pandavas and Kauravas between the good and the evil.' The man from the south captivated a full house for 30 enchanting minutes.[146]

As there was a split in the Lok Dal during this time, NTR said he was only appealing to the people to defeat the Congress, without specifying which party he was supporting. However, he met Lok Dal (B) leader Devi Lal at Panipat, and they addressed a meeting together. NTR declared that Devi Lal would be the next chief minister of Haryana. Local newspapers such as *Jansatta* and *Punjab Kesari* wrote that Devi Lal's faction received a boost due to NTR's campaign. His party indeed wiped the Congress out in the polls.

NTR was now an important voice in national politics. All critical decisions by the Opposition were being vetted by him. The candidature for the presidential election in 1987 was one such. However, the Opposition disunity during such crucial moments caused him much distress. NTR was part of the three-member committee along with CPI (M) General Secretary E.M.S. Namboodiripad and Janata Party President Chandra Shekhar for finalizing the Opposition candidate. NTR tried to put up a joint Opposition candidate against the Congress's official candidate R. Venkataraman. The Opposition tried to prevail upon Zail Singh, who had completed his term, to be the Opposition candidate. But the CPI (M) put spokes in the plan. Namboodiripad despatched a letter to NTR, withdrawing from the committee since his party was committed to V.R. Krishna Iyer. NTR and Chandra Shekhar were aghast. They wrote back, reminding him that the communist leader had agreed that 'the position regarding Giani Zail Singh's candidature should be ascertained before we finally announce the name of Sri Krishna Iyer'. Finally, Krishna Iyer was chosen as the Opposition candidate, but he lost the election.

NTR mulled over a mechanism to come up with a common agenda for non-Congress parties. The common plan, according to him, should have guiding principles that included protecting national integrity, restructuring Centre–state relations, developing BCs and maintaining secularism. In the wake of the Congress (I) defeat in the Haryana elections, another attempt to come up with a common platform was made under the aegis of Devi Lal, the new Haryana chief minister. NTR was invited to the Surajkund conclave, which had the BJP but no communists. The hurdles for Opposition unity remained the same—the question of leadership, the issues to be highlighted, and mutual suspicion between the BJP and the communists.

But NTR was not ready to give up. As part of his single-point agenda to defeat the Congress, NTR took along a contingent of TDP leaders in 1988 for the crucial bypolls in north India. V.P. Singh was also in the fray for the Allahabad by-election. NTR launched his northern campaign quite seriously. He toured Udhampur (Jammu), Faridabad, Allahabad, Chaproli (Uttar Pradesh), Sirsa (Rajasthan) and Godhra and Pali (Gujarat) constituencies on his Chaitanya Ratham. He had sent a few lakh posters of himself, some in his mythological avatars, to these places. As always, NTR attracted good gatherings. The southern leader was able to get a feel of the crowd response in north India at a time

NTR's forays into north India were a huge success. Few regional leaders campaigned as extensively across India as NTR did. Here is a news item on NTR's roadshow in Haryana, reported by the *Telegraph* of Calcutta on 15 June 1987.

when he was seriously planning to foray into national politics. The Congress (I)'s rout in Uttar Pradesh was complete when it lost all three by-elections. These were the first elections after the Opposition parties achieved a semblance of unity by putting up a joint candidate against the Congress in every seat. They won resoundingly. NTR was enthused by the victories. He stepped up his efforts for Opposition unity, and even the Opposition leaders saw the possibilities in a unified front.

While V.P. Singh emerged as the Opposition mascot post-Bofors, NTR came to be the most acceptable face among the disparate non-Congress parties. NTR, who consistently worked for Opposition unity, played host to them in 1988—on the fifth anniversary of his government and for Mahanadu. Prominent leaders of the Opposition parties were present on both occasions in Hyderabad and Vijayawada. Devi Lal, A.B. Vajpayee, Bangaru Laxman, Madhu Dandavate, M.N. Gurupadaswamy, Ramakrishna Hegde, Biju Patnaik, S. Jaipal Reddy, K.P. Unnikrishnan, Sarath Chandra Sinha, Ram Dhan, Bhrigu Kumar Phukan, Bhim Singh, M. Karunanidhi, Ram Jethmalani, Ajit Singh, Ram Naresh Yadav and Ramu Walia participated.

NTR used this occasion to insist that all Opposition parties should form one political unit under a federal umbrella to take on the Congress in each constituency. This federal party should have a common manifesto and field candidates on the same symbol for Parliament elections. Each party could contest on its symbol in assembly elections. 'On my part, I insisted that unless all of us come together, there is no way of defeating Congress,' he told the media. But the Opposition meeting, despite NTR's hopes, did not make much progress at Vijayawada. Each one of the leaders held on to the belief that their party had an opportunity to make an all-India impact. Besides, the stand-off between the communists and the BJP stood as a hindrance to Opposition unity.

The emergence of Singh and his Jan Morcha by the second half of 1988 provided a fillip to the Opposition unity efforts.

NTR seized the opportunity. He could finally play a decisive role in the complicated process of putting together a strong front at the national level against the Congress. At the meeting organized at Andhra Pradesh Bhavan in Delhi in August 1988, NTR used his charisma and political tact to work out a consensus among the parties. He did not mince words in condemning the internal squabbles among the Opposition stalwarts, warning they would perish without unity. In an ultimatum, he said he would not be a part of unity efforts in future if the bickering Opposition leaders did not give up their bloated egos. He held discussions with Singh, Karnataka Chief Minister Ramakrishna Hegde, Janata Party leader Chandra Shekhar and Lok Dal President Hemwati Nandan Bahuguna. The recalcitrant Bahuguna and Chandra Shekhar, who had stayed away from all the previous unity talks, fell in line. The leaders of the regional parties, as well as non-Congress chief ministers, supported NTR to the hilt.

The formation of the National Front on 6 August 1988 was a triumph of NTR's efforts. The front came into existence following a tie-up among seven parties—the Lok Dal, Janata Party, Jan Morcha, Congress (S), DMK, AGP and the TDP. 'It was his show all the way,' remarked journalist Prabhu Chawla. 'Rama Rao's long-cherished dream of acquiring national status seemed to have come true.'[147] For his crucial role in bringing together the Opposition parties a year and a half before the general elections, NTR got unanimously elected as chairman of the front. Singh became the convener.

According to Upendra, originally only Singh was to head the newly formed National Front. Upendra claimed he had convinced the regional parties to push for two posts—of a convener and a chairman—for balanced representation between the north and the south. Once it was agreed, NTR emerged as the best fit for the position of chairman, given his long-standing efforts at Opposition unity.[148] The National Front had its first massive public meeting at Marina Beach in Madras on 17 September

1989, with NTR presiding over the function in which Opposition stalwarts participated. It was a memorable day for NTR. 'My dream of bringing all the Opposition parties together has come true,' NTR gushed. Praising the TDP's role in the formation of the National Front, Vajpayee remarked that the development was a partial fulfilment of NTR's dream since 1983. It was a high point in NTR's barely six-year political career when he returned to Hyderabad as chairman of the National Front. He was treated to a grand welcome amid cries of 'Desh ki Neta NTR' at Begumpet Airport.

NTR's long-standing goal of unifying the Opposition to unseat the Congress appeared closer. There was open talk among TDP cadres that NTR was eyeing the prime minister's post. NTR prepared for his future role in Delhi by taking lessons in Hindi from Vemuru Radhakrishna Murthy of Dakshina Bharat Hindi Prachar Sabha in Hyderabad and later from Yarlagadda Lakshmi Prasad, a Hindi professor. His growing importance at the national level was visible at the launch of the film *Brahmarshi Viswamitra* in Hyderabad. The leaders of all major Opposition parties were in attendance.

But NTR's growing graph at the national level did not match his government's deteriorating image back home. A belligerent Opposition and many controversies rocked NTR's carefully crafted image.

He, however, had something up his sleeve. Or at least, he thought so.

~

Act IV

The Reel and the Reality

The Ramakrishna Horticultural Studio at Nacharam on the outskirts of Hyderabad was buzzing with activity after a long gap. A potent mix of politics and cinema was waiting to play out. Elaborate sets replicating forest dwellings of ancient rishis or sages had been set up. Hindi and Telugu songs recorded in Bombay by well-known Hindi music director Ravindra Jain were playing in the background. After a gap of more than six years, the artiste-turned-chief-minister was back where he felt the most comfortable—under the arc lights. NTR had been preparing for what he thought was the role of his lifetime—of sage Viswamitra of the Hindu Puranas.

The reel and the real coalesced on this day, 18 June 1989. NTR's make-up man Muthu gave finishing touches to the thick coat of paint on his face, and he appeared satisfied with the look. He had knotted hair with a streak of silver, flowing beard and thick eyebrows befitting a sage. Wearing bright saffron clothes in the manner of a *rajarshi*, a king who turned into a royal sage in Hindu tradition, he was heavily accessorized with a pair of earrings, a string of *rudraksha* around the neck and a gold belt around the waist (*vaddanam*). A necklace resembling a five-headed serpent (*panchamukha sarpam*), an anklet with a snake's head (*nagabandham*) around the right ankle and a *kamandalam* (an oblong water pot) completed the look. He then drove to the film set in his Packard car, sporting his favourite four 9s number plate. Putting on the wooden footwear (*pavu kollu*), the traditional shoe worn by the saints in Hinduism, reverentially brought by his son Harikrishna, NTR posed for the waiting photographers.

Bollywood actress Meenakshi Seshadri, playing the divine danseuse Menaka, drove into the studio in her flashy costume. Cameramen vied with one another to click pictures of the celestial nymph. Fans who had thronged in large numbers were watching the proceedings on about fifty closed-circuit television sets that had been installed outside the studio floors. The mahurat shot, for which NTR's son Balakrishna sounded the clapper board, was a teaser. The scene was: Menaka, the temptress, employing her charms to seduce Viswamitra, who was in deep penance. She wanted to lure him away from his intense ascetic practice. A couple of Menaka's bewitching poses and Viswamitra's vain attempts at self-control constituted the opening shots.

This was the first time a chief minister in office was acting in a film. NTR's move was naturally seen as an unprecedented event. But what made it more interesting was the presence of national Opposition leaders who constituted the newly formed National Front. NTR, only a regional satrap till recently, was now the proud chairman of the Front and hence the honour. Once again proving that cinema and politics were one and the same for him, NTR had turned the launch of his much-talked-about film *Brahmarshi Viswamitra* into a national political event. Opposition luminaries V.P. Singh, Biju Patnaik, Haryana Chief Minister Devi Lal, Tamil Nadu Chief Minister M. Karunanidhi, his colleague Murasoli Maran, Assam Chief Minister Prafulla Kumar Mahanta, and Congress (S) leaders S.N. Sinha and K.P. Unnikrishnan had flown down to grace the event.

This was probably the first time the veteran leaders (except Karunanidhi, of course) were experiencing the glitzy and gaudy world of cinema from such close quarters. They awkwardly watched Meenakshi Seshadri gyrating in garish costumes before an aged and overly made-up NTR against the backdrop of a cardboard set piece. After the shot was over, the leaders walked towards NTR and self-consciously congratulated him.

How did a man who wanted to transform politics end up putting on greasepaint once again? That too at a time when he was all set to be catapulted on to the national scene? A host of issues had prompted NTR to try this, what critics dubbed as a gimmick. By 1989, the mercurial chief minister had landed himself in a series of controversies, many of them of his own making. His image took a severe beating. Senior party leaders who fell out with him became a thorn in his side. Caste conflicts and Naxalite violence created fissures in his governance. His iron grip over the party and the administration seemed to loosen. The Opposition stepped up its attack. The Congress (I) was able to pin him down on his home turf when he thought he was close to realizing his ambition of taking on the establishment at the national level. The chief minister was feeling stifled by the negativity around him.

Enmeshed in the political quagmire, NTR found solace in the idea of making a movie that allowed him to project himself the way he perceived himself. Since he became chief minister in 1983, NTR always ardently talked about his movie career and how people wanted him to continue to showcase his histrionics. He sincerely believed that his absence was a great void in the field. The character of Viswamitra, a temperamental sage in Hindu mythology, caught his attention a long time ago. He first announced plans for a film on the rishi in January 1987.

Whenever an opportunity presented itself, NTR spoke animatedly about the venerated sage, his Gayatri mantra and his radical personality. The chief minister also revealed his plans to have a Hindi version of *Brahmarshi Viswamitra*. As the National

Front chairman, NTR must have considered it a golden opportunity to make a mark among the north Indian voters. The film became a hot topic for both the media and political circles, at least in AP. NTR liked to indulge the press with tantalizing titbits about the film, especially over the role of the celestial danseuse, Menaka. He would go into raptures talking about the persona of Viswamitra.

NTR was fascinated with the mythological character for a reason. He saw a kinship with Viswamitra, whom he visualized as his alter ego, taking on the gods of the establishment. NTR viewed the self-obsessed gods as the Centre. He was like Viswamitra, a Kshatriya who achieved the same powers as the rishis of Brahmin lineage and used them for the welfare of the society. When Rishi Vashishta refused to send King Trishanku to heaven in his bodily form, Viswamitra created an alternative heaven known as Trishanku Swarga. The politician NTR, in his mind, was building an alternative world for the benefit of the common man. It was this message that he apparently wanted to drive home through the film. 'Viswamitra is the inspiration for TDP policies and principles. Creating a casteless and classless society was the ideal of Viswamitra, which inspired me,' NTR said during the inauguration of the film.[1] NTR firmly believed that the film was his Brahmastra (the ultimate weapon in Hindu mythology) to create a positive impact in the next elections. He thought that the film would take him to the pinnacles of his political ambition.

The TDP chief took the decision to undertake the movie project on the banner of NTR Trust at the end of 1988. NTR's mark was all over the film. He was involved in the screenwriting, editing and direction besides producing and taking the lead role in the movie. Dialogues for the Telugu film were written by Nagabhairava Koteswara Rao and for the Hindi version by Vishnu Malhotra. His sons became involved, with Balakrishna playing a character in the movie and Mohana Krishna wielding the camera. In August 1989, NTR organized an audio release function for the film at Hotel Krishna Oberoi in Hyderabad with veteran film personality Dilip Kumar as the chief guest. The cassettes, containing six songs, written by C. Narayana Reddy, rendered by K.J. Yesudas, P. Susheela, S.P. Balasubrahmanyam and Kavita Krishnamurthy, with music composed by Ravindra Jain, had record sales of reportedly one hundred thousand on the day of the release. They were rendered in Hindi by Lata Mangeshkar, Asha Bhosle, Anuradha Paudwal and Suresh Wadkar and recorded in Bombay.

A dismayed Opposition launched a tirade against NTR for his brazenness in pursuing this unpolitical endeavour. He should resign and appoint his replacement before putting on make-up, they demanded. The CPI dubbed the move as NTR's `shameful' gambit to regain his lost political clout.[2] Rajiv Gandhi, who visited the state during this time, found fault with NTR for 'prancing around Menaka', leaving the state to the dogs.[3] As NTR was busy shooting, officers visited the film sets with their files. NTR's

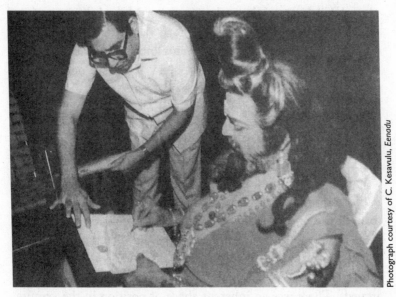

Photograph courtesy of C. Kesavulu, *Eenadu*

NTR signing government files during the shooting of the film *Brahmarshi Viswamitra*. The Opposition parties criticized the chief minister for pursuing his acting career against all norms.

pictures of signing government files in Viswamitra's get-up were published all over the papers. 'Should we consider these signatures as those of NTR or Viswamitra?'[4] Nadendla questioned. The state Congress president Channa Reddy said he wouldn't be surprised if NTR were to attend office in the Viswamitra attire. K. Rosaiah took exception to senior officers being forced to meet NTR on cinema sets. Actor Krishna alleged that NTR had turned the state into his own production house. Government employees denounced NTR as 'Nero at Nacharam', who had no time for their grievances. But NTR was unfazed.

Meanwhile, Dasari Narayana Rao, a film director, announced plans for a television series on Viswamitra in Hindi. He had worked with NTR earlier in movies but was now close to the Kapu leaders in the Congress. The leaders of the TDP reacted strongly to the announcement, condemning the attempts to undercut NTR's efforts in making a classic. Doordarshan gave Dasari the slots. Well-known Hindi television actor Mukesh Khanna played the character of Viswamitra. The story was written by Kamalakara Kameswara Rao, a yesteryears director known for his mythological films, while dialogues were penned by Rahi Masoom Reza of *Mahabharat* fame. The sixteen-part serial was also targeted to be telecast before the upcoming Lok Sabha elections. The mythological soap was clearly intended to steal NTR's thunder.

As NTR began shooting, his move was challenged in the AP High Court. Congress activists moved the court for the issuance of a writ of quo warranto against NTR. The party argued that NTR had committed a constitutional infraction and forfeited the right to hold the office of chief minister by pursuing the commercial activity of producing a film. 'Acting in and directing a film by a chief minister is incompatible with the office,' S. Ramachandra Rao, a known legal baiter of NTR and counsel for the petitioner, argued.[5] There was an inherent abuse of position in the venture, he said. NTR went ahead with the shooting, while TDP leaders agonized over the legal implications.

The people and the media took enormous interest in the case as NTR's undertaking was uncommon. NTR's lawyers contended in the court that he had undertaken the film to propagate the ideals of equality, brotherhood and egalitarianism. The life and philosophy of Viswamitra symbolized the said doctrines, and the most effective way of conveying the ideas to the people was through the medium of film. The proceeds of the film would go to a charitable trust, and hence the chief minister was not involved in any business activity. They also argued that there was no statutory provision prescribing a code of conduct for ministers that could be enforced by the court.

The high court concurred that the oath of office did not say that a minister shall devote all his time to his official duties. It was a matter left to his good sense and conscience. Dismissing the petitions, the high court bench said that the rules of conduct applicable to civil servants did not apply to ministers. 'This Court has no power to inquire into the desirability or otherwise of the respondent's conduct, nor has it the power to restrain him from engaging himself in the said activity. Much less can it declare him to be disqualified from holding the office of chief minister on the said ground,' the judgment said.[6]

NTR came out unscathed legally. But his obsession with the movie at a time when a mandal president, Malhar Rao, was brutally killed by Naxalites did not go down well with the people. When the state was beset with calamities—drought in one region and floods in another—NTR was speaking of the film, teasing the press over Menaka's role. For some time, Viswamitra and Menaka were the flavour of the season for even mainstream newspapers. The Opposition, as well as the media, lampooned NTR's rather unusual pursuit. Congress legislature party leader M. Baga Reddy referred to NTR's frequent absences during the assembly session, remarking tongue in cheek, 'Looks like NTR may not come to assembly till Viswamitra finds his Menaka.'[7]

Unperturbed, NTR went about the shooting schedule, which started early in the morning. He would spend time on the sets till afternoon and then return to his official duties. He was sixty-five years old at the time with a heavyset body. But he was following a strict diet to reduce his weight for the film. He slept on the floor, eating only fruits and vegetables, a habit he had carried throughout his cinema life. He was working hard to release the movie around the Vijaya Dasami festival in October 1989 and make the most of it for the elections that would follow. But *Brahmarshi Viswamitra* could not be completed as election dates were unexpectedly advanced, and NTR had to plunge headlong into the campaign. But at the time of making the film, NTR must have thought that he could arrest his sliding popularity through his cinematic appeal.

NTR was hoping to turn the political tables with his histrionics on the screen, but it was a tall order. By the end of 1988, NTR's image lost much of its sheen due to various allegations of misgovernance. Several of his decisions turned controversial. The Congress, through its relentless attack, put NTR on the defensive.

NTR, a Casteist?

One of the tools that the Congress (I) employed to attack the ruling TDP was the alleged caste favouritism by NTR. What started off as a whisper in power corridors in 1983 became shrill and open by 1987. Many Opposition leaders, especially in the Congress party, repeatedly spoke of NTR's alleged bias in favour of people of his caste in the government. The Reddys in the Congress were at the forefront of this criticism. Brahmins, both in bureaucracy and in politics, played a significant role in promoting this perception, as they had been on the receiving end during NTR's administration. A good part of the Dronamraju Satyanarayana petition against NTR in the AP High Court filed in 1987 dealt in detail with the chief minister's alleged casteism. 'In the State of Andhra Pradesh ruled by Sri N.T. Rama Rao, nothing but caste matters,' the petition charged.[8]

Undoubtedly, more persons belonging to the Kamma caste were found in prominent positions in the government during the NTR period as compared to the earlier Congress regimes. The figures quoted by the Congress (I) in this regard, however, were generally inflated. While the locus of power indeed stayed with the Kammas, caste domination was not as entrenched in the government as it was during the Congress regime. But the unrelenting campaign by political opponents did leave the slur of casteism on the NTR government.

NTR always had high regard and respect for people with talent and merit. He was generally on the lookout for achievers and persons of character and integrity, and sought their help and advice for innovative policies and schemes in the government. Yelavarthy Nayudamma, Dr Kakarla Subba Rao, Justice Avula Sambasiva Rao, Justice Challa Kondaiah and Prof Koneru Ramakrishna Rao were some of the respected personalities NTR had picked for important positions in the government. However, the fact that they all belonged to the Kamma caste did not go well with NTR's image.

Nayudamma, an internationally reputed scientist-bureaucrat who held such distinguished positions as director of CSIR and CLRI, was appointed as an honorary industrial adviser to NTR. It was Nayudamma's advice to 'concentrate on large programmes that are visible to the public'.[9] He was the inspiration behind NTR's crusade against corruption and corrupt officials. He died in the 1985 Kanishka plane bombing in Canada.

Koneru Ramakrishna Rao was an internationally reputed academic scholar, philosopher, psychologist, educationist and researcher. He was made vice chancellor of Andhra University and later chairman of the higher education council. Rao, a Fulbright scholar who had worked with leading institutions in the US, was brought in by NTR in 1984 to head Andhra University. 'Even though I had not met NTR before, we instantly took a liking to each other, and I soon became a principal advisor on education,' Rao recalled.[10] As vice chancellor, he initiated major reforms in the university administration, introduced several new academic programmes and worked to improve standards of research. NTR, after his return as chief minister in 1994, inducted Rao as head of the state planning board with the cabinet rank, 'a position few non-politically involved academics in India could dream of'.[11]

Dr Kakarla Subba Rao was an American citizen and an internationally renowned radiologist, whom NTR brought to the state after much persuasion to start a speciality hospital in the government sector. During his treatment in the US in 1984, NTR had noticed that many of the leading Indian doctors in the country were from his own state. Dr Kakarla, who was also the founder-president of the Telugu Association of North America (TANA), was one such medical personality. He was invited by the chief minister to do his bit for the country.[12] NIMS in Hyderabad was conceived and set up in December 1985 under Dr Kakarla's stewardship. The facility rose to be one of the premier super speciality hospitals in the country.

The appointment of retired judges Avula Sambasiva Rao and Challa Kondaiah as Lokayukta and chairman of the endowments commission respectively was also cited as a case of casteism. Justice Avula Sambasiva Rao had retired as chief justice of AP High Court by the time NTR came to power. He was well known for his progressive views and radical humanist philosophy. He was the vice chancellor of Andhra University when NTR chose him as the first Lokayukta of the state. As Lokayukta, Justice Sambasiva Rao was widely acclaimed for strengthening the new institution. He indicted three former ministers, and in the first two years of operation, managed to clear as many as 3800 of the 7000 complaints received. 'Despite the constraints, its [Lokayukta] track record has been impressive so far, something that its counterparts in eight other States cannot begin to match,' *India Today* complimented Justice Rao's contribution.[13]

Justice Challa Kondaiah was also a retired chief justice of the AP High Court, who was appointed as chairman of a commission to recommend reforms in Hindu religious endowments. Justice Kondaiah brought about radical changes in the administration and functioning of Hindu temples. His recommendation for divesting hereditary rights of priests in temples and allowing non-Brahmins to be temple priests made him an object of hatred in the priestly community.

The induction of another retired judge of the high court, Justice P.A. Chowdary, known for his landmark judgments, as the legal adviser to the state government ran into controversy with advocate general E. Manohar resigning in protest. A petition was also filed against Justice Chowdary's appointment, but the high court upheld the government decision.

The NTR government sought and obtained the services of several retired judges of the Supreme Court and high courts for various assignments, and all of them, except the above three, were from other communities. Justice Koka Ramachandra Rao, Justice P. Ramachandra Raju, Justice A. Gangadhara Rao, Justice A.D.V. Reddy and Justice T.L.N. Reddy headed various statutory commissions of inquiry. The services of judges from outside the state, such as Justice V.R. Krishna Iyer, former judge of the Supreme Court, Justice A.R. Desai and Justice R.N. Agarwal, were also requisitioned.

The continuation of Narla Tata Rao, known as the doyen of the power sector in the country, as chairman of the state electricity board, was criticized as another instance of favouritism, though Tata Rao was retained in his position after retirement even by the earlier Congress governments. Thumati Donappa, a professor of Telugu, who had done extensive research on literary contributions of Andhra kingdoms, was made the first vice chancellor of Telugu University. Many of these gentlemen enjoyed a distinguished record in their fields, though they all belonged to the same caste as the chief minister.

NTR craved people with integrity and intelligence and sought them without any prejudice. He had several others as advisers or in important posts who did not belong to his community. N. Devanathan, a chartered accountant and a Sanskrit pundit, was his adviser as well. C. Narayana Reddy, the well-known writer, held several important positions during NTR's time. E.V. Rami Reddy was specially chosen by NTR as Dharma Maha Matra. Prof T. Navaneeth Rao and Prof R.V.R. Chandrasekhara Rao, vice chancellors of Osmania University and Open University, were also NTR's choices. He picked Reddy Labs' K. Anji Reddy to advise on vocational education. He selected the banking sector expert O. Swaminatha Reddy as the head of the state financial corporation. Prof V.L.S. Bheemasankaram, a well-known geophysicist, was nominated as the chairman and managing director of the AP mineral development corporation.

P.V.R.K. Prasad, an IAS officer, recalled that he had informed NTR that he was inducting two officers on deputation in the culture department, who were Brahmins. The chief minister was quick to correct him. 'Brother, what do you mean? I don't have anything against Brahmins. If you have felt like that, I am sorry. What matters is efficiency. Please go ahead if you are confident.'[14]

Impressed by legal luminary Nani Palkhivala's erudition, NTR wanted to elevate him to the Rajya Sabha from the TDP. The eminent lawyer, however, could not accept the honour since he was not a resident of AP, a residency requirement rarely adhered to by politicians.

'He was constantly on the vigil to find the best men and women to head the universities. He never went by caste or other considerations in choosing the vice-chancellors,' Koneru Ramakrishna Rao said.[15] Rao recalled that when NTR wanted to appoint a Dalit to Jawaharlal Nehru Technological University, he wanted the best person in the country. A group set up for the purpose came up with the name of P. Dayarathnam, who had served earlier at IIT, Kanpur. 'No one knew where he was after retirement. We had a lot of difficulty in finding his address and getting his CV. He was appointed as the VC of JNTU,' Rao said.[16]

The composition of various cabinets under NTR could be a more accurate reflection of the caste bias or lack of it in his government. If the distribution of the ministries was any indication, clearly Kammas did not have the lion's share in the TDP's power structure in the early days. In fact, the number of Reddy ministers was consistently more than their Kamma counterparts in all NTR cabinets. The first ministry of NTR in 1983 had no Kammas except the two founders, NTR and Nadendla. But out of the fourteen ministers, as many as four belonged to the Reddy community. In 1984, NTR's second cabinet had only two Kammas besides himself, while the Reddys had six portfolios. By 1994, the Kammas had better representation with six of them in the ministry besides the chief minister, while the Reddys too had six cabinet members. Clearly, NTR, who was the sole arbiter of ministerial selections, did not make his cabinets Kamma-heavy.

Caste had been a significant factor in AP politics even before Independence. But since it was mostly one-party politics till 1983, the issue of a few castes cornering all political or administrative posts was not contested. However, after the TDP's arrival on the scene, those who had near monopoly in politics (Reddys) and in bureaucracy (Brahmins) acutely felt the rising profile of Kammas in these fields. The Reddys initially did not openly talk about caste bias, because they remained the alternative to the TDP to capture power. But the Brahmins, who were co-opted by the Reddys over time, came out publicly to target NTR and his party. Decisions like lowering retirement age, arming ACB to the teeth, the abolition of karanam posts, recasting the cultural establishment, removal of government laureates and banning hereditary priesthood were perceived as anti-Brahmin. This accumulated anger was the underlying factor behind Dronamraju Satyanarayana, the Congress (I) organizing secretary, mounting a legal attack against NTR.

The implementation of the Challa Kondaiah Commission report was widely seen as causing irreparable damage to the Brahmanical hold on Hindu temples and institutions. NTR's actions were anti-Brahmin in the DMK mould. Brahmins were numerically not as strong as other communities in AP. But their sociopolitical standing in Telugu society was disproportionate to their numbers. Many social and administrative structures were dominated by them. In the bureaucracy, from village officer to secretary in the administration, they were the undisputed leaders. In religious and spiritual matters, they enjoyed the last word. As NTR went about dismantling their sway, the Brahmins felt choked. The Congress had always been their political sanctuary.[17] They used all their points of influence such as the media to shape public opinion against NTR's alleged perversions.

The Reddy political leadership turned vociferous in pointing out NTR's perceived caste bias in the TDP government. The Kapus later joined the Congress chorus in tossing allegations of caste chauvinism against the government.[18] Many senior TDP leaders who fell out with NTR complained of caste bias in the party. Leaders such as Srinivasulu Reddy and Mudragada Padmanabham, who had held important positions in his government, imputed caste motives to NTR's various actions.[19] Along with Vangaveeti Mohana Ranga, Mudragada emerged as the leader of the Kapu community on the plank of opposing alleged Kamma-dominated TDP policies. Aided by the Congress, they were successful in projecting NTR as anti-Kapu.[20] The SC leaders of the Congress too dubbed the NTR government anti-Dalit. The Karamchedu killings and other incidents of caste carnage had already stained the party's standing. In this scenario, the detractors increasingly found the TDP's Kamma association a soft spot for censure.

While political motives were undoubtedly the immediate cause for these imputations, elements of casteism in the government did lend credence to the propaganda.

Since NTR was the first Kamma chief minister, politicians and bureaucrats from the caste had better access to power corridors. The hold enjoyed by NTR's sons-in-law, Chandrababu Naidu in particular, on the administration also contributed to the perception of Kamma bias. There were certainly many Kammas at the helm during this time as compared to the past. While caste preference was nearly absent in the early period of the TDP, the same could not be said as the years passed by. NTR himself had an eclectic approach and rarely did caste considerations sway him. He was aware of the criticism and asserted in 1984, 'To start a Kamma Raj I need not have sacrificed everything and come here.'[21]

While the earlier regimes were heavily Reddy and Brahmin dominated, it never became an issue because of the single-party rule. The moment the TDP emerged, the Kamma dominance came under intense scrutiny by the erstwhile power holders. The Congress party's political strategy to project the TDP as a Kamma party in a bid to wean away various sections also contributed to the caste-branding. The message was drilled so hard and non-stop that it was the first time in AP that the ruling party's caste bias was debated so brazenly.

Interestingly, many important Kamma leaders continued to sail with the Congress even at the height of the TDP's power. N.G. Ranga (later Rayapati Sambasiva Rao) and Kavuri Sambasiva Rao were Congress MPs from Guntur and West Godavari Districts who actively resisted the TDP dominance. Maganti Ravindranath Chowdary, Pinnamaneni Koteswara Rao and Alapati Dharma Rao were all Kammas who opposed the TDP in the Kamma heartland.

The role played by several Congressmen was one of the reasons for caste becoming an exacerbating factor during NTR's period. Punjala Shiv Shankar was one such leader, a man Friday to Rajiv Gandhi, who used all his power at the Centre to put the NTR

government to discomfiture. Despite his defeat in Medak, Shiv
Shankar was made a member of the Rajya Sabha from Gujarat
by Rajiv, who entrusted him with various important jobs. Shiv
Shankar, along with other Congress leaders, played a crucial role
in reconfiguring caste equations and inflaming caste conflicts to
weaken the TDP stranglehold and turn different caste groups
against its administration.[22]

Judicial Attack by Congress

The Congress employed every trick in the book and some more
to weaken NTR and topple his government. The constitutional
coup in 1984 was the first attempt. Later, riding on various
controversial issues such as lowering the retirement age, the
Karamchedu incident and reservations for BCs, it did everything
possible to undermine the TDP government. It tapped into the
discontent among different sections of the society and mobilized
various caste groups against NTR's alleged anti-people policies.
Their last weapon was the judicial ambush.

Thus came the infamous writ petition by Dronamraju
Satyanarayana, who was the then organizing secretary of the
Congress (I) committee for coastal districts of AP. A Congress
MP and MLA in the past, Dronamraju, born into a family of
karanams, typified the anti-TDP segments in society that abhorred
NTR and his government. An out-and-out Congressman,
Dronamraju was known for his uncanny political sense. He filed
four writ petitions in the high court in August 1987, alleging
various violations of laws and constitutional provisions by NTR.
His lawyer, Sriramagiri Ramachandra Rao, who hailed from the
same social background as Dronamraju, and was known for his
tenacity and resourcefulness, gave NTR a hard fight in court.

A common affidavit running into 193 pages was filed
in support of the relief sought through four writ petitions—
essentially praying for NTR's removal as chief minister. The

petitioner sought a writ of quo warranto against NTR, declaring that he was a usurper of the office of chief minister. He sought a writ of mandamus directing the Central government to appoint a judicial commission for inquiring into the misdeeds of 'corruption and abuse of authority'. In another writ, the petitioner sought a direction to the Centre for the chief minister's prosecution for violations under the income tax, wealth tax and foreign exchange regulation. The fourth writ prayed for directing the Centre to exercise its constitutional power to consider imposing President's Rule in the state.

Even before the court took up the matter, a rattled NTR chose to answer the people on the allegations. He placed on the floor of the assembly his rebuttal to all the accusations in the affidavit. The ninety-seven-page statement carried the allegations and denials in brief, while two volumes of 487 pages, distributed along with it, contained supporting government orders.

Such a recourse to courts for a chief minister's dismissal was unprecedented. 'Never has a high court been moved, or allowed petitions, demanding a chief minister's removal and the imposition of President's rule in a State,' *India Today* remarked.[23] NTR chose no less than the veteran constitutional lawyer Nani Palkhivala to defend him at the admission stage. Besides questioning the locus standi of the petitioner, Palkhivala cautioned that the court must not allow its process to be abused by politicians and others to gain a political objective. Calling the petition 'a political interest litigation', the well-known jurist also apprehended that the 'court will have to encroach upon the spheres reserved for the legislature and the executive' to grant the relief prayed for by the petitioner.

The bench, describing that several of the allegations in the petition were 'grave', averred, 'A writ petition containing serious allegations touching upon matters of great public importance cannot be thrown out on the short ground that it is filed by a political rival and for political considerations.' The bench concluded that the petitioner, even though a Congress politician, had locus standi, and the issues raised were justiciable.

'This is one of the extraordinary cases without any parallel,' the bench remarked, even as it admitted two out of the four petitions—seeking a writ of mandamus for the appointment of the commission of inquiry and another seeking direction to the Central government to prosecute NTR for fiscal offences. Because of the importance of the complex questions of law raised, a larger bench of five judges—Chief Justice K. Bhaskaran, Justices K. Ramaswamy, M.N. Rao, Y. Bhasker Rao and A. Venkatrami Reddi—was constituted to look into the case.

But before throwing out two writ petitions out of the four, the court made some unusually harsh remarks against NTR. Rejecting the plea for a writ of quo warranto to remove NTR, Chief Justice Bhaskaran observed, 'It is for the chief minister himself to make up his mind regarding the path he should follow in the face of the allegations. No gratuitous advice, much less specific direction, from this court is necessary.'[24] The court's observations were enough reproof for the Opposition, especially the Congress, to demand NTR's resignation. But NTR refused to yield.

The hearings in the remaining two writ petitions were intensely followed by the public as NTR's fate seemed to hang on the outcome of the verdict. The affidavit, prepared meticulously by S. Ramachandra Rao, contained an exhaustive list of allegations against NTR. It included economic crimes, corruption, political patronage, misappropriation of public funds, the breakdown of constitutional machinery, killing of extremists in fake encounters, deaths in police lock-up and instances of strictures passed by courts against NTR. By any standard, it was a comprehensive, sweeping and thorough listing of NTR and his government's alleged infractions since 1983.

NTR's lawyer for the hearings before the larger bench was the renowned legal eagle Ram Jethmalani, who argued that personal rights could not be enforced in the garb of public interest litigation. Calling the petition 'a perplexing misjoinder of disparate complaints, grievances and alleged causes of action',[25] he submitted that in the process of correcting executive errors, the court should not enter into the political arena on policy decisions which were, by the Constitution, exclusively vested in the executive. He added that the court must guard itself against interfering in respect of executive and statutory orders without affording the opportunity to the parties likely to be affected.

Attorney General K. Parasaran, the well-known legal luminary, was called in by the court to act as amicus curiae to help the bench because of the complex issues involved. Parasaran, who was sympathetic to the Congress cause, said that in a public interest litigation, the jurisdiction of the court was not adversarial but inquisitorial. 'What is required is the necessary factual material,' he opined.[26] The counsel for the petitioner, Ramachandra Rao, pleaded that the common man's sense of justice should not be allowed to be shattered by placing primacy on procedural aspects.

The court, stating that the writ petition on scrutiny did not answer the description of political questions, then chose some of the allegations in the affidavit for critical examination. And to the ruling party's chagrin, the AP High Court found there was enough material on record to enter prima facie findings. The hearings that went on for nearly two months gripped the attention of the people of the state. NTR's actions were discussed and argued threadbare in the court and reported widely in the media. The court finally delivered its judgment on 2 January 1988. It found prima facie evidence that NTR had abused his position on five counts. The action of the state government on two other charges was considered arbitrary and illegal.[27]

The first charge of abuse of official position related to the choice of a co-promoter for making electronic cordless telephone instruments. The court concluded that the process of selection was manoeuvred to confer a benefit on NTR's youngest son-in-law Naren Rajan. The co-promoter was initially KCP Ltd, but later L'Avenir Telecoms Ltd, owned by Naren Rajan, came into the picture in a manner that was 'shrouded in mystery'. Rajan was married to NTR's youngest daughter Uma Maheswari. The court found that KCP Ltd, which had all the requisite qualifications to be a partner, was used to clandestinely award the project to Rajan. 'We, therefore, consider that the material available on record warrants prima facie finding that in securing the advantages to his son-in-law Sri Naren Rajan, the first respondent abused his power as chief minister,' the court said.[28]

The second charge related to Ramakrishna Studios at Musheerabad. This was a complicated matter that had been under scrutiny by the Opposition since 1983. NTR had purchased land in 1975 measuring 8000 square yards in Musheerabad near Golconda crossroads in the heart of the twin cities of Hyderabad and Secunderabad to construct Ramakrishna Studios. Around the same time, he applied for purchasing 1200 square yards of government land situated next to his own site. Since Musheerabad had been declared a residential zone, he asked for zonal relaxation for building a film studio, which was permitted. The government also ordered allotment of 1200 square yards of adjacent land at the rate of Rs 40 per square yard.

As soon as the TDP came into power, the government approved changing the use of the land into 'local commercial use' for building cinema theatres, etc. The agreed rate of Rs 40 per square yard for the assigned land was slashed to Rs 15 per square yard. The court questioned how the rate of land which was Rs 40 per square yard in 1976 could have gone down years later in 1983. The court also found the change in classification of Ramakrishna Studios land from industrial use to commercial use indicative of abuse of official position.

The exemption of the land at Nacharam Ramakrishna Horticulture Studio from the Urban Land (Ceiling and Regulation) Act, 1976, was another issue in which NTR's family, according to the court, had benefited. The bench found that even after Ramakrishna Studios ceased to be a film production centre, the exemption granted under the land ceiling act was not withdrawn.

The exemption from entertainment tax of Rs 1.57 lakh, granted to the cinemas owned by NTR's sons, was also found irregular by the court. NTR's family owned Ramakrishna 70 mm, Ramakrishna 35 mm and Tarakarama cinema theatres in Hyderabad.[29] There was a provision for exemption from tax during natural calamities, national disasters, breakdown in law and order, etc. The court, however, said that the applications for exemption were made after the period of limitation.

Naren Rajan figured in another charge. Loans were granted to him among others to set up mini steel plants although loans for such units were banned by the Industrial Development Bank of India (IDBI). The government suspended the ban, invited applications and granted financial assistance to the tune of Rs 75 lakh to each applicant. The process showed prima facie that power had been abused by the first respondent, the judgment said.

Rajan hailed from a Kamma business family based out of Coimbatore in Tamil Nadu. It seemed he had given a great deal of trouble to NTR, even in personal matters. He and Uma Maheswari had marital issues very early on. Later, she obtained a divorce from him. But before that, Rajan figured in another sensational case, where he abducted the daughter of a Hyderabad-based lady, Uma Reddy, claiming that he was the child's biological father. Uma Reddy approached the Supreme Court, which restored her daughter to her. NTR's lawyer Jasti Chelameswar and senior cop V. Appa Rao were present in Delhi to ensure the chief minister's name was not dragged into the unsavoury issue. Uma Maheswari's divorce proceedings had already been moved by that time, and hence few suspected that NTR had any interest in protecting Rajan.

The high court, however, dismissed the two writ petitions seeking direction to the Central government to act against NTR for the alleged violations of various financial acts and to appoint a commission of inquiry to look into his misdeeds. The court recorded its prima facie findings concerning seven allegations and said it had 'chosen to adopt this course in view of the fact that the persons who are likely to be affected by final orders, if any passed by us, are not before us'.[30]

Establishing prima facie guilt based on preliminary material even while dismissing the petitions appeared strange to many observers. 'The judgment was unusual and the haste with which it was delivered even more so,' *India Today* remarked.[31] Upendra wondered at the speed with which the case was handled. 'The court has passed its order based on the material supplied by the petitioner and a sketchy counter-affidavit—given only for the purpose of denying the allegations—with extraordinary efficiency. This is not normal for our courts,' he said.[32] Conspiracy theories also floated suggesting a link between a special leave petition in the Supreme Court over Chief Justice Bhaskaran's age and the NTR case heard by his bench. Union Law Minister Shiv Shankar reportedly helped Bhaskaran in the matter of his birth records, and the latter allegedly paid back his debt by putting NTR in the dock.

Since NTR had emerged as a national leader by then, the case created unease among the federal parties. Opposition MPs questioned the unusual haste displayed in delivering the judgment. 'The oddities of the case are so many as to create disquiet,'[33] remarked Arun Nehru, Arif Mohammad Khan, Satyapal Malik (Jan Morcha) and K.P. Unnikrishnan (Congress [S]). In a stinging editorial, the *Indian Express* castigated the high court for performing the incredible feat of rejecting the plea before it and yet keeping it open in a disguised form by a colourable exercise of judicial power. 'The chief minister's conduct, to adjudicate which a commission of inquiry was sought and rejected, has already been pronounced on. It is a patent injustice,' the paper said.[34] The court coming to conclusions without giving the parties involved an opportunity to defend themselves was indeed strange.

The high court ruling finding NTR prima facie guilty of abuse of official position was politically combustive material. The Congress demanded that NTR step down immediately. But, more importantly, the disclosures made during the hearings, which showed NTR in the most unflattering manner, caused damage to his reputation. For example, it was claimed that NTR had declared unaccounted income under the Voluntary Disclosure of Income Scheme in 1975, showing that he had accepted black money during his film career. Hence, he was described in the petition as 'a self-confessed criminal', though he was immune from prosecution. NTR did not commit any felony, but the court spent considerable time on this matter.

Many such allegations raised in the affidavit lacked substance and the court didn't get into them. But the exaggerated details presented in the petition painted a tainted picture of NTR to the general public. The Congress (I) later nominated Dronamraju, who inflicted maximum damage to NTR's image, to the Rajya Sabha.

The case was freely used to throw mud at NTR's character, though the court's prima facie findings lacked legal rigour. For example, NTR did not obtain land from the government for his film studio. On the other hand, his counterparts in the industry, ANR and Krishna, got land parcels at a nominal price from the government. NTR chose to buy land in the open market. He did not expect any concessions or incentives for his film theatres either. He built them all on his own. A deeply upset NTR appealed in the Supreme Court against the strictures. The case, however, got stuck in the apex court for a long time and was closed following NTR's demise.

The Congress and other Opposition parties raised the pitch in demanding NTR's resignation. NTR refused to budge. His response was to organize a massive bash to mark the fifth anniversary of his government in 1988. Hundreds of thousands of people attended the celebration at Hyderabad Exhibition

Grounds, with national Opposition leaders gracing the occasion. For NTR, his popularity was enough of an affirmation of the legitimacy of his rule. 'The people are with me. Why should I resign?' he questioned rhetorically.

NTR's brush with the judiciary throughout his tenure was bitter. At times, the face-off between the executive and the judiciary threatened to snowball into a major constitutional crisis.

Almost every critical decision of the TDP government was challenged in the courts. While the courts struck off a few like the BC reservation law, others like the abolition of hereditary rights of priests were stuck in appeals for years. By the time of the Dronamraju petition, NTR's government was at the receiving end of strictures passed by the courts in issue after issue. In more than sixty cases, the courts made critical comments on the NTR government. Most of the cases were politically targeted, and nearly all of them were filed by Congress leaders and activists. Writs and appeals, at least a couple of hundred, were filed against NTR by the end of 1989.[35]

NTR expressed anguish at the judicial intervention, which resulted in halting various programmes of the government. 'No wonder, the lady is blindfolded,' said an exasperated NTR referring to the image of the Lady of Justice. 'So many cases are pending in courts, and the inordinate delay is causing strain on the State. The system is moving at snail's pace,' he bemoaned.[36] To overcome the issue, he proposed a law academy to effectively argue cases on behalf of the government.

Expressing his unhappiness, NTR sought to dub the verdicts as being against people's interests.[37] 'These verdicts are not against NTR but against six crore Telugus,' he said. Soon after the court strictures in the Dronamraju petition, NTR, while participating in a meeting of Opposition leaders on the fifth anniversary of the Janata government in Bangalore, demanded that states should have a say in the appointment of high court judges. While clarifying that it was not his intention to interfere in judicial institutions,

NTR said it was his view that the opinion of the states should carry some weight in these appointments.

The Opposition Congress had opened several fronts against the TDP government by this time. NTR proved equally adept at countering them with a dramatic response. What came to be known as NTR's theatrical acts were targeted at stealing the wind out of the sails of his detractors. As the Congress and the Centre tried to embarrass the chief minister, he turned the tide in his favour through apparently farcical actions.

The most famous of NTR's histrionics was his dramatic sit-in in the middle of the road outside the secretariat. The Congress was trying to derive political mileage by raising the Rayalaseema[38] issue at the time. As a climax to the agitation, the Congress leaders wanted to organize a dharna at the secretariat before handing over a representation to the chief minister. The Opposition Congress had planned to create a ruckus within the secretariat during their meeting with the chief minister. The cops had prior information

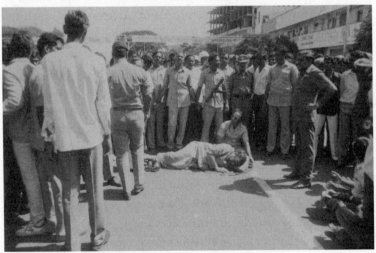

Photograph courtesy of C. Kesavulu, Eenadu

NTR was always a step ahead in countering the Opposition Congress party's tactics. Here, he is seen lying in the middle of the road opposite the government secretariat when Congress leaders wanted to gatecrash the CM's chambers.

about such a possibility. The officials decided that the chief minister would receive the representation at the secretariat gate itself to prevent large crowds inside. It was 1 November 1988, the AP Formation Day. After unveiling the statues of prominent Telugus installed on Tank Bund, NTR proceeded to the secretariat. But the belligerent Congress leaders demanded to be allowed to hand over the memorandum at the chief minister's chambers. On refusal, the MLAs, leaders and workers of the Congress, numbering a few thousand, tried to gherao NTR. Even the cops were helpless as they had not anticipated such a situation.

The ever-resourceful NTR was not to be outdone. Furious at being surrounded, he came out of the car and to everyone's surprise, squatted on the road. The Congress leaders, as well as the cops, were taken aback at this unexpected act. He sat tight amid slogans by the Congress agitators. After some time, he spread his kanduva on the road and pretended to take a nap in the hot sun. The farce went on for quite some time. After a while, even the protestors got tired. The chief minister abruptly got up, walked up to the place where the Congress leaders had assembled, snatched the memorandum from one of them and left in his car. Crestfallen, the Opposition leaders had no option but to leave, raising slogans against the chief minister.

The brief bonhomie between Rajiv and NTR waned after the 1984 Parliament elections. Egged on by his partymen, the prime minister caused much disquiet to NTR. He often visited AP without prior information and addressed press conferences criticizing the state government. NTR reacted equally strongly to Rajiv's barbs. After Rajiv's visit to drought-affected areas in the state, NTR rapped the prime minister. 'He was racing in a jeep with Sonia Gandhi on one side and Governor Kumudben Joshi on another, cruising at 100 km speed, stopping wherever Congress flags were waved. Is this the way to visit the affected people?' he questioned.[39] Relations remained sour between the two throughout.

The Murder that Shook Vijayawada

The murder of Congress MLA Vangaveeti Mohana Ranga Rao, known simply as Ranga, at the fag end of 1988 was a dark chapter in the TDP rule. NTR failed to grasp the calculated caste mobilization being actively pursued by the desperate Congress to wean away certain castes from the TDP and Ranga's crucial place in this scheme of things. He did sense that the main Opposition was trying to stoke caste embers in the state, as he spoke about the conspiracy of the Congress to topple his government through caste divisions. However, he failed to take adequate steps to tackle the looming threat, leading to a caste conflagration that would cost both NTR and the TDP government dearly.

Given his humble origins, Vangaveeti Mohana Ranga Rao had a chequered history. Krishna District, in which Vijayawada is located, was dominated by Kammas with better economic and social standing, while the Kapus were numerically strong. Till 1983, the clout of Ranga, a Kapu, was limited to Vijayawada, and he was mostly treated as a minor gangster. His rise as a caste and political leader subsequently coincided with the TDP's emergence. The caste equations underwent a dramatic change in the city as the Congress and TDP played polarized politics.

By 1985, Ranga became an MLA from Vijayawada. He was projected as a Kapu leader with encouragement from several Congress leaders, including P. Shiv Shankar and Y.S. Rajasekhara Reddy. The frail-looking don emerged as the unlikely champion of the underprivileged. He projected himself as the face of resistance against the perceived Kamma domination in the city. As the TDP became a powerful political force in the late 1980s, the Kapu vs Kamma tug of war turned into a frightening reality in Vijayawada. The development was mainly because of the growing hostility between Ranga and Devineni Rajasekhar, alias Nehru, another ringleader-turned-TDP-MLA; also a Kamma.

But Ranga's history did not begin as a chronicle of caste confrontation. His wife, Chennupati Ratnakumari, was a Kamma. Ranga's brother, Radhakrishna Murthy, known as Radha, came to Vijayawada from West Godavari in the 1960s to make a living. Radha became an aide of Chalasani Venkataratnam, a city CPI leader, who ran local transport unions. Radha worked as a taxi driver, while Ranga was a cycle mechanic. The city was growing during this time as a trading and transportation hub. There was money to be made in controlling the unions. The CPI, which once had a powerful presence in Vijayawada, having sent poet Harindranath Chattopadhyay as MP to the Lok Sabha in 1952, was now reduced to leading labour unions. When Radha wanted to strike out on his own in the union politics of the booming transport business, he fell out with Venkataratnam in 1969 and launched his shady private enterprise. Venkataratnam was later eliminated in 1972, and Radha became dominant in the underbelly of the city.

At this point of time, Devineni Chandrasekhar, alias Gandhi, was working with Radha and his gang. Gandhi came out of the shadow of Venkataratnam along with Radha. Caste was not an issue at this time, though both Venkataratnam and Gandhi were Kammas. Radha and Gandhi began organizing auto drivers, rickshaw pullers and daily wage earners. They also started a students' organization called United Independents and used them for their nefarious, mostly 'collection', activities. Later, Gandhi, along with brothers Devineni Nehru and Murali, separated from Radha and floated another outfit, United Students Organization. These so-called students' organizations were nothing but a cover for extortion, mostly in the form of protection money. For some time, both the gangs appeared to have avoided any mutual confrontation. They made use of muscle power and intimidation to carve out their respective territories in the city.

Not long after, in 1974, Radha had to pay for Venkataratnam's murder. He was hacked to death in an auto shed, allegedly by communist supporters. That was when his brother Ranga took over the family 'business'. Ranga proved to be more street-smart and quickly rose to become a celebrated 'rowdy'. Having built his little empire of crime, he took it upon himself to eliminate the competition. In 1979, Devineni Gandhi was stabbed to death, allegedly by Ranga's henchmen, in an ambush while escaping into the compound of Andhra Loyola College. Gandhi's brother, Devineni Nehru, now took over the reins. Nehru's fortunes took a dramatic turn when he got a ticket from the newly established TDP to contest from Kankipadu on the outskirts of Vijayawada in 1983. Nehru became an MLA.

In the meantime, Ranga made an effort to make his political debut. He succeeded in 1981 when he won as a municipal councillor from Krishna Lanka, an urban slum. In 1985, he contested assembly elections on a Congress ticket and was one of the few candidates who overcame the NTR onslaught. He became a loud voice against the ruling party in the city. The police's high-handedness in the city during this period was much resented, especially by the poor and the working class. Ranga emerged as a Robin Hood by standing up to the cops.

Though he was jailed several times for his alleged role in various criminal acts, including murders, Ranga's image continued to be in the ascendant. The more cases that were slapped on him, the more popular he became. Gradually, he transformed into a hardcore politician and began cultivating the image of a Kapu leader. That made him politically more valuable for the Congress. He was considered the right material to take on the TDP. His increasing clout was evident when Congress leaders in coastal districts relied on his image for party gatherings.

The city politics now revolved around Ranga and his fight against the Kamma-dominated TDP. But not everyone in the Congress liked him. Jalagam Vengala Rao, who was the state Congress president at the time, was against a hoodlum playing an important role in the party. Gokaraju Subbaraju, popularly known as Siri's Raju, after his company South India Research Institute

(SIRI) Private Ltd, had a similar opinion. He was the city Congress president who resented Ranga's show of muscle power in the party. He complained to the party leadership that Andhra Ratna Bhavan (the Vijayawada city Congress office) had turned into a den of antisocial elements. Ranga was barred from entering the Congress office by Vengala Rao. Ranga took up cudgels with both and organized meetings deriding Jalagam's leadership, who in turn suspended him along with his followers from the party. Ranga's defiance of the leadership emanated from the mass following he enjoyed as well as from the increasing support of a large section of Kapus in the coastal districts. He also had the backing of Shiv Shankar and Y.S. Rajasekhara Reddy. His position remained unassailable in local politics.

In the other camp, though Nehru was the MLA, it was his younger brother Murali who emerged as the belligerent one. The Ranga group saw him as a threat. Devineni Murali and his friends were ambushed in March 1988 at Edlapadu in Guntur District when they were returning from Nellore in a van. He, along with four of his companions, was brutally killed after a dramatic chase. Ranga was the prime suspect in the case. He was arrested and jailed though he claimed he was in Delhi at the time of the incident, undergoing treatment at Ram Manohar Lohia Hospital. But Ranga thought it wise to surrender to the police back home rather than expose himself to retaliatory attacks. Reportedly, an attempt was already made on him in Delhi. As Ranga was taken into custody, personal rivalries assumed political connotations. The turf war now turned into a caste confrontation. A massive rally of Kapus was organized in Guntur in support of Ranga while he was in jail. Congress Kapu leaders, such as P. Shiv Shankar who was the Union minister then, were actively pushing the caste agenda.

Ranga came out on bail soon, but he had reason to believe that he would be an easy target for the Nehru group, given that the TDP was the ruling party. He was in hiding for some time and sought police protection. Meanwhile, the Kapu sentiment was being consolidated by the Congress against the TDP. The fault lines had already formed. Kapu caste gatherings were being regularly organized. The atmosphere in Godavari, Krishna and Guntur Districts, which had large Kapu populations, became charged, with Kapu leaders threatening to pull down the NTR government if Ranga was harmed.

The uneasiness among Ranga and his followers—and other Kapu leaders—over possible retaliation for Murali's killing was not without basis. The situation was beyond NTR's control as local rivalries had reached a point of no return. It was perhaps naive on Ranga's part to have thought that the Devineni family could be checked by applying political pressure on the TDP government. Since Murali's killing, the air was thick with rumours of revenge.

The worst fears of Kapus and Ranga's followers did not take long to come true. Eight months after Murali's murder, in the early hours of 26 December 1988, Ranga, at the age of forty-two, was bludgeoned to death. He was at the time sitting on a dharna near Raghavaiah Park at Nirmala Hrudaya Bhavan, opposite his residence, protesting, among other things, against police high-handedness. The attack on the hunger strike camp was carried out by two busloads of assailants draped in black attire, traditionally worn by Lord Ayyappa devotees for the Sabarimala pilgrimage. They threw smoke bombs and in the ensuing melee attacked Ranga with knives, axes and spears and killed him along with two others at about 3.20 a.m.

As the news of the murders spread, the state went into violent convulsions. The resulting mayhem was unprecedented in the annals of AP history. A one-sided caste war broke out in many parts of the state as Kapus saw the killing of Ranga as an offensive against their community. In a fit of uncontrolled rage, mobs targeted Kammas, causing enormous damage. Vijayawada was in flames, as scores of shops and establishments owned by Kammas were looted and torched. Targeted attacks were carried out against Kamma businesses and houses. Public property including RTC buses were burnt to ashes in several places in coastal areas, more so in Godavari District. *India Today* wrote:

> On the morning of December 26, the State woke up to the unholy cries of murder and revenge and within minutes the districts—East and West Godavari, Krishna and Guntur—were convulsed by riots.[40]

Paramilitary forces were called in to contain the rioting mobs even as more than two dozen people were killed in police firings in a single day, most of them in Krishna District.[41] Hundreds were grievously injured in the riotous attacks. The city burnt for days together, and the property losses were estimated variously as between Rs 200 and 300 crore. Around 400 RTC buses were reduced to rubble across the state, while a thousand were damaged. The continued instigation by political leaders ensured that incidents of arson and looting continued in Vijayawada even after fifty platoons of police forces were deployed.

Kamma houses, shops and properties were identified for arson and looting. Residential areas such as Mogalrajapuram, Krishna Lanka and Gunadala, and commercial shopping areas such as Eluru Road, Prakasam Road, Bandar Road, Ring Road and Besant Road were mainly targeted. The Vijayawada Super Bazaar faced plunder to the tune of Rs 70 lakh. A popular textile shop owned by TDP legislator Ravi Sobhanadi Chowdary in neighbouring Gudivada suffered a loss of Rs 2 crore due to daylight burglary. Many cinema theatres, including Durga Kala Mandiram, Annapurna, Sakunthala and Apsara, were damaged beyond recognition. Besant Road in the shopping district with its line-up of showrooms such as Roopam's, Manohar Prince, Maharani Textiles and Kamadhenu was ravaged. The images of the burning theatres, such as Alankar, Kalyana Chakravarthy and Jai Hind, the smouldering Roy Tyres, the shattered Peacock Bar and Restaurant, and the ransacked Mangaldeep and Raymond's showrooms remained etched in the minds of the people. Curfew was imposed in the city off and on for more than a month amid continuing attacks. *The Hindu* recalled the aftermath of the gory scenes, 'The poisonous effluvium emanating from the fire engulfed the city for several months and the nostrils inhaled harmful gases.'[42]

During the frenzied attacks, the miscreants killed Dr Uppalapati Srihari, a medical doctor. He was known to have stood up to some lumpen followers of Ranga in the past. The occasion was used to settle scores. Dr Srihari was a friend of the director general of police (DGP) P.S. Ramamohan Rao who had called him just a while ago from Hyderabad to find out the ground situation in Vijayawada. Rao recalled he had offered to arrange protection for him and his family, but tragically Dr Srihari had said it was not necessary.

The police utterly failed to contain the violence immediately after the dastardly act. The police top brass claimed the sudden flare-up caught them unawares and that it took time before forces could be mobilized to quell the rioting. The cops were outnumbered and ill-prepared for the fallout of the killing. Dora recalled that DGP P.S. Ramamohan Rao sat in the police control room in Hyderabad and gave instructions to the police—the first time such a thing happened. However, victims recalled that the police did not arrive on the streets to stop the rioters and arsonists as they went on a rampage for at least five hours. DGP Rao felt that 'the strong political overtones of the murder inhibited normal responses from field police'.[43] A report in *Andhra Patrika* stated:

> Police presence in the city was almost nil during the looting. The rioters had a field day for hours together. Violence and vandalism were everywhere. There was no power in many parts. Telephones did not work. People were stuck in different places and had no clue what was happening. The entire city was full of billowing smoke and raging fires. The miscreants swarmed wine shops, drank as much as they wanted and destroyed the remaining stock.[44]

That the violence was not as spontaneous as it was portrayed was evident from the targets that were chosen. 'There was clear evidence of prior planning in the violence,' the DGP said. He explained:

> Fire tenders were first immobilized by deflating tyres. Police stations were put under 'siege' by attacking them, with sufficient numbers of agitators, at each place. Repeated attacks were mounted on targets, identified with the ruling party.[45]

While most cinema theatres in Vijayawada were torched during this period, Raj-Yuvaraj, theatres belonging to the Y.S. family, were not touched. Kalyana Chakravarthy, a theatre belonging to NTR's brother Trivikrama Rao, was burnt to ashes. *Eenadu*'s was the only newspaper building that was attacked. The long campaign against Kammas and the TDP by the Congress and Kapu groups seemed to have had its effect. It was unlikely that the violence against the Kammas and TDP activists would have reached such intensity in the absence of such a campaign, said D. Parthasarathy in his doctoral thesis on Vijayawada violence.[46] The role played by 'the organised rioting engineered by Congressmen and Ranga's henchmen' was no less.[47] The political motive to further accentuate the caste divide and the Congress's intention to destabilize the TDP government by hook or by crook were factors in the incitement to lawlessness.

The looting and arson could partly be attributed to the pent-up anger of the lower-income classes. The police brazenness against ordinary people before the murder was rampant. Kapus, who were mostly working class, faced this harsh behaviour daily. The Kammas were relatively well-to-do in the city, and this class divide was another reason for the attacks on people who were unrelated to the incident.

NTR was unnerved by the murder and its gory aftermath. The chief minister quickly got into action to bring the situation under control. But the inconvenient fact that both the home minister, Dr Kodela Siva Prasada Rao, and the DGP, P.S. Ramamohan Rao, belonged to the Kamma caste did not provide good optics in this scenario. NTR pulled Kodela out of the home portfolio and transferred Ramamohan Rao. He had already ordered the prime suspect, Devineni Nehru, to surrender to the police.

Despite the overwhelming sentiment against the TDP among Ranga supporters, NTR dared to visit Ranga's house in Vijayawada to console his grieving widow, Ratnakumari. However, at the residence, he was booed and not allowed to meet the widow by Ranga's highly charged followers.

The Congress was unabashed in making political capital out of Ranga's murder. The party saw the first major crack in the TDP's political armour. Leader after leader from Delhi and Hyderabad visited Vijayawada to squeeze the last ounce out of the horrid situation by making provocative statements. A bandh was called to protest the government's alleged role in the killing. The funeral was delayed, enabling Union Ministers Sheila Dikshit and Mohsina Kidwai besides Congress (I) General Secretaries Ghulam Nabi Azad, Jagannath Pahadia, and treasurer Sitaram Kesari to fly down to Vijayawada. Leaders such as the Union human resources minister, P. Shiv Shankar, the state Congress president, N. Janardhana Reddy, and the Rayalaseema strongman Y.S. Rajasekhara Reddy delivered vitriolic speeches against the TDP government.

The then DGP recalled that Shiv Shankar's 'conduct during those difficult days, fell far short of the standards of dignity and decorum expected of such highly placed and responsible persons'.[48] Abetted by the Congress, Ratnakumari sat on a fast at the same spot where Ranga was killed, demanding a CBI inquiry into the murder. The venue of the fast became a political pilgrimage centre for Congress leaders who tried to inflame passions around the issue. As a counter to the Congress's attempts to impart political colour to the incidents, the TDP brought national leaders of non-Congress parties. L.K. Advani, Madhu Dandavate, Mufti Mohammad Sayeed, Amal Datta, Dinesh Goswami and Jaipal Reddy visited Vijayawada and surrounding areas. They condemned Ranga's murder and the caste-based violence that followed. The non-Congress parties in the state, including the Janata, BJP and CPI (M), condemned the Congress's attempt at drawing political mileage out of the murder. The Editors Guild of India sent a team, comprising Kuldip Nayar, S. Sahay, K.R. Malkani and N.S. Jagannathan, to visit the ravaged town and assess the situation. After the visit, Malkani likened the scenes in Vijayawada to 'one of those in the partition days'.[49]

The Ranga episode remains a blot on NTR's political career. He was certainly not the one who had created the conditions for the rise of gangsters in politics. But his folly was to give political legitimacy to the Nehru group in his eagerness to take on the Ranga gang. This move was used to the hilt by the Congress which gave political colour to what was mainly a turf war between two rival mobsters. NTR shared the blame with the Congress for giving cover to such elements. The TDP acted like a mirror image of the Congress, proving, in the words of Balagopal, that, '. . . the street gangs can be appropriated and adorned with the hallowed symbols of Parliamentary democracy: hoodlums become legislators, their gang fights become political battles, their murder becomes national news, and in their death they become martyrs in the cause of socialism, national integrity or Telugu pride'.[50]

For the TDP, the Ranga murder threw up one of the most challenging situations the party faced during NTR's second term. The political and caste turns the incident took exasperated NTR at a time when he was preparing to play a crucial role in national politics as the National Front chairman. The unchecked violence eroded trust in the ability of his government to ensure law and order.

The role of NTR and the TDP in the murder continues to be an acrimonious topic to this day. No evidence has been unearthed till date that connects NTR to this incident. But allegations that the TDP government facilitated the killing through its acts of omission and commission got stuck, especially among Kapus. Chegondi Hararama Jogaiah, a Kapu, wrote in 2015 that a few partymen had approached NTR with their plans to eliminate Ranga, but the latter had snubbed them.[51] But the role of local TDP leaders in the attack, specifically the Devineni family, was public knowledge.[52] There were also rumours that local Congress leaders opposed to Ranga were involved in the killing.

Over the years, the courts did not convict a single person for any of the murders committed during the gang wars in Vijayawada. From Chalasani Venkataratnam, Vangaveeti Radha, Devineni Gandhi to Devineni Murali, every homicide was dismissed for lack of evidence. The Ranga murder did not see a different outcome. All the forty-four charged, including the prime accused, Devineni Nehru, in the CBI case were acquitted in the judgment delivered in 2002. Incidentally, Ranga's wife, Ratnakumari, did not support the trial. Most of the other witnesses too turned hostile. Subsequent developments proved that caste was only incidental in the game of political opportunism and personal aggrandisement. Ratnakumari, whose fast demanding a CBI inquiry was used by the Congress to corner NTR, and Devineni Nehru, whose alleged involvement in the killing resulted in the attacks on Kammas in coastal districts, changed their political loyalties later.[53]

Nearly 2000 cases were registered relating to the post-Ranga-murder violence, while 592 rioters were taken into custody in coastal districts. During a recovery drive of stolen goods by the police, it was reported in the media that fearing raids, items such as television sets and expensive alcoholic drinks were thrown into the canals in Vijayawada. The Congress activists and Ranga followers who were arrested by the NTR government in the aftermath of the violence were unconditionally released and all cases against them lifted by the later Congress government.

The Image Trap

While NTR was very conscious of his image, the Congress became adept at running him down. The Mallela Babji case in which an unemployed Dalit Christian youth from Guntur had made an attempt on NTR's life in 1984 cast a shadow on his reputation. The episode turned out to be more curious than was imagined. NTR had earlier acted magnanimously in court, pleading that the judge take a lenient view of the 'innocent youth'. The judge had found him guilty anyway. 'I have little doubt in concluding . . . that the accused had intended to voluntarily cause bodily harm to the chief minister.' Babji spent a year in jail.[54] He was later found hanging from a ceiling fan in a room at Durga Lodge in Vijayawada in November 1987, causing an uproar.

As the Congress raised doubts over the death and demanded an inquiry, a commission headed by retired justice C. Sriramulu was instituted by the NTR government. During the investigation, two letters, said to have been found with the victim, were leaked. They revealed, the Congress alleged, that the entire episode of the attack was an elaborately orchestrated drama. One letter was purportedly written by Babji to his parents. The second was addressed to the Agarwal Commission, which at the time was looking into various matters, including NTR's acts as chief minister. According to the second letter, the person behind the drama was allegedly Chandrababu Naidu, besides NTR himself. Babji claimed in the alleged dying declaration that he was a fan of NTR and that Chandrababu had cajoled him to enact the fake attack to draw sympathy for NTR. For this act, he was promised Rs 3 lakh but was allegedly paid only Rs 30,000.

The issue figured in the assembly several times with the Congress blaming NTR for the 'staged attack'. Home Minister Kodela Siva Prasada Rao alleged that the Congress was behind the letters. He said that the language in the letters could not have been that of Babji who had little education.[55] NTR himself submitted an affidavit to the Sriramulu Commission, denying all the charges in the letter. The contents of the alleged letters, however, did inflict damage to NTR's reputation. 'In his quest for dramatic effect, N.T. Rama Rao may finally have gone too far,' *India Today* remarked on the turn of events.[56] The ruling TDP alleged that Babji was murdered and that the deceased was forcibly made to write the letters before he was hanged.

Much later in 1992, the Congress government made the Sriramulu Commission report public. In a damning indictment, Justice Sriramulu concluded that the attack on NTR was orchestrated to draw sympathy and executed for political purposes. He blamed NTR for luring Babji to enact a fake attack on him at Lal Bahadur stadium 'as per an understanding' between them. Justice Sriramulu, in his 246-page report, was scathing in his exposure of the events surrounding the 'stage-managed affair':

> The medical evidence does not support the possibility of causing so much bleeding from the trivial, simple and superfluous self-inflicted injury to the left thumb . . . Sri N.T. Rama Rao himself would have manipulated blood on the spot . . . which we generally find in film shootings . . .[57]

Interestingly, the commission concurred with the NTR government's contention that Babji's death was forced. (By the time the Sriramulu Commission report came out, NTR was out of power.) The report said, '. . . the death of Mallela Babji was out-and-out a homicide and not a suicide, and he was done to death while he was in a state of intoxication.'[58] While nothing came of the case in the end, Justice Sriramulu's report spoke very poorly of NTR. He or his cohorts apparently enacted the entire episode of the attack on him 'to boost up his image in the eyes of the public'.[59]

The Congress government in Delhi also used the tax regime to sling mud at NTR. As one of the top stars of Telugu cinema for decades, NTR had faced several tax issues during his career. These were later used by the Congress to tarnish his reputation.

Income tax cases against NTR were proposed by the Congress government at the thick of his debut political campaign. The proposal to prosecute NTR 'for wilfully failing to file his return' for the assessment years 1980–81, 1981–82 and 1982–83 was made in December 1982. The file was put up to the then finance minister in June 1983 after NTR was already the chief minister. But the proposal did not get a go-ahead from the ministry. However, it was sought to be activated once again in the late 1980s. J. Vengala Rao, the Central minister at the time, would repeatedly mention income tax cases which would 'expose' NTR.

There was a serious attempt to drag NTR into tax cases at the height of his power. In April 1988, NTR had to attend the special court for economic offences in Hyderabad in a case related to the failure to submit wealth tax returns for 1985–86 and 1986–87. NTR, who came to the court with a host of his ministers and MLAs in tow, used the occasion to create dramatic interest around himself. The court hearing turned into a spectacle, as he played the victim. NTR alleged the Centre was hounding him for trying to bring a change in the system. The cases were indeed filed to harass NTR. The income tax department rarely launched action against anybody for not filing returns in the absence of taxable wealth. Another tax case was slapped on NTR for allegedly failing to declare income as a member of HUF (Hindu Undivided Family) even though, by this time, he did not have the HUF status.

While charity was not one of his virtues, NTR genuinely believed politics was not for making money. 'I was the king of filmdom. I have entered politics only to serve the people, not to make money,' he said.[60] But his protestations lost some of their edge due to the continued allegations of corruption against him. Though not even his detractors said that he took money for any undue favours, NTR appeared lax in the application of the law when it came to his family properties. He was always prepared to institute commissions of inquiry on every allegation of corruption thrown at him, but they did not help his cause in the public perception.

Since he was waging war against corruption in the government and scrutinizing every action of his ministers, legislators and senior officers, NTR's every little lapse was blown out of proportion. The level of corruption was minimal in his government compared to the earlier ones. Several senior officers who worked with him and political leaders associated with him vouched for his brutal honesty in the affairs of the government. Nobody would dare to approach him with pay-offs for approvals or policy changes. 'He would give a dressing down of a lifetime to his ministers or party men if he had the slightest information about their shady deals,' recalled N. Jayaprakash Narayan, an IAS officer who worked closely with NTR.[61] 'His forte was the ability to remain totally incorruptible,' Mohan Kanda, another senior officer who worked as the chief secretary of AP said.[62]

But all that came to naught after the court judgment in the Dronamraju case. The Congress (I) was able to project NTR as a hypocrite whose war against corruption was shallow. As his reputation took a beating, his government's image too took a nosedive.

While the Congress dragged him down, NTR was liberal in deploying government resources to boost his popularity. He retained the portfolio of information and public relations (I&PR) for the most part, from 1984 to 1989. He took a personal interest in the design of advertisements released by the department on various government schemes. As could be expected, he was the prominent face on all such publicity material. They carried his stamp to reflect Telugu culture and language. Instead of the prosaic style of typical government communications, these ads were written in an ornate style using a mix of chaste Telugu and high-sounding Sanskrit. The level of his interest in the quality of the publicity material was so great that once, elated at a picture of his which had been used for an ad in papers, he invited

K.V. Ramanachary, the I&PR commissioner, for lunch to express his appreciation.[63]

Like in every sphere, NTR wanted to experiment with the Department of Information and Public Relations (DIPR) too. In 1985, he hit upon the idea of creating a government advertising agency. Telugu Samacharam (Telugu Information) was created in April 1986 to save the commission paid to advertising agencies. It prepared the artwork and the copy for all government publicity material and released it to newspapers. The advertisements, supervised by NTR himself, were arguably well done in terms of creatives. But the Indian Newspaper Society rejected accreditation to the government agency. The newspapers refused to pay commission to the government. The agency was later closed after NTR's term was over.

Velivelli Saidulu, the then I&PR commissioner, came up with the idea of a magazine to bolster the chief minister's image. The fortnightly magazine was titled *Telugu Samacharam*. Different from the advertising agency of the same name, *Telugu Samacharam*, which began publication in March 1987, lasted less than a year. But during its short existence, the magazine was used to project NTR through Saidulu's enthusiastic efforts. The twelve-page newspaper-size magazine, was priced at just 10 paise first, then 25 paise and 50 paise later. The initial circulation of *Telugu Samacharam* was 20,000 copies. In six months, the circulation zoomed to a million copies.

As much as Rs 50 lakh was spent a month on the publication, printed on glossy paper. Government departments and public limited companies advertised in it, but still, the magazine incurred a loss of Rs 4.75 per copy. The fortnightly was criticized heavily for its unabashed projection of the chief minister and for the considerable expenditure it entailed. *India Today* called the publication a 'vehicle for Rama Rao's narcissism'. The experiment did not last long, and the *Telugu Samacharam* fortnightly closed by February 1988.

NTR's unpredictable behaviour often kept the ministers as well as the party leaders on tenterhooks. But even by the chief minister's oddball standards, the rather unprecedented and arbitrary sacking of all thirty-one ministers in February 1989 was stupefying. The unusual step was triggered by leaks in the media of the coming budget. NTR did not even heed the advice of confidants that the step might destabilize the government. Upendra recalled that even Chandrababu tried his best to dissuade NTR from taking such a drastic decision but in vain. The move dealt a blow to the TDP government's image. NTR's whimsical action did not go down well with the people.

The government was in suspended animation as there was no ministry for a week. Though an infuriated NTR ostensibly decided to act on the budget leaks, it appeared the TDP chief wanted to show the world who the boss was. NTR was bothered by the indiscipline that had seeped into the party. He suspected his sons-in-law encouraged groups. In 'cleansing' the entire cabinet, he believed he was administering shock treatment to the 'establishment'. There was also talk that the unsavoury developments in the family at this time drove NTR into this rash action. The marriage of his youngest daughter was on the rocks.

NTR left for Delhi immediately after his capricious decision. There was a void in the government without a cabinet. The sacked ministers, who included Daggubati Venkateswara Rao, were in shock. They felt humiliated and insulted but observed restraint in the hope that as and when NTR chose to recast his ministry, they would stand a chance. It was pathetic to see the former senior ministers vying with one another to prostrate themselves before him to gain his attention. A week after keeping everybody on tenterhooks, NTR replaced every one of them with an entirely new and inexperienced lot.

NTR inducted twenty-three ministers—all first-timers—into his cabinet. Observers were dumbfounded at the audacious way NTR went about his ministry formation. 'Selflessness was the only

criteria. There is no senior or junior; all are cabinet rank ministers,'
NTR grandly said.[64] So inscrutable was NTR's selection process
that even some of the legislators who were inducted in the cabinet
were surprised at their elevation. The way NTR sacked all thirty-
one ministers with the stroke of a pen caused deep resentment
among the senior party leaders. The damaging effect of the move
continued for long with dissidents harping on the lack of internal
democracy within the TDP. These developments caused anxiety
in the National Front that was still in the making.

Unable to take the humiliation, three sacked senior
ministers—Vasantha Nageswara Rao, K.E. Krishna Murthy and
K. Jana Reddy—declared a revolt against the party leadership.
They quit the TDP as well as their assembly membership and
floated a new party, Telugu Nadu. They joined Nallapareddy
Srinivasulu Reddy, Mudragada Padmanabham and other
former TDP leaders in launching a frontal attack against NTR's
despotism. Nallapareddy lampooned NTR's action, calling him
'Samuhika Rajakeeya Sirachcheda Apoorva Drama Rao [The
Extraordinary Drama Rao of the Mass Political Beheading]', a
satirical take on the 1960s Telugu folk film *Sahasra Sirachcheda
Apoorva Chinthamani*.[65] NTR's brash attitude was helping swell
the ranks of the Opposition day by day. The wholesale sacking of
the cabinet was the last straw that broke people's faith in NTR's
political prudence and administrative sagacity.

Rising National Stature

Despite the mess in his backyard, NTR continued to focus on
building a viable alternative to the Congress government in
Delhi. He extensively campaigned for Karunanidhi's DMK in the
January 1989 Tamil Nadu assembly elections. It was a time when
NTR smelled the real possibility of ousting the Congress from
everywhere. Already fluent in Tamil due to his long years in Tamil
Nadu, NTR brushed up on the language. He was a big hit. The

DMK's victory in the face of the Congress party's aggressive bid for a comeback on its own delighted NTR.

As founder-chairman of National Front, NTR devoted more time to national politics. He often flew to Delhi, while Hyderabad became a hub for national Opposition activities. NTR inaugurated the National Front office in Delhi on 16 November 1988. The presidium of the National Front was held in June 1989 in Hyderabad, and V.P. Singh and NTR addressed the media from the latter's residence at Abids. NTR's single-point agenda of removing the Congress from power gained traction after the Bofors scandal. NTR aggressively pursued this line of attack against the Rajiv government.

The TDP chief famously ticked off Rajiv Gandhi for buying 'rusted' guns for the army for kickbacks. Calling him a traitor, he demanded that the prime minister resign in view of the strictures issued by the comptroller and auditor general (CAG) on the Bofors deal. Even as NTR upped the ante on Bofors, the state Congress turned aggressive, with Union Industries Minister Jalagam Vengala Rao calling NTR a 'CIA agent'. Nadendla even alleged that NTR's bypass surgery was fake and that he was meeting foreign agents. An alarmed US consul general in Madras reportedly wrote a protest letter to Nadendla against the charges.[66]

As an outsider to traditional politics, NTR's fresh perspective on issues came to the fore even in his national foray. It was NTR's idea that the Opposition MPs of the Lok Sabha should resign en masse as a protest against the prime minister's refusal to step down. NTR came up with this game plan even though he was beset with Naxalite kidnappings and their demands back home. He was 'the master-schemer who worked behind the scene to bring about the resignations and a stunning show of Opposition unity'.[67] As the National Front chairman, NTR announced to reporters in New Delhi on 23 July 1989 that 106 members from twelve parties would resign from the 538-member Lok Sabha. The TDP, with its largest contingent of twenty-nine MPs, quit five months ahead of the term along with seventy-seven MPs from other Opposition parties, further raising NTR's profile. The historic move cemented NTR's position among national Opposition leaders. The Congress's information and broadcasting (I&B) minister, K.K. Tiwari, lamented that NTR had reduced the entire Opposition to a drama company. But the smart move created ripples, as Rajiv Gandhi came under intense political pressure after the resignations.

Competitive politics between NTR and the Congress reached a zenith in the election year. Both tried to outwit each other, resorting to gimmicks. In 1989, NTR created drama around the Bofors scandal in his Independence Day speech, which he delivered at Parade Grounds. NTR was always more dramatic and rhetorical than solemn and serious on such occasions. However, this time he went overboard with his speech, which was to be telecast on Doordarshan. Apart from his usual diatribe about the common man not gaining anything after Independence, NTR made an indirect but provocative reference to the Bofors scandal. 'Why are we providing the soldiers with substandard guns? By this, we are playing with the future of the country. We are risking the lives of the brave soldiers,' NTR said.[68] Alarmed DD news staff notified the same to Delhi, and the I&B ministry asked NTR to remove the reference to soldiers and guns.

NTR refused and made it an issue of freedom of speech and the rights of the states. The Congress alleged NTR was inciting the army to mutiny. Union Minister H.K.L. Bhagat criticized him for causing unrest among the defence forces and damaging the morale of the soldiers. The Congress paper, the *Deccan Chronicle,* dubbed NTR's speech 'subversive'. The CPI's Nallamala Giriprasad denounced NTR for talking about mutiny in the army. His defence was that he was merely recounting the CAG report on Bofors. He clarified that he had only said that mutiny might rise in the army due to scandals such as Bofors. Rajiv Gandhi asked Union Home Minister Buta Singh to look into the reports of NTR calling for rebellion against the Centre.

As Rajiv Gandhi was inextricably linked to the Bofors scandal, NTR saw an opportunity to strike when the iron was hot. Along with other National Front leaders, NTR was of the view that Rajiv was in no mood to hold elections to the Lok Sabha on time because of the Bofors scam. He repeatedly demanded that elections be conducted as per the schedule and wrote to the Election Commission of his willingness to go for simultaneous elections to the state assembly. While parliamentary polls were due in early January 1990, those of the state assembly were to happen in March. NTR's game plan was that his party would have a smooth sail in both the elections, riding on the anti-Congress sentiment in the country following the tainted Bofors deal.

But in an unexpected development, Rajiv called for early elections in the third week of November in 1989, even as the Election Commission approved simultaneous polls to the AP assembly. The announcement came as a shock to NTR, as many of his plans, including his campaign film, *Brahmarshi Viswamitra,* were still in the pipeline. The sudden announcement poured cold water on NTR's elaborate plans to use his movie as a propaganda vehicle for his party. An unprepared NTR appeared to have been caught off guard. He had to suspend the shooting of the film and focus on the campaign plan and candidate selection. He also had to take part in the National Front meetings as its chairman, finalizing the manifesto and electoral tie-ups. He quickly drew up a list of candidates for both the Lok Sabha and the assembly.

Both sons-in-law were in the race for the assembly. Chandrababu Naidu was in the fray for the first time after 1983, when he lost from Chandragiri as Congress candidate. Daggubati chose to contest from Parchur again. Practising what he preached at the national level, NTR brought all non-Congress Opposition parties in the state together for an electoral tie-up. The TDP was able to strike an alliance even with the CPI, which had been a long-standing and strident critic of NTR's government. After the seat adjustments, the TDP was finally in the race for 245 assembly seats, leaving forty-nine seats (CPI [M]—15; CPI—18; BJP—12; Janata Dal—4) to allies. NTR contested from Kalwakurthy (Mahabubnagar) and Hindupur (Anantapur). For the Lok Sabha, TDP fielded candidates for thirty-three seats, leaving the rest for partners. The Congress was in the fray for all 294 assembly and forty-two Lok Sabha seats.

In Delhi, NTR released the front manifesto along with V.P. Singh. Despite his increasing profile in national politics and the role he was expected to play, NTR declared that he would not personally contest Lok Sabha elections. 'I will not leave my people and go out of this State,' he said.[69] The TDP prepared cassettes for its publicity containing NTR's speeches. NTR himself vetted the script for the one on Bofors. Campaign vehicles for all twenty-three districts had stills and the trailer from *Viswamitra*.

Wearing a saffron slack suit to give himself a more youthful look, NTR began his roadshow on his Chaitanya Ratham. As the campaign peaked, NTR would have felt a little uneasy at the lack of enthusiasm in the crowds. He had been so focused on the national scene all these days that he had failed to grasp the pulse of the public back home. The anti-incumbency was widespread, and a resurgent Congress was able to capitalize on this discontent. For a change, the Congress buried all its internal feuds to make one last-ditch effort to unseat NTR.

NTR seemed to have heavily banked on the Bofors scandal for re-election. 'Give your judgment on the Bofors corruption,' NTR asked the voters in his roadshows. However, the voters of AP were more interested in the affairs of the state than issues affecting the nation. Many people appeared to have little clue about the Howitzer guns and the alleged corruption behind their procurement, despite NTR's strenuous efforts at highlighting the issue.

NTR's decision to contest from Kalwakurthy in Mahabubnagar District, apart from Hindupur in Anantapur District, was symptomatic of the overconfidence that he had in his victory. Media reports indicated that there was no TDP wave in this constituency. But NTR did not even bother to visit the place till the last day of the campaign. He was apparently swayed by the talk in the party that the Lambada tribe of Telangana worshipped the chief minister. Lambadas constituted about 30,000 people in the Kalwakurthy constituency. According to media reports at the time, P.K.S. Madhavan, who ran an NGO, 'Aware', through which he wielded influence on Lambadas, supported the Congress candidate Chittaranjan Das. More film actors campaigned for the Congress this time around, and they received a good response. Actors Krishna and Jamuna contested for the Lok Sabha from Eluru and Rajahmundry on Congress tickets. At the height of the campaign, the media reports indicated that the Congress enjoyed an edge everywhere even as the TDP lost its previous fervour..

The Debacle

When the results poured in, the drubbing was comprehensive for NTR and the TDP. The party lost in all its traditional strongholds. NTR personally suffered the ignominy of defeat at the hands of a lightweight opponent in Kalwakurthy. J. Chittaranjan Das, the Congress candidate, briefly shot into prominence following this David vs Goliath fight. NTR's newly acquired profile as the chairman of the National Front and his party's electoral alliance with all other non-Congress Opposition parties did not come to his rescue. The ruling TDP tasted bitter defeat at the hands of the Congress, which single-handedly swept the polls after a gap of nearly seven years. 'Andhra Pradesh voters reject Rama Rao's eccentric politics and incompetence,' *India Today* commented.[70]

It was a double whammy for the actor-politician who till date had the best of both worlds. The TDP received a thumbs down both in the assembly as well as Parliament polls. Losing power in the state was a jolt. But more damning was the loss he suffered in the Parliament election at a time when the national alliance he had worked for with such enthusiasm all these years finally bore fruit. The National Front formed the government at the Centre with the support of the BJP. NTR realized his dream of stripping the Congress of power at the Centre, but he was not part of the brave new world. He wanted to play the kingmaker at the Centre. Now he was reduced to a cameo role.

The Congress, which contested all alone, bagged 181 assembly seats in a House of 294 members, while the TDP was reduced to seventy-four seats.[71] The non-Congress parties which sailed with TDP were cut down to twenty seats.[72] The Congress secured 48.21 per cent of the vote. The TDP was in the race for 241 constituencies, polling 44.49 per cent of votes in these seats.

The outcome of the parliamentary election was worse for the TDP. The party, which rose to national prominence after having emerged as the single largest Opposition group in the Lok Sabha in the 1984 polls with thirty MPs, was nearly decimated. The TDP could barely scrape through in two constituencies—Bobbili (Kemburi Ram Mohan Rao) and Narsapur (Bhupatiraju Vijaya Kumar Raju). The Congress was back with a bang in the Lok Sabha elections, sweeping thirty-nine of the forty-two seats.

What must have crushed NTR were the resounding victories of his detractors both within and outside his party. Jalagam Vengala Rao, K. Vijayabhaskara Reddy and Y.S. Rajasekhara Reddy, his bitter critics in the Congress, won hands down in the Parliament polls. His long-time foes from the film industry, actor Krishna and actress Jamuna, had a smooth sail in Eluru and Rajahmundry Lok Sabha seats. All those who left him at different stages after acrimonious fallouts such as Nadendla, Nallapareddy Srinivasulu Reddy, K.E. Krishna Murthy, K. Jana Reddy and Mudragada Padmanabham came out with flying colours. Chinta Mohan, the MP from Tirupati who had deserted the TDP earlier, was

re-elected on a Congress ticket. On the other hand, TDP allies
S. Jaipal Reddy (Mahabubnagar), P. Babul Reddy (Secunderabad)
from the Janata Dal and M. Venkaiah Naidu (Bapatla) from the
BJP bit the dust. The only saving grace for NTR was the election
of Chandrababu Naidu from Kuppam. Chandrababu went on to
lead the party in the assembly in its new avatar as the Opposition.

The defeat shocked NTR, but he did not show it publicly. He
was at home with a few people when his assistant Mohan conveyed
the news of the debacle. 'Let's have some tea,' he ordered. But the
cook came to tell him nervously that the cow had refused to give
milk that day. 'So, our cow that we feed daily kicked us,' NTR said
with a wry smile before retiring to his room.[73]

However, NTR did not withdraw into a shell but faced
reality. 'Lord Krishna said do your duty and don't worry about the
consequences,' a philosophical NTR maintained. He was quick to
dispel the rumours that he would give up politics and go back to
Madras. 'I am not going anywhere. I am here and will rebuild the
party,' he asserted.[74]

The results of the 1989 elections in AP were more a rejection
of NTR's idiosyncrasies than an affirmation of Congress policies.
Anti-incumbency was at its peak. The writing on the wall was
clear to everybody else but the self-absorbed NTR. The whimsical
attitude he had displayed and the political excesses that he had
committed were too many by this time to rescue him from
imminent disaster. The eroding popularity and fading image of the
chief minister were widely felt even within his party. However, the
one-man show that the TDP was, nobody dared to mention the
same to NTR. As S. Sahay of the *Statesman* had feared as far back
as 1983, NTR frittered away his advantages by 'bullheadedness'
and 'his messianic zeal'.

NTR's term as chief minister was marked by his tendency
to create crisis after crisis and then try to wriggle out of it. The
situation always looked as if he was at the edge of the political
rope. His tenure was characterized by building up tension and

suspense from time to time, and then when it seemed he had been pushed to the end of the road, he would come out unscathed with his one-upmanship. But that worked only up to a point. People increasingly became fed up with his style.

NTR found himself in a multi-tiered offensive launched by the Congress. An unending series of court strictures caused severe damage to his image. The relentless campaign by forces inimical to NTR converged towards the end of his tenure.

A crucial mistake that NTR committed was calling for simultaneous elections. He was caught off guard when the Centre announced early elections. In a bid to protect his flock on the home ground, he decided against personally contesting for the Lok Sabha. Even then, he could not contain the seething discontent among people. While Rajiv's government was in a shambles over the Bofors scandal, NTR did not fully understand the extent of anti-incumbency against his government in the state.

Role Reversal

NTR might have lost both assembly and Lok Sabha polls, but he was still the chairman of the National Front which was all set to form the government at the Centre. Having lost political capital back home, NTR could only be a nominal participant at the meetings of the National Front held in Delhi in preparation for the formation of the government. As the chairman, he did his part in negotiating with the BJP to support the Front in forming the government.

Though he did not expect any position in the National Front government, NTR seemed to have taken offence over the elevation of Devi Lal as the deputy prime minister without a word to him. Upendra recalled that he had brought up the subject, but NTR had expressed disinterest in joining the Front government. The TDP chief said that he was not inclined to move to Delhi at a time when the party was in the doldrums in the state. Besides, he was not keen to play second fiddle to anybody. 'If at all, I would prefer to be number one as and when it happens,' Upendra quoted NTR.

There are different versions of what happened over the offer of deputy prime ministership made to NTR. Though NTR was unwilling, party leaders persuaded him to accept the position, saying he had made a substantial contribution to the victory of the National Front. The party drafted a letter conveying NTR's consent to the position, and a TDP team consisting of Daggubati Venkateswara Rao, Yalamanchili Sivaji and B. Satyanarayana Reddy handed over the same to Devi Lal at Haryana Bhavan. However, Upendra, who was a general secretary of the Front, allegedly influenced the Front leaders to change the plan. He, along with others, pushed the agenda of accommodating general secretaries of the National Front, who represented various regional parties, in the cabinet. Accordingly, the TDP, DMK and Asom Gana Parishad received berths in the ministry. As a result, the proposition to make NTR the deputy prime minister lost traction.

However, Chandrababu Naidu was not willing to give up on the prospect of making NTR the deputy prime minister. He kept asking Upendra to lobby for the post. When approached, Prime Minister V.P. Singh was not forthcoming. He told a TDP delegation that the situation might get complicated if one more post of deputy was created. 'He [NTR] might not even like such a post. We want a better position for him. In any case, I will talk to him,' he told them. Nothing happened for a few days, even as Chandrababu in Delhi kept phoning NTR and telling him he would get a call from V.P. Singh any moment. According to Upendra, 'It all happened in a very unseemly manner.' Finally, when Singh spoke to NTR, it was about inducting Upendra into the Union ministry.[75]

NTR felt embarrassed at the turn of events. Devi Lal's unexpected elevation and V.P. Singh shaking hands with Rajiv Gandhi before greeting him at the swearing-in added insult to the injury. NTR felt humiliated. He left the function in a huff.

When Upendra came to meet him at AP Bhavan, a rattled NTR refused to see him. But the TDP leaders coaxed him, saying that the Front government would suffer if the differences were leaked to the media.

All through his short political career, NTR was at the top of his game, winning elections and enjoying a position of power. After seven years of being continuously in power, he suddenly found himself in political wilderness. He had become used to being in the limelight. Now, he had to play the uninspiring role of Opposition leader. M. Channa Reddy, who took over as the chief minister after the Congress win, quipped that he was sure that NTR wouldn't like to sit in the Opposition benches. 'I will be happy to be proved wrong,' he said.[76]

Though disappointed at the people's rejection, NTR did try to play his new role with sincerity. Congress members, mainly the defectors from the TDP, sought to belittle him during the proceedings of the legislature. The ruling party MLAs resorted to various tactics to throw him off balance.

More than the loss of power, NTR felt dejected as seven years of hectic life had abruptly come to a standstill. He felt unwanted and disconsolate. To get away from his depressing surroundings, NTR announced that he would make three movies—including the partially completed *Brahmarshi Viswamitra*—during the year. The second film was on Telugu poet Srinatha while the third was on emperor Ashoka. He worked hard for the completion of *Viswamitra*, shooting in the cold climate of Kullu-Manali in Himachal Pradesh.

NTR's propaganda film *Brahmarshi Viswamitra* was finally released later in 1991 and proved to be a box office dud. Though NTR had great expectations from the film, both in terms of its box office and political leverage, it succeeded in none. *Viswamitra* came across as a laboured effort of an ageing actor who looked like a poor imitation of himself. The way Viswamitra's character was changed to suit NTR's political message attracted criticism. NTR reshot several portions of the film for its Hindi release, spending a considerable amount of money, but it never saw the light of day. The other two films, *Samrat Asoka* (released in May 1992) and *Srinatha Kavi Sarvabhowmudu* (October 1993), also did not do well at the box office.

Though divested of his earlier stature, NTR expected to play a role, however limited, as the chairman of the National Front which was the ruling coalition at the Centre. However, given the internal contradictions within the Janata Dal, Prime Minister V.P. Singh had little leeway in policy decisions. The pulls and pressures from various regional parties as well as the ongoing brawl between the communists and the BJP constantly threatened the stability of the government. Besides, with just two MPs in the Lok Sabha, NTR could not be persuasive on any issue with the coalition government. Not surprisingly, no advice or suggestions were sought by the Front government from NTR despite his ceremonial position. He supported V.P. Singh during the Om Prakash Chautala crisis when Devi Lal rocked the Front boat, but nursed a grudge at being sidelined.

NTR was already peeved that Singh did not even formally offer the deputy prime minister position to him. He was later upset that the Front government did not bother to consult him on various issues such as the implementation of the Mandal report and dismissal of Devi Lal. NTR also took it to heart that the Singh government did not take the TDP into confidence over the grants, approvals, funds, etc., given by the Centre to the state. He expressed unhappiness over Krishna Kant, the Front-appointed governor, cosying up to the Channa Reddy government. He resented that the Front government did not withdraw the income tax cases slapped by the Congress regime against him. He sulked at not being taken seriously by the other Front leaders during the presidium meetings. NTR poured out his frustrations to Upendra, but never publicly gave vent to his feelings.

As the Front chairman, NTR campaigned in the Bihar, Rajasthan, Madhya Pradesh and Gujarat assembly polls in 1990 for the Janata Dal and BJP. He often visited Delhi for Front presidium meetings though his presence did not make any difference to the ongoing political rumblings in the Janata Dal and other Front constituents.

NTR, however, did try to make himself useful when he sought to defuse the heat around the Ram Mandir issue that was causing communal convulsions in the country. When Advani was in the midst of his Rath Yatra, NTR made efforts to convince the BJP leader against escalating the situation. He went to Advani's house and, taking the BJP leader's hands into his, almost begged him to find a solution, recalled Upendra. Having already sensed the political benefits of his yatra, an unwilling Advani continued with his pilgrimage. NTR stood by Prime Minister Singh when the Centre disrupted Advani's Rath Yatra and arrested him. NTR's support to V.P. Singh's stand on both the Ram Janmabhoomi issue and the Mandal report led to his party's estrangement with the BJP.

A Comeback of Sorts

The National Front government lasted less than a year, and general elections were announced to be held in May 1991 in two phases. A year and a half into the Opposition stint in the state, NTR had an opportunity to prove his mettle sooner than he had expected. The Congress government in the state already had a second chief minister in N. Janardhana Reddy, who had replaced M. Channa Reddy.

Nothing energized NTR as going to the people. Given that the voters were already getting tired of the Congress government's inability to provide better governance, NTR campaigned vigorously to retrieve lost ground. He may have made a massive dent in the Congress vote bank by repeating the 1985 performance, but fate intervened. The dastardly killing of Rajiv Gandhi in the middle of the polls, on 21 May 1991, unleashed a sympathy wave for the Congress, which enabled the party to recoup its losses in the second phase of elections held after the assassination.

The TDP registered a stupendous victory, winning ten out of fourteen Lok Sabha seats for which polls were held in the first phase on 21 May. But in the second phase, the tide turned in a different direction, and the TDP won just three seats. In the final tally, Congress won twenty-five out of the forty-two seats. Despite the setback, the TDP made significant gains—it increased its numbers from two in 1989 to thirteen in 1991. Film actors Krishna and Jamuna who had an easy win in 1989 bit the dust, along with U. Krishnam Raju, another actor-turned-politician, who contested on a Congress ticket from Narasapur. TDP allies, CPI and CPI (M), won one seat each. Had it not been for Rajiv's assassination, the TDP would possibly have swept the polls. It was a clear sign that NTR was making a comeback. But as the National Front failed to secure enough seats to form the government, it was the Congress which cobbled up a minority government under the leadership of Pamulaparthi Venkata Narasimha Rao.

The 1991 general elections proved that the TDP and NTR had the tenacity to rebound, despite doubts over the regional party's ability to sustain itself after the crushing defeat. His party's fortunes, however, did not increase much in Delhi. Instead, he was to face another setback not long after.

On the day Rajiv Gandhi was assassinated, NTR was in Visakhapatnam, staying at Hotel Apsara. Local officials quickly moved NTR to the guest house of the Port Trust because of the tensions in the city. He was alone in the guest house till the next morning. Meanwhile, news reached him that miscreants led by some Congress leaders had targeted his family-owned film theatres, Ramakrishna 70 mm, Ramakrishna 35 mm and Tarakarama, and Aahwanam Hotel in Hyderabad.[77] NTR was upset as Ramakrishna 70 mm had many souvenirs of his mythological roles on display. When he took the flight the next day to Hyderabad, Uma Gajapathi

Raju, the Congress MP from Visakhapatnam, who was on the
same plane reportedly hurled abuses at him. At the Hyderabad
airport, the Congress workers who came in large numbers to receive
Hanumantha Rao, the state Congress president, menacingly
approached NTR on seeing him.[78] TDP workers and police
escorted him out, but when he reached home it was empty, with
neither his family members nor police and security staff present.

NTR was upset at the damage done to his properties as well
as those of his party sympathizers. He and his party were victims
of Congress-backed political hooliganism once again. The NTR
Estate in Abids had been deliberately targeted. M.V. Bhaskar
Rao, who was the Hyderabad police commissioner at the time,
was lax in taking precautionary measures. He did not even register
a case against the Congress MLAs, P. Sudhir Kumar and Mukesh
Goud, who were behind the violence.[79] Justice M.R.A. Ansari
headed the commission of inquiry into these incidents of violence.
'The attitude of the commissioner is certainly open to criticism,'
Justice Ansari remarked.[80]

NTR decided to fast unto death to protest the premeditated
attacks and demand reparations. He chose Tank Bund in the
middle of Hyderabad to take up his protest. His silent fast soon
turned into a sort of pilgrimage site with women coming to see
him in large numbers. A worried Janardhana Reddy government
forcibly shifted him to NIMS given his deteriorating health. NTR
continued his fast in the hospital. Party leaders requested Upendra,
the Union minister in V.P. Singh's government, to intervene on
behalf of the Centre so that NTR could end his fast on his terms.
(Singh had continued as the head of the caretaker government.)
But Upendra expressed his helplessness. NTR was administered
fluids and later discharged. The fast happened between the two
phases of Lok Sabha elections in June 1991. But it did not impact
the outcome of the second phase of elections.

When the dark horse P.V. Narasimha Rao emerged as the
prime minister following the 1991 split verdict, NTR was one

of the few politicians who rejoiced. He was happy at a Telugu occupying the pivotal position. So enthused was NTR that he decided to not field a TDP candidate against P.V. in the Nandyal by-election subsequently. NTR went ahead with his decision, though the National Front constituents and the communists were opposed to such an idea. 'For the first time after Independence, a Telugu assumed the office of prime minister. We consider it a matter of pride for the Telugus,' NTR justified his decision.[81] P.V. won with a record margin amid allegations of booth capturing by over-enthusiastic local Congress leaders. Despite such a gracious gesture from NTR, P.V. and his political henchmen had no qualms in engineering defections from the TDP and causing a vertical split in the TDP's parliamentary party.

When the Opposition parties, including the Left and the BJP, decided to move a no-confidence motion against the minority regime headed by P.V. in March 1992, only four out of thirteen

NTR played a key role in uniting the disparate Opposition parties under the umbrella of the National Front. NTR, along with V.P. Singh, Devi Lal, Karunanidhi and others at a Front meeting in 1989.

TDP MPs in the Lok Sabha voted against the government. Those who acted under the party whip were Daggubati, Vadde Sobhanadreeswara Rao, Lal Jan Basha and Ummareddy Venkateswarlu. The party leaders in the Lok Sabha, Bhupathiraju Vijayakumar Raju, G.M.C. Balayogi and Indrakaran Reddy abstained from voting. The remaining six—M.V.V.S. Murthy, Bolla Bulli Ramaiah, K.P. Reddaiah, K.V.R. Chowdary, Gaddam Ganga Reddy and Thota Subba Rao—failed to even land in Delhi.

What came in handy for P.V. and his operators was that Vijayakumar Raju, the Telugu Desam Parliamentary Party leader, was a former acolyte of the prime minister. It was a loss of face for NTR that so many of his MPs deserted him at a crucial time. He had given his word to the National Front and V.P. Singh on the vote, but now he was left embarrassed.

NTR was enraged at the fraud committed against the party by the MPs. But he could not immediately act as the party would be reduced to just four members if he were to expel the rebels. The Congress managers allegedly 'managed' some of these MPs who were industrialists and business persons.[82] To escape possible expulsion by NTR, the rebel MPs got together to form a splinter group of the TDP in the Lok Sabha. Initially, eight of the nine MPs met Speaker Shivraj Patil and claimed that they constituted the original TDP. As Chandrababu Naidu and Daggubati stayed put in Delhi to sort out the squabble, two MPs chose to return to the party. However, a split could not be averted as six of the MPs were finally recognized by the speaker as a separate group.

Upendra was expelled as a result of the episode, along with rebel MPs from the TDP. Sidelined by NTR for some time now, Upendra had been unhappy after he was removed as the leader of the Telugu Desam Parliamentary Party. He was shut out of important meetings with national leaders and National Front constituents. A disgruntled Upendra contributed his part in influencing his Lok Sabha colleagues to cooperate with the P.V. government. It was Upendra who suggested to the Vijayakumar

Raju group a way out from attracting the anti-defection law, by
leading them to Chidambaram to draft a letter to be submitted
to the speaker. 'I had no role in the rebellion except that I had
introduced Raju to Chidambaram for help in drafting the letter,'
Upendra claimed.[83] However, after confirming Upendra's hand in
the sordid episode, NTR booted him out.

NTR's political journey was marked by tears, sweat and blood.
But what caused much distress in his life was the periodic betrayals,
such as the split in the Telugu Desam Parliamentary Party. He
could not fathom how P.V. could have done what he did, even
after his big-hearted decision to support him in the Nandyal by-
election. Regretting his gesture, NTR blasted P.V. at a press meet
in Delhi, 'The Prime Minister who talks about values has exposed
his true nature. He lured our MPs with money to keep his seat by
hook or crook. He has backstabbed the people of Andhra Pradesh.'
P.V.'s ingratitude rankled NTR for a long time.

As the TDP's pointsman in Delhi since his elevation to the
Rajya Sabha, Upendra did an admirable job in helping NTR
create a national profile for the regional party. When the TDP
emerged as the largest Opposition group in Parliament after the
1984 general elections, Upendra was made the leader of the Telugu
Desam Parliamentary Party. He quickly transformed himself as
the back-room boy, ably supporting NTR's continuous efforts
to bring non-Congress Opposition parties together. Upendra
already had some good contacts in Delhi, and his fluency in Hindi
and Bengali further helped his cause. The former railway PRO
proved to be a smooth political operator, serving both his and his
party's interests. During the several Opposition conclaves that the
TDP hosted, Upendra efficiently coordinated the participation of
Opposition stalwarts and leaders of regional parties.

However, Upendra's meteoric rise was resented by many in
the party. NTR suspected that Upendra was not as critical of
Rajiv Gandhi as he should have been. NTR was also not thrilled
at V.P. Singh's choice of Upendra for a berth in the ministry.

The party leaders accused him of using his proximity to national leaders to get himself appointed as the Union minister. The TDP had two members elected to the Lok Sabha, but Upendra, even though a Rajya Sabha member, was a natural pick for Front leaders. However, given NTR's disappointments with the Front government and resentment at Upendra's role, the newly anointed minister for I&B and parliamentary affairs was fast losing his stock in the party. There was a strong feeling that Upendra, as Union minister, did not do much to strengthen the TDP back home. He, however, got a second term in the Rajya Sabha from the party after much dithering in April 1990.

Following the midterm polls in 1991, Upendra was replaced by Bhupathiraju Vijayakumar Raju as the Telugu Desam Parliamentary Party leader. He was slowly sidelined as Daggubati, now an MP, became the pointsman for NTR in Delhi. However, Daggubati was unable to get a hold on his colleagues as a result of which several TDP MPs voted for P.V.'s government during the trust motion. Upendra was expelled from the party, along with defiant MPs, on the suspicion he was the kingpin in the episode. He was already prepared for the worst, and hence took it in his stride.

With this, Upendra's eight-year-long eventful stint in the TDP ended abruptly. Upendra proved to be a resourceful politician with an understanding of the nuances of the ever-changing politics of the country. He contributed much to the emergence of the TDP as a regional party with a national outlook. As minister for I&B and parliamentary affairs, he acquitted himself creditably. His one contribution to NTR's image while a Union minister was telecasting his leader's film *Daana Veera Soora Karna* in the regional slot on Doordarshan on a Sunday. He personally handed over the cheque for Rs 5 lakh from Doordarshan to NTR. But Upendra's critics in the party accused him of enriching himself using his clout in Delhi and promoting his political career at the cost of the party.

After expulsion from the TDP, Upendra attached himself to the BJP but later joined the Congress in 1994. He was elected as MP from Vijayawada on a Congress ticket in the 1996 and 1998 elections. He lost in the following year's elections. In the 2004 elections, his son-in-law Lagadapati Rajagopal grabbed the Congress seat from Vijayawada with the help of Y.S. Rajasekhara Reddy. Upendra receded into oblivion only to surface in 2009 to join Chiranjeevi's Praja Rajyam Party, which fared miserably in the polls. He died in November 2009. Upendra's best years in politics were indeed with the TDP.

Meanwhile, NTR vowed in August 1993 to return to the assembly only as the chief minister. His melodramatic pledge was triggered by the blanket suspension of all TDP MLAs, including NTR, from the assembly session at the behest of the ruling Congress. The TDP legislators were demanding action against the daylight murder of the Jammalamadugu (Kadapa) MLA Ponnapureddy Siva Reddy in Hyderabad. As some TDP MLAs rushed into the well of the House, the speaker suspended all the TDP members, though NTR did not take part in the protest. An upset NTR vowed not to return to the assembly till the anti-people government was thrown out.

And he redeemed his pledge in the 1994 elections, but not before raising the curtains for another drama.

~

Act V

The Unkindest Cut

'Punya Bhoomi naa desam namo namami, Dhanya Bhoomi naa desam sada smarami,' a rousing patriotic song enacted by NTR in the blockbuster film *Major Chandrakanth* was renting the air. It was NTR's last but one film.[1] The 100-day-run celebrations of the box office hit were taking place at the municipal high school grounds in Tirupati on 10 September 1993. It was more than a routine cinema function in the film-crazy state. The expected attendance of thespian and TDP chief NTR, who essayed an important role in the movie, was a special attraction. Mohan Babu, a long-time follower of NTR, who hailed from Chittoor District in which Tirupati is located, was the lead character as well as the producer of the film.

Amrish Puri, Nagma and Ramya Krishna, the cast of the film, were present along with a host of other artistes. The guest of honour was the Congress MP and veteran Hindi film actor Sunil Dutt. Now the Opposition leader in AP, NTR, clad in a bright white dhoti and kurta with Telugu-style kanduva on his shoulder, got a rousing welcome as he stepped on to the stage.

As the proceedings began, the invitees paid rich encomiums to NTR's acting career, his discipline and dedication. Sunil Dutt said that though he belonged to the Congress, he was participating in the event as a mark of respect for NTR, entertainer par excellence. When the time came for NTR to speak, he began in a measured tone without the usual histrionics. *Major Chandrakanth's* success at the box office had given joy to the beleaguered politician. In the film, he was a retired army man who sets out to reform his son and in the process the society. Recounting how he had exerted himself while dubbing for the film in Madras in April of the same year, he suddenly became emotional:

> I became dizzy and was rushed to the hospital. Doctors said my sugar shot up to 350. I returned to Hyderabad, and within a few days, I had a heart attack. I suffered another attack later. It was my third time as I had already experienced one in the past. I was hospitalised, and doctors were surprised that I survived three attacks. During this challenging period, I was nursed to health with care and affection by an anonymous woman. But for her, I would not have been alive today. I am grateful to my saviour. I owe her, and I want to repay her. She is present here amidst you. *(clamour in the audience as people get up to see her.)* Today I seek, with your permission, to propose to her. *(NTR pointing to the front row.)* Parvathi, come on . . .[2]

As NTR took a few steps forward to invite on to the dais the mysterious lady who was sitting in the front row, there was commotion on the stage. His voice choked, but he kept mumbling. Mohan Babu rushed to him and helped him back to his seat. A nervous and confused Lakshmi Parvathi, the woman that NTR was referring to, stood up but did not move. Immediately the mics were muted, and the lights on the stage switched off. An agitated Chandrababu Naidu, who was sitting on the dais, left in a huff.[3] The event was abruptly over, even as fireworks lit up the sky—prearranged to celebrate the success of the film. Shock and dismay followed NTR's announcement that he wished to marry again and that too a woman half his age. While it was breaking news for many on and off the stage, it was not entirely so for the family. They had all been aware of an obscure woman's presence in NTR's life for some time now. However, they did not expect him to publicly announce his intention to marry her. In fact, Lakshmi Parvathi did not go with NTR to Tirupati. But apparently, NTR decided a day before that he would announce his second marriage on the public stage. On landing in Tirupati, he told Mohan Babu to book a flight for Lakshmi Parvathi to the temple town. She was put up at a hotel along with some actresses who had arrived for the film event. On instructions from NTR, she was brought to the venue in a separate car. Suspecting something unusual due to her presence in the front row, Chandrababu spoke to NTR on the stage before the proceedings began. But NTR didn't tell him about his intentions.

After the celebratory function was hurriedly wound up, NTR along with Parvathi flew back to Hyderabad. The next day, the former chief minister addressed a press conference with a bashful Parvathi by his side. 'We tied the knot this morning,' he announced grandly, and smugly declared, 'we are a wedded couple from today.' The widower was unperturbed over the political consequences of his late marriage. *The Hindu* reported:

> Asked whether his marriage would not attract criticism, he said he had committed nothing wrong. He said he had not thought of formalities like solemnising the marriage. She had faith in him and 'from now on she is my wife', a beaming Mr Rama Rao said.[4]

The salacious story of the septuagenarian marrying his young biographer made headlines. Only NTR could have pulled off such a theatrical saga in his already drama-filled life. Lakshmi Parvathi's entry into NTR's life and the subsequent dramatic developments would remain a testament to the cliché 'truth is stranger than fiction'. The episode, as it unfolded, had all the trappings of a Shakespearean tragedy with fate looming large in all its omnipotence over the protagonist.

A Cinderella Story

Lakshmi Parvathi's circumstances in comparison with those of NTR's were unexceptional. She hailed from a lower-middle-class family from Patchala Tadiparru village in Guntur District. Her family fell on bad times when she was growing up. Veeragandham Subbarao, a successful *Harikatha* artiste from Tenali in Guntur District, became a family friend during one of his performances in the village.[5] A married man with three children, Subbarao supported Parvathi's education. Due to the family's penurious circumstances and out of gratitude to him, Parvathi accepted the proposal to marry him, a widower by this time, in 1978. Parvathi was twenty-three, and he was about seventeen years older than her. Both lived together for more than a decade and had a son. A studious person, she completed her post-graduation and began working as a lecturer in Telugu at Raghuramaiah Degree College in Narasaraopet, Guntur District.

Contrary to the widely held view, Parvathi was not part of Subbarao's Harikatha troupe. Having done Ubhaya Bhasha Praveena, a course in Sanskrit and Telugu, at Sri Bhavanarayana Swamy Sanskrit College in Ponnur, Parvathi developed an interest in spiritual texts. Before every Harikatha performance, she would give a talk on Hindu scriptures.[6] She became famous for her spiritual speeches, laced with references to Telugu literary texts. Both visited various places across the state for their performances, and even went to the US. Parvathi recalled that she had first met NTR in 1985 at AP Bhavan in Delhi along with her husband. They performed on State Formation Day. The couple was felicitated by NTR. They continued their association with the TDP by participating in the party campaign during several elections. Meanwhile, Parvathi joined Telugu University in Hyderabad to do her MPhil. During this period, she made efforts to meet NTR. Her persistence paid off, and NTR was apparently charmed by her devotion to him. He was attracted to her proficiency in Telugu classical literature and Hindu Puranas, of which NTR himself was a keen student. This was towards the end of his tenure in 1989.

The association took a significant turn after NTR lost power. Following the rout of the TDP in 1989, NTR was disheartened. He was living at the Nacharam Ramakrishna Horticultural Studio, feeling old, sick and lonely. It was more than five years since his wife Basavatarakam had died at a relatively young age of fifty-eight. Her departure had left a void in his life. All through his career, NTR put in long hours at work, and it was the patient and uncomplaining Basavatarakam who took care of the large family. NTR fulfilled all his obligations to his children, but he was never very close to them in their growing years. As a result, none of them had a strong bond with their father. They were respectful of him but maintained a distance. This was the reason why NTR felt desolate upon his wife's death. As long as he was the chief minister, he had a hectic life, engaged in both party and government activities. However, with the trappings of power gone, NTR suddenly found himself deserted and abandoned. Signs of deteriorating health caused further distress.

NTR had a large family. But by this time, all his surviving eleven children, except for Jayashankara Krishna, were married and living separately. Immediately after losing the elections, NTR focused on completing his film *Brahmarshi Viswamitra*. He set up a shooting schedule in Kullu-Manali. During this time, a lot of family issues bothered him. He arranged to bring all his extended family members to Kullu, where he settled many quarrels among them. Back in Hyderabad, he shuttled between his kuteeram at Nacharam Studios and his house in Abids. He met party workers and visitors at Abids, where his son Ramakrishna stayed.

NTR had already given away the property to Ramakrishna. He sensed his son and daughter-in-law were uncomfortable with the party workers and visitors trashing the place. So, in 1992, he built a small and inexpensive house at Banjara Hills and moved there.

However, he had nobody to look after him. Cooks and other workers were irregular. Journalists recall that after his campaigns during this time, 'he returned to his Road No. 13 Banjara Hills residence at night to find practically none waiting for him, including the cook and servants'.[7] His health began to fail, living as he was with a host of ailments, including diabetes and hypertension, for more than three decades. Besides, his long career in the film industry and the marathon roadshows following his political entry had taken their toll on his body. He had already undergone a bypass. His right arm and leg were partially immobilized due to a stroke he had suffered in the past.[8] All these factors compounded his sense of helplessness. But he had no one with whom he could share his innermost feelings. He badly needed help in his daily chores and in taking care of his health. He sorely wanted a personal aide who could be relied upon. More than that, he yearned to have someone by his side to provide emotional succour and intellectual companionship.

Lakshmi Parvathi was an everyday person with none of NTR's fame or charisma. She had neither the looks nor the star quality of NTR. In 1990, when they started meeting regularly, she was about thirty-six, thirty-one years younger than him, leading an ordinary and prosaic life. What brought her closer to NTR, according to Parvathi, was her infatuation with him. NTR had always shown affection to the most ordinary of his fans. She claimed to have idolized him since childhood. It is possible that her accounts of a lifelong fixation with NTR were dramatic afterthoughts. But the fact remains that Parvathi touched emotional chords in NTR when he was at his most vulnerable. He was not an easy person to get close to. Parvathi persevered for his attention, and, over time, he found a soulmate in her.

When Parvathi sought permission to write his biography in the early days of their conversations, NTR did not take her seriously. He thought she was too inexperienced to understand the gamut of his rather eventful life and told her as much. But as the two kept exchanging views, NTR found her articulation and thoughts on Hindu philosophical traditions impressive. Her ardour and devotion to him touched NTR. She once again pleaded with him for permission to write his biography. After a time, NTR yielded. Like many people at the top, NTR, despite his haughty demeanour, was brittle inside. He would never share his failures and frustrations with others, and hence felt burdened by the bottled-up bitterness. Feeling lonely and isolated at his Nacharam ashram, NTR kept in touch with Parvathi on the phone.

He would frequently call her at the college in Narasaraopet where she worked. 'We would talk at least for an hour every time,' Parvathi recalled in her biography of NTR.[9] When she told him of the embarrassment of taking his calls in the college office, NTR got a telephone installed at her home. NTR later teased her that his long-distance romance cost him Rs 2 lakh in phone bills!

Throughout 1991, Parvathi kept regularly visiting NTR on weekends in Hyderabad where he provided a separate room for her in the studio premises. Later, he also gave her a job in the trust that he had set up for building a cancer hospital. Her extended stays increasingly brought them together. NTR began seeking her company more than ever. He found in her unconditional love and uncomplicated nature a great relief from the stress of his life. 'As I get ready to leave after the weekend, he looks forlorn,' Parvathi recalled. NTR strained himself during the campaign for the 1991 midterm Parliament elections. That's when she started tending to him. He gradually became dependent on her. The courtship continued for a couple of years. Parvathi claimed that it was NTR who proposed to her first. She had already told him about her unhappy marriage with Subbarao and that they had been living separately. One morning, during her regular weekend stays with him, NTR asked her whether she would be willing to be his companion for the rest of their lives. An overwhelmed Parvathi happily accepted his proposal and proceeded to file for divorce from her husband. This was her version. NTR's family, however, always insisted that Parvathi pressured him to marry her.[10]

According to Parvathi, the couple secretly got married on 22 February 1992, in the puja room of NTR's kuteeram with no witnesses but the gods. 'We showered early in the morning and wore traditional white clothes. NTR, chanting the wedding mantra "mangalyam tantunanena", tied the knot around my neck in front of the statue of goddess Gayatri,' Parvathi recalled.[11] However, there was no other confirmation about these private nuptials. Interestingly, NTR underwent another sartorial transformation around this time. He shed saffron and took up a new white, signifying his switch from a rajarshi (royal saint) to a grihastha (a family man). At the time, few guessed the reason behind the change. Soon, the couple moved to his Banjara Hills residence, which was witness to many dramatic developments during NTR's last days.

NTR was shooting for the film *Samrat Asoka* at this time.[12] During one of the schedules in Ooty, he had told his sons about his wish to make Parvathi his life partner. Though they were aware that she was living with their father, his children were aghast and refused to accept his proposal. Parvathi alleged she was even abducted once to prevent NTR from continuing his relationship with her.[13] But he refused to yield to their threats and secretly solemnized his wedding with Parvathi. The family soon came to know of the furtive marriage. Parvathi alleged that Chandrababu Naidu tried to find loopholes in her 'character' and 'expose' them before NTR. He challenged NTR that he would prove his allegations, but, according to Parvathi, he could not substantiate them.[14] Gradually, amid the family's vociferous protests, NTR and Parvathi began to settle down, though their marriage was still a secret as far as the public was concerned. The family, including

NTR's sons, daughters, daughters-in-law and sons-in-law, refused to come to terms with the patriarch's decision. The fiercest opposition came from his sons Harikrishna and Ramakrishna, and sons-in-law Chandrababu and Daggubati.

NTR told his family that his relationship was a done deal. 'Whether you accept or not, I have taken a liking to her. She is not expecting anything from me. I have already fulfilled my responsibilities towards all of you. Now, I need a person who understands me and who will always be by my side. You have your own lives. Who will take care of me in this old age? I hope you will appreciate my decision,' he explained, according to Parvathi.[15]

Not long after, NTR suffered a paralytic stroke. 'We were talking to each other casually, when suddenly he complained of illness,' Parvathi recalled. He had multiple strokes before doctors attended to him. According to Parvathi, NTR felt dejected in the face of his failing health. And in a fit of emotion, advised her to lead her own life since he was not sure of his own longevity. He assured her he would make provisions for her and her son to lead a comfortable life. Parvathi was taken aback. She had just received her divorce papers.[16] 'I was dumbfounded and started crying. I said I wanted to be with him through thick and thin, in sickness and health. I pleaded with him not to entertain such thoughts.' A deeply moved NTR took her in his arms, collected himself and expressed his determination to get back on his feet for both their sakes. She accompanied him, for the first time publicly, for his medical tests to NIMS. Seeing them together agitated the family. There was a minor ruckus in the hospital, and on the insistence of the family members, Parvathi had to leave.

Once again, the family tried to convince NTR that it was suicidal for his public image to be with a divorced woman with a son. 'If you want, we will look for a young woman you can marry,' they reasoned with him. But NTR rejected their suggestions. He said he did not need conjugal pleasures and would not like to ruin the life of a girl. 'I am looking for a companion, and Parvathi fits the bill. Try to understand my situation and help with my decision,' he cajoled them.[17]

Doctors advised NTR that he needed further treatment for the blood clots that had formed during the paralytic attack. He went to the US in July 1993 (not accompanied by Parvathi), got treated and returned home.[18] During his convalescence over several months, Parvathi nursed him with care and affection. Their bond strengthened. By the middle of 1993, the news that NTR was living with a woman found its way into newspaper columns. Kanna Lakshminarayana, a Congress minister, first spoke about a woman in NTR's life in early 1993. Later, in May 1993, the *Deccan Chronicle* sensationalized the story. NTR would have preferred to make his marriage public himself but couldn't do so because of the resistance from his family, mainly from his sons-in-law who were worried about the political fallout. The TDP leaders were mortally afraid that the party would not survive in the face of the publicity disaster if the 'affair' came out into the open. 'It threatens to destroy his image of a clean, disciplined politician and pious social crusader and puts on the skids his comeback bid which had just begun to gather momentum,' *India Today* predicted.[19]

For outsiders, especially his large and extended family, Parvathi's entry into NTR's life was outrageous. She was no match for NTR's stature, the family lamented. This spelt nothing but disaster for NTR, both personally and politically, they bemoaned. The family was also concerned that the development would badly reflect on them—the sons and daughters who were provided substantial wealth from NTR's large earnings—as the situation conveyed that none of them was taking care of the man in his silver years.

Though Parvathi was from the same community as NTR, the Kamma elites strongly disapproved of the liaison as beneath NTR's station in life. It was the class that mattered more than the caste. An awkward and unimpressive woman—at least by the standards prevailing in Telugu society—and a divorcee to boot, slithering her way into the life of a bumbling but larger-than-life personality in his sunset years reinforced many of the age-old prejudices against the unlikely union. Parvathi was simple, almost rustic, in her upbringing, lacking the sophistication the middle and upper classes associated with filmdom and NTR. This inherently prejudiced view was further accentuated by the rich and the powerful of NTR's community who looked at her as a wily temptress plotting to gatecrash into glory. A pompous but senile old man falling for a dubious young woman to catastrophic consequences had an allegorical ring to it.

NTR paired with many a good-looking actress in his long film career—from Anjali Devi, B. Saroja Devi, Savitri, Jamuna, Jayalalitha, Vyjayanthimala, Waheeda Rehman and Krishna Kumari of the 1960s and 1970s vintage to Rati Agnihotri, Vani Viswanath, Jayaprada, Jayasudha and Sridevi of the later days. And he had his own—but not sustained—flings. Some accounts say he was ready to take his co-star Krishna Kumari as his second wife, but for a last-minute change of mind.[20] According to his film biographers, NTR rarely wavered from his pursuit of acting and did not allow his temporary infatuations to distract him. In this backdrop, it was difficult for many to accept, even to this day, that NTR chose such an unexceptional woman as Parvathi.

What the family failed to appreciate was that NTR needed not only the care that she could give him, but also stimulating companionship. Parvathi appealed to him in her cultural sensibilities as much as she drew him with her selfless service. Recalled a former aide of NTR:

How dearly NTR had loved LP or was influenced by her had to be seen to be believed. NTR held people's durbar at Hindupur while Lakshmi Parvati was at nearby Lepakshi. She gave a graphic account of the sculptural splendour and other features of the place to the small audience consisting of two close aides of her husband and this writer. NTR, himself well informed on Gods, Goddesses and mythology, listened to her in utter awe, like a child in grandma's lap. No wonder he defied the world for his love.[21]

The Congress did everything to get political mileage out of this sensational episode. In an interview, Subbarao, Parvathi's first husband, recalled how he was hounded by leaders in the Congress government immediately after NTR publicly announced his marriage with Parvathi.[22] He was woken up in the dead of night by Guntur District police and was told he was wanted by the home minister. Despite his reluctance, Subbarao was taken to Hyderabad, where he was forced to tell the media that he feared for his life from NTR and the TDP.[23] He poured out his troubles to Alapati Dharma Rao, the home minister, who also hailed from Subbarao's native Tenali. The minister regretted that political compulsions had led to the artiste's predicament. Relentlessly pursued, Subbarao went into hiding in Gudiyattam in Tamil Nadu. He surfaced only after one of his sons from his first marriage filed a habeas corpus petition in the high court. He told the press that he was being forced by Congress leaders to accuse NTR of hatching plans to murder him.[24] He also accused NTR and the ruling Congress of causing distress to him. Subbarao was provided protection by the court.

There was no love lost between Subbarao and NTR because of the fate that befell him. But he genuinely feared that he might become a victim in the political game NTR's detractors were bent on playing. NTR himself demanded protection for Subbarao. Media outlets opposed to the TDP portrayed NTR as a lustful leader. But after a while, Congress leaders realized that they could do little to damage NTR's reputation. They understood that people had taken the development in their stride. Subbarao was finally spared from being a casualty of cut-throat political games.

NTR had a talent to see dramatic possibilities where others saw only disasters. Politicians and the media were certain that his rather late marriage would be revolting to the people. But NTR instinctively knew that the public would welcome his decision to make his relationship open. And indeed, the people seemed to appreciate NTR courageously announcing his second marriage to the world. They treated NTR's action as a refreshing episode in the amoral world of politics. People's interest rekindled in the TDP, and soon the new couple was treated as an item by fawning fans. They admired how he doted on her despite her 'lower stature'. His family and well-wishers were scared that his choice of a 'lowly' divorcee would damage his glamour and charisma, but this very act made him more human and relatable.

To the consternation of both his partymen and detractors, especially the Congress, NTR's image received a further boost among women, who saw him as a person who did not care for skin-deep beauty. His being upfront about his relationship contrasted with the hypocrisy of politicians who preferred to keep such things under wraps.

NTR now took Parvathi along with him wherever he went and appeared relaxed and reinvigorated in her company. Party leaders such as Renuka Chowdhury issued statements supporting NTR's action. Over time, there was widespread approval for the marriage. Partymen were now eager to invite the couple to various functions and celebrate their wedding as if it were a royal affair. Parvathi became a star guest in many literary and cultural events. Their house at Banjara Hills became a new centre for fans, well-wishers, party workers and leaders. They vied with one another to meet and greet the newly married couple and pose for pictures with them.

The developments that unfolded from then on were probably the most unusual not only in the political history of AP but also in India. What happened during this episode differs widely according to the points of view of the central characters in the drama. Like in *Rashomon*, the psychological thriller by renowned director Akira Kurosawa, any attempt to understand the 'truth' behind this dark chapter in NTR's life ends up as an exploration of multiple realities. The differing accounts by Parvathi, Daggubati, Chandrababu, NTR and the media reflect the subjectivity of the truth.

Parvathi's Rise

A rejuvenated NTR now went about his task of rebuilding the party. He decided to hold regional public meetings across the state to mark a new beginning for the party. Besides revitalizing the party cadre, these meetings were organized to seek public feedback about his marriage. At this stage, there was nothing to suggest that NTR wanted Parvathi to play a political role. Soon after their wedding, he told the party politburo that Parvathi would have no part in the TDP. He repeated the same in the press meet that followed.[25] However, the family's overreaction to her presence at anything remotely political made NTR defiant. Even the party cadre had no issues. 'What difference does it make to us whether we have to go through Chandrababu or Daggubati or now Lakshmi Parvathi?' the party workers were quoted by the media about the entry of the new person in NTR's life.[26]

To activate the party cadre, NTR planned the first regional public meeting in Rajahmundry. It was a grand success with lakhs of people turning up to see the new couple. Towards the end of the programme, there were demands from the public that Parvathi should speak. NTR asked her to. She stood up and addressed the large and enthusiastic crowd, proving to be a better speaker than many party leaders. She asserted she was not interested in politics but wanted to see NTR return to power. With the help of Chandrababu and Daggubati, NTR would snatch victory, she said amid applause. An elated NTR took her around the stage, waving to the huge gathering that greeted them with warmth. A report in

Eenadu noted, 'NTR's wife Lakshmi Parvathi turned out to be a special attraction during his Rajahmundry tour. As it was the first time that he came out along with Parvathi, the party workers vied with one another to have a look at her.'[27]

Two other meetings attended by the couple in Telangana (Nalgonda) and Rayalaseema (Kurnool) regions were also hugely successful. Two more sessions dedicated to women and farmers held in Nellore and Guntur, respectively, also received a thunderous response. The Opposition TDP seemed to be on a surge once again.

The tensions in the family escalated further as Parvathi seemed to inexorably emerge as a potent force in the party. The more NTR guarded her from the attacks of the family, the more worried they became about her increasing influence on him. The family in general and the politically active sons-in-law in particular had every reason to be concerned over their dwindling influence. Parvathi was assuming the role of a power centre within the party. The party was already known to be divided into two groups headed by Chandrababu and Daggubati. Many disgruntled partymen now found a better way to reach NTR. It was understandably difficult for Chandrababu and Daggubati to stomach the new development at a time when they were hopeful of a return to power.

Chandrababu had worked hard for the party without enjoying a formal position in the government. Since December 1989, when the TDP began sitting in the Opposition benches, he had been leading the party's fight from the front, even as NTR remained slightly indifferent. Now, it all seemed like an effort gone waste. He had invested too much in the party to let it go. Predictably, he did everything possible to put hurdles in Parvathi's way.

Initially, Chandrababu and others were genuinely fearful of the repercussions of NTR's late marriage on the party. But once the NTR–Lakshmi Parvathi relationship became public and started generating positive vibes, the family members felt resentful of Parvathi's increasing clout. Both the sons-in-law knew how NTR viewed them. While he thought of Chandrababu as an efficient organizer, he was wary of his political ambitions and personal integrity. He regarded Daggubati as good-natured but ineffectual. It was against this backdrop that they feared that NTR was trying to mentor Parvathi to succeed him.

Palace intrigue started in earnest. NTR's increasing dependence on Parvathi meant that the sons-in-law were kept at a distance. They saw Parvathi as an ambitious young seductress out to destroy the grand old man's legacy for her own self-aggrandizement. That was how the political heirs of the family portrayed Parvathi in public perception.[28] Since such a patriarchal bias against women was deep-rooted in society, their task was not difficult. And Parvathi contributed no less to shore up such an image through her own excesses. She was a political novice. She took everything at face value, not realizing that opportunism was inbuilt in the system.

As NTR wanted her to share the burden of managing the party, she undertook the task rather brashly. She took it upon herself to bring everybody together so that NTR could return to power. But she was not immune to the trappings of power that automatically accompanied her as the wife of an indulgent NTR. She did not try to hide her new-found celebrity status and wallowed in the reflected glory. Many of those who had felt left out in the party now found a saviour in her. Others saw a shortcut to party positions by pleasing her. Felicitations, offerings of sarees, jewellery and other gifts became the order of the day. She enjoyed being arm candy for the magnetic personality that NTR already was. Parvathi was a showpiece that he presented proudly as his wife.

Soon newspapers, especially *Eenadu*, began caricaturing her as a wily woman in whose hands NTR was now a helpless pawn. The primeval images of a henpecked husband in declining years under the evil influence of a young and conspiring wife were transmuted into the public consciousness ever so surely. The truth, however, was more complicated. While Parvathi enjoyed his confidence, NTR took most of the decisions himself. But in public, Parvathi played the doting wife, and NTR teasingly put his hands around her shoulder, giving the impression of being a lovesick husband. Parvathi claimed in her biography that though NTR's health had improved, he was still weak and unsteady. He would find it difficult to stand onstage for long hours during public events and hence would lean on his wife. Ever an actor, NTR would do it playfully to mask his lack of physical strength. But that made the couple look like a sassy pair, playing to the gallery. A picture that soured the mood in the family. Perceptions matter more than reality in politics.

News reports began to appear regularly of Parvathi's imminent induction into the party. Parvathi was eyeing the post of Telugu Mahila (the women's wing of the party) president, one report said. Another surmised she was seeking a party ticket to contest as an MLA. Parvathi was cited as being responsible for keeping the sons-in-law out of the loop on various decisions of NTR, though the party supremo had always taken unilateral decisions. Parvathi, for her part, did try to win over the family to acquire legitimacy. She was able to make amends with some of NTR's clan, including Balakrishna, Mohana Krishna and Jayakrishna, though Harikrishna remained hostile. The easily excitable Harikrishna was with the sons-in-law in their fierce opposition to her presence. As more and more party leaders started meeting Parvathi to get through to NTR, the chasm between her and the family only grew bigger, though it was yet to explode.

The Renuka Chowdhury episode also contributed to Parvathi's negative image. Renuka's story in the TDP stands out as an example of how ordinary persons with no connection to the world of politics became stars due to NTR's unconventional approach. Her entry into politics was entirely accidental. She was one of the many citizens who came on to the streets in Hyderabad to protest NTR's removal by Governor Ram Lal in 1984. The story of a pregnant housewife leading the protests caught the attention of local newspapers. NTR immediately took a liking to her, a daughter of an Indian Air Force doctor. She was educated, intelligent, articulate and above all daring. She was picked up by the party to contest for the Banjara Hills ward as a corporator in the MCH (Municipal Corporation of Hyderabad) elections in 1986. Her courage in confronting Congress MLA P. Janardhan Reddy, a mass leader in Hyderabad who commanded local support, further enhanced her image in NTR's eyes.

Renuka had a meteoric rise in the party. Appreciative of her guts in standing up to tough Congress leaders, NTR promoted her from a corporator in Hyderabad municipality to a member of the Rajya Sabha, not once but twice, in 1986 and 1992. She was also made the chief whip of the Telugu Desam Parliamentary Party. When the party was in the doldrums after the 1989 defeat, Renuka came forward to contest against Chief Minister K. Vijaya Bhaskara Reddy in his den in Kurnool District. Reddy, a Lok Sabha member, was required to be elected to the assembly and contested from Panyam seat. Though Reddy won, Renuka gave him the jitters. NTR, who chose her for tough assignments, bestowed her with special recognition in the party, calling her in one of the public meetings 'the only man' in the party.

Meanwhile, Parvathi's arrival on the scene changed the equations. Renuka was one of the first few party leaders who had welcomed NTR's decision to marry her. However, things soon changed. Parvathi alleged that it was because of Chandrababu's prompting that Renuka turned hostile towards her.[29] Renuka already had a running feud with Daggubati. A party delegation, seen as being close to Parvathi, reported Renuka's alleged demeaning comments against the couple during a party meeting.[30] The TDP chief was miffed and demanded a public apology. When she refused, Renuka was expelled from the party.[31] Reacting sharply to her dismissal, Renuka alleged that NTR was planning to anoint Parvathi as the chief minister. NTR suspected that Chandrababu was behind the fracas. Later, in an interview, Renuka clarified that Parvathi's role was insignificant in her expulsion and that she quit because she was tired of the family feud within the TDP.

In Renuka's removal, the party lost a very articulate leader. Renuka, who achieved national recognition in a short time, was one among many leaders who owed their political birth to the TDP. Despite the bitter incident, she continued to have high regard for NTR whom she considered one of the finest leaders AP had produced. The fiery politician subsequently joined the Congress and rose to be a member of the Union cabinet.[32]

The Renuka imbroglio was the outcome of the internal tensions in the TDP. The more NTR acted independently, the more it perturbed the sons-in-law. News leaks about Parvathi's interference in party affairs became almost regular in papers, with *Eenadu* coming up with tendentious stories. Daily cartoons were used to drill the message of a malleable NTR being manipulated by Parvathi. One picture showed NTR busy cooking in the kitchen, while Parvathi ran the party affairs. Parvathi's name cropped up as being the cause for every disturbance in the party. Parvathi said Chandrababu was behind many of these stories which found their way in the media. But her own political ambitions were becoming evident.

As Parvathi began helping NTR in consolidating the party cadre, her role started to expand. NTR would take inputs from her interactions with party activists from districts, though the final decision on any appointment would always be his. Because of his fragile health, NTR deliberately encouraged her to pitch in for him in public meetings, as he had been advised by doctors to cut down on his tours and speeches. The roaring success of the public meetings, which were attended by thousands, cemented her place as a crowd-puller. Neither Chandrababu nor Daggubati could boast of oratorical skills, besides lacking NTR's charisma. Parvathi's relevance in the TDP was thus established.

Senior leaders such as P. Indra Reddy, G. Muddu Krishnama Naidu and G. Butchaiah Chowdary grew close to her and were branded as her clique. Most of the partymen who sought to cultivate Parvathi as a leader were those who did not get along with Chandrababu. Many of them had tried to protect their turf earlier by supporting Daggubati. Now, they found in Parvathi someone who had the eyes and ears of the party supremo. Thus encouraged, Parvathi began entertaining the disgruntled in the party. She emerged as a foil to the sons-in-law rather quickly. While reports about Parvathi's ambitions continued to appear periodically in the press, the sons-in-law were now more worried about the forthcoming assembly polls. They made peace with Parvathi for the time being.

The Congress regime in the state repeated the same mistakes that it was known for all along. It was riven by groups and dissidence throughout, giving little time to the incumbent chief minister to bear any meaningful impact on governance. It was widely believed that M. Channa Reddy's exit as chief minister was choreographed by his detractors in the party by triggering communal disturbances in the old city. He was ousted in December 1990, after barely a year in power. The rule of N. Janardhana Reddy, who succeeded him as chief minister, became known for nepotism and corruption. Strictures by the AP High Court against the sanction of private medical colleges led to his resignation, clearing the path for Kotla Vijaya Bhaskara Reddy in October 1992.

The soft-spoken Vijaya Bhaskara Reddy, despite his best efforts, failed the expectations of the people. The caste equation in the Congress once again came to the fore as the three Reddys ruled the state during the five-year term. 'Andhra Pradesh without a Reddy at the helm is like a bullfight without a bull,' *India Today* remarked.[33]

The historic anti-arrack agitation by women across the state, which gathered momentum midway through the Congress rule, proved a significant threat to the government. Vijaya Bhaskara Reddy ordered a ban on the sale of arrack from 1 October 1993. The move was intended to dilute the militancy of the non-political movement. The protestors, however, demanded a total ban, including on Indian Made Foreign Liquor (IMFL). The issue came in handy for NTR who supported the agitation. NTR's promise of total prohibition carried weight because he was a teetotaller and was known as a man of his word. The women once again flocked to NTR.

The December 1994 assembly elections were crucial for Prime Minister P.V. Narasimha Rao since failure in his home state would dent his reputation within the party. But paradoxically, P.V., though a son of the soil, was not as big a vote catcher as Indira or Rajiv had been for the Congress in the state. His campaign was vigorous but did not help the Congress gain any traction with the electorate. 'If the Congress (I) started out the campaign by taking Andhra Pradesh for granted, as the pocket-borough of its party president, he faces the threat of getting his pocket picked,' commented Shekhar Gupta in a pre-poll analysis.[34]

On the other hand, NTR was an invigorated man. In just a year, he had been able to reclaim much of his lost ground. With Parvathi by his side, NTR organized a series of public meetings across the state culminating with Praja Garjana (Roar of the People) in Hyderabad. This was attended by unprecedented crowds, estimated to be a million. His new Chaitanya Ratham, a tweaked DCM Toyota truck with an ABT 4242 number plate, once again rolled across the state with the added attraction of Vadina (sister-in-law) along with Anna. Back in his khaki trousers and shirt, topped by a felt hat, NTR had lost none of his dramatic touches.

But due to his nagging physical condition, the seventy-one-year-old was far from his earlier sprightly self, despite the 'boisterous expression of his newfound virility through the display of his young new wife'[35] in public. As a result, he had to cut down on his campaign trail. In comparison with his earlier campaigns, the 1994 elections saw NTR limiting his roadshows drastically. The public, though, went crazy when they saw the ageing politician with his new wife atop the Chaitanya Ratham. Even a sober Vijaya Bhaskara Reddy could not resist commenting about the 'cavorting couple'.[36] In the aftermath of such a dramatic campaign, elections to the 294-seat assembly were held in two phases on 1 and 5 December 1994.

Back with a Bang

When the results came out, the outcome was one-sided, marking a triumphal return for the TDP. Surpassing its own record of the 1983 and 1985 elections, the party created a new benchmark for the state. It won the largest-ever majority in the AP assembly—219 on its own and more than 250 seats along with allies in a House of 294. His partners did well too. The CPI's nineteen and the CPI (M)'s fifteen seats were their highest in AP since 1967. NTR himself breezed through the Tekkali and Hindupur seats he contested from. At least five rebel candidates who had won, later returned to the party, further boosting the TDP's numbers.

The ruling Congress was mauled beyond recognition. The party won a paltry twenty-six seats, not even qualifying to be the Opposition party. Except for Vijaya Bhaskara Reddy, thirty-three of the thirty-nine-member outgoing cabinet were washed away in the TDP tsunami. The Congress was wiped out in seven out of ten districts of Telangana and two out of nine districts in coastal Andhra. Sons of stalwarts—P.V. Ranga Rao (son of P.V. Narasimha Rao), Sudhir Kumar (son of P. Shiv Shankar, the Manipur governor at the time) and Jalagam Prasada Rao (son of former chief minister Jalagam Vengala Rao)—bit the dust. N. Janardhana Reddy, the former chief minister, and Speaker D. Sripada Rao were among those who lost. Nadendla, who had made a comeback in 1989, was now back to square one, losing in Tenali. K. Rosaiah, the finance minister, was humbled in Chirala.

The BJP, which fielded candidates for 281 seats, ended up
with just three. It had contested independently after the TDP
snapped ties with the party in the wake of its role in the fall of the
National Front government. Kanshi Ram's Bahujan Samaj Party,
which was predicted to make inroads into the state, lost deposits
in most of the 235 seats it contested. For all the hype, the party
scraped 1.42 per cent of votes polled.

Parvathi's contribution in the TDP's unprecedented victory
was undeniable. Despite all the negative publicity she had got in the
press, it was crystal clear that the voters stood by NTR's marriage
with her. People also seemed to have given their hearty approval
to her supportive role during the campaign. The overwhelming
majority the party secured gave much-needed legitimacy to Lakshmi
Parvathi in the TDP.

This naturally rang alarm bells in the minds of the sons-in-law,
especially the more ambitious Chandrababu Naidu. But putting

NTR's second marriage to Lakshmi Parvathi was vehemently opposed by the
family. The public, however, seemed to have endorsed NTR's decision. The
couple during the 1994 assembly election campaign.

to rest the raging speculation about her future role in the party, Parvathi, a day before the TDP government was formed, clarified in an interview that she would remain a quintessential housewife.[37] She tried to avoid controversy, refuting suggestions that the stupendous victory was due to her campaign. NTR, however, was not so coy about admitting Parvathi's role. 'She has already been rendering services to the party. Hasn't she campaigned along with me for the party?' he shot back when asked about her role.[38] But the tempest that awaited the party did not go unnoticed. Amarnath K. Menon of *India Today* anticipated that NTR's victory 'may signal the beginning of veritable Mahabharata'.[39]

The spectacular swearing-in of NTR seemed like déjà vu. Hundreds of thousands of people from across the state were present at the elaborately decked up Lal Bahadur Stadium, where NTR, wearing a golden-hued dhoti, kurta, kanduva and gold-framed spectacles, took oath as the chief minister for the fourth time in eleven years in the presence of the who's who of India's non-Congress Opposition. Chief ministers of Tamil Nadu and Orissa, J. Jayalalitha and Biju Patnaik, CPI and CPI (M) leaders Indrajit Gupta and Harkishan Singh Surjeet, Janata Dal leaders S.R. Bommai, Sharad Yadav, S. Jaipal Reddy, and Akali Dal leader Surjit Singh Barnala were present at the grand event, evocative of the nostalgic days of the National Front.

With a dramatic flourish, NTR signed the file to impose total alcohol prohibition in the state, announcing that he was redeeming his pledge given to his 'sisters'. The crowd responded with thunderous applause. Showing his commitment to the cause, NTR created a separate ministry for implementing the ban.

Despite his apprehensions, Chandrababu had the best deal among the ministers. He was rewarded with plum postings in the cabinet—finance and revenue. Rarely were two such important portfolios handed over to one minister in the state. But at the same time, NTR denied berths to some Chandrababu loyalists. NTR was evidently trying to balance the political equations in the party.

But Parvathi accompanying NTR wherever he went continued to cause anxiety to Chandrababu. She was present at the swearing-in ceremony, mingling with the top leaders of the non-Congress parties. She accompanied him during the Delhi trip to meet Prime Minister P.V. Narasimha Rao. She was carving out her own niche by attending many cultural, film and literary functions in Hyderabad and other parts of the state. The ministers were in attendance wherever Parvathi was present. The media reading was that the back-seat driver in the Chaitanya Ratham had taken on the steering wheel in NTR's life.

NTR's style of functioning as chief minister underwent a sea change this time. He was more circumspect. Ministers noted that NTR was now taking every decision after careful examination. One thing that did not change was his sincerity in keeping his word on poll promises. Besides total alcohol prohibition, he brought back the Rs 2 per kg rice scheme and implemented subsidized power for agriculture. NTR showed a more restrained approach in tackling Centre–state relations, unlike in the past when he was always itching to take up the cudgels against Delhi.

He was, at the same time, ready to get back into national politics. NTR resumed his mission of reviving the faded National Front. He campaigned in Bihar for Laloo Prasad Yadav in the 1995 assembly elections. After Laloo's victory, another Front meet was held at AP Bhavan in Delhi with Opposition regulars such as Biju Patnaik, Chandra Shekhar, V.P. Singh, Ram Vilas Paswan, Sharad Yadav and Laloo Yadav. He was raring to campaign in other states where elections were due. In AP, he wanted to literally bring the administration to the doorsteps of the people, for which he planned a new programme. But he would be stopped in his tracks.

Despite several setbacks and challenges in his political career, Chandrababu Naidu made a mark by digging his heels in. He was the kind of politician who would not say or do anything in the heat of the moment. By the time Parvathi came into NTR's life, Chandrababu had come into his own as a seasoned politician. He wielded enormous clout in the party, but he had his detractors too. Parvathi and Daggubati were wary of him. Both claimed that Chandrababu was continuously manipulating the party and NTR to ensure that he had the upper hand. Daggubati said it was Chandrababu who created discord between NTR and Nadendla. Likewise, he was accused of playing a dubious role in Renuka's expulsion. NTR blew hot and cold at his son-in-law all through, but Chandrababu always managed to make himself needed.

Chandrababu was also media-savvy. He effectively used the media, especially the Telugu media, to serve his political interests. *Eenadu* had been critical of him in the early days. The paper had found fault with NTR's decision of admitting him into the party. However, by 1990, Ramoji Rao, not too happy with the mercurial NTR, put his eggs in Chandrababu's basket. The media mogul felt NTR had become fickle and erratic, and even advised him in 1991 in an editorial to step down from party leadership and hand over the reins to young blood. 'If NTR retires from politics, it would be good for the party, for NTR himself and for Andhra Pradesh,' *Eenadu* said caustically.[40]

Daggubati alleged that Chandrababu perfected the art of creating a crisis in the party and the government and later emerging as the troubleshooter. Even during the 1984 stalemate, Chandrababu was projected in the media as the crisis manager which, according to the elder son-in-law, was not true. NTR was not unaware of the situation and would snub him at times.

After the Renuka fracas, Chandrababu approached Parvathi to diffuse the tension between him and NTR. Parvathi, recalling this conversation, said a distressed Chandrababu sought her good offices for allaying NTR's apprehensions about him. 'He has been upset with me for some time now and keeps me at a distance. If this continues, I will have to go back to Chittoor and look after my businesses. I had worked all these years for the party for eighteen hours a day. Unless you can prevail upon him, I am all lost,' he said. Later, when a conciliatory Parvathi told NTR about the conversation, NTR apparently laughed knowingly and said, 'Oh, you are such a naive woman. He is crafty.'[41]

Despite such an unflattering picture portrayed by Daggubati and Parvathi, NTR considered Chandrababu to be indispensable in running the party because the latter was committed and hard-working. Chandrababu exhibited an enormous amount of patience through the ups and downs he faced in the party. Even in the face of tough challenges, he never lost his cool. Unlike Parvathi and even Daggubati, Chandrababu was never flippant in public. He came across as focused and goal-oriented. He played a crucial role in the organizational development of the TDP and was always in close contact with the party workers and leaders. In fact, NTR was as dependent on him as he was wary of him in running the affairs of the party. Chandrababu was devoted entirely to the party even though he did not enjoy any important post in the government throughout the TDP regime. For twelve years, from 1983 till 1995, Chandrababu did not have any ministerial position, even though he wielded power in the party as the general secretary between 1985 and 1989. It was this perseverance and fortitude that set Chandrababu apart as a long-distance runner in politics.

But Chandrababu felt uncomfortable with Parvathi's constant presence around NTR. Contrary to her earlier statements that she would limit herself to her household, Parvathi became a permanent fixture in NTR's private as well as public activities. She started taking a tiffin carrier to the secretariat to serve him lunch in the office. Even NTR's first wife, Basavatarakam, used to carry lunch to the secretariat in early 1983, but only a few officials in the chief minister's office were aware of her presence. Parvathi's every action received extensive press coverage, and she too seemed to enjoy the attention. She took great pride in feeding NTR with her own hands.

According to Daggubati, NTR allowed her to indulge in such displays to convey the message that he needed her to take care of him. But Parvathi's overindulgence conjured up the image of an old and infirm patriarch who was literally eating out of his young wife's hands. Daggubati recalled that during a party thrown in Delhi by the newly elected chief minister of Bihar, Laloo Prasad Yadav, after a meeting of the National Front, Parvathi revelled in her act of feeding him in the presence of hundreds of guests. It was splashed all over the national press. 'We were all expecting that the next day's papers would write about the role NTR was going to play in reviving National Front, but Parvathi's affected actions ruined all of it,' Daggubati said.[42] Dr Kakarla Subba Rao, who visited NTR to congratulate him on the electoral victory in 1994, 'was truly shocked to see Lakshmi Parvathi feeding him with her hands and almost bragging of her care for the old man'.[43]

Parvathi increasingly became assertive of her position and was not coy about her celebrity status. She started acting on behalf of NTR. She did try to mediate with some of those who had had a falling-out with NTR in the past. She prevailed upon Carnatic musician Mangalampalli Balamuralikrishna to forget the past misunderstanding with NTR and visit the state. Due to her intervention, NTR himself felicitated the maestro at Ravindra Bharathi.[44] Parvathi claimed that it was due to her good offices that the ailing Kondapalli Seetharamaiah, the Naxalite leader, was released from jail. She also bridged the widening gulf with the film industry by arranging a meeting of prominent movie personalities, such as Akkineni Nageswara Rao, Krishna, Chiranjeevi and Dasari Narayana Rao, with the chief minister. Parvathi also did her bit in defusing the tension that had existed for long between NTR and sections of the Brahmin community. She regularly attended cultural and literary meets and became a popular figure in those circles. She even prevailed upon the chief minister to participate in such gatherings. It became known that it was easy to get access to the chief minister through his wife. Lakshmi Parvathi was the consort of the deity through whom the devotees sought the lord's grace, a tradition in Telugu devotional poetry.

It became more and more difficult for family members to access NTR. Those who were privy to the inside happenings also recalled that NTR did not pay attention to issues brought to his notice by Chandrababu. According to senior officials at the time, NTR began showing disinterest towards anything that Chandrababu had to say about the party or government matters. 'Chandrababu was the senior most leader in the party as well as the government, but he was not getting the respect he deserved,'[45] recalled a close aide of NTR during this time.

Parvathi followed NTR to election campaigns in Orissa, Bihar and Karnataka. Media reports continued to predict her imminent political elevation. Speculation was that she was all set to contest from Tekkali in Srikakulam District, for which a by-election was due. NTR's son Harikrishna, who had been the driver for his father's Chaitanya Ratham since 1984, had never showed interest in politics in the past. But now, after having stiffly opposed his father's second marriage, he met NTR and sought a ticket for the same seat. He had already dashed off an open letter to Parvathi, duly released to the press, questioning her credentials. Neither Parvathi nor Harikrishna finally got the ticket.[46] The TDP won hands down all three by-elections to the assembly—Tekkali (Srikakulam), Bhimavaram (West Godavari District) and Gorantla (Anantapur District).

But the family politics and media reports continued to make NTR uncomfortable. His bitter son Harikrishna kicked off a tour of the state to tell people how NTR had become a helpless pawn in the hands of a wily Lakshmi Parvathi. His meetings, which attracted huge crowds, were allegedly supported by MLAs loyal to Chandrababu with the tacit support of Daggubati. NTR was strangely tolerant of his son's open defiance despite the damage being caused to his reputation. Harikrishna was paving the way for the final assault against his father, perhaps unwittingly.

Dr Jayaprakash Narayan, the IAS secretary to NTR, enjoyed the chief minister's respect and confidence. NTR often sought his advice on various matters, both administrative and political. Parvathi said that, concerned over the reports about her, JP, as he was known, brought some of them to the chief minister's notice. NTR called Parvathi and let JP raise his objections. The officer referred to complaints about Parvathi accepting jewellery, sarees and other valuable gifts. 'Such things will bring a bad name to NTR garu,' JP said. Parvathi protested saying they were all rumours.[47] However, such allegations continued unabated in the press. When businessman T. Subbarami Reddy, a Congressman, invited the couple for dinner, it was hinted in the media that NTR, known for keeping contractors and industrialists at arm's length, was now friends with them because of Parvathi.

Though there was not much to substantiate the charge that Parvathi was acting as an extra-constitutional authority in the government, she was actively involved in party affairs. NTR deployed her to campaign in the municipal elections. The TDP did not fare well. But her graph within the party saw only an upward trend. Soon a clique formed around her. Party leaders such as P. Indra Reddy, G. Muddu Krishnama Naidu and Gorantla Butchaiah Chowdary, for their own political interests, projected her as a leader in her own right. Statements made by these leaders, for example, that it was because of Parvathi's campaign that the party had won the recent elections, caused discomfiture all around. Muddu Krishnama Naidu even declared that NTR would become the prime minister after the 1996 Lok Sabha polls and that Parvathi would be his successor in the state. NTR did not seem to mind such statements.

As more and more wannabe politicians began flocking to her, the image of an upstart going overboard stuck to Parvathi. She seemed blissfully unaware of the disgust the sycophancy around her caused in the party and among the people. She was being hailed as a superwoman by all and sundry who saw in her an opportunity to reap political benefits. The CPI (M), voicing concern over her 'increasing role', said, 'We are not sure to what extent these reports are correct. But it is time the ruling party mended its ways.'[48]

Parvathi lacked the subtlety and sophistication required to handle the enormous amount of attention being bestowed upon her. She came across as crass at times, accepting awards and titles from all kinds of dubious organizations. One of the awards she received was 'Woman of the Millennium' presented through the hands of Tamil Nadu Chief Minister Jayalalitha. NTR, who attended the event, expressed his wish to see Parvathi as a people's representative. It was a confirmation for his family and partymen that NTR was planning to anoint her as his successor. They were now sure that Parvathi was manipulating the old man. The family's hatred of her was so palpable that they asked their father to come alone for two family functions. Strong rumours floated around at this time that NTR was being administered folk remedies to keep him under Parvathi's spell.

But NTR's debilitating health meant he needed her continued help in daily chores such as feeding, clothing and washing. He apparently wanted her to be his representative in the party, since he was not prepared to rely entirely on his sons-in-law. NTR's weakness had always been to elevate his diehard fans at the expense of other deserving leaders. While his own MLAs could not easily approach him, his fans still had access to him. He made his fan from his cinema days, T. Ramesh Reddy, an MLA. Sripathi Rajeshwar, the president of the All India NTR Fans Association, was even picked as a minister. NTR seemed to have considered Parvathi his most ardent follower and reposed faith in her. The more his family and the media denigrated him over his wife, the more NTR seemed to want to project her as his heir, however indirectly. It was part defiance and part exigency.

Parvathi certainly seemed to have a hold on NTR by this time. According to some senior officials, NTR often spoke in glowing terms about Parvathi's care of him. The extent to which Parvathi could influence NTR was narrated to this author by a senior official close to NTR. According to him, NTR as chief minister came to know in 1995 that a minister in his government was allegedly involved in a ransom demand of Rs 2 crore from an industrialist over a piece of disputed land. The chief minister asked the senior police officer to trap his cabinet colleague. The minister was an NTR loyalist and now a staunch follower of Lakshmi Parvathi. But given his antipathy to corruption, NTR was prepared to catch his own minister red-handed as he had once done in 1984. Apparently, NTR was elated at the prospect of apprehending a big fish and sending a strong message across the party. 'This would be a piece of Hollywood-level news,' he gushed in his cinematic jargon.[49] All was set for the entrapment. But when Parvathi found out the reason for NTR's elation, she quickly called the official involved and ordered the withdrawal of the move. NTR, contrary to his nature, reportedly acquiesced to her decision. While there were many other such allegations against Parvathi, very few were proved.

Another senior IAS officer, C.D. Arha, described how Parvathi was able to win over NTR's affections through her acts of fidelity. He was in Delhi on deputation when he was called by NTR for a meeting immediately after the TDP won the 1994 elections. He wanted to bring the officer back to the state. The officer called on NTR at the latter's home. The incumbent chief minister sat with Arha in the drawing room. Meanwhile, Parvathi strolled in with a copper vessel which was filled with water and floating rose petals. She bent down and washed NTR's feet in the container and sprinkled the water on her head. All this happened even as NTR continued to talk to the officer. Such acts apparently satisfied an ageing NTR's narcissistic tendencies.

The family suspected Parvathi of harbouring political ambitions when they came to know of her recanalization operation to have a child with NTR. She underwent surgery at the government maternity hospital in Hyderabad before the elections. The procedure was carried out under the watch of the superintendent of the hospital, Dr Mahalakshmi. There were rumours that Parvathi was giving steroids to NTR so that the couple could have a successor.[50] For the family, it was a confirmation of their worst fears that Parvathi was out to claim NTR's legacy at the cost of his kith and kin.

A few months into governance, Chandrababu, who always saw himself as the natural successor to NTR in politics, was convinced of the need to rid the TDP of Parvathi. She was chipping away at his support base and baiting his followers with positions of power. Her own support base, consisting mainly of fringe elements in the party, was swelling by the day. The increasing assertion of her sycophants troubled Chandrababu. He realized that he stood little chance in the current circumstances to inherit NTR's political legacy.

With eyes on the future, he began cultivating his own group of legislators and waited for the right moment to strike. At this point of time, the idea was to put pressure on NTR to cut Parvathi's role in the party to size.

Coup Unfolds

Amid all this political shadow-boxing, NTR and Parvathi found a way to get away from it all and left for England in June 1995. NTR's medical check-up was done in London, and it was found that the blood clot formed during one of his heart strokes still posed a threat. Despite this news, NTR, along with Parvathi, participated in various programmes, both official and non-official. Parvathi said that NTR watched with great interest Shakespeare's plays staged in London for three days. The couple was hosted by several Telugu families as well as by the Indian high commissioner and the mayor. 'NTR did a lot of shopping like a child, buying hats and jackets,' Parvathi recalled.[51]

Back home, a mutiny was brewing. An incident related to approval of new distilleries was the first whiff of that revolt. Before leaving for London, NTR had signed a file approving a licence for fourteen distillery units. In the middle of the tour, Chandrababu called up NTR to tell him that all hell had broken loose back home because of his decision. The step was painted by the media as a dilution of the liquor law. NTR explained that he had given the nod on an appeal by the farmers growing sugar cane, but reports appearing in papers projected him in a bad light. Parvathi's hidden hand in NTR's decision was also speculated. *Eenadu* carried an editorial, condemning NTR as a 'betrayer' of people's trust.[52]

NTR and Parvathi were back in Hyderabad. NTR once again was wholly immersed in the administration and had no clue about the mounting dissonance in the party. The trigger, when it occurred, was unexpected. NTR suspended eight MLAs from the party for working to defeat some of the official candidates for the offices of presidents of District Cooperative Central Banks (DCCBs). The dissident MLAs obviously had the blessings of the finance minister to go against the party line. The cross-voting was orchestrated because some of the candidates in the fray were allegedly Parvathi's men. Following the swift action by the party president, Chandrababu took up the cudgels on behalf of the suspended MLAs, but NTR refused to relent.

August was the 'Ides of March' for NTR. After the earlier crisis in August 1984, the party experienced momentous developments once again in August 1995. The media, especially *Eenadu,* influenced the readers' understanding of the goings-on in the TDP at this critical juncture.

On 16 August, newspapers splashed the suspension of the eight MLAs. Disciplinary action was kept pending against two ministers, Kadiyam Srihari and Godam Nagesh. NTR told a party meeting that he would rather go for fresh polls than allow indiscipline in the party. 'Flare up in TDP,' the *Eenadu* headline screamed.[53] The report said that the party was hurtling towards a catastrophic crisis. Protests erupted as most of the suspended MLAs were from the Chandrababu group. The MLAs on whom the axe had fallen demanded that the Telugu Desam Legislature Party (TDLP) meeting be convened immediately.

The disgruntled legislators met Chandrababu at his home and expressed their strong displeasure at the way 'unilateral actions are being resorted to in the name of disciplinary action'.[54] The suggestions embedded in the media coverage, especially *Eenadu,* implied that Parvathi was taking control of the party and promoting inconsequential people. Under her influence, NTR was ignoring the majority view of the party. NTR's actions and Parvathi's role would spell disaster for the TDP government. Chandrababu and his group were trying to save the party from disintegration. This was the tone and tenor of the reports.

During this period, NTR talked only about national politics and the National Front's chances in the next Lok Sabha elections. He was focused on defeating the Congress at the national level. On 15 August 1995, he spelt out a three-point plan for the National Front—linking the Ganga and Cauvery rivers, rewriting the Constitution to strengthen federalism and bringing in welfare schemes for the poor.

NTR was aware of Chandrababu exerting his influence on the party legislators, but he chose to ignore the signals. He refused to believe that Chandrababu or his MLAs would ever go against him.[55] Even while pushing Parvathi into the political vortex, NTR busied himself in day-to-day administration. He launched an ambitious programme, Prajala Vaddaku Palana, which literally meant taking the administration to the doorsteps of the people. NTR left Hyderabad with his wife Parvathi on 17 August 1995 for Srikakulam on a week-long trip to north coastal AP. He was to have a one-on-one with the local people in the presence of various departmental officials to resolve issues on the spot. Almost all the ministers participated in the programmes which were part of Prajala Vaddaku Palana held in Srikakulam, Vizianagaram and Visakhapatnam Districts. Chandrababu accompanied the couple. He, along with the supporting MLAs, lodged at Dolphin Hotel, Visakhapatnam, owned by Ramoji Rao, apparently finalizing the last details of the strategy to take on the patriarch of the party.

Even as he was touring the north coastal districts, NTR received inputs from intelligence that MLAs were getting together in groups in Hyderabad. But he was not worried because Chandrababu was with him. Chandrababu participated in the programmes with the chief minister during the day and prepared for the impending mutiny at night. NTR was under the impression that the group led by his son-in-law was trying to build up pressure to extract some concessions. He was concerned but not panicky.

Meanwhile, Harikrishna continued with his blitzkrieg against his stepmother. He conducted several public meetings with large cut-outs of NTR with his first wife Basavatarakam in Vijayawada and its surroundings. Vijayawada was in Krishna District from where NTR hailed. Harikrishna declared in one of the meetings that he would 'oppose even my father for justice'. Justice for him was to remove Parvathi's presence from NTR's life. This was the first time Harikrishna had spoken against his father in public. While Chandrababu opposed Parvathi for political reasons, Harikrishna's antagonism was emotional. All the family members who could not accept Parvathi in Basavatarakam's place threw their weight behind Harikrishna in this public spat. Harikrishna had been going around the state for some time now, berating Parvathi and turning the family feud into a political battle.[56] This was the first time anyone among NTR's sons and daughters had talked politics in public.

Yarlagadda Lakshmi Prasad, a Hindi teacher with a gift of the gab, played a crucial role during this period. He grew close to some of NTR's sons, especially Harikrishna. He was the guiding force behind the garrulous son in his public fight against Parvathi. Lakshmi Prasad, like many others, was convinced that NTR was not his earlier self and that Parvathi was an undesirable influence on him. 'NTR was losing his faculties, and Parvathi was exercising control over him. I believed he was no longer in command,' Lakshmi Prasad told this author. Prasad, who was with Harikrishna during his Krishna District tour, conveyed to

Chandrababu that the son had spoken about his readiness to fight against his own father. Following this communication, the son-in-law, staying at Nagavali Hotel in Srikakulam, was apparently emboldened in his plans.

On the same day, the Chandrababu group took a firm decision to mobilize legislators to stop Parvathi in her tracks. Chandrababu managed all these developments even as he took part in various programmes in north AP. He was with NTR and his wife all along and reiterated his loyalty to the party chief in public meetings. At Vizianagaram, located at one end of AP, all the ministers and senior officials sat in different tents from morning till evening to receive petitions from the public. Chandrababu, then the minister for finance and revenue, was supervising the public interaction to ensure everything was in order. The chief minister and his wife had been put up at a tastefully erected kuteeram in the premises of the Sri Durga Prasad Saraf College of Arts and Applied Sciences in Vizianagaram. The Chandrababu camp was tying up the logistics and calling up MLAs from all regions to reach Hyderabad, even as the power couple was being treated to sumptuous dinners by local MLAs and ministers. P. Ashok Gajapathi Raju, the minister from Vizianagaram District with royal ancestry, hosted a dinner for the couple at his home only to topple NTR a couple of days later.

Interestingly, Chandrababu gave more than a hint of his plans to NTR during this period. In Vizianagaram on 19 August, Chandrababu took the intelligence IG R.P. Singh aside and gave vent to his frustration over Parvathi's political interference. He was upset that she was enticing his loyalists with offers of positions. He made it clear that he would not allow Parvathi to have her way. He said he had no other option but to take over the reins from NTR as and when the time came. But he was quick to add that he would not take any hasty steps as long as NTR was alive. He appeared worried that Parvathi might precipitate some unforeseen development at any moment.

Chandrababu was concerned that Parvathi might pressure NTR into anointing her officially as his successor any time. Both Parvathi and Chandrababu knew that NTR was not well. Both camps were apparently nervous about what the future might hold for them. It was against this backdrop that Chandrababu was preparing for any eventuality. Meanwhile, Singh immediately conveyed to NTR what his son-in-law was up to. He told the chief minister that Chandrababu was ready to launch an offensive for transfer of power if he continued to be sidelined. 'Ok brother, don't worry,'[57] an unruffled NTR responded to his intelligence sleuth and went about his business as usual. He apparently thought Chandrababu's attempts were aimed at resisting Parvathi, which was something he could handle.

NTR stated at Narsipatnam in Visakhapatnam District that he would contest for the Lok Sabha. The statement came at the wrong time for the Chandrababu group, which interpreted it as Parvathi replacing him in the state. NTR certainly had his eyes on national politics at this time, though few had an inkling of his plans for the state. At the fag end of the tour, a public meeting was held in Visakhapatnam. As a precursor to the power struggle, Chandrababu was taken to the venue in a huge procession by his supporters, even as NTR and Parvathi were stranded behind. Before the return journey, Chandrababu, who was on the same flight as NTR and Parvathi to Hyderabad, had already set the stage in the state capital for the final showdown. The couple had little inkling that the rug would be pulled from under their feet as soon as they landed.

Even after returning to Hyderabad on 23 August, NTR apparently continued to be under the impression that it was all a storm in a teacup. He had no clue that it was going to be a nightmare from which he would never recover. A delegation from the Chandrababu group consisting of P. Ashok Gajapathi Raju, S.V. Subba Reddy and T. Devender Goud met NTR. The chief minister was open to their request to reconsider suspensions.

When they told him that the legislators wanted Parvathi to be kept out of politics and government, an enraged NTR blasted them. 'Who are these people who want to control my wife? Haven't all of them consulted their wives on some issue? In any case, what has she done? She campaigned for the party at my insistence. All candidates in the election benefited from her participation. And what makes you think that I go by her recommendations on anything? Do I look like a fool?' he said at the top of his grave voice. He spat fire at Chandrababu at whose behest, he said, these ministers and legislators had gone against the party candidates in the DCCB elections. He reiterated that he intended to take stringent action against such indiscipline.[58]

It is difficult to say whether the Chandrababu group expected to find an amicable solution through this mediation. They would have known that given NTR's proclivity to respond emotionally, he would react the way he did. But NTR's rebuff was interpreted as his refusal to climb down over Parvathi's role in the party. The mediation was considered to have failed, and Chandrababu decided to bite the bullet. He moved with agility and set about executing the plan. *Eenadu* reported that as many as 110 MLAs met Chandrababu at his chambers in the secretariat. 'The MLAs were in a defiant mood and were not afraid to speak out against NTR in the presence of the press,' the report said.[59] At this point, the theme on which the party MLAs rallied behind Chandrababu, according to Rajendra Prasad of *The Hindu*, was that Parvathi had created a situation in which NTR was no longer able to act according to his judgement.[60]

But while Chandrababu had the support of a considerable number of MLAs, what the shrewd politician needed was legitimacy. He could get it only with the help of the family, especially Daggubati and Harikrishna. This was where Chandrababu displayed his famed managerial skills. Once again, Yarlagadda Lakshmi Prasad came to the rescue.

On a request from Chandrababu, he brought Balakrishna, who was shooting for a film in Visakhapatnam, to Hyderabad.

Balakrishna was not aware of the political developments in his father's party. It so happened that the shooting was cancelled due to technical problems. Lakshmi Prasad, on Chandrababu's suggestion, prevailed upon Balakrishna to go to Hyderabad in view of the political uncertainty. 'It was purely a coincidence that Balakrishna was in Vizag at the time and the shooting schedule was cancelled. This gave me the opportunity to fly him to Hyderabad. Nothing was pre-planned,' Lakshmi Prasad told this author.[61]

On landing in Hyderabad, Balakrishna was taken to Chandrababu's chambers at the secretariat. He was talked into the urgency of saving the party from Parvathi's clutches. It was again Lakshmi Prasad who told Chandrababu to get in touch with Harikrishna at Aahwanam Hotel in Hyderabad. Following a call from Chandrababu, Harikrishna also went to the secretariat, where the MLAs were already meeting. He was quickly convinced of the need to organize a revolt to protect the interests of the 'real party workers'. NTR's sons were not politically savvy and were swayed by their animosity towards Parvathi.

Lakshmi Prasad, known for his oratory skills, had been associated with non-Congress parties during his student days. He grew close to NTR after the TDP lost power in 1989. NTR took a liking for his literary flair in Telugu and Hindi. The teacher from Andhra University helped NTR finalize the script and dialogues of the Hindi version of *Brahmarshi Viswamitra*. He also accompanied NTR to the US in 1993 for a medical check-up at St Louis. A Padma Bhushan awardee (2016) for his literary contributions, Lakshmi Prasad claimed he opposed NTR's marriage with Parvathi from day one. He said Parvathi made use of NTR's fragile health to wield undue influence on him even in political matters. She began controlling access to NTR, resulting in several party loyalists getting distanced from the leadership. Lakshmi Prasad, who played an important part in the coup, believes to this day that what he did during this period was right. According to him, the TDP would not have survived as a party, if the situation was allowed to deteriorate any further. His role in bringing Harikrishna and Balakrishna into the rebel camp was a big morale booster for Chandrababu, who now had an ace up his sleeve.

The stage was set the next day, 24 August 1995, for the final showdown. Harikrishna, Balakrishna and another son Ramakrishna went to NTR's residence to try to convince him one last time. Chandrababu followed them later. What transpired there is unknown, but they left in a huff at around 7 p.m. Parvathi said that contrary to media reports of heated arguments, Chandrababu mumbled something incoherently in front of NTR and left the place within a few minutes. Harikrishna and Balakrishna hovered around the house for a bit but, apparently, they could not bring themselves to directly confront the patriarch.

Daggubati, who was the Telugu Desam Parliamentary Party leader in the Lok Sabha, arrived from Delhi late that evening. It is interesting that he stayed put in Delhi at a time when far-reaching developments were occurring in Hyderabad. Once again, he showed that he lacked the political instinct to effectively react to a developing situation. This tentative attitude costed him later. He rushed to Hyderabad on Chandrababu's call, who picked him up from the airport. When Daggubati and Chandrababu reached the former's home, not far from NTR's, Harikrishna and Balakrishna, along with Lakshmi Prasad and Jasti Chelameswar, were waiting for them. NTR's secretary Jayaprakash Narayan, and senior cops H.J. Dora and R.P. Singh were also present. The officials were there to get a sense of what was happening.

Chandrababu took Daggubati aside and after some private talk was able to persuade him to join hands. All of them, along with his group of ministers, trooped to Viceroy Hotel near the secretariat. All the collaborators would stay put in this star hotel for the next week. The hotel was owned by P. Prabhakar Reddy, the brother-in-law of Bojjala Gopalakrishna Reddy, a TDP MLA and a close associate of Chandrababu. Bojjala, son-in-law of the former Janata leader Babul Reddy, played a vital role in the coup. The MLAs who gathered around Chandrababu's chambers in the secretariat were initially sent to Viceroy Hotel on Tank Bund for dinner. The Chandrababu camp subsequently thought it wise to keep all the MLAs in the hotel to meet any eventuality. The guests who were already staying there were asked to leave, and all the rooms in the hotel were occupied by the rebel camp.

Apparently, till 23 August Chandrababu was only interested in standing up to NTR against Parvathi's role in the party. He also seemed to be intent on resisting NTR's 'unilateral decisions', especially concerning actions against party legislators and other leaders. He was keen to be recognized as NTR's political successor. According to Ummareddy Venkateswarlu, a senior leader who was with Chandrababu at the time, the idea at this juncture was for all the MLAs to confront NTR. They wanted to organize a protest at the chief minister's residence, demanding that he give his word to keep Parvathi out of politics. However, NTR came across as unrelenting, leading them to change their plans. The rebel group believed, according to Ummareddy, that NTR was all set to make his second wife deputy chief minister and had set 9 September as the mahurat (auspicious time) for the ceremony. The Chandrababu camp was now desperate. There was a sense of urgency to act.

Once the rebel forces began gathering, it was evident to Chandrababu that he had more backing than he had imagined. The ambitious son-in-law was spurred on by the overwhelming support he was receiving from the party. Viceroy Hotel was overflowing with legislators and party functionaries. A good number of MLAs were prepared to get rid of NTR and choose Chandrababu as their leader. The earlier idea that the MLAs should confront the patriarch to fulfil their demands was now replaced by Chandrababu's desire to succeed NTR as the chief minister.

Many MLAs harboured seething discontent against NTR, who had always treated them as mere appendages. Besides,

Parvathi's emergence as a power centre in the party caused much discomfiture to the legislators. They started feeling insecure about their place in the TDP. Chandrababu was able to tap into this sense of insecurity. Things fell into place in a way that even Chandrababu could not have imagined. The contours of the revolt underwent a dramatic change in a matter of just twenty-four hours.

It is difficult to determine the exact point at which Chandrababu decided to turn his spar with his father-in-law into a full-fledged battle with irreversible consequences. It was most likely on 23 August at Viceroy Hotel when the events shaped up frenetically overnight. The backing he received from the family sealed Chandrababu's resolve to effect a change of leadership. According to one version, even then, Chandrababu, not known to be intrepid, dithered at one point over going all out against his father-in-law. He flinched at the idea of toppling NTR right away, probably because of the severe repercussions that would befall his camp if he failed. He was aware of what had happened to Nadendla's political career.

'Chandrababu turned panicky at one time,' Lakshmi Prasad recalled. But some of his colleagues, who included Ashok Gajapathi Raju and Kotagiri Vidyadhara Rao, warned that if Chandrababu were to step back at this stage, then the MLAs, who were in a defiant mood, would be forced to go ahead with the formation of a government on their own. Journalist I. Venkata Rao wrote that MLAs were prepared to elect Ashok Gajapathi Raju if Chandrababu were to back out. Even the legislators were aware that they had come too far to go back. It was a psychological game in which each—Chandrababu and his coterie—pushed the other to take the leap. The full-fledged support extended by *Eenadu* and Ramoji Rao in this dicey power game undoubtedly acted as a fillip to Chandrababu.

24 August was a crucial day in the TDP's history. A clutch of events took place one after another. Three senior officials, N. Jayaprakash Narayan, H.J. Dora and K. Durga Prasad, were

present at Daggubati's house where the latter, Chandrababu and others were huddled to thrash out a plan. Having sensed that something alarming was in the offing, they tried to dissuade the family members from taking any hasty decision. The senior officials told them they were young and that they could wait for their turn to run the state. They also advised the family against causing suffering to the patriarch in his sunset years. However, Chandrababu came across as unrelenting. The officers had to leave without any assurance. They rushed to NTR's house to tell him about the changing political equations.

When they arrived, NTR was soundly asleep even as the plot against him thickened in the darkness of the night. Nobody, including Parvathi, dared to wake him up. The officials waited, and when NTR got up in the early hours, briefed him about the ominous developments. But none of them had a clue as to the endgame of the rebel group, except that it was to stiffly oppose Parvathi. Jayaprakash advised the chief minister that a quick statement by him about limiting Parvathi's role in the party might defuse the situation. A meeting of the TDLP could be convened immediately after, where the same message could be conveyed directly to the MLAs to put them at ease.

But NTR was averse to the suggestion. 'If I were to yield now, they would play around with me. It's a matter of my self-respect. It's not about Parvathi at all; I know their target is me,' he told them. Even when Jayaprakash hinted that his government might be in jeopardy if he were not ready for a compromise, NTR remained nonchalant. 'I don't care for power. I lived like a king and will die like one,' he retorted.[62] Unable to prevail upon NTR, Jayaprakash and his colleagues left. This was the moment when NTR had an opportunity to amend the situation, but he chose to remain inflexible. Dawn was already breaking.

When an agitated Parvathi pleaded with NTR to give in to what the rebel group wanted, NTR shouted at her and asked her to stay out of the matter. A panicked Parvathi, apparently on the advice of Jayaprakash, called up an *Eenadu* reporter and gave an apologetic statement in the hope of reversing the alarming developments. 'If I am the reason for the current crisis, I would like to declare publicly that I will have nothing to do with politics from now on,' she entreated. 'Madam changes the tune,' *Eenadu* heckled.[63]

The battle lines had, however, already been drawn by the Chandrababu group, and these events were playing out at Viceroy Hotel. The intervening night of 24 and 25 August had been in the grip of a swift tide of developments. A good number of MLAs—*Eenadu* put the figure at 157—declared that Chandrababu had been elected as their leader. No less than Daggubati, a long-time adversary of Chandrababu, made the announcement in the dead of night. He later sheepishly said that it was Chandrababu's ploy to make him issue such crucial statements to the press. A letter addressed to the governor to this effect—Chandrababu having been elected as the leader of the Telugu Desam Legislature Party in place of NTR—was signed by all the 157 MLAs present. Effectively, NTR was replaced as the chief minister. All through that cataclysmic night, Harikrishna and Balakrishna stood by Chandrababu. 'Unless something totally miraculous happens, there is no way NTR government would survive after this development,' *Eenadu* declared.[64] The paper, in its editorial titled 'A Self-Made Calamity', justified the undermining of NTR, calling him and his wife Parvathi names.

NTR, asleep at the time, was completely unaware of the unexpected turn of events. He learnt of them from the three officials only in the early hours of 25 August by which time it was already too late. Clearly, NTR did not expect that his son-in-law would go to the extent of toppling him as chief minister and party leader. He could not foresee that Chandrababu had the guts to rebel against him, despite being warned by various sources in the past few days. He did not care for the alert sounded by his advisers just a few hours ago. He was now clearly caught off guard. The intelligence failure in this episode also contributed to the situation. The overnight election of Chandrababu as the TDLP leader came as a shock.

The day, 25 August, saw a flurry of developments that sealed NTR's fate. But the battle-scarred veteran did not go under without a fight.

- At 5.30 a.m. on that day, NTR, already briefed about the developments at Viceroy Hotel, recommended the immediate dismissal of five ministers leading the revolt, namely, N. Chandrababu Naidu, P. Ashok Gajapathi Raju, T. Devender Goud, A. Madhava Reddy and K. Vidyadhara Rao. The recommendation was accepted, and the ministers were dismissed by Governor Krishan Kant.

- Quickly realizing the gravity of the unfolding situation, at about 8 a.m. NTR called on the governor and handed over a letter requesting him to dissolve the assembly. 'Owing to certain unhappy circumstances in my party, I have felt my moral duty to go back to the ultimate sovereign in a democracy, to the people,' NTR said in his letter.[65] Some observers are of the opinion that this was NTR's first crucial misstep. While NTR and his advisers probably believed that the recommendation for dissolution of the assembly would scare away the defecting MLAs, it had the opposite effect. Most of the legislators were now forced to sail with Chandrababu to save their skins. The Chandrababu camp made effective use of the threat to keep the flock on its side.

- The Chandrababu group, well prepared for all eventualities, proved to be nimble. Two of Chandrababu's emissaries, K. Vidyadhara Rao and T. Devender Goud, had met the governor at 7.35 a.m. before NTR reached him and submitted a list of 140 MLAs, including eleven ministers, in support of Chandrababu Naidu, the new Telugu Desam Legislature Party leader.

- After that, at about 9.30 a.m., Chandrababu and his group of legislators went to Raj Bhavan in four buses in a show of strength. They called on the governor and submitted two resolutions dated 24 August 1995 purported to have been passed by the legislators of the Telugu Desam Party: i. Expressing a lack of confidence in NTR as the leader of the party and; ii. resolving to elect Chandrababu as the leader of the Telugu Desam Party. They also opposed the dissolution of the assembly.

- Chandrababu also got in touch with Speaker Yanamala Ramakrishnudu who was on tour in East Godavari District. He arranged a private helicopter to bring him to Hyderabad. Yanamala reached the capital by 8.30 p.m. and plunged himself into the task of counting the number of legislators supporting Chandrababu. He issued a bulletin declaring that 164 MLAs were backing Chandrababu.

Meanwhile, NTR's well-wishers tried to compromise through mediators, but the Chandrababu group was riding high by this time.[66] Chandrababu, who till then had operated in the shadows, came out in the open and dismissed the possibility of any talks with NTR. He also triumphantly declared at a press conference at Viceroy Hotel that he was now the leader of the real TDP as most MLAs and MPs supported him. Earlier that day, NTR had addressed a press conference at his residence. He said he was prepared to 'renounce' his wife if any allegation of corruption or improper conduct against her was proved.

P. Ashok Gajapathi Raju, who enjoyed several key positions, including the party general secretary, under NTR, made the most telling comment against the couple. Puffing away on a cigarette in the spacious lobbies of Viceroy Hotel, he wryly declared, 'We do not subscribe to the ideology of Love Me and Love My Dog.'[67]

On the same evening, in a fit of unthinking emotion, NTR and Parvathi, along with some ministers loyal to them, climbed atop Chaitanya Ratham and went to Viceroy Hotel. It proved to be the most humiliating experience for NTR. His own MLAs, ensconced behind the imposing gates of the hotel, heckled, taunted and jeered at him. A dreaded leader of the party till the other day, he was now reduced to an object of ridicule. Excerpts from a report in *Eenadu* of the incident painted a picture of NTR who had become a caricature of himself:

> NTR stayed put for two hours in front of the gates of the hotel, calling out hoarsely, 'legislators, come out, don't trust the backstabbers'. As he went on speaking emotionally, Chandrababu's supporters, gathered behind the hotel gates, mocked and shouted at him, throwing empty water bottles, even slippers, at the Ratham. The police did not care for his repeated orders to bring the MLAs out of the hotel. 'As CM, I am ordering you. Go, bring all those who are staying in the hotel against their will. Why don't you heed my words?' a flustered NTR went on and on. Meanwhile, a fretful Lakshmi Parvathi was cursing the MLAs, pointing fingers at them. Chandrababu supporters began abusing her in unprintable language. NTR and his supporters beat a retreat.[68]

Things were clearly not going NTR's way. The humiliation that he faced that day was something that not many of his fans and admirers have been able to stomach to this day. Renuka Chowdhury, who had left the TDP by this time, was livid when she recalled the incident much later in 2017, 'One time I felt bad was during the Viceroy incident. I wished I was there for him on that unfortunate day. He was humiliated by them. It should have never happened. There is no excuse for what they did to him.'[69]

Parvathi's presence on Chaitanya Ratham gave the defecting MLAs the perfect ruse for sticking to their guns. Parvathi later regretted her decision to go along with NTR to Viceroy Hotel against her own wish. 'It was all confusing at the time. All kinds of

24 August 1995 was a black day in NTR's life. When he went to Viceroy Hotel
on his Chaitanya Ratham along with Lakshmi Parvathi, the MLAs supporting
Chandrababu rebuffed him in the most humiliating manner.

people were coming to us and advising us,' she said. On the advice
of some well-wishers, NTR had decided to go alone to Viceroy
Hotel that evening and talk things out with the rebel group in
private. Nobody knew what would have happened in such a case,
but that was not to be. Plans changed somehow in the afternoon.
The decision to take Parvathi and other loyal ministers along, and
ride on Chaitanya Ratham to the hotel in attack mode came a
cropper for NTR.

Parvathi's Climbdown

Efforts were still being made by some family members for a patch-
up. NTR's sons Saikrishna and Ramakrishna were among those
who met NTR with a compromise formula. The proposal was that
NTR should give up power in favour of Chandrababu, continue as
the party president and play a greater role in national politics. NTR
curtly rejected the suggestion. Daggubati said Balakrishna also

came to Viceroy Hotel and told Chandrababu and his supporters that he had convinced NTR of many of the conditions and that his father should be retained as the party president. But they said it was too late by then for any compromise.[70]

Meanwhile, a disheartened Parvathi issued a lengthy statement of apology in Telugu on 26 August, regretting any mistakes she might have committed in the past due to lack of experience. 'Let the past be past. From today, I will have no connection whatsoever with politics. I will remain a mere servant to NTR.' She went on:

> I was a commoner, and it was a turning point in my life that I came in contact with him and married him. I assert that I never wilfully did anything that was despicable or wrong. As the saying goes, when the lamp grows, the shadow under it also lengthens. This happened in my case. I regret that I acted in haste, and this feeling always haunts me. I apologise for the mistakes I had done and appeal to the Telugu people to pardon me.[71]

In a way, Parvathi's letter met the primary demand of the rebel group that she quit politics. In a bid to meet other requirements of the Chandrababu group, the NTR camp also asked forty-odd chairmen of government corporations to resign to assuage the rival group's feelings that they were all Parvathi's men. Five ministers, G. Muddukrishnama Naidu, G. Butchaiah Chowdary, P. Indra Reddy, M. Narasimhulu and Dadi Veerabhadra Rao, branded as Parvathi acolytes, also submitted their resignations. But the rebel group, swelling in numbers, was in no mood to back down. Chandrababu's associates were not prepared to take NTR's belated actions at face value. They were afraid that NTR would go back to his old ways once the dust settled. He would then ensure, they feared, that everyone who had opposed him was politically decimated.

Meanwhile, both the parties were pressing for their demand—NTR for dissolution of the assembly and Chandrababu for the call to form the new government. Adding to NTR's travails, Governor Krishan Kant was not inclined to heed his recommendation for dissolution. NTR dashed off another letter to the governor, urging him that a fresh mandate was the only option. 'When a mandate is being thwarted, the only fair and appropriate forum for decision is the people, who are the ultimate sovereign in a democratic polity,' he asserted.[72]

The governor, however, took into consideration the enormous strain and expenditure on state resources. 'In my judgment, it is the constitutional obligation of the governor that every effort should be made, which would obviate the extreme consequences of the dissolution of the assembly,'[73] the governor said later in his affidavit in the high court. The governor's decision to go against the chief minister's advice sealed the latter's fate.

What strengthened the governor's stand were the views expressed by the leaders of the legislature parties of the CPI, CPI (M) and the BJP. All of them told the governor in writing that they opposed the dissolution of the assembly. While expressing sympathy for NTR, the leaders of the communist parties justified Chandrababu's claims, saying, 'It is an open revolt and a spontaneous reaction.' The Congress, under the leadership of P.V. Narasimha Rao, issued strict directions to its state wing to keep away from the power struggle within the TDP. The prime minister took the stand that the governor should be allowed to take a view on the developments. Meanwhile, the Chandrababu group was getting restive and increased pressure on the governor to invite their leader to form the government, claiming the majority support.

Taking cognisance of the leadership crisis in the ruling party, the governor asked NTR in the early hours of 27 August to seek a vote of confidence on the floor of the assembly by Wednesday, 30 August 1995. Since he had barely three days left, NTR requested the governor to convene the assembly after 15 September. NTR was aware that he did not have the numbers on his side. He thought he might be able to get his legislators back if there was enough time before the assembly met. But the governor was willing to extend the date only by a day, to make sure a stable government was in place as soon as possible. By this time, the Chandrababu group was claiming support of 173 MLAs, much more than the 148 needed to cross the halfway mark in the House. In a bid to overcome any problem that might arise out of NTR issuing a party whip for the floor test, Chandrababu sought recognition as the new leader of the TDLP, which was promptly granted by the speaker.

The contender to the throne organized not only MLAs but even MPs to back him. Mohan Babu, the film actor, had maintained close relations with NTR and Parvathi. NTR had nominated him to the Rajya Sabha. But now he joined the MPs who wanted the governor to invite Chandrababu to form the government.

Mohan Babu visited NTR's residence on 27 August, taking Tamil superstar Rajinikanth along with him. Having come to know of Mohan Babu's support for Chandrababu, the restive crowds outside NTR's residence shoved and pushed him. It was with great difficulty that they could be escorted out. Rajini, who had been nominated by NTR as the TTD board member only recently, surprisingly threw his weight behind Chandrababu. He even went to the assembly premises where he addressed the rebel MLAs. In his speech, he painted Parvathi as the villain of the piece. She had proved what damage a woman could do, he alleged, describing her as 'an evil force'.[74]

Rajini's support at this crucial juncture, apparently egged on by his friend Mohan Babu, helped Chandrababu's cause further. Three days later Rajinikanth resigned from the TTD board. Interestingly, he later clarified he did not support Chandrababu Naidu.[75] But it did not matter by then.

Having proved unequal in dealing with the covert politics of his rivals, NTR chose what came naturally to him—going to the people. On the evening of 27 August, he left by the

Falaknuma Express on a tour of coastal AP 'to seek justice from
the people'. His aim apparently was to create a wave of public
sympathy for himself, forcing the MLAs to mend their ways. This
time, a chastened Parvathi was not by his side. Beginning from
Vizianagaram District, NTR, despite his failing health, went on
a whirlwind tour for three days across the state, addressing public
meetings and narrating the sordid tale of deception and betrayal.

Even amid these calamitous developments, NTR's sartorial
instincts remained sharp. During the tour, he wore black trousers
and a full-sleeved black shirt, symbolic of his protest against
the 'murder of democracy'. He didn't mince his words against
Chandrababu, whom he described as Duryodhana, adding that
he gave him only his daughter, not the party. NTR's impromptu
public meetings in this period of crisis did receive a good response,
even though not many party leaders were left to mobilize the
crowds. *The Hindu* reported that about 20,000 people attended
the Vijayawada meeting, braving an incessant drizzle and heard
the fifteen-minute speech with rapt attention. 'They clapped and
raised slogans against Mr Chandrababu Naidu.'[76] However, the
crowds were moderate compared to the overwhelming support he
had received in 1984 during the Nadendla episode. R.J. Rajendra
Prasad of *The Hindu* analysed the situation thus:

> In 1984, Mr Rama Rao received almost unanimous press
> support while today the Telugu press is completely antagonistic
> to him. The earlier crisis was due to a political manipulation
> with the active participation of the Congress (I) but today the
> 'backstabbing' was by Mr Rama Rao's own son-in-law and the
> general public perceives it as Mr Rama Rao's personal problem
> to be resolved at his family level.[77]

NTR was so comprehensively deserted at this time that even his
own advocate general, S. Ramachandra Rao, advised the governor
to invite Chandrababu to form the government. Arguing before a

division bench of the AP High Court on a writ petition filed during the crisis, Ramachandra Rao said that NTR had 'no legitimacy or constitutional authority to continue as chief minister' after the speaker recognized Chandrababu's claim of legislators' support. This was the same Ramachandra Rao who had unleashed a legal ambush against NTR in the previous tenure.[78] NTR, still the chief minister, terminated Ramachandra Rao as advocate general, but the high court stayed the order.[79]

The leadership struggle in the TDP caused much disquiet in the National Front, and its leaders sought to find an amicable solution to the crisis. V.P. Singh, the former prime minister, arrived in Hyderabad on 28 August to work out a compromise. He was joined the next day by the Janata Dal president S.R. Bommai and the Karnataka chief minister Deve Gowda. But by this time, unity efforts appeared remote because the demand that NTR should distance himself from his wife had receded into the background. The refrain of the Chandrababu group now was that NTR should quit as the chief minister and stay only as a figurehead of the party. 'What began as a campaign against Mrs Lakshmi Parvati's overbearing attitude has ended as a revolt against Mr Rama Rao himself,' Rajendra Prasad of *The Hindu* wrote.[80]

With the mediation efforts failing, NTR pledged at his last public meeting at the Nizam College grounds on 30 August, a day before the floor test, to 'fight back' and rebuild the party. V.P. Singh and Akali leader Baldev Singh Talwandi, who were present at the meeting, appealed to NTR to 'leave the State behind' for which he had done so much and to play a role in national politics. 'Honour awaits you at the national level,' they said.[81]

Having been elected as the TDP president the same day at the defunct Basant Talkies theatre at Lingampally, Chandrababu was now in an unassailable position. A resolution was also passed to amend the clause in the party constitution that enabled NTR to be president for life. Daggubati and Harikrishna were present during the announcement. A torrent of abuses was poured on

Parvathi by the leaders, calling her names like *'deyyam* [devil]'.
Daggubati, in his speech, infamously castigated Parvathi as a
country bumpkin who came in a 'red bus' but was now flying in
chartered planes.[82] Harikrishna broke down while talking about
the 'evil influence'.[83]

A day earlier, Speaker Yanamala Ramakrishnudu had issued
a bulletin recognizing Chandrababu as the TDLP leader. This
gave authority to Chandrababu to issue a whip to all TDP MLAs
to vote against NTR during the confidence motion. This also
meant that all those who supported NTR on the floor could be
disqualified. The speaker's action thus ensured that the number of
supporters behind NTR dwindled rapidly.

Things took a dramatic turn on 31 August, the day the assembly
was to be convened. Early in the morning, NTR's official secretary
Dr N. Jayaprakash Narayan sought an appointment for NTR with
the governor at 11 a.m., informing that the chief minister wished
to submit his resignation personally. NTR apparently had decided
to resign after consultations with his loyalists. The appointment
with the governor was fixed. Meanwhile, NTR suddenly collapsed
around 9.20 a.m. while talking to his colleagues. According to
MLA G. Butchaiah Chowdary, NTR was discussing the next
course of action when he suffered an incessant cough for nearly
fifteen minutes followed by breathlessness. He was rushed to
Mediciti Hospital. The doctors said that he had suffered from
secondary coronary infarction.

At about 1 p.m., the chief secretary to the government, M.S.
Rajajee, arrived at Raj Bhavan and informed that the chief minister
had requested the governor to go over to the Mediciti Hospital to
receive the resignation letter as he was not in a position to travel to
Raj Bhavan for the said purpose.

At about 1.20 p.m., Krishan Kant, accompanied by the chief
secretary, visited NTR, who handed over his letter of resignation.
The governor accepted the same and requested NTR to continue
to be in office till the new government was sworn in. Harikrishna

and his sisters, Purandeswari and Bhuvaneswari (wives of Daggubati and Chandrababu respectively), were among those who visited NTR in the hospital. Many NTR supporters gathered at the hospital, some of them sobbing. Harikrishna was jeered by the agitated fans, 'We are his sons, not you. You can go back.'

The assembly, convened to test NTR's strength, was adjourned by the speaker, given NTR's inability to attend the House. By evening, NTR recovered and went back home against the advice of the doctors. He was resting at home when Ramoji Rao with his wife Ramadevi visited him to inquire about his health. NTR thanked them for the visit. Parvathi recalled that as they came out, she fell on Ramoji's feet and cried. 'I have not done anything wrong. They concocted all these rumours. You are the only one capable of finding a solution to this issue. NTR's health is terrible. Please do something,' she pleaded.[84] Ramoji said bluntly that she was the cause of all that had happened, and that he had information that she had taken money from party leaders.[85] When Parvathi wanted a trial to prove her innocence, Ramoji apparently withdrew saying it was anyway a family issue and that he would not like to interfere. NTR later consoled Parvathi, saying that both (Ramoji and Chandrababu) were partners in the crime, and hence there was no point in seeking his help.

Following NTR's resignation, Chandrababu immediately staked his claim to form the government. The governor invited Chandrababu to form the government the next day, 1 September 1995. The forty-five-year-old Chandrababu, the second youngest chief minister in AP's history, was sworn in along with ten other ministers in a low-key ceremony at Raj Bhavan.[86] After more than seventeen years of relentless pursuit of power, Chandrababu finally realized his dream of becoming the chief minister. Harikrishna, who was not an MLA, was also inducted. Immediately after the ceremony, Chandrababu went to NTR's residence with his wife Bhuvaneswari, son Lokesh and brother-in-law Harikrishna to seek the patriarch's blessings. Stripped of his power after barely eight and a half months in the government, NTR, still recovering from his bronchitis spasm, did not wish to see them.

The architect of the TDP was devastated at the turn of events. A man who had seen so many battles in his life finally lost the one with his family. He was left vulnerable as his entire brood ganged up against him. His chair was snatched from right under his nose. The TDP was his baby, and he had shed blood, sweat and tears to conceive, create and nurture it. But now he was a persona non grata in his own party. 'Even for a consummate comeback artist like NTR, the damage could be too much to repair,' *India Today* said.[87]

Even while he was gravely wounded by the course of events, NTR's personality shone through. Jayaprakash Narayan recalled that he, along with other senior officials who served him, met him to take leave a day after Chandrababu assumed office. 'We went there early in the morning. He was sitting there like every day afresh in his crisp clothes. He appeared unaffected by what all happened a day before. He always regarded himself above the chief minister's chair. Today was no different,' he said.[88]

During this period, NTR often talked about the need for a presidential system, wherein the prime minister and the chief minister were directly elected by the people. He also wanted the 'right to recall' clause to be incorporated so that the electorate could exercise it if their elected representatives subverted democracy. He wanted to make this part of the National Front manifesto.

The saga of humiliation did not end for NTR, with the Chandrababu camp ensuring that he was comprehensively beaten on every front. A weakened NTR decided to attend the assembly session on 7 September convened for Chandrababu to win a vote of confidence. He wanted to speak on the momentous political developments. His mic was cut as he began to talk. Speaker Yanamala Ramakrishnudu denied NTR an opportunity to give a statement on the circumstances that had led to his resignation. 'Sir, I have been thrown out of office. I should explain to the

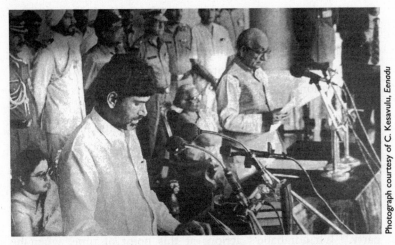

Nara Chandrababu Naidu, who replaced NTR in the most unusual circumstances, was the second youngest chief minister of united AP. The manner in which he replaced NTR remains controversial.

people, through this assembly the reasons for that. Please give me a chance. That is my privilege,' he pleaded.[89] Even for those sitting in the overflowing media gallery, the scene appeared improbable.

The chief minister and founder-president of the TDP till barely a week ago, NTR was now pleading for permission to speak. The speaker disallowed NTR's request, saying it could be taken up after the vote of confidence, triggering protests from the twenty-eight MLAs who had remained with NTR. Even as NTR's supporters demanded that he be allowed to speak, the speaker asked Chandrababu to move the confidence motion, which he did. 'I beg to move that this house expresses its confidence in the Council of Ministers headed by Sri N. Chandrababu Naidu,' he read out amid the din. Since NTR loyalists continued to protest by storming the podium of the House, they were all suspended for the day, and the vote of confidence was taken in their absence. The motion for Chandrababu was supported by 227 members with the backing of the CPI, CPI (M), MIM and some independents.

On assuming office, Chandrababu tried to dampen the already broken spirit of NTR. He criticized the slow pace of development allegedly witnessed during the past eight months under his father-in-law. He ruled out any patch-up with NTR. He expressed his determination to get the TDP symbol for himself. He visited Delhi in the first week after assuming office and there he denigrated his mentor as having given a go-by to all democratic principles. He said that he had to topple NTR to protect democracy. 'People did not vote for NTR; they had voted for TDP,' he asserted. He ridiculed NTR, saying that the days of film glamour working in politics were long over. He declared that the people had welcomed the split in the TDP and recognized him as the leader of the party.[90] Chandrababu's actions at this point of time, when he needed to assert his position, were driven by immediate political compulsions. But they appeared as if he was trying to throw NTR into the dustbin of history.

While Lakshmi Prasad played a key role in getting NTR's sons Harikrishna and Balakrishna to align with the opposite camp, how did Chandrababu manage to convince his long-time rival Daggubati? According to Daggubati, Chandrababu offered him the position of deputy chief minister. The elder son-in-law had been equally troubled with Parvathi's role. But as an MP, he was not as involved in undermining Parvathi and NTR as Chandrababu, who was up to his neck in running the party and government affairs. The only common ground between them at this stage was their antipathy towards Parvathi.

Against this backdrop, what made him sail with Chandrababu as his second-in-command remained unclear. The entire family saw Parvathi as the bigger threat. There was talk that his wife Purandeswari, NTR's second daughter, prevailed upon him to string along. The Chandrababu group later gave currency to this rumour, and Parvathi too in her book accused Purandeswari of colluding with other family members against the couple. Daggubati, however, rubbished these allegations, insisting that

NTR's daughter, on the contrary, pleaded with him to not go against her father.[91]

Whatever the truth was, Daggubati acquiesced rather meekly and joined forces with Chandrababu with or without his wife's goading. When Daggubati queried about Harikrishna, who had been literally waging war against his father, Chandrababu apparently said the temperamental son could be appeased with the post of party secretary. Balakrishna was at the top of his career in Telugu films, and hence was not in the race for any position.

The impression given by the media during the palace coup was that the entire family was behind Chandrababu in his fait accompli. Except for Harikrishna, nobody in NTR's family ever spoke about their feelings in public. Balakrishna was seen with Chandrababu during this crucial period, but he too never made any public comments.

NTR's seven sons and four daughters generally kept away from politics and were rarely seen in public. During the coup, Jayakrishna, Saikrishna and Mohana Krishna remained neutral, while Jayashankara Krishna was opposed to it. Harikrishna and Ramakrishna sided with Chandrababu, while Balakrishna, though with Chandrababu, tried to salvage the situation to find a middle ground. Among his daughters, Lokeswari and Uma Maheswari lived outside of Hyderabad and had no role in the developments, while Bhuvaneswari followed her husband, Chandrababu. Purandeswari's part, as mentioned earlier, remained unclear. Thus, the reports about NTR's entire family supporting Chandrababu were not exactly true. However, the fact that Daggubati and Harikrishna, the two prominent faces in the family, stood behind Chandrababu served the optics well for the rebel group.

NTR had hopes of relief from the courts, but he was in for a disappointment. His writ petition against the actions of Governor Krishan Kant, Speaker Y. Ramakrishnudu and N. Chandrababu Naidu was dismissed in December 1995 by a bench of the AP High Court, consisting of Chief Justice Prabhashankar Mishra,

Justice Lingaraja Rath and Justice B. Sudershan Reddy.[92] NTR's counsel in the case, G. Ramaswamy, a former attorney general, raised several contentions in the course of the hearing, revolving around the governor not taking notice of the advice of the council of ministers headed by NTR to dissolve the assembly, and the speaker publishing a bulletin declaring Chandrababu as the TDLP leader. NTR alleged that the governor and the speaker acted in league with Chandrababu to remove him and install him as the TDLP leader.

The judges, however, said it was difficult to see any legal mala fide in the governor's actions. But the court found fault with the actions of Speaker Ramakrishnudu. 'The issue as to who was the president or leader of the Telugu Desam Party obviously is not one to be decided by the Speaker,' the judges agreed. But in the event the majority of TDP legislators supported Chandrababu Naidu, these issues became irrelevant. 'Since Sri N. Chandrababu Naidu has the support of majority of the members of the Legislature, whether he belongs to Telugu Desam Party or not and whether he is the leader of the Telugu Desam Legislature party or not, the governor has committed nothing wrong in the eye of law in appointing him as the chief minister,' the bench concluded.[93] Reputed legal eagles Ramaswamy and Rajeev Dhavan for NTR, K. Parasaran for Chandrababu Naidu, Soli Sorabjee for Governor Krishan Kant and Kapil Sibal for Speaker Yanamala Ramakrishnudu argued the case.

Reasons for NTR's Downfall

Legally, NTR did not stand a chance as Chandrababu Naidu clearly had a majority supporting him both in the government and the party. But in moral and political terms, it was a travesty of justice to deny NTR his position in a party he had founded. The party would not have thrived but for his charismatic leadership. Even legally speaking, many scholars maintained that the governor should have abided by NTR's advice, when he had the majority support, for dissolution of the assembly. 'If the precepts of British Parliamentary polity were to be strictly followed, the Andhra Pradesh assembly must have been dissolved when the chief minister recommended its dissolution,' Subhash C. Kashyap, the former secretary-general of the Lok Sabha opined.[94] *The Hindu*, while recognizing the reality of the greater support for Chandrababu from within the party, underlined that the mandate in the 1994 polls was for NTR. 'It was within everybody's knowledge that but for the personal appeal of Mr Rama Rao the party could not have done half as well as it did in the previous elections, and he was fully within his right politically to ask for a dissolution.'[95]

Chandrababu succeeded where Nadendla failed because the former was able to destroy NTR's moral high ground through the adroit use of Parvathi's alleged sins. The leading Telugu papers of the time successfully projected a sinister persona of Parvathi in the public mind, which helped justify the overthrow when it happened.

Mobilizing the family on his side was a master stroke that further strengthened Chandrababu's hands. The animus of some of NTR's own blood towards Parvathi was so severe that they were prepared to cast off the patriarch along with his partner. Unlike during the Nadendla episode, the plot this time was planned meticulously. Chandrababu's trusted lieutenants helped him net many MLAs and other party leaders with promises of better positions in the government. The political management on his side was swift and resolute.

Too many players in this sordid drama, from the speaker to the advocate general, acted in a way that was clearly harmful to NTR's interests. His loyalists, regaining their wits after the shock of the coup, later alleged that NTR was a victim of wrong advice by Ramachandra Rao. The senior counsel, a Congress sympathizer earlier, had filed dozens of cases during the 1983–89 period against NTR and his government. To everybody's surprise, he was made the advocate general after the TDP government was formed. Some say it was Parvathi who brought him into NTR's circle before the 1994 elections. Ramachandra Rao had won some cases against the Congress government between 1989 and 1994 and thus apparently gained NTR's confidence.

Chelameswar, who had been associated with the party from the beginning and who took care of NTR and the party's legal matters, appeared to have been estranged due to these developments. He was the standing counsel of AP Lokayukta during 1985–86 and worked as the government pleader for home affairs in the high court during 1988–89. He threw his weight behind the rebel group and was appointed as the additional advocate general in October 1995. He subsequently became a high court judge and later a judge of the Supreme Court of India. Yarlagadda Lakshmi Prasad, another dramatis persona in the coup, tilted the scales by bringing together the family members against NTR.[96]

There were allegations by the NTR camp that business interests and the liquor lobby worked against NTR because he was universally known as not amenable. Chandrababu, on the other hand, was known to be pragmatic. Barely a year after he scrapped even health permits to prove a point to NTR, Chandrababu boldly did away with total prohibition, opening doors to the liquor business once again. Prabhakar Reddy, the owner of Viceroy Hotel, the venue that had played a key role in the transfer of power, became a close confidant of Chandrababu during his term as chief minister, between 1995 and 2004, and was also made a Rajya Sabha member. The new chief minister also opened doors to the corporate world in a big way.

NTR's fall was attributed to his failure to live up to the expectations of the rising social class that was eager to expand its economic footprint. 'It was not a simple event of a change of guard of the TDP but a contestation that involved different social classes, especially the entrepreneurial class which successfully directed the crisis to a finale,' stated a CESS paper.[97] The leadership crisis in the TDP was effectively used by the disgruntled capitalist class which was restless with the populist policies and obsessive self-image-driven governance of NTR, according to the paper. NTR's policies since he took over in 1983—such as the ban on capitation fees, spending on welfare, nationalization of bus routes, reservations for BCs and prohibition on liquor—did not go down well with the business class, of which Kammas were a significant part.

The facile way the CPI and CPI (M) parties abandoned NTR and embraced Chandrababu without so much as a blink remained an enigma. Egged on by the state leaders, even their national leadership urged NTR to 'leave the State to your children'[98] and concentrate on national politics.

The media role, especially that of *Eenadu*, in the transfer of power was by no means insignificant. Ramoji Rao ran his paper in campaign mode against NTR and Parvathi. The reason was his frustration with NTR's maverick attitude. According to analyst K. Balagopal, NTR was found wanting in 'the social urge represented by *Eenadu*'s politics' for economic and industrial modernization. Chandrababu was a better bet for the new market regime. In its effort to displace NTR, the paper resorted to 'copious use of the patriarchal distrust of an ambitious woman who gets married to a wealthy and powerful old man whose brain is suspected to have gone soft of late'.[99]

That NTR and Ramoji had fallen out was evident even before the TDP came to power in 1994. Ramoji did not seem to have appreciated NTR acting as his own boss throughout his earlier tenure. He considered the TDP chief whimsical and unstable. For him, NTR was no longer the best bet for the state. Ramoji had extended only tentative support to the TDP in the 1994 assembly polls. He was not even sure that NTR would win this time, given his erratic behaviour in the recent past, especially regarding his second marriage. Parvathi narrated how her efforts to bring the two together just before the 1994 state elections ended in a fiasco:

With great difficulty, I could make NTR and Ramoji agree to meet. We were to join him at 5.30 am at the latter's residence in Begumpet. We went in an Ambassador car, unaccompanied by security people. We entered past the huge gates, got down and went to the main door, which was closed. There was nobody around. No signs of opening the door either. Seconds were turning into minutes. NTR was already getting impatient. I was scared to death inside. I was feeling guilty because I had pushed him against his will for this meeting. But why is this gentleman Ramoji behaving like this? He gave us time and now makes the guests wait. Is he trying to convey a message? NTR's face turned red with anger as the clock ticked away. I was afraid even to look at his face. At last, after the longest five minutes of my life, Ramoji opened the door. He did not seem to be unduly bothered about the awkward situation. 'Was walking on the terrace, hence the delay,' he said in a casual tone, without a hint of apology. NTR had a grave look on his face. Both went inside a room and stayed closeted for 15 minutes. Before leaving, I tried to win Ramoji over once again. 'Annayya garu, this is a party encouraged and promoted by you. Don't allow personal issues to creep into our relationship. Please cooperate like always'. He did not respond much to my plea. 'The party might get through barely, and the government, even if formed, may not even survive,' he said dryly. NTR nodded his head but did not say a word. I was terrified. Would the party lose because of our marriage? With a heavy heart, we returned home. Despite my apprehensions, NTR did not say a word of rebuke to me, but he was withdrawn throughout the day. My efforts to bring together two big egos fell flat.[100]

Ramoji was not the only one displeased with Parvathi's role in the TDP affairs. A whole lot of people around NTR, including TDP leaders and the media, were tired of Parvathi's shenanigans and NTR's seemingly thoughtless support for her. Parvathi was the *shikhandi* (the transgender in Mahabharata deployed to defeat Bhishma, the supreme commander of Kuru forces), the bogey through which the Bhishma Pitamaha of the TDP was politically slain.

In spite of the widely held view that Parvathi nursed political ambitions, NTR actively encouraged her participation in party affairs. He even reportedly wanted to make her the party general secretary to strengthen her position. Furious over his son-in-law's attempts at undermining his authority, NTR also considered removing Chandrababu from the cabinet several times in those eight months (January to August 1995). Getting wind of such a possibility, Chandrababu and his supporters finally decided that it was not Parvathi, but NTR himself who needed to be removed.

Jayaprakash Narayan, the IAS officer who was a close confidant of NTR, affirmed that Parvathi had no role in the administration despite the hype around her alleged 'extra-constitutional role' in the government. 'Only on one occasion, she was present when we were to discuss official business with NTR. I suggested Parvathi should leave the room. She hesitated a bit, but NTR asked her to move out,' he recalled. She might have played whatever role in the party, but in the government, she never got involved, he added.[101]

An overwhelming impression was that Parvathi manipulated NTR into choosing her as his political heir and that he was entirely under her sway. She was even suspected of using magic spells and potions to gain control over him. Dr Kakarla Subba Rao, considered a tall figure among the medical community both in AP and the US, was upset at the change he saw in NTR after his marriage with Parvathi:

> In earlier days, he used to call me late at nights on trivial issues such as to confirm whether he should take a particular pill that had been prescribed to him by another doctor. But when I asked about his health this time, he very curtly said, 'What has happened to me? I am all right.' With my years in medicine

behind me, I could feel something terribly wrong in him. Was he avoiding discussing his health? Was he taking certain medicines he secretly knew he should not be taking? There was evil in the air of the house of this demigod.[102]

This sense of intrigue haunted many observers because of Parvathi's seeming hold on NTR who otherwise was known as inflexible. But from Parvathi's own accounts, NTR came across as the domineering husband. She was terrified of his disapproval. At the height of the crisis when Parvathi wanted to withdraw from politics as demanded by the rebels, NTR was furious. 'I put you up at the top, but you talk like a sissy,'[103] he shouted. In a way, Parvathi acted out as the typical Indian wife, treading the path that her husband had chalked out for her. But for NTR's explicit backing, Parvathi would not have made the political moves that she did.

But the image of a modern Kaikeyi (the proverbial stepmother in Ramayana) who could bend her husband's will to hers was overpowering. Sociologist Kalpana Kannabiran stated: 'Very soon, all the decisions were being taken by her while NTR became symbolic of the old, ageing, infirm king, who allowed himself to be manipulated by the machinations of a scheming wife.'[104] Such an image was skilfully manipulated even though no proof was unearthed by the media of Parvathi's 'undue' influence concerning any major policy matter benefiting any person or group.

Many women activists found fault with the way Parvathi was being portrayed. A group of twenty-four women activists criticized 'the totally unpardonable dimension' that the ire against Parvathi had taken. In an open letter, these intellectuals, including Susie Tharu, Rama Melkote, Veena Shatrugna and D. Vasantha, said:

> The way the attack has been orchestrated by the Opposition groups seems to be emerging as a no-holds-barred attack on women in general in the most feudal, gender and caste

discriminatory terms . . . We feel that political differences should be discussed in political terms.[105]

However, it was widely felt that Parvathi became too ambitious for her own good. The enormous clout she came to wield as NTR's wife made her overconfident. Many senior officials and partymen claimed that she immaturely behaved as if she were the next chief minister, though no major decision in the government was made by NTR according to her wishes. She loved being the wife of Caesar but never bothered to keep herself above suspicion. The vulgar display of sycophancy around Parvathi put off the public as well as party leaders.[106] She also underestimated the strength of her detractors. Parvathi was no match to Chandrababu in the political arena.

Chandrababu was a driven politician with a network of loyalists nurtured over a long period. He was not a charismatic personality, but his political skills were legendary. Parvathi was a greenhorn, and all her strength was derived from NTR. Without NTR by her side, she was a political nonentity.

The public perception that after all those years his son-in-law deserved to be his political heir tilted the scales in Chandrababu's favour. He enjoyed political credibility among the party legislators. Parvathi was catapulted into the much-vaunted position due to a curious turn in her destiny, but she fell woefully short of the role she was thrust into. She had no quality except being NTR's wife to be even seen as claiming his political legacy.

The second-rung party leaders deserted NTR as they regarded him as a weakling relying on a political ignoramus like Parvathi. Chandrababu, on the other hand, was considered a legitimate and capable politician who could steer the boat through stormy waters.

Another important element that played a part in this catastrophic episode was NTR's declining health. Many officers who worked with him said that NTR was not his former self in his third term. His faculties were not as sharp. His precarious health condition was one of the factors that lent an urgency to the rival camps to realize their respective goals.

People, including the media, continue to be divided in their stand over the change of leadership in the TDP. While a section is of the opinion that the Chandrababu-led group backstabbed NTR in a pre-planned coup, others see the development as forced by circumstances. While critics seek to portray Chandrababu as an opportunistic politician to this day, others feel that he had little choice in the prevailing situation. Most observers agree that Chandrababu was prepared to take up the mantle in the natural course after NTR. He would have waited as long as it was required to inherit NTR's legacy in the ordinary course. But the turn of events apparently led him to act sooner than he anticipated.

Chandrababu never gave his side of the story. Critics see Chandrababu's admission of guilt in this reticence. Admirers attribute it to his aversion to digging up skeletons from the past.

During the height of the crisis, NTR tried to get Prime Minister P.V. Narasimha Rao's help in wriggling out of the situation. Both NTR and Parvathi spoke to him on the phone, seeking his support. A desperate NTR reportedly offered his cooperation in Lok Sabha elections if P.V. could see that the assembly was dissolved. According to Upendra, NTR was even ready to give up all Lok Sabha seats in P.V.'s favour if he were to rescue him from his predicament.[107] While Vijaya Bhaskara Reddy, who was the Opposition leader at this time, supported the dissolution, other Central ministers from the state such as G. Venkataswamy and P.V. Rangaiah Naidu opposed it. The latter contended that it was the right opportunity to weaken NTR, who was the Congress's primary political rival. Meanwhile, Chandrababu was said to have pulled some strings in Delhi through a secretary close to the prime minister. The name of P.V.R.K. Prasad, P.V.'s media adviser, was mentioned by Lakshmi Parvathi in this context.[108] In any case, P.V. chose not to act in the matter.

NTR was left with less than thirty MLAs out of the 219. In the early days of his forced exit, NTR was mostly trying to grapple with the legal implications. He still asserted he was the TDP's legitimate president. However, the Chandrababu group, with its better resources and support base, aggressively pursued the process of acquiring ownership of the party. The group approached the Election Commission to recognize the party under the leadership of Chandrababu Naidu as the real TDP. They submitted an affidavit with signatures of all MLAs, MPs, ZP chairpersons, ZP members and mandal parishad presidents, asserting their leader was Chandrababu. As many as 2000 individual affidavits were said to have been gathered as part of the exercise.

National Front leaders, worried over the implications of the split in the TDP at the national level, made one more effort to bring about a rapprochement. Janata Dal leader Biju Patnaik flew to Hyderabad in the first week of October in 1995 but made little progress as both sides stuck to their guns. NTR refused to reconcile because of the personal affront caused to him and said he was confident of turning the people to his side. The National Front finally gave up the mediation and decided to stick with NTR. Chandrababu declared that he would not join the Front if NTR continued to be its chairman.

Meanwhile, Daggubati, the parliamentary party leader, failed to get a berth even in the cabinet expansion and realized he had been taken for a ride. Chandrababu's stand was that since Harikrishna was already in the cabinet, it was improper to have one more family member as a minister. 'I never promised him the post of deputy chief minister. People would have detested us if Daggubati were installed in the post,' he said.[109]

Daggubati was now a dejected person. He felt he was being treated as an unwanted person in Chandrababu's party. Sensing the situation, NTR's son Jayakrishna mediated with Daggubati. Finally, the elder son-in-law went back to NTR along with fourteen MLAs on 16 October 1995, a month and a half after the coup. Chandrababu, of course, was ready for the eventuality. He had more than enough TDP MLAs, MPs and other party functionaries supporting him. He was now free of the burden of another power centre in the party.

The return of the elder son-in-law was a shot in the arm for NTR, though the former failed to bring along a significant number of MLAs. He addressed the media regularly, castigating the Chandrababu government's policies. He said like Lord Krishna, he was counting the sins of this Sisupala.[110] Continuing his tirade against him, NTR came up with an audio cassette titled *Jamata Dasama Graham*, 'exposing' how Chandrababu Naidu, whom he compared with the killer of Mahatma Gandhi, Nathuram Godse, conspired to dethrone him.[111] The cassette began with 'This is your brother NTR speaking . . .' and went on to explain how he was 'backstabbed'. By this time, NTR's dentures had a mumbling effect when he spoke. NTR strained himself considerably to get the right effect for his speech.

The wounded patriarch was now focused on the big fight. The only way for him to redeem himself from his ignominy was to show who called the shots at the hustings. That could happen only in the Lok Sabha elections due in a few months. He wanted early elections to Parliament so that he could bounce back from the political wilderness and teach a lesson to all those who had betrayed him.

In one of the most exhaustive interviews given on the occasion of the launch of *Vaartha*, a Telugu daily, to journalists Y. Kasipati and N. Sitarama Raju just ten days before his death, NTR expressed his sense of deep hurt at the way his son-in-law had plotted against him. He also expressed his disappointment with the behaviour of his sons. 'Nobody ever behaved so badly with his parents as Hari [Harikrishna] did with his father,' he remarked.[112] He, however, was determined to fight it out. In the same interview, he recalled a dialogue from the Hindi play *Jay Parajay* (1937) written by Upendranath Ashk. He said Parvathi had told him about the play, which captured his own personality. 'Jeevan mein aaraam kahaa? Tahernaa aur sustanaa kahaa? Nirantar athak chalte reh nahi toh jeevan hai, tahernaatoh mrityu hai [There is no respite in life. No waiting and relaxing. Being relentlessly on the move is what life is; stopping is death],' he recited the lines and said the words reflected his own state of mind.

NTR started planning for what he called the Simha Garjana (Lion's Roar) public meeting to be held on 2 February 1996, at Vijayawada, to kick off the campaign for the forthcoming Lok Sabha polls, as early as the first week of January. He reviewed the arrangements almost daily. On 17 January, barely twelve hours before he breathed his last, NTR addressed a marathon press conference, detailing how he would 'unmask' Chandrababu Naidu at 'the mother of all public meetings'.

Curtains

When the end came the next day, in the early hours of 18 January 1996, it was totally unexpected and certainly untimely. 'See, I am hale and hearty,' NTR had assured the press at a packed media conference a few hours earlier. He wanted to scotch rumours that he would not be able to campaign for the Lok Sabha elections because of his ill health. But before dawn broke, the seventy-two-year-old breathed his last. He died between 3.30 and 4 a.m., after suffering a massive heart attack. Unlike hundreds of his celluloid dramas, NTR's life story ended on a tragic note. He left the stage before the curtains were drawn in a proper finale.

I was working for the *Deccan Chronicle* at the time and distinctly remember the day NTR died. I was woken up at around 5 a.m. on that Thursday by my editor P.N.V. Nair. A man of few words, Nair broke the news that NTR had passed away and wanted me to rush to the latter's residence on Road No. 13, Banjara Hills.

That house was very familiar to me, as I used to visit it almost daily. At the time, I was covering NTR's TDP for the paper, and hence used to spend quite a bit of time at NTR's residence. I had met NTR barely twenty-four hours ago on 17 January in his private room, and he had looked as grand as ever. No wonder, initially it was hard to believe my editor's words. I felt sure it was just a rumour. I rushed to NTR's residence, which was a little more than a kilometre away from where I stayed at the time.

Even as I entered the house, I could feel a sense of sickness enveloping me. There was some activity near the home, though there weren't too many people around. I rushed into the front hall of the house when the body was being brought down the steps from the upper floor. Only a chest-beating Lakshmi Parvathi and a few domestic staff were present at the time. NTR looked peaceful in his eternal sleep. I almost felt that he was still alive. The dark reality descended on me slowly, as hundreds of people soon started crowding the place, many of them shell-shocked at the unexpected death.

NTR was in his element when I had met him a day earlier. A correspondent from the international news agency Reuters was in Hyderabad to interview him. On a request from him, I had sought an appointment with NTR, who had agreed to meet at 7 a.m. the next day, 17 January.

A day earlier, that is on 16 January, during a routine chit-chat, NTR had animatedly talked about the forthcoming Lok Sabha polls. He was very keen on these elections as these would provide him with an opportunity to establish that he was still the darling of the people and that his party was the real TDP. He was also aware that the fluid political situation in the country on the eve of the 1996 Lok Sabha polls meant that a regional leader might emerge as the kingpin in Delhi. During the conversation, he told me that he would personally be in the race for a parliamentary seat. Towards the end of the tête-à-tête, I checked with him whether I could do a story on his decision to contest. He asked me to wait.

During my briefing to the correspondent from Reuters, I prompted him to ask NTR whether he would personally be in the race for the Lok Sabha polls, which he did. 'Yes, I am going to contest,' NTR declared in his grandiose style. I used the opportunity to file the story I knew all along. It was published in the *Deccan Chronicle* the day he died with the caption 'NTR to Contest LS Polls'.

NTR looked his best during the thirty-minute interview with the Reuters correspondent. He was energetic all through and went high pitch while talking about the August crisis. He compared Chandrababu to Aurangzeb, who killed his brothers and jailed his parents to grab the throne. 'But nobody can keep me away from the people for too long. I will come back sooner than later,' he told the Reuters correspondent, who filed the story the same day. It appeared in newspapers on the day of his demise. I spent half the day mourning his death along with scores of people who came to pay their last respects.

When I reached the office, I found my editor waiting. He wanted me to write a piece on the political implications of NTR's death. 'He died barely a few hours ago. Don't you think it would be in bad taste to write about post-NTR TDP politics already?' I protested. 'People already know he has passed away. That won't be news tomorrow. We have to talk about what is going to happen,' he said in his awkwardly focused style. 'Fierce Feud Likely to Inherit NTR's Political Legacy,' was published the next day.

While his last days were tempestuous, even in death NTR had no peace. His final journey was marked by scuffles and fist fights. Political opportunism between the two groups of the TDP ensured that the funeral was a noisy and contentious affair. Hundreds of thousands of his grief-stricken fans and supporters who wanted to pay condolences were left to fend for themselves in the melee that ensued during the solemn occasion. The moment his death was announced, the ruling camp went on a blame game pointing fingers at Parvathi.

When Chief Minister Chandrababu Naidu rushed to the Banjara Hills residence, he had to face the ire of NTR's supporters.

Many of NTR's family members had to take police protection to enter the house. Chandrababu's ministers and supporters came face to face with the wrath of NTR's fans. Actors Mohan Babu and Jayaprada who had sided with Chandrababu were nearly lynched by the agitated crowds gathered at the residence. A host of personalities from the world of politics, the film industry, culture and business came in droves to have a last look of the departed icon.

After some wrangling, the body was moved to Lal Bahadur Stadium for the public to have a last glimpse. Prime Minister P.V. Narasimha Rao flew down to Hyderabad to pay his respects. Thousands of people lined up at the stadium to catch a glimpse of one of the most popular Telugu personalities in the modern era. The police, however, failed to control the crowds. As the pushing and jostling continued unabated, they had to resort to lathi charge. Many people, including the VIPs, could not get a proper last view of the body. The tension between the Chandrababu group and the NTR group who had gathered around the mortal remains of NTR under a shamiana was palpable. It soon turned into a scuffle with camp leaders entering an altercation. The place echoed with shouts and screams, even as some miscreants threw footwear at the ruling party functionaries. The police could bring the situation under control only by evening. *The Hindu* captured the scene thus:

> The melancholy sentiment among the vast throng turned to anger and frustration thanks to the breakdown in the arrangements for the orderly flow of mourners past the body. Several people who entered the stadium could not make it to the spot while many more waited patiently in the stands.[113]

An inconsolable Lakshmi Parvathi was initially prevented from accompanying the cortège to the stadium. She and her supporters, however, insisted and followed the procession. After Harikrishna's arrival from abroad the next day, he dominated the proceedings.

He pushed Parvathi and her supporters away from the body and planted framed pictures of his father and mother Basavatarakam near the body.

Despite these unsavoury scenes, the who's who of Indian politics gathered in Hyderabad to pay their last respects to one of the most colourful and forceful political personalities of the 1980s and early 1990s. Former prime ministers Chandra Shekhar and V.P. Singh; Chief Ministers Deve Gowda, Manohar Joshi, Laloo Prasad Yadav; Governors M. Channa Reddy, Krishan Kant; Lok Sabha Speaker Shivraj Patil; former Union Minister Balram Jakhar; former J&K Chief Minister Farooq Abdullah; Union Minister Rajesh Pilot; BJP leader L.K. Advani; Janata Dal leaders S.R. Bommai, S. Jaipal Reddy, Sharad Yadav, Ram Vilas Paswan, Mufti Mohammad Sayeed; MDMK leader V. Gopalaswamy; and CPI (M) leader Sitaram Yechury, besides all state leaders of the Congress, BJP and communist parties attended the funeral.

The state cabinet decided to cremate the body at the Buddha Purnima site opposite Hussain Sagar Lake with state honours. Nandamuri Jayakrishna, the eldest son, lit the pyre at 5.21 p.m. on 19 January 1996 at the specially erected platform as tens of thousands of mourners assembled at the place.

Leaders paid rich tributes to the Telugu Desam patriarch. P.V. described NTR as 'a man of many parts—a learned and deeply religious person, a very fine and powerful actor who swayed millions of people, a forceful orator and above all a man of the masses'.[114] J. Jayalalitha, the Tamil Nadu chief minister, said NTR 'was one of the most courageous political leaders the country had ever known'.[115] Jyoti Basu, the West Bengal chief minister, recalled NTR's 'dauntless fight against the undemocratic dismissal of his Government in 1984 forcing Indira Gandhi to resurrect him as a chief minister within a month' which was 'a unique event in the constitutional history of the country'.[116] Advani described NTR as 'one of the chief architects of the anti-Congress wave of 1989 which led to irreversible changes in national politics'.[117]

Telugus across the globe were deeply grieved at the death of not only a political but a cultural icon. For Telugu-speaking populations across the country and the world, NTR was not merely a political leader who became the chief minister thrice. Before that, he was an actor par excellence who played a significant role in constructing the cinema aesthetics of the Telugus.

The *New York Times*, reporting on the outpourings of grief on the streets of Hyderabad, wrote in its obituary on NTR, 'In death as in life, Mr. Rama Rao was at the center of emotional scenes that could have been written for some of the 330 melodramas that made him a mythic figure among the Telugu-speaking people of Andhra Pradesh.'[118] The *Independent* of London remarked, 'During his three terms as chief minister, he proved as durable a politician as he had been an actor.'[119]

NTR's family, supported by the ruling TDP, raised doubts about the nature of his death. They suspected that the death was unnatural and somehow caused by Parvathi. A day after he was cremated, five of his sons filed a complaint at the Banjara Hills police station, urging the cops to conduct a search of the house and seize all the documents pertaining to his illness. The complaint said, 'The nature and circumstances of his death are highly suspicious, and we have reasonable doubts to apprehend that his sudden death is unusual.'

The central allegation of the family, especially Harikrishna, was that Parvathi made NTR take steroids to have a child with him, leading to complications in his health. She was accused of giving stimulants to him in a bid to increase his virility.[120] 'When he was under the spell of steroids, he gave statements in her favour at her instance,' Harikrishna alleged. According to them, NTR's health began declining since she entered his life. She blackmailed him into marrying her, the stress of which caused a paralytic stroke in 1993. The immediate cause of his death, Harikrishna alleged, was the pressure she put on him for two days before his unfortunate end to adopt her son, Koteswara Prasad.[121]

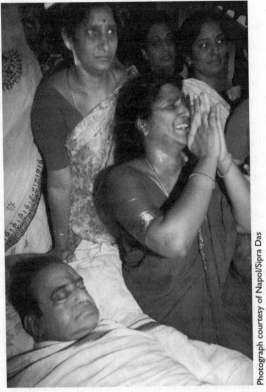

The end of an era. NTR's death was untimely and
tragic.

While Parvathi refuted the accusations, she admitted that NTR
wanted to have a child with her. She claimed she had conceived
but lost the pregnancy at an early stage. After that, according to
Parvathi, the couple did not pursue the idea due to NTR's fragile
health. The family suspected that it was her pressure that made
NTR accept the idea of having a child. They believed that it was
one more of her tactics to legitimize her claim over NTR's legacy.

The timing of NTR's death and Parvathi's behaviour
immediately after were also questioned by Harikrishna. Parvathi
claimed that she found NTR snoring loudly when she got up in

the small hours of 18 January. When she tried to wake him up, he did not respond. He began foaming at his mouth. Panicked, she immediately called Dr Mahalakshmi, the gynaecologist who had conducted her operation earlier. Later, she asked the telephone operator to call Dr B. Somaraju and Dr D.N. Kumar, the team that had treated him for a long time. Dr Mahalakshmi and her husband, along with another doctor, came rushing. Even as they were trying to revive NTR, Dr Somaraju and Dr Kumar arrived and after an examination declared NTR dead.

Curiously, the next person Parvathi called was Congress leader Kotla Vijaya Bhaskara Reddy. Parvathi later justified her action, saying she had called him up because she feared her life was in danger from the ruling TDP. Reddy apparently advised her to intimate the family first. It was almost 5 a.m. before the family members came to know of the death. Dr Somaraju later stated that NTR died of a massive heart attack. 'Given NTR's medical history, his demise did not come as a surprise,' he said.

Chief Minister Chandrababu Naidu also raised suspicions about the circumstances leading to NTR's death and hinted at an inquiry. He kept the conspiracy angle alive, remarking, 'There are many unanswered questions [over NTR's death].'[122] However, the government neither conducted a post-mortem of the body nor ordered an inquiry into the death. The lingering doubts about the end and Parvathi's role in it were left open. The way NTR had met his end, apparently without medical aid, caused pain among his admirers. 'A man who created NIMS, who was only second to God to an entire generation of physicians in India and the United States, died without getting any medical assistance,' wrote an anguished Dr Kakarla Subba Rao. He went on:

His death was certainly not instantaneous. There was a time before he breathed his last. That his wife called none of us would remain a very disturbing fact of history and a big hole in my consciousness. That I could not do anything to save my mentor from his fiendish end would ever remain a tormenting guilt in me.[123]

While the fight for NTR's political legacy clearly lay ahead, the feud for his money broke out almost immediately. On the day NTR died, as Parvathi accompanied the body, some of the family members stayed back at the house in Banjara Hills and sought keys to NTR's bedroom. But many party workers objected to their attempt, and the family members were forced to leave. By the time NTR came into politics, there was little money or any assets in his name, since he had distributed all of them among his children. But the family clearly suspected that the patriarch had stashed currency that came as party funds and were probably looking for it.

The funeral was barely over when the family members alleged that Parvathi sent away suitcases from the house even as NTR's body lay there. Parvathi admitted she had already sent suitcases to the chairman of Kakatiya Cements, P. Venkateswarlu, industrialist Kalidindi Krishnam Raju and MLA Gadde Baburao. She alleged only Venkateswarlu returned the bag intact, while the other two cheated her.[124] The suitcases reportedly contained cash—a few crore rupees—mainly party funds for the 1994 elections received from well-wishers. Another bag containing gold and other valuables was sent to Dr Anil Kumar, a family friend of Lakshmi Parvathi. But he also allegedly failed to return it.[125]

Parvathi admitted that NTR never discussed money matters with her. She said there was a locked room in the house in which money and valuable ornaments were kept. Only NTR, who always kept the keys with him, had access to the room. It was rumoured that Biju Patnaik and Jayalalitha had sent funds to NTR to fight the 1994 elections.[126] Whatever remained of this fund was apparently sent away by Parvathi after NTR's death, but she did not receive all of it back. The house on Road No. 13, Banjara Hills, where NTR and Parvathi lived and where the former breathed his last, was claimed by the family. After NTR's death, the family filed a case, seeking to evict Parvathi from the premises. She lost the case in the courts, leading to her eviction from the house in 2011.

NTR lived barely for four and a half months after he was unceremoniously dislodged as chief minister and TDP president. The shock of being thrown out of power by his own offspring obviously precipitated NTR's end. NTR was distraught throughout this period but also determined to reclaim his legacy. As a man of high self-esteem and pride, NTR refused to bow down before adversity and considerably strained himself both physically and mentally to prepare for a long-drawn fight. But setbacks continued to haunt him. He lost the case against his toppling in the court, and then the Chandrababu group legally gained control over the TDP.

He was bravely swimming against the tide when, on what was to be his last day, he faced another blow. On 17 January 1996, NTR was as usual up and about by 3 a.m. and went through his routine—exercise, massage and meditation. He had his breakfast and gave an interview to the Reuters correspondent in which he predicted that Chandrababu's days were numbered. Then NTR and Parvathi, along with some party leaders, discussed the arrangements for the proposed Simha Garjana meeting. NTR gave instructions about cut-outs, arches, pamphlets, etc., and estimated that Rs 30 lakh might be required for the event.

NTR had deposited Rs 75 lakh in March 1995 in the name of the TDP in the Khairatabad branch of Bank of Baroda. This was mainly the fund collected through membership drives. Chandrababu, on being elected as the TDLP leader on 26 August, had written a letter to the chief manager of the bank, staking his claim over the deposit. He also asked the bank to not honour cheques or permit withdrawals by NTR from the account. As a result, the bank authorities instituted a civil suit for adjudication. NTR filed a petition before the banking ombudsman, who reportedly was inclined to pass an order enabling NTR to withdraw Rs 25 lakh.

Chandrababu filed a writ petition in the high court against the proposed move, alleging that the ombudsman, R.K. Ragala, was earlier appointed as the DGP during NTR's tenure. The high court stayed all further proceedings before the banking ombudsman for AP till 25 January. This meant NTR had no way of raising money for his proposed public meeting. NTR, who had just finished addressing a lengthy press conference about the Simha Garjana meet, was enraged by the news. He began shouting invectives at Chandrababu. All those present were terrified by his uncontrollable anger. 'He stole my chair, my party and now even my money. The poorest of the poor gave their hard-earned money to this party because of their faith in me. He wants even their money,'[127] he went on and on. Parvathi said she gestured to all those present to leave and tried to calm him down. After a while, at around 6.30 p.m., he went upstairs, had a bath and put on his evening clothes, a starched lungi and shirt. He lay on the massage mattress, relaxing for a few minutes, but he was still sullen. When asked by Parvathi whether he would like to see a doctor, NTR said, 'Oh, my body is alright, it is my mind that is troubled.'[128]

NTR's eldest son Jayakrishna, along with his wife Padma, visited the house and handed over a dish of keema balls (minced lamb curry) for his father. The couple was one of the few family members who had maintained close relations with NTR. Meanwhile, another former minister and MLA B.V. Mohan Reddy, whose company NTR liked, visited him. Reddy was an amateur astrologer who entertained NTR with funny stories. Parvathi switched on the TV, and a programme on veteran film personality L.V. Prasad was airing. Turning nostalgic, NTR asked Parvathi to call up ANR. When she gave him the phone, he said, 'Brother, are you watching the programme on TV? I went down memory lane seeing it. Those were the golden days. Come to our place someday, we will have dinner.'[129]

By this time, the dinner was ready. NTR had chapatti, fish curry and the keema balls. Mohan Reddy pepped up NTR with his stories. After Reddy left, NTR was getting ready to sleep when the operator called up on the intercom and said film producer D. Ramanaidu had come to see him. The meeting lasted only a few minutes. The producer had come to invite NTR for a film function. Before going to sleep, NTR once again talked about the bank issue. 'Lakshmi, how to manage the Simha Garjana meeting? This fellow has stopped us in our tracks . . .' Parvathi tried to reassure him that everything would be all right. 'How can we manage the show without any money?' he sighed.[130] NTR closed his eyes and was soon snoring softly. Six hours later, he got up at his regular hour only to go back to eternal sleep.

Fight over NTR's Legacy

The triumph of the rebellious son-in-law in the battle for NTR's political legacy points to the complex nature of Indian politics. That Chandrababu Naidu should have firmly entrenched himself as NTR's legatee even after engineering his downfall appears, on the face of it, the most baffling phenomenon in modern Indian political history.

But it is not inexplicable. With NTR not around, it was not difficult for Chandrababu to consolidate the party under his leadership. More and more party workers veered towards the ruling TDP with the patriarch gone. Chandrababu changed tracks and quickly began owning the legacy of NTR. 'He always liked me. He was like my father, and he would always stay my leader,' he said. A week later, he garlanded the portrait of NTR in the TDP party office. He announced the development of a forty-four--acre Buddha Purnima site where NTR was cremated. He named the University of Health Sciences after NTR and announced the installation of NTR's statues in all twenty-three districts.

The Lakshmi Parvathi group, now left with less than forty MLAs, decided to fight it out on its own. Her supporters believed they would be able to ride the sympathy wave for the late NTR under the leadership of Parvathi and Daggubati Venkateswara Rao. The battle of wits continued between the two camps, each vying to claim NTR's legacy. But neither Parvathi nor the other family members who periodically made attempts at seizing NTR's political inheritance could browbeat Chandrababu in the end. One after another, all the contenders in the race fell by the wayside.

The first one to fall flat in this fight was the lead challenger Lakshmi Parvathi. She failed miserably to cash in on the expected sympathy wave in the Lok Sabha elections that took place after NTR's death in April–May 1996. Her newly floated NTR TDP with a Lion as the election symbol initially appeared to pose a serious threat to Chandrababu's TDP. She attracted better crowds at election rallies compared to the ruling TDP. The image of the wronged widow, pleading for justice, seemed to have the desired impact on voters. But the result came out to the contrary. Parvathi, who fielded candidates in all forty-two parliamentary constituencies in the state, managed 10.66 per cent of the votes polled but could not win a single seat. The resounding defeat meant she could not keep her flock from crossing over to the ruling camp. From forty-odd legislators at the time of NTR's demise, the demoralized party was soon down to just seven members.

Parvathi briefly gave Chandrababu the jitters when she won against all the odds in a three-cornered contest from the Pathapatnam assembly seat in Srikakulam in a bypoll five months later in October 1996. The chief minister failed to stop her from entering the assembly despite deploying all his resources. That was the first and last victory in Parvathi's turbulent political career. The decline of her party was rapid from then on as NTR TDP drew a blank in the 1998 (Lok Sabha), 1999 and 2004 (assembly) elections. When personally all she could muster were just 946 votes in the Atmakur (Kurnool) assembly seat in the 2004 elections, she became a political nonentity.[131] Parvathi later merged whatever was left of her party with Y.S. Jagan Mohan Reddy's YSR

Congress Party. She continues to wage her relentless battle against Chandrababu Naidu, firing from the shoulders of his enemies.

Why did Parvathi fail despite her fervent invocations to NTR's legacy? Parvathi did not have what it took to be in the ruthless world of power politics. She was unable to rise above the immediate circumstances that had thrust her into the top rung of political power. She was content wielding clout as NTR's wife, without partaking in his political philosophy. She played her role strictly within the framework of mainstream patriarchal politics and proved unequal in operating efficiently in the same system. She did not even try to follow principle-based politics, running to the BJP for a tie-up when NTR had scrupulously kept away from the party. Her single-point agenda was to restore NTR's legacy. But she did not seem to have a clue about what NTR stood for. Not only did she flounder in truly representing NTR, but she also did not offer anything fresh to the people who were already tired of the family antics. The media-created image of the wicked stepmother might have worked against her to some extent. But more realistically, the political bubble in which she had floated during NTR's life popped once the source disappeared.

NTR's eldest son Nandamuri Jayakrishna contested as a Parvathi candidate from Srikakulam constituency in the 1996 Parliament elections. He lost to K. Yerrannaidu, the official TDP candidate. Jayakrishna withdrew from politics after this fling.

Harikrishna had earlier resigned as minister in the Chandrababu cabinet after he could not get elected to the assembly. Later, he got elected from Hindupur, his father's constituency, but Chandrababu did not induct him into the cabinet. Soon, he fell out with his brother-in-law. Raising the banner of revolt, he founded Anna TDP in January 1999 along with Daggubati. Alleging that 'the TDP leadership wanted to bury NTR's legacy',[132] Harikrishna fielded a good number of candidates for both the Lok Sabha and assembly seats in the elections held the same year.

The party flopped big time, securing less than 2 per cent of the votes polled. The humiliation was complete when Harikrishna himself lost in the Gudivada assembly seat, his father's native place. He became inactive in politics for almost a decade and later joined the TDP again when it was in the Opposition. He was sent to the Rajya Sabha by Chandrababu in 2008. In an emotional decision, he resigned as MP in August 2013, protesting the proposed bifurcation of AP. His relations with the TDP by this time seemed to have soured once again. His son, NTR Jr, who campaigned for the TDP in the 2009 polls, was conspicuous by his absence in the 2014 elections. Harikrishna died in a road accident in August 2018.

Daggubati did not take much time to fall out with Parvathi. He was furious that she had double-crossed him in the Rajya Sabha elections held in April 1996. She allegedly had cut a deal to support the Congress candidate T. Venkatram Reddy, chairman of the *Deccan Chronicle*.[133] Daggubati scraped through with the help of votes from TDP MLAs who were once his supporters. After breaking ties with Parvathi, he chose to sail with the BJP for some time.

He left the party a year later to join Harikrishna's new party. Following the Anna TDP fiasco in the 1999 polls, he went into hibernation only to emerge in 2004 to join the Congress. Daggubati contested and won as Congress MLA in the same year and once again in 2009. All through, he fought on the anti-Chandrababu plank. In 2014, he announced his political retirement but came back in 2019 to join hands with Chandrababu's bête noire Jagan Mohan Reddy of YSR Congress and contested unsuccessfully for the assembly.

An unexpected development in this family drama was the emergence of Purandeswari, the second daughter of NTR and Daggubati's wife. At the age of forty-five, Purandeswari jumped into the electoral fray as Congress candidate for the Lok Sabha elections from Bapatla in 2004. Her rather sudden entry into politics was to prevent Chandrababu from being anointed as the sole inheritor of NTR's political legacy. The Congress welcomed the husband-and-wife duo as it would show cracks in NTR's family. Purandeswari won the seat and turned out to be a star parliamentarian. An impressed Congress leadership made her state minister for human resources in the Union cabinet within two years. She was elected on a Congress ticket once again in the 2009 general elections and this time held portfolios of commerce and industry and later textiles. The suave and well-spoken Purandeswari quickly carved out a name for herself in politics.

In the bifurcation blues of 2014, Purandeswari along with husband Daggubati left the Congress. She chose to join the BJP and lost twice, in the Lok Sabha elections of 2014 and 2019. As BJP spokesperson in the residual AP, she continues to be a thorn in the side for Chandrababu, especially after the TDP severed its ties with the NDA government in the second half of 2018.

For all the dramatis personae, it was antipathy to Chandrababu that primarily dictated their political leanings. And in the process, most of them ended up with parties that NTR did not approve of. Lakshmi Parvathi, like a woman possessed, had always been ready to sail with the devil himself if only to see the political end of Chandrababu Naidu. Her choice of Jagan Mohan Reddy, the dominant force in the residual state of AP taking on Chandrababu, then did not come as a surprise. But it was unbelievable for many when Purandeswari chose to pick the Congress for her political entry. That her father fought tooth and nail against the grand old party did not stop Purandeswari. That he had refused to ally with post-Babri BJP, the party she chose later, did not deter her either.

Despite the challenges, Chandrababu Naidu credibly emerged as NTR's political successor. The efforts to 'call his bluff' by his detractors at every opportunity failed to stall him from stepping into NTR's shoes. NTR's legacy today rests on his shoulders, whether one likes it or not. Over time, Chandrababu and his colleagues came to be viewed as, to use a Shakespearean expression, 'villains by necessity', as far as the August coup was concerned.

Had NTR lived for a few more months, Chandrababu's political future certainly would have been in jeopardy. The raging old man would certainly have made a mark in the Lok Sabha elections, and the ruling TDP under Chandrababu would have faced an uphill task in containing the wounded lion to his den. NTR's sudden end, however, brought about significant changes in the political situation. The TDP workers, sympathizers and its traditional voters chose Chandrababu over all other claimants because he was regarded as the most capable and deserving despite the stain of betrayal.

If the TDP were to survive, many felt, only Chandrababu could lead it. The first test for his leadership came in the 1996 parliamentary elections when the party won sixteen seats (polling 32.59 per cent of the votes) even as Parvathi's outfit drew a blank. Though the Congress won more seats, twenty-two, from the state, it was clear who had inherited the TDP's legacy. Chandrababu was able to project an image of continuity as NTR's successor, even though he later brought about fundamental changes in the party's political philosophy.

The victory in the 1999 assembly elections firmly cemented Chandrababu's position. He won 180 seats out of 294, continuing for another term as chief minister.[134] In the Lok Sabha elections held at the same time, the TDP secured twenty-nine out of forty-two seats, enabling him to play an important role at the Centre. The BJP, as TDP ally, won seven seats, the highest ever for the party in AP. During the nearly nine years between 1995 and 2004 that he was in power, Chandrababu strengthened the TDP to the extent that the regional party played the 'kingmaker' role in Delhi.

It was not always smooth sailing though. He faced many an ordeal for nearly a decade from 2004 till 2014 when the TDP was voted out of power and suffered a series of setbacks over the issue of a separate Telangana state. But it was due to the political

stamina of Chandrababu Naidu that the regional party survived
the many ups and downs.

New Leadership Style

As soon as he captured power in 1995, Chandrababu Naidu began
determined efforts to efface NTR's memory. He wanted to carve
out a niche for himself as a leader in his own right. It was from
this urge that the new chief minister soon fashioned himself as the
poster boy of economic reforms and the private sector. He took bold
steps, ending the welfare-oriented regime of NTR and heralding
a market-oriented government. He quickly transformed into the
darling of the corporate world and global funding agencies, calling
himself the chief executive officer of the state. He carefully nurtured
a media image of himself as a modern, pragmatic and progressive
political leader. He spoke of technology and communication as key
to social and economic transformation. He brought in reforms in
the power sector and privatized the education and health sectors.

Through these policy shifts, Chandrababu not only moved
away from NTR's core ideology of welfarism and populism but
also succeeded in building a name for himself as the torchbearer of
the global liberalization agenda at the regional level.

During his first stint between 1995 and 2004, Chandrababu
single-mindedly focused on being hailed as the icon of economic
reforms. But the political wilderness he suffered for the next
decade taught him a lesson or two on the pitfalls of blindly
pursuing market economy. As a result, Chandrababu now talks of
balancing development with welfare. But there is a difference even
in the way NTR and Chandrababu looked at welfare measures.
'Welfare schemes for Chandrababu were only a matter of political
expediency—taking a step backwards or sideways from the logic of
economic market to meet the compulsions of the electoral market,'
said K.C. Suri.[135] For NTR, populist measures were the fulcrum of
his political philosophy.

Despite his attempts at completely supplanting NTR, Chandrababu had to go back to invoking NTR's name, especially after being thrown out of power in 2004. Though himself lacking in the emotional core, Chandrababu realized that voters did not live by bread alone. Even after all this time, NTR stirred Telugus in ways that he could scarcely comprehend. He made amends to his political philosophy accordingly.

As a hard-working politician, he continues to appeal for electoral support for the performance of his government. But he now uses the old NTR rhetoric of Telugu pride, besides using NTR's portraits and cut-outs at public meetings. The change of heart was because Chandrababu found it useful to restore the patriarch to his place, however figurative that imagery might be.

The TDP has come a long way from what it was under NTR's leadership, but the party still clings to his memory to connect with the average Telugu person. It may sound paradoxical but TDP followers who still deify NTR as a demigod are the ones who also stand by Chandrababu today. He made conscious efforts to successfully edit out the unsavoury episode of the coup from public memory and rewrite the event as a necessary step in public as well as party interest. And as for the family, he made sure blood continued to be thicker by entering his son into a matrimonial alliance with the family of Balakrishna, NTR's son.[136]

Chandrababu, in comparison with the TDP founder, has been more successful in emerging as a long-lasting political leader. He was able to craft for himself the role of a kingmaker twice in the past—during the stints of the United Front (1996) and NDA (1999). NTR did much more to bring together disparate Opposition parties, but luck was not on his side.

Chandrababu, though hailed as a visionary for his reform-oriented governance, failed to follow a principled stand on any issue, unlike NTR. For example, on the momentous decision regarding the division of AP in the wake of a separate Telangana movement, NTR would have stood by the integrated state even if it cost him his political career. Chandrababu was not willing to take such political risk and ended up pleasing none and offending all. Likewise, he was in and out of an alliance with the BJP, depending on immediate political interest. NTR stands tall in Indian politics because he did not allow political survival to determine his outlook.

The complete loss of Telangana in the 2018 assembly elections for the TDP, where once the party enjoyed extensive support, is a failure of the leadership of Chandrababu in sustaining the base that was laid by NTR. The party, for all practical purposes, is now confined to AP, where it ruled for five years between 2014 and 2019. But here too, Chandrababu faltered once again. After the crushing defeat in the 2019 assembly and Lok Sabha elections in AP, the TDP is facing an existential crisis.

Many of the genetic infirmities in the TDP can be traced to NTR's leadership. But while Chandrababu continued with the personalized style of NTR's politics, he was found sorely wanting in many of his mentor's sterling qualities, especially the latter's ability to read the pulse of the people and connect to the common man. NTR was a great communicator, and Chandrababu, despite his many admirable traits, is not. Besides, under Chandrababu's leadership, the TDP has not only lost its ideological underpinnings but has also turned into a family outfit, like so many other regional parties in the country.

Chandrababu has great willpower and a never-say-die attitude. But as a septuagenarian, he does not have age on his side. Many believe that only another NTR can ensure the future of the TDP. That is saying a lot about NTR himself.

~

Epilogue

Nandamuri Taraka Rama Rao, seventy-two, strode the cultural and political life of Telugus like a colossus for decades. Indeed, it is difficult to sift the man from the myth. He transcended the image of a screen personality to become a symbol to his people.

There is no denying that he imbibed some of the qualities and characteristics of the mythological characters that he played with such finesse. Like Duryodhana, he was imperious, but always vulnerable. He was self-righteous like Ravana and shared his deep religiosity. Like Lord Krishna, the role for which he would be remembered for generations, he was a great showman, and remained a child at heart till the end. As in his portrayal of Krishna, the divine and the mundane merged in him effortlessly.

When he entered politics in 1982 to become the most popular man of the masses in the state, his driving force was passion, not ambition. Indeed, few politicians can match NTR's dynamism and energy. His means and methods might appear awkward, but his motives were always genuine. In fact, the familiar concept of 'scheming politician' did not fit him.

He wanted to run politics according to his rules and most of the time succeeded. Flawed though it might be, he had a vision

of his own for the betterment of his people. He was a fighter
to the core and had an indefatigable spirit. He fought four
assembly elections, two Parliament elections and was tipped to
make a comeback in the 1996 Lok Sabha polls. All his election
campaigns in the state were the greatest spectacles of democracy
in action.

Despite the aura he built up over the years, NTR was the most
accessible of all the politicians of his stature in the country. In
fact, he was such an incorrigible campaigner that few would have
had the kind of interactions he had with people. He inspired awe
but at the same time charmed the people around him. Even the
high and the mighty were intimidated by his apparently whimsical
persona, but strangely the common man felt a certain warmth in
his presence.

The irony of NTR's politics was that he had always been a
darling of the masses, notwithstanding his totally personalized
style of functioning.

NTR's political career spanned less than fourteen years, but
the imprint he left in that rather short period was remarkable. He
straddled the worlds of cinema and politics with equal aplomb. Many
actors came into politics, but none of them dominated like him.
A trailblazer in many ways, NTR emerged as a disruptive force in
regional politics and a factor to be reckoned with at the national level.

What is impressive is that he did all this and more without any
formal grounding in politics. NTR had little prior understanding
of political ideologies, though he quickly summoned up one of
his own during his short political career. His political philosophy
was home-grown. Like most of the leaders who emerged as an
answer to regional problems and aspirations, NTR's political ideas
were geared to cater to the basic needs of the poorest of the poor.
His ideology was rooted in the immediate context of his political
entry. And he was spot on in his instinctual understanding of the
historical role that he was called upon to play. 'He defies everything
that is written in political textbooks. For one thing, he hasn't read

those venerable tomes,' said Venkat Narayan, his first biographer, with a tinge of irony.[1]

NTR was ridiculed often for calling himself 'the biggest leftist in the world'.[2] But NTR's approach to issues was certainly left of centre. He put a premium on taking care of the bare necessities of the poorest, rather than planning long-term development goals. Reacting to the criticism that development got short shrift during his rule, NTR told *India Today*, 'What is development if we can't fill the stomach of the hungry man today? For whom is this development? I believe in building today because tomorrow is based on today.'[3] It was more than just rhetoric for NTR. One must also understand that poverty and hunger were more pronounced in the India of the 1980s than we can appreciate today.

NTR's socialist credentials, however unpolished, lay in the fact that besides being a welfarist, he was generally in favour of state control of big industry. 'The 'ism' of TDP is to help establish a society based on equality. Natural resources, big industries should be under the control of the State. There should be no place for capitalists,' he said.[4] It might appear sanctimonious for somebody like NTR to talk of capitalists when he thrived in the system. But NTR apparently had such ideas even during his film career. In one of the interviews to *Vijayachitra*, a film magazine of the Vijaya Studios, NTR passionately argued in the 1970s that the state should take over all private properties in the country. When asked whether the same applied to him, NTR replied he was no exception. However, this part of the interview was not published as the magazine's management feared that NTR's emotional responses might land him in trouble.[5]

NTR opposed the economic reforms undertaken by the Narasimha Rao–Manmohan Singh duo. 'Is the Government a private-sector enterprise or a business that it should be run in a profit-making manner? Whatever money the Government has should be spent on the poor,' he asserted in an interview with journalist Shekhar Gupta.[6] In his condemnation of free markets,

NTR seems to have anticipated the antiglobalization movement and the rise of crony capitalism. He believed economic reforms benefited only developed countries and would cause job losses to the natives. 'I am not going to accept a so-called reform that benefits foreigners at the cost of the natives,' he asserted.[7]

Interestingly, NTR was opposed to government investment in non-welfare areas. For example, he expressed reservations over the expansion plans of the state government undertaking the Allwyn Nissan company. 'Why should the government get into manufacturing scooters, cars or blades? I think we should get rid of this unit,' NTR said. When told about a possible backlash from workers' unions, he was not dissuaded. 'We can't waste money like this. There is no need to pour money into such ventures when we need to invest in schools and hospitals,' he said. Allwyn became one of the early cases of disinvestment in AP.[8]

NTR favoured the Nehruvian mould of a mixed economy but without the same suspicion against private enterprise. There were several instances where NTR was willing to bat for privatization. However, he wanted a certain amount of self-reliance for the country which revealed his ingrained socialist approach. 'Swaraj,' he said in the same interview with Shekhar Gupta, 'is taking money from the rich and giving it away to the poor and not taking it from the poor and giving it to the foreigner.'

NTR had no political pedigree unlike many regional stalwarts ranging from MGR to Laloo Prasad Yadav. He lacked formal ideological grounding like many of his contemporaries. But what distinguished NTR was that he developed his own native political outlook and stuck to it through thick and thin.

If there was one thing that actively constituted NTR's political philosophy, it was the anti-Congressism that he propounded all through. It could be said that he was the original proponent of 'Congress-mukt Bharat' philosophy. NTR waged an uncompromising fight against Congress all through his political life. 'In the past, the Congress freed the country and now the time has come to free the country from the Congress misrule,'[9] he said at the inaugural rally of the National Front in Madras. NTR spiritedly questioned the assumption of unbridled powers by the Centre, while making energetic efforts to bring the non-Congress Opposition together to break the one-party dominance in the country. 'What I especially liked about NTR,' veteran BJP leader L.K. Advani wrote in his autobiography *My Country, My Life*, 'was his genuine concern for forming a democratic and stable alternative to the Congress at the Centre. In pursuit of this objective, he tirelessly strove to mobilise Opposition parties on a common platform . . .'[10]

NTR's most significant contribution was in the area of Centre–state relations, which constituted his core political philosophy. NTR was not the first politician to talk about federalism in the Indian context. There were regional parties in Tamil Nadu, Punjab and the Northeast even before NTR, but the credit for pushing Centre–state relations into the mainstream agenda should largely be accorded to him. NTR repeatedly talked of the need to rewrite the Constitution to ensure a better balance of power between the Centre and the states. The states' rights were getting whittled down with every Constitutional amendment, he alleged. 'The States ought to enjoy fiscal, economic, political and administrative autonomy,' he asserted.[11]

NTR's arguments on violation of the federal spirit of the Constitution continue to have relevance against the backdrop of the bifurcation of united AP and the abrogation of Article 370 in Kashmir. 'There is a need to take a relook at the provisions in the Constitution that enable the President's rule in the States. There should be no scope for misusing these provisions to political ends,'[12] NTR said in his speech at Rajaji Institute of International Relations and Public Administration in 1983.

'The Centre is a myth,' was the most popular and succinct postulate that NTR enunciated on the federal structure of the country. NTR used the expression 'mithya' which translates more appropriately as 'false, unreal'. Speaking at the Calcutta meeting of the Opposition parties in 1984, he explained his concept that India was a union of states, and the Centre existed only through the states. 'The Centre on its own does not possess any geographical boundaries; it lacks a physical body,' he said. The Centre, according to him, was only an agency to carry out prescribed tasks on behalf of the states.[13] However, the Centre treated the states as its branch offices, as a result of which their autonomy and cultural identity was under threat, he said. NTR was firmly in favour of the abolition of the institution of the governor, which acted as an agent of the Union government.

At a time when the homogenized and centralized concept of nationalism pursued by the right-wing governments has caused fissures in the country, NTR's finely articulated stand on 'co-operative federalism' is more relevant than it was in the past. His call in the 1980s to build 'a powerful and united Opposition on true federal lines'[14] continues to resonate in twenty-first-century India.

True Nationalist

At a time when 'nationalism' has become a controversial construct, it is interesting to see how NTR balanced his stand on regional autonomy with patriotism. NTR was a nationalist to the core and stood firmly for the integration of India. His Telugu sub-nationalism did not have even a whiff of the secessionist tendencies that marked the DMK's initial years. He always ended his speeches with 'Jai Telugu Nadu, Jai Hind'. His emphasis on Telugu identity was bereft of any hostility towards outsiders. As early as May 1983, Girilal Jain, the veteran editor of the *Times of India*, recognized that NTR was 'different in that he alone among the south Indian chief ministers has taken the initiative to forge ties with Opposition parties which have support in the north'.[15] L.K. Advani said, 'Though a votary of Telugu *atma gouravam* (regional self-pride), NTR was a patriot to the core. Indeed, he set a fine example of harmonising legitimate regional aspirations with strong and unshakeable nationalist commitment.'[16]

NTR was more nationalistic in spirit than many national leaders. Jayaprakash Narayan, a former IAS officer and civil society activist, recalled how NTR reprimanded his partymen when they wanted to counter the then Karnataka chief minister Deve Gowda's statement on Tungabhadra River. 'Just because Deve Gowda gave a provocative statement, I would not react. Karnataka is also in India, and they are also our people. We will sort out the issue through discussions,'[17] NTR admonished. This was unlike many of his contemporaries and successors who jumped at every opportunity to derive mileage out of incitement. It was this broad outlook that pushed him to play a role at the national level.

An important aspect of NTR's fight for strong federation was that he consistently remained a nationalist while advocating a more equitable distribution of resources between the Centre and the states. 'A strong Centre is possible only with strong States. But if a secessionist force raises its head anywhere in the country, I will fight against such tendencies till the last drop of my blood,' NTR declared at the Calcutta Opposition meeting.[18] In tune with his true nationalism, NTR refused to talk ill of the Centre in a foreign land. During his US visit in July 1984, Madhu Trehan of *India Today* asked whether the Centre would not come in the way of NRIs establishing industries in AP given his strained relations. 'I can't forget I am in New York and I am meeting the press here. So, no comments about the Union Government whom we respect,' he replied.[19]

It was this nationalist instinct that propelled NTR to serve as a catalyst in organizing the non-Congress Opposition conclaves in the 1980s. NTR was the architect of coalition politics at the national level after the Janata experiment. I am a regional leader of a national party, while NTR is a national leader of a regional party, S. Jaipal Reddy, then in the Janata Party, liked to say.

He was the only regional leader who campaigned extensively across the nation in his efforts to build a national political alternative.

NTR also remains the only regional party leader who was able to attract huge crowds in north India. The TDP chief campaigned in sixteen states including J&K, Punjab, Haryana, Rajasthan, Gujarat, Uttar Pradesh, Madhya Pradesh, Bihar, Orissa, West Bengal, Assam and Nagaland in support of the National Front. And NTR conducted most of his campaigns across India alone on his Chaitanya Ratham, with no local leader accompanying him.

It was because of NTR that in the 1980s, Andhra Pradesh Bhavan in Delhi became the hub for non-Congress coalition activities. NTR's efforts were substantial in paving the way for the formation of the National Front government led by V.P. Singh in Delhi. No other chief minister or regional party president spent so much time and energy on strengthening the Opposition. He remains the only leader who brought the antagonistic Left and the BJP on the same platform in pursuit of a single goal. It is, however, unfortunate that NTR did not receive due recognition for his crucial role in forming and sustaining the National Front. Political journalist Kalyani Shankar commented on how NTR did not get deserving credit for his contribution to the defeat of Congress in Delhi in 1989.

Many of his admirers consider it a stroke of bad luck that he died just before the 1996 Lok Sabha elections. That he would have emerged as the consensus candidate in place of H.D. Deve Gowda in June 1996 to occupy the prime-ministerial chair was not entirely in the realm of fantasy. Even in 1989, NTR would have been a contender for the top post along with V.P. Singh and Devi Lal, had he not lost so badly in the state.

Saffron Secularist

The TDP under NTR was secular to the core. Though saffron-clad, he consistently exhibited a secular streak in administration. NTR was not afraid of upsetting the Hindu traditionalists through many of his administrative decisions. He took it upon himself to ensure that communal politics were not encouraged in the state. He was against alienating the minorities through demands such as building a temple on the disputed site in Ayodhya.

Conspicuously religious outwardly, NTR was neither communal nor orthodox. Asked to choose between science and religion, NTR was surprisingly rational. He said he gave priority to science and held that religion was purely personal. 'We are secular people,' he said in the midst of the Ayodhya row.[20]

He matched his actions with his words when he refused to ally with the BJP for its stand on the Ram Janmabhoomi controversy.

He was referred to as the 'Saffron Caesar' by English media commentators during his heyday, mistaking his saffron attire for his religiosity. But NTR was as secular as they come. 'Labels don't stick easily to Nandamuri Taraka Rama Rao,' journalist Shekhar Gupta commented.

Ideologically, it is difficult to pin down NTR into any existing categories. He transcended class consciousness; however bizarre it might appear. For the Left, he was a rightist, and for the rightists, he was a populist. The conservatives considered him strangely radical, while the progressives regarded him as an obscurantist. 'I am the biggest leftist in the whole world,' NTR declared grandly several times. In a flight of fancy, he even dreamed of a socialist society: 'The CM and the chaprasi (peon) should have the same salary. There should be equality among all. Caste, class and religion should go away. Like Adi Sankara, who travelled from Kerala to Kashmir, one day, I might even go around the country to re-establish moral principles and awaken people.'[21]

NTR did not regard himself as a career politician. 'I am not a politician and will never be one,' he maintained. He believed he came into politics only to do good for the poor but felt that he was being stifled with bottlenecks. G.S. Bhargava of the *Indian Express* wrote in the early days that NTR was apolitical and there was a moral aspect to his thinking and approach. He often expressed unhappiness with his own performance. NTR would vent his frustration at not being able to deliver on his promises and policies. 'I have not been able to achieve what I had intended to. There is too much red-tapism in the bureaucracy, and it is dragging down all my plans,' he said three years into governance.[22] Another time, he blurted out, 'What is the point of my staying as CM if I can't bring about changes in the system? I wanted to do many things. But when I look back, [what I could do was] a big zero.'[23]

NTR repeatedly talked about eliminating the role of money in politics. 'I am not for spending money in elections and then trying to get back that money through misappropriation. I don't want such power,'[24] he said with conviction. During NTR's regime, it was unthinkable that anybody could get a nomination to any post by offering money. He gave seats to ordinary persons whose only qualification was their integrity, competence and loyalty. 'Several big shots queued up with money bags for Rajya Sabha seats, but he never cared for them. It was because of his incorruptibility that unknown people like me and several of my colleagues at the time, who were all young, idealistic and ready to fight, shot into prominence,' Renuka Chowdhury, who is now in the Congress, recalled with nostalgia.[25]

Electoral reforms were close to NTR's heart and he initiated a debate on the issue in 1988 by holding a meeting in which all political parties except the Congress participated. He held detailed discussions in this regard with eminent personalities such as S.L. Shakdher, the former chief election commissioner, H.R. Khanna and V.M. Tarkunde, retired judges, and C. Subramaniam, the former Union minister. NTR supported holding simultaneous polls to the Lok Sabha and assemblies and practised what he preached in 1989.

NTR had iconoclastic views on dismantling the governance systems with which he grappled during his time. He was impatient with the bureaucratic slackness in the administration. Having spent a major part of his life in the film industry, a private and individual initiative, NTR could not come to terms with the governance behemoth. 'Poverty is still an issue because of the way our systems run. It appears to me that unless a revolution happens like in Russia, nothing will ever change,' he observed.[26] This confusing mix of socialist instincts and belief in individual initiative characterized NTR's political views.

The quintessential quality of NTR that many of his contemporaries acknowledged was his genuine desire to do good for the common man. Almost all those who came in contact with him vouched for his passion for changing the ground rules and his dedication to finding solutions to complex problems. In this effort, he ruffled many feathers, especially the entrenched bureaucracy, used to soft handling in the long years of the Congress rule. He was insistent on delivering goods despite tremendous challenges—an approach that did not amuse some officers. And the fact that he came straight from the world of cinema did not go down well with many of them. 'NTR was used to solving problems in three hours—the average length of a Telugu movie,' said Narendra Luther, an IAS officer. 'He had no understanding of the complexities of political and social issues.'[27]

One view was that NTR's lack of administrative experience, coupled with his zeal, resulted in his rather inept handling of some senior officers, leading to disquiet in the bureaucracy. However, some of the best officers who worked with him paid rich encomiums to NTR for his deep concern for the betterment of the lives of the poor. Y.V. Reddy, the former RBI governor, who devoted an entire chapter to his experiences with NTR in his autobiography, assessed him thus: 'NTR was a man with a vision, flair, imagination and great instincts; he was dynamic, disciplined and had iron resolve. He was known to value honesty and he was hardworking.'[28]

NTR had high regard for officers whom he considered intellectual, competent and honest, and displayed great respect towards them. U.B. Raghavendra Rao, a well-regarded IAS officer, was specially picked by NTR to be his secretary though he had worked in the earlier Congress regime. 'UB won the trust of NTR because he was a man of outstanding moral and intellectual calibre, and remarkable courage,' said Reddy, who himself was called back from Washington to be his planning secretary. K.R. Venugopal, a highly committed civil servant who supervised the subsidized rice scheme during NTR's government, praised NTR's commitment towards eradicating hunger. Mohan Kanda, another civil servant of repute who held several important positions in the state and the Centre, admired NTR's sense of impartiality. 'His only weakness, if there was any, was his total devotion to the cause of the development of his State.'[29] Though he departed in unpleasant circumstances, G.V. Ramakrishna, who later held important positions such as the chairman of Securities and Exchange Board of India (SEBI), recalled that NTR had personally called him to be the chief secretary though he had never met him. Prathipati Abraham, who retired as Union power secretary, said that NTR 'encouraged honest and hardworking officers who were committed to the development of the State'.[30]

Two IPS officers, H.J. Dora and Ravulapati Seetharama Rao, wrote books exclusively on their association with NTR, paying rich tributes to him. Those who fell out with him such as P. Upendra and Chegondi Hararama Jogaiah dedicated their autobiographies to NTR, recognizing him as the one who rekindled the spirit of the Telugus.

Political Awakening in Andhra

The history of united AP could easily be divided into the pre-NTR and post-NTR period. The actor-turned-politician strode into the commanding heights of the state's political landscape on his debut. The arrival of NTR irreversibly changed the political landscape of the state for the next many decades, and the seeds sown by him continue to shape the political discourse in Telugu-speaking lands. The domination of regional parties in both AP and Telangana is largely due to the political culture that NTR introduced in the region.

NTR's entry brought about a fundamental change in the way politics was conducted in the state. Politics was no more an esoteric power game played in the corridors of Delhi but amid its dusty villages and towns. Nor was it the exclusive preserve of a few well-heeled and the well-connected but a field wide open to one and all. NTR truly transformed the existing power politics into people's politics. A year after NTR stormed into power, Bhabani Sen Gupta of *India Today* credited him with 'creating a political movement the like of which India had not seen for many decades'.[31]

He was genuinely the man of the masses. It was NTR who triggered the process of mass political participation in Andhra and Telangana. He empowered the common man by creating political awareness through his historic campaigns. At a time when elections were dictated by vote banks, NTR communicated with the voter directly. Fixers and dealers of the previous regime lost their relevance. He brought a new vigour, spontaneity and participative culture into the election campaign.

NTR's contribution to the recognition of Telugus as a distinct group of people with their own language and culture has been widely recognized. He awakened self-esteem among Telugus by his evocative recall of past glory and his passionate call for its revival in the present. Even those who did not share his political views acknowledged the paradigm shift he brought in the way Telugus looked at themselves and were regarded by others.

But in his construction of Telugu identity, NTR observed moderation that was refreshingly different from similar regional political movements elsewhere in the country. While he was a firebrand, NTR was never incendiary. What distinguished him from other similar regional satraps was that while he constructed Telugu identity based on the unity of all Telugus, he never indulged in demagoguery. Unlike the movements based on language and subnationalism in Tamil Nadu, Maharashtra and

Karnataka, NTR's Telugu pride did not constitute opposition to non-Telugus. Or for that matter, against any group of people. His ire was targeted explicitly against the political leadership of the frozen Congress high command in Delhi.

He stands miles apart in this regard from Bal Thackeray of the Shiv Sena, and is significantly removed from the Dravidian parties in Tamil Nadu.[32] NTR's assertion of Telugu unity also contrasts with the ideology of K. Chandrashekar Rao (or KCR as he is known), the founder of Telangana Rashtra Samithi. He was another prominent political leader who rewrote the geography of the united AP and marked a new phase in the politics of Telugu-speaking regions. In his fight for a separate state of Telangana, KCR deliberately targeted Andhra—its people, geography, culture, language, food, and, of course, its political leadership.[33] KCR's success in realizing a separate state for Telangana was no mean achievement, but he did not necessarily bring about a qualitative change in the politics of the region, the way NTR fundamentally altered the political culture. NTR transformed the political landscape, while KCR changed the geographical profile.

In the heat of the Telangana movement, arguments were advanced about the alleged subjugation of the region by Andhra people. NTR, who had not been spared in this no-holds-barred diatribe, was acutely aware of the fault lines. He was very sensitive to regional sentiments. He always referred to the state as 'Telugu Nadu (Telugu Land)' rather than its official nomenclature 'Andhra Pradesh', stressing cultural identity rather than geographical identity. Many commentators pointed to the decline of the separate Telangana movement, however temporarily, as a result of the Telugu subnationalism that NTR preached and practised.

Complex Personality

Everyone who met NTR was mesmerized by his imposing personality. The aura that he radiated left a lasting impression on all those who interacted with him. 'I had been witness to many scenes when battle-hardened veterans in politics, prominent industrialists, eminent scientists, media Mughals and many great achievers in their respective fields became diffident, subdued and almost reverential in his presence,'[34] remarked P.S. Ramamohan Rao, an IPS officer and former governor of Tamil Nadu who worked closely with NTR. He went on to describe the regal air about him:

> He was generally convivial and yet few would dare take any
> liberties with him. He was seldom given to temper or anger but
> could convey his unhappiness or disapproval with a mere glance
> or cryptic comment. Such was the theatre of the man.[35]

NTR's reference to himself in Telugu as 'we' even in day-to-day interactions further accentuated his grandiose personality. He was known to address his wife and children with the suffix 'garu', a term of respect in Telugu. He also extended the same deference to others. If he liked somebody, he would call him 'brother', and if he were angry with somebody, he would slip into English. 'I am sorry' meant he was peeved at something.

His personal integrity was beyond reproach, and his visceral hatred for corruption was well known. Everyone who worked with him—politicians and bureaucrats—spoke about his incorruptibility. 'We can't even begin to understand his intense dislike for corrupt politicians and corrupt bureaucrats,'[36] said Jayaprakash Narayan. His uncompromising stance alienated him somewhat from the administration as well as the political class, but he did not waver in his resolve. NTR truly considered himself a trustee of public money. In 1994, intelligence officials conveyed that the official Ambassador car that the chief minister travelled in was in bad condition and recommended a replacement. At the time, an Ambassador car cost around Rs 3.5 to 4 lakh. When told about the same, NTR was reluctant. 'Why waste money on a new car when we can repair it?' he said. Alcohol prohibition had been enforced, and money was tight for the government. The chief minister, who had given the green signal to close down distilleries to implement a ban on liquor in toto, making the treasury poorer by Rs 100 crore, was not willing to buy a new car. Likewise, NTR wrote a personal cheque on the spot when told that travel bills for his wife, Lakshmi Parvathi, who accompanied him, needed to be paid.

NTR's socialist inclinations coupled with self-projection neatly dovetailed with his personalized style of politics. He was not a Stalinist dictator, but he exhibited autocratic tendencies. His intentions were never suspect, but he entertained a self-centric view of the world. He behaved as an emotionally charged benevolent dictator. The CPI's Giri Prasad criticized NTR as being a Hitler fan.[37] It was not without any basis that critics called him Hitler. The German dictator was undoubtedly a decisive leader for NTR. Speaking on the eve of Mahanadu in 1988, he equated Adolf Hitler with nationalist personalities such as Napoleon Bonaparte of Italy, Joseph Stalin of Russia, Winston Churchill of England and Franklin Roosevelt of the US. He believed such a personality was the need of the hour for India. 'We can't say such a personality would not emerge in our country,' he said. NTR seemed to hint that he was such a figure who would impact the country.[38] While NTR quickly grasped political and administrative issues after his entry into politics, he had large gaps in his understanding of history and political philosophies. Clearly, NTR was taken in by Hitler's purposefulness, without a perspective of the latter's alarming legacy.

The feudal streak was solid in NTR. He exhibited his feudal qualities both in his personal and political life. When he married Lakshmi Parvathi, he presented it as repayment of his gratitude for her service. In his political life, NTR exhibited the positive as well as negative values of a feudal mindset. Personal honour for him was paramount, and this involved keeping his word at any cost. Unlike other politicians, NTR took his poll promises very seriously, and they were a commitment to the people that he fulfilled in all earnestness. He also considered himself as royalty who was ordained to rule his people with fairness and justice. However, this also meant that NTR believed in personalized politics, leading to centralization of power and sycophancy. While the TDP was built around NTR's persona, it continued to exist around his whims.

Man of Opposites

NTR was a man of strange contradictions. He believed in the power of the people, and his entire political life revolved around gaining their trust. But at the same time, his democratic credentials were suspect because he had no qualms in turning his party into a one-man show. He was secular to the core but exhibited a peculiar religious streak. While he was democratic to the extent that he considered the will of the people supreme and felt accountable to them, NTR had little faith in decentralized or collective leadership. He was authoritarian in his decision-making and dictatorial in the management of the party affairs. He acted as the be-all and end-all of the party, treating it as merely an instrument to carry out his mission.

His narcissistic tendencies were striking not only in his sartorial immodesty but also in his highly personalized style of politics. From making his birthday as the party foundation day to the way he allowed fans and acolytes to prostrate before him on all fours, NTR's obsession with grandiosity came across as obnoxious. The theatrics he introduced into politics left a bitter aftertaste. Some critics believe the consecutive electoral victories in 1983, 1984 and 1985 made him extremely arrogant and intoxicated with power.

The split personality of NTR threw up paradoxical outcomes during his administration. NTR's old-fashioned outlook, for example, never came in the way of his interest in modern technology. He was at the forefront of computerization in government departments as early as in 1986. 'Ironically, the foundation for modern e-governance, for which Andhra Pradesh became a leader in the country, could be attributed to this initiative, led by a man who dressed in saffron robes and talked like he was Lord Krishna,'[39] former RBI governor Y.V. Reddy recalled.

Since NTR was an amalgam of different personas, his character readily lent itself to critical interpretations. His inflated sense of self and his need to be the centre of attention was even a subject of psychoanalysis in a Telugu book. 'One moment he is hopelessly incoherent and then, in a flash, charmingly articulate,' found journalist Shekhar Gupta.

The complexity in NTR's personality arose primarily due to the confusing nature of his transaction with reality. His character was significantly impacted by the long years he had spent in the film industry—a world many layers removed from the social and the political realities of the society. Over time, he was used to treating the reality of the film world in the same way as that of the real one. He carried this role play into his politics. Whenever he said or reacted to anything, it appeared as though NTR was transforming into a character at that instant and speaking from the point of view of the role that he was required to play in the context. Not surprisingly, quite a lot of things that NTR said or did might have come across as incongruous due to this role play in which he would swing between characters. His performance-style utterances in public convey that unmistakable mark of role playing.

By the time he came to politics, NTR was in the firm grip of cinematic consciousness that propelled him to play the role of a saviour. He was genuinely baffled as to why his detractors were trying to derail his government all the time, though it was very clear to him that he had been playing his character as a saviour with utter sincerity and dedication. His personal sterling qualities combined with his role play brought out a distinct personality that could easily be perceived as maverick.

Given the largely linear thinking within his own radical, anti-establishment streak, NTR was not suited to the world of politics that required constant compromise on every issue and belief. It was probably for this reason that throughout his political career, NTR seemed to have spent most of his time grappling with political realities and feeling frustrated at not being able to execute his thoughts the way he would have been able to do in cinema.

NTR is seen by some as the archetypal tragic personality who lost his kingdom because of blind love for his woman. What sets NTR apart from such figures is his conscientious approach to the issue and his refusal to stand down even when offered a compromise. He would rather be stripped of his power than allow the stigmatizing of his wife and in the process himself. His own sense of self was far more critical to NTR than the material—in this case, political—rewards. His commitment to his wife till death-did-them-part was rather condescendingly viewed by some as being 'within the framework of upper caste patriarchal traditions'. But the fact remains that NTR chose to stand by Parvathi against the same patriarchal traditions which would have sided with the family rather than with the stepmother. It is, of course, debatable whether NTR should have pushed an amateur like Parvathi into politics in the first place. NTR shares the fatal flaws of many of the Shakespearean tragic heroes. He was prone to flattery, was self-delusional at times and blindly loved his kith and kin. Like the Bard's protagonists, NTR's hubris contributed to his downfall.

His legacy, however, lies in his gutsy fight against the hegemony of a single party, his bold stand over the historical necessity of regional political parties and his spirited advocacy of the autonomy of the states—all of which continue to be relevant today. His inspired efforts in bringing together the disparate Opposition parties and his unswerving commitment to secular principles make him a much-needed model in today's India.

And in his genuine commitment to the welfare of the poor, Nandamuri Taraka Rama Rao rises many notches above his contemporaries and successors.

Acknowledgements

I would like to place on record my gratitude to former IPS officer A.S. Bose for meticulously going through the draft and making useful suggestions. His encouragement and help throughout the writing has been immense.

Several people associated with NTR spared their time to speak to me about their experiences. They include Dr N. Lakshmi Parvathi, Dr Y. Lakshmi Prasad, Dr Daggubati Venkateswara Rao, V. Appa Rao IPS (Rtd), R.P. Singh IPS (Rtd), C.D. Arha IAS (Rtd), Dr Y. Sivaji and Vasantha Nageswara Rao.

My grateful thanks to Dr N. Jayaprakash Narayan (former IAS), Parakala Prabhakar and K. Padmanabhaiah (IAS Rtd) for reading the book and offering their encouraging comments.

Political commentator and policy analyst, Sanjaya Baru, was kind enough to offer his insightful remarks on the draft.

I thank journalists Dr Narisetti Innaiah, Suresh Dharur and Annapaneni Gandhi for going through the manuscript and offering suggestions.

But for the interest shown by Mita Kapur of literary agency Siyahi, this book would not have seen the light of the day. Much obliged to her.

I cannot thank enough Executive Editor Elizabeth Kuruvilla and Senior Copy Editor Saloni Mital at Penguin Random House India for enhancing the readability of the book through their attention to detail.

Needless to say, I am responsible for any inaccuracies or inadequacies in the book.

Notes

Act I

1. The former Andhra Pradesh state was bifurcated into Andhra Pradesh and Telangana in 2014 by an act of Parliament.
2. As the Janata government fell due to internal squabbles, Indira stormed back to power in the 1980 midterm polls to the Lok Sabha. The Congress (I) swept AP once again, winning the same forty-one out of forty-two seats.
3. Pupul Jayakar, *Indira Gandhi: A Biography* (New Delhi: Penguin Books, 1995), p. 446.
4. Editorial, 'Test of Charisma', *Indian Express*, 3 January 1983.
5. 'Na bhadhanta mee bhavishyathu gurinche [I Am Only Worried Over Your Future]', *Eenadu*, 3 January 1983.
6. 'Calling through Cassettes', *Indian Express*, 1 January 1983. Also, 'Inca duragataala tera dinchaali [Bring curtains down on Congress (I) atrocities]', *Eenadu*, 4 January 1983.
7. Ravulapati Seetharama Rao, an IPS officer, reported this conversation in his memoirs. Ravulapati Seetharama Rao, *Police Sakshigaa— Udyoga Vijayaalu* (Hyderabad: Emesco Books, 2010), p. 98.
8. The Telugu-speaking region, now called Andhra Pradesh (then referred to as Andhra), was part of Madras Presidency since the British era.

9. The Madras Province, which succeeded Madras Presidency, included the whole of Tamil Nadu and Andhra and parts of Odisha, Kerala, Karnataka and the union territory of Lakshadweep.

10. The survey was conducted in 2013, nearly seventeen years after NTR's demise.

11. S. Venkat Narayan, *NTR: A Biography* (New Delhi: Vikas Publishing, 1983), p. 78. Narayan, associate editor with *India Today*, based in Delhi then, was the first journalist to write the full-length biography of NTR.

12. The incident occurred in 1980, at least a year and a half before NTR formally took up politics. *Shashtipoorthi* is an event marking the completion of sixty years in a person's life in the Hindu tradition. This incident was reported in the film magazines of the time, later picked up by general publications.

13. Nadendla Bhaskara Rao, *Walking with Destiny* (Hyderabad: Sarva Dharma Nilayam, 2008), p. 73. The autobiography provides a history of the TDP from Nadendla's point of view.

14. The newly formed Congress (I) was left with only second rankers or newcomers with most of the senior leaders choosing to stay with the official Congress or join the Janata Party.

15. AP was the only state where Indira Gandhi's newly founded party was in power during this time in the entire country.

16. The local papers reported it only two days later.

17. H.J. Dora, *NTR tho Nenu* (Hyderabad: Emesco, 2011), p. 21.

18. B.K. Eswar, *Vijaya Chitra Gnapakalu* (Chennai: Vijaya Publications, 2016). Eswar, a film reporter in Madras at this time, mentioned how NTR had always expressed distaste at the topic of politics.

19. In his first public meeting on 11 April 1982, NTR confirmed he was offered a position by the Congress government. In an interview to *Vaartha* Telugu daily in 1996, NTR recalled that he was invited by Neelam Sanjiva Reddy to join politics, while Brahmananda Reddy had offered him an MP's seat if he were to join the Congress.

20. Mallemala Sundara Rami Reddy, *Idi Naa Katha* (Hyderabad: Mallemala Prachuranalu. 2011), p. 150.

21. Daggubati Venkateswara Rao, *Oka Charitra—Konni Nijalu* (Hyderabad: Nivedita Publications, 2013), p. 11. NTR's son-in-

law says that NTR discussed his political entry with very few of his family members. His memoir tells the story of the TDP from his point of view.

22. Since the Telugu film industry was still based in Madras, the capital of Tamil Nadu, film personalities such as NTR probably suffered this sense of alienation and unfulfilled potential more acutely than Telugus back home.

23. But to call the TDP the first example of a political party that set up as a business concern with its own money, resources and men, as Inukonda Thirumali did in his *Telangana-Andhra: Castes, Regions and Politics in Andhra* (2013) is rather misleading.

24. J. Mahesh, *Telugu Desam Charitra* (Hyderabad: Pinakini Publications, 1983), p. 33.

25. Parvathaneni Upendra, *Gatham-Swagatham-Part I* (Hyderabad: Satya Ridhima Prachuranalu, 1992), p. 79.

26. Kalyani Shankar, *Gods of Power: Personality Cult and Indian Democracy* (New Delhi: Macmillan, 2012), p. 122.

27. Ibid., p. 123.

28. Inaganti Venkata Rao, *Oke Okkadu* (Hyderabad: Monica Publications, 2014), p. 47.

29. Daggubati Venkateswara Rao, *Oka Charitra—Konni Nijalu* (Nivedita Publications: Hyderabad, 2013), pp. 4, 5.

30. Interview with C. Narayana Reddy in 1998.

31. NTR Estates, a landmark in Abids areas of Hyderabad even now, consists of Ramakrishna 70 mm, Ramakrishna 35 mm theatres, Hotel Aahwanam and a shopping arcade.

32. 'Indira Rashtraaniki Emi Chesaru [What Has Indira Done to the State]?', *Andhra Patrika*, 12 April 1982.

33. 'Naku, NTRku polika yekkada [No Comparison between Me and NTR]', *Andhra Patrika*, 13 May 1982.

34. 'Rashtra rajakeeyalanu kalushitam chese maro malupu [A Development that Poisons State Politics]', *Andhra Patrika*, 13 April 1982.

35. 'Prajalanu rechagotti adhikaramloki ravalani prayatnistunna Telugu Desam [TDP Provoking People to Capture Power]', *Andhra Patrika*, 21 April 1982.

36.   Even during the pre-Independence period, the Kamma elite was part of non-Congress formations such as the South Indian Liberal Federation, popularly known as Justice Party, and later Swatantra Party. Ranga and Rajagopala Naidu were in the Swatantra Party before moving back to the Congress.

37.   Selig Harrison, 'Caste and the Andhra Communists', *American Political Science Review*, Vol. 50, No. 2 (June 1956): 381.

38.   M.N. Srinivas, *Caste in Modern India: And Other Essays* (New Delhi: Asia Publishing House, 1962), p. 28.

39.   Prakasam and later P.V. Narasimha Rao were the only Brahmin chief ministers Andhra and Andhra Pradesh had.

40.   It is important to note that many stalwarts of the communist parties were from the Reddy community such as Puchalapalli Sundarayya and Neelam Rajasekhara Reddy, but the backbone of the Left parties in Andhra was formed by the Kamma peasantry.

41.   The five Reddy chief ministers are N. Sanjiva Reddy, Kasu Brahmananda Reddy, M. Channa Reddy, Bhavanam Venkataram Reddy and Kotla Vijayabhaskara Reddy. The others are Damodaram Sanjeevaiah (Dalit), P.V. Narasimha Rao (Brahmin) and Jalagam Vengala Rao (Velama). Interestingly, T. Anjaiah, widely considered a Backward Class (a caste classification) member, claimed he was a Reddy (an upper caste) and that his original name was Ramakrishna Reddy Talla—this after he became the chief minister!

42.   K. Balagopal, 'A False Resurrection, the Rise and Fall of Rama Rao', *Leaders Beyond Media Images* (Hyderabad: Perspectives, 2013), p. 27.

43.   'Kamma Party Kadu [Not a Kamma Party]', *Andhra Patrika*, 12 April 1982.

44.   'Venkataswamy bangarame tappa notlu muttukoru [Venkataswamy Accepts only Gold]', *Andhra Patrika*, 14 April 1982.

45.   K.C. Suri, 'Andhra Pradesh: From Populism to Pragmatism 1983-2003', *Journal of Indian School of Political Economy*, Vol. 15, Nos. 1&2 (Jan–June 2003): 54, 55.

46.   K. Balagopal, 'A False Resurrection, the Rise and Fall of Rama Rao', *Leaders Beyond Media Images* (Hyderabad: Perspectives, 2013), p. 27.

47. 'Prakasampai aaropanalu chesinavariki charitra teliyadu [Those Who Criticize Prakasam Don't Know History]', *Andhra Patrika*, 24 April 1982.

48. Turlapati Satyanarayana, TDP founder general secretary, in an interview with the author.

49. *'Pranthiya party desa samaikyataku hanikaram kaadu [Regional Party Not Harmful to National Integrity]'*, Andhra Patrika, 4 May 1982.

50. B.K. Eswar, *Vijayachitra Gnapakalu* (Chennai: Vijaya Publications, 2016), pp. 16, 17.

51. 'NTR mayasabha bhranthi [NTR under Mayasabha Illusion]', *Andhra Patrika*, 14 April 1982. One of the iconic scenes in *Daana Veera Soora Karna* highlights NTR's histrionics as Suyodhana after entering 'Maya Sabha' of the Pandavas and feeling humiliated by its dazzle.

52. Editorial, 'Kotha Party', *Andhra Patrika*, 31 March 1982.

53. According to R.J. Rajendra Prasad (*Emergence of Telugu Desam, and an Overview of Political Movements in Andhra*: 2004), these papers were pro-Congress. N. Innaiah (*Saffron Star Rising in Andhra Pradesh*: 1984) also mentioned that there was a pro-Congress tilt in reporting in Telugu media, except for *Eenadu*.

54. 'Asantruptulaku NTR party asrayam [NTR Party a Refuge to Dissidents]', *Zamin Ryot*, 26 March 1982. *Zamin Ryot*, published from Nellore, has been running without a break since 1930.

55. Amarnath K. Menon, 'Of Cherukuri Ramoji Rao, *Eenadu* and Telugu Desam', *India Today*, 15 February 1983.

56. Interview with film journalist Bhagiratha, 2017.

57. Eswar, *Vijayachitra*, p. 18.

58. Amarnath K. Menon, 'Of Cherukuri Ramoji Rao, *Eenadu* and Telugu Desam', *India Today*, 15 February 1983.

59. Menon reported that 'Ramoji Rao also did his bit in preparing the party's manifesto while his advertising agency designed hoardings and other publicity material for the new-born party'.

60. G. Krishna Reddy, 'Forging Public Opinion: The Press, Television and Electoral Campaigns in Andhra Pradesh', *Media and Mediation*, Volume 1, ed. Bernard Bel, Jan Brouwer, Biswajit Das, Vibodh Parthasarathi, Guy Poitevin (New Delhi: Sage Publications, 2005), p. 320.

61. Sambaiah Gundimeda, 'Caste, Media and Political Power in Andhra Pradesh: The Case of *Eenadu*', *History and Sociology of South Asia* 11 (2017): 192–203.

62. Praveen Donthi, 'Chairman Rao', *Caravan*, 1 December 2014. Jalagam Vengala Rao belonged to the Velama caste.

63. There is no evidence that Ramoji businesses had directly benefited during NTR's tenure, though the media baron enjoyed clout as kingmaker.

64. Upendra, *Gatham-I*, p. 78.

65. *Mahanadu* became an annual feature subsequently, conducted in the last week of May coinciding with NTR's birthday on 28 May.

66. Suman Dubey, 'Matinee Idol and Telugu Desam Leader N.T. Rama Rao Challenges Congress(I) in Andhra', *India Today*, 15 January 1983.

67. Justice Chelameswar, then a young lawyer, not only helped NTR with party matters but also was his lawyer in personal and family matters.

68. Daggubati Venkateswara Rao, *Oka Charitra-Konni Nijalu* (Nivedita Publications, 2013), pp. 29, 30.

69. Inaganti Venkata Rao, *Oke Okkadu* (Hyderabad: Monica Publications, 2014), p. 64.

70. Daggubati Venkateswara Rao, *Oka Charitra-Konni Nijalu* (Hyderabad: Nivedita Publications, 2013), pp. 11, 12.

71. Daggubati, *Oka Charitra*, p. 12.

72. M.L. Fotedar, *Chinar Leaves* (Noida: HarperCollins Publishers India, 2015).

73. Government of Andhra Pradesh, *White Paper on State Finances*, 10 July 2019.

74. The incident, which happened on 2 February 1982, was widely commented in the media as an affront to an elected chief minister. The Congressmen saw the incident only as a setback to Anjaiah.

75. Anjaiah's sudden removal as CM was linked to this incident by the newspapers of the time. M.L. Fotedar also hints at this in his book *Chinar Leaves*. According to Fotedar, Pranab Mukherjee asked for Anjaiah's resignation as CM at P.V. Narasimha Rao's behest.

76. Kotla was sent as chief minister on 20 September 1982. Assembly elections were due in February 1983.

77. Chief Minister Vijayabhaskara Reddy went one step ahead and fixed the price at Rs 1.90 per kilo rice.

78. S. Venkat Narayan, 'It Is only with Service Motivation that I have Taken to Politics: N.T. Rama Rao', *India Today*, 15 October 1982.

79. Andhra Pradesh High Court, *V.R. Sreerama Rao vs Telugu Desam, A Political Party*, 3 December 1982.

80. Ibid.

81. Ibid.

82. *Eenadu*, 9 October 1982.

83. K.R. Venugopal, 'Two CMs, One Scheme', *The Hans India*, 2 March 2014.

84. The TDP manifesto was prepared by former communists and socialists, according to N. Innaiah (1984). Many analysts also pointed to the role of *Eenadu*.

85. Juergen Neuss, 'The NTR Phenomenon Reconsidered', Internationales Asienforum, Vol. 29 (1998), Nos. 1-2, pp. 23–45. Juergen Neuss, who calls it Desham instead of Desam, makes several other errors, both factual and interpretive. Nara Chandrababu Naidu is referred to as Naravaripalle Chandrababu Naidu. Naravaripalle is the name of the village. His reference to an 'imaginary Telugu nation' is also surprising, since, by this time, there is certainly a Telugu-speaking state with political and geographical boundaries.

86. By the time he entered politics in 1982, NTR had acted in 300-plus films.

87. S.V. Srinivas traces NTR's interpretation of the epics to 'the influence of the early-twentieth-century non-Brahmin movement in Coastal Andhra'. S.V. Srinivas, *Politics as Performance: A Social History of Telugu Cinema* (Ranikhet: Permanent Black, 2013), p. 284.

88. Many of NTR's films, both mythological and social, were simultaneously made in Tamil such as *Sri Krishnavataram* (1967), *Lava Kusa* (1963), while a few like *Raja Sevai* (1959), *Karnan* (1964) were straight Tamil films. K.V. Srinivasan, a dubbing artiste, told *The Hindu* (12 April 2012) that he gave voice to NTR in Tamil for fifty-five straight and dubbed films.

89. NTR's food habits were legendary. Jagga Rao, who acted in many of NTR's films, recalls that during the shooting of the film *Eka Veera*, NTR easily devoured fourteen different kinds of sweetmeats. NTR could have twenty-five mirchi bhajis in one go.

90. NTR owned a collection of the heavy jewellery and weapons used in his mythological films.

91. B.K. Eswar narrated an incident in which NTR flew from Madras to Bangalore wearing his entire make-up and costume for the shooting of a mythological film to save time. He was playing the role of Lord Krishna. Eswar, *Vijayachitra*, p. 16.

92. A lot of inputs went into transforming NTR into Lord Krishna. For example, for his first major role as Krishna in *Maya Bazaar*, director K.V. Reddy advised NTR to practise a stylized walk that had a feminine touch to it.

93. NTR attempted five roles—Lord Krishna, Arjuna, Duryodhana, Brihannala and Kichaka—in *Srimad Virata Parvam* (1979).

94. NTR reprised the role thirty-three times; if short plays within the movies are included.

95. Viswam, *Nannatho Nenu* (Chennai: Vijaya Publications, 2015), p. 226. According to Vijaya Studio's patriarch B. Nagi Reddy, around 40,000 calendars of NTR as Krishna were printed in their press during the release of *Maya Bazaar* (1957).

96. Chidananda Das Gupta, 'Seeing and Believing, Science and Mythology: Notes on the "Mythological" Genre', *Film Quarterly* Vol. 42, No. 4 (Summer, 1989): 12–18.

97. Ibid.

98. T. Vishnu Vardhan, 'After Godhood: The Political Career of NTR', paper presented at the international conference on Asian Cinemas organized by CSCS, Bangalore.

99. Srinivas, *Politics*, p. 290.

100. 'Rama Rao garu, endukintlanti daurbhagyapu chitralu tistaru?', *Zamin Ryot*, 22 August 1980.

101. Daggubati, *Oka-Charitra*, p. 101.

102. 'Na party box-office hit: NTR [My Party is Box office Hit]', *Andhra Prabha*, 10 April 1982.

103. Srinivas, *Politics*, p. 259.

104. Ibid.

105. These are *Anuraga Devatha, Kaliyuga Ramudu, Justice Chowdary, Bobbili Puli, Vayyari Bhamalu—Vagalamari Bhartalu, Naa Desam* (all released in 1982); *Simham Navvindi* and *Chanda Sasanudu* (released in 1983).

106. This was supposed to be his last film. However, NTR later went on to act in five more films. Review by Amarnath K. Menon in the 15 July 1983 issue of *India Today*.

107. Amarnath K. Menon, 'Chandasasanudu, Starring N.T. Rama Rao, Is a Typical Formula Film', *India Today*, 15 July 1983.

108. 'The social capital of stars is immense, and it has been translated into political power with regional stars like N.T. Rama Rao in Andhra and M.G. Ramachandran and Jayalalitha in Tamil Nadu forming governments in respective States,' says Brian Shoesmith. 'Our Films, Their Films: Some Speculations on Writing Indian Film History', *The SAGE Handbook of Film Studies*, ed. James Donald, Michael Renov (London: Sage Publications, 2008), p. 82.

109. Interview with Turlapati Satyanarayana, the first general secretary of the TDP, in 1998.

110. 'Bhuswamya, pettubadidari vargalaku NTR maddatu [NTR Supports Feudal, Capitalist Classes]', *Andhra Patrika*, 5 December 1982.

111. Though the party was yet to be recognized, it managed to get a common symbol for its candidates from the Election Commission.

112. Indira Gandhi, for example, addressed forty-three public meetings between 15 and 17 December, twenty-nine meetings on 23–24 December and sixty-five meetings between 30 December and 3 January.

113. 'Na badhanta mee bhavishyattu gurinche [My worry is about your future]', *Eenadu*, 3 January 1983.

114. M.L. Fotedar, *The Chinar Leaves, A Political Memoir* (Noida: HarperCollins India, 2015), Chapter 18, Kindle edition.

115. 'Aidellu Chintinchali, Alochinchandi [Will Have to Regret for Five Years]', *Zamin Ryot*, 24 December 1982.

116. Editorial, 'Splintered Opposition', *Deccan Chronicle*, 26 December 1982.

117. Sumit Mitra and S. Venkat Narayan, 'As Andhra Pradesh Election Approaches, Congress (I) Feels the N.T. Rama Rao Heat', *India Today*, 2 August 2013.

118. Sanjay Vichar Manch candidates contested on TDP's Cycle symbol.

119. Ramachandra Guha, 'States of the Nation', *Telegraph*, 10 March 2012.

120. S. Venkat Narayan, 'Leaders Should Not Forget What They Have Been Voted For: N.T. Rama Rao', *India Today*, 31 January 1983.

121. NTR announced the TDP on 29 March 1982. Election results were out by 7 January 1983. That makes it nine months plus a week between the party's formation and its capture of power.

122. Editorial, 'Gone with the Wind', *Indian Express*, 8 January 1983.

123. K.C. Suri, 'Telugu Desam Party—Rise and Prospects for Future', *Economic and Political Weekly*, Vol. 39, Nos. 14–15 (3–16 April 2004), 1487.

124. Ratna Naidu, 'Symbolic Imagery Used by the Telugu Desam', *Shift in Indian Politics*, ed. George Mathew (New Delhi: Concept Publishing, 1984), p. 135.

125. Kuldip Nayar, '*Eenadu* Did Its Duty: Andhra CM Suppressing Press Freedom', *Tribune*, 30 December 2006.

126. Backward Castes (BCs) is a collective term used by the Government of India as well as state governments to classify castes which are educationally or economically disadvantaged. These are intermediate castes between the so-called Upper Castes (or Other Castes) and SCs and STs.

127. NTR was elected to the assembly from two seats in the 1983 elections—Gudivada and Tirupati.

128. In 1978, the last election before the TDP came on to the scene, forty-one Kamma MLAs got elected.

129. S. Venkat Narayan, 'Leaders Should Not Forget What They Have Been Voted For: N.T. Rama Rao', *India Today*, 31 January 1983.

130. YSR Congress Party, founded by Y.S. Jagan Mohan Reddy in March 2011, captured power in the 2019 assembly elections in residuary AP. Praja Rajyam of Chrinajeevi had a short life. Jana Sena of another actor Pawan Kalyan, set up in March 2014, could make little progress.

131. Devanik Saha, 'AAP Is Unique, but It Isn't India's Best Political Debutant', Scroll.in, 25 January 2015, https://scroll.in/

article/702187/aap-is-unique-but-it-isnt-indias-best-political-debutant.

132. B.P.R. Vithal, *A State in Periodic Crises: Andhra Pradesh*, (CESS Monograph, Hyderabad, 2010), pp. 95-96.

133. The cover story in the *Week*, 19 September 1992.

134. K. Rama Rayalu, 'Chiranjeevi's Entry into Andhra Politics', *Economic and Political Weekly*, Vol. 43, Issue No. 41, (11 October 2008): 17.

135. Suresh Krishnamoorthy, 'It was God's decree: Chiru', *The Hindu*, 18 August 2008. The political press meet was staged in the manner of a film promotion.

136. K. Rama Rayalu, 'Chiranjeevi and the Coming Polls in Andhra Pradesh', *Economy and Political Weekly*, Vol. 43, No. 48, (29 November 2008), pp. 16–17.

137. J. Balaji, 'Chiranjeevi Joins Congress', *The Hindu*, 6 February 2011.

138. Narayan, 'Leaders Should Not Forget', *India Today*, 31 January 1983.

Act II

1. R.J. Rajendra Prasad, *Dateline Andhra* (Hyderabad: RS Prasad, 2010), pp. 224, 25.

2. 'Rashtram ika Telugu Nadu [State Henceforth to Be Called "Telugu Nadu"]', *Andhra Bhoomi*, 8 January 1983.

3. NTR disclosed his decision on 3 February 1983, during his Delhi visit. *Andhra Patrika*, 3 February 1983.

4. Bhabani Sen Gupta, 'NTR Has Awakened the Self-esteem of the Telugu People', *India Today*, 31 May 1983.

5. 'NTR Mollifies Secretariat Staff', *Indian Express*, 9 February 1983.

6. Amarnath K. Menon, 'More than Three Lakh Andhra Govt Employees Go on Indefinite Strike', *India Today*, 15 August 1983.

7. The strike by the NGOs was called off on 4 August 1983.

8. 'Hakkulu teese uddesam ledu [Don't Want to Suffer Employees]', *Andhra Patrika*, 4 August 1983.

9. NTR shared his experience with many senior officials such as Y. Venugopala Reddy, former RBI governor, and N. Jayaprakash

Narayan, another IAS officer who worked with NTR. S. Venkat
Narayan also recounted the incident in his biography of NTR.

10. NTR created Dharma Maha Matra after the existing State
     Vigilance Commissioner T. Lakshmaiah refused to quit to enable
     E.V. Rami Reddy to take over. The vigilance commission was
     abolished.

11. 'Appointment of First Andhra Pradesh Lokayukta Causes Crisis
     in State Administration', *India Today*, 15 December 1983.

12. Amarnath K. Menon, 'Andhra Pradesh Govt Suspends Three
     High-ranking Officials, Faces Bureaucratic Heat', *India Today*,
     15 June 1983. Also, 'Appointment of First Andhra Pradesh
     Lokayukta Causes Crisis in State Administration', *India Today*,
     15 December 1983. And, Y.V. Reddy, *Advice and Dissent: My Life
     in Public Service* (Noida: Harper Business, 2017), Chapter 9, 'My
     Days with NTR', Kindle.

13. P.V.R.K. Prasad, *PMs, CMs and beyond: Wheels behind the Veil*
     (Hyderabad: Emesco, 2012), p. 62.

14. Amarnath K. Menon, 'AP Chief Minister N.T. Rama Rao
     Alienates Officials', *India Today*, 15 December 1987.

15. P.V.R.K. Prasad, *PMs, CMs and beyond: Wheels behind the Veil*
     (Hyderabad: Emesco, 2012), p. 70.

16. Y.V. Reddy, *Advice and Dissent: My Life in Public Service* (Noida:
     Harper Business, 2017), Chapter 9, 'My Days with NTR', Kindle.

17. Amarnath K. Menon, 'Andhra Pradesh CM Rama Rao Traps
     "Corrupt" Minister into Taking Bribe to Sack Him', *India Today*,
     15 March 1984.

18. Venkat Narayan, Amarnath Menon, 'I Have Failed in Rooting
     out Corruption: N.T. Rama Rao', *India Today*, 31 January 1984.

19. The TDP government's affidavit in the High Court. Andhra
     Pradesh High Court Judgment, Dasarathi vs State of Andhra
     Pradesh, 13 July 1984.

20. Andhra Pradesh High Court, *Dasarathi vs State of Andhra Pradesh*,
     13 July 1984.

21. Ibid.

22. Balamurali underplayed the issue later. 'There was nothing
     personal between me and NTR. We were good friends and I sang
     more songs for him in his mythological films than for any other

actor. But I had to do something when the government announced the move and I did it,' he was quoted in *The Hindu Business Line* (23 November 2016).

23. 'Asthana vidwamsulu, akademila raddupai councillo dumaram [Uproar in Council over Scrapping of Poet Laureateships, Academies]', *Andhra Patrika*, 20 August 1983.

24. Amarnath K. Menon, 'Andhra Pradesh Cabinet Deliberates on Winding up Directorate of Cultural Affairs', *India Today*, 15 August 1983.

25. However, Prasad was soon transferred out of the Information, Public Relations and Culture Department after, he said in his book, he sought to encourage arts and culture through grants to the tune of Rs 3 crore a year. NTR thought Prasad was doling out money as a favour. Apparently, NTR later found nothing amiss.

26. S. Venkat Narayan, *NTR: A Biography* (New Delhi: Vikas Publishing, 1983), p. 107.

27. Ibid., p. 109.

28. S. Venkat Narayan, 'Leaders Should Not Forget What They Have Been Voted For: N.T. Rama Rao', *India Today*, 31 January 1983.

29. P.S. Ramamohan Rao, 'NTR—Phenomenon and Paradox', *Souvenir* (Hyderabad: NTR Memorial Trust, 2013), p. 39.

30. Sumit Mitra, 'Conclave of CMs, Opposition Leaders Meet to Hammer Out Common Future Strategy', *India Today*, 30 June 1983.

31. Girilal Jain, 'Mr Rama Rao's Politics', *Times of India*, 31 May 1983.

32. NTR's interview with PTI published in *Andhra Patrika*, 7 January 1984.

33. Bhabani Sen Gupta, 'NTR Has Awakened the Self-esteem of the People', *India Today*, 31 May 1983.

34. 'Karuvu nivaranaku nidhlu: Pradhaniki NTR vignapthi [NTR's Plea to PM on Drought Relief]', *Andhra Patrika*, 18 April 1983.

35. 'Sasana mandalilo chalokthulu, sarasokthulu [Repartees in Legislative Council]', *Andhra Patrika*, 23 August 1983.

36. 'Sanyasulu Rajyam Yelavachchuna [Can a Sannyasi Rule a State?]', *Andhra Patrika*, 23 August 1983.

37.   'Annagariki Bhuswamulapai Abhimanam Minna [Anna Loves Landlords]', *Andhra Patrika*, 18 October 1987.

38.   Amarnath Menon, 'MLA's Imitation of NTR's Attire Leads to Fisticuffs on Floor of the House', *India Today*, 15 September 1983.

39.   Nadendla Bhaskara Rao, *Walking with Destiny* (Hyderabad: Sarvadharma, 2008), p. 165.

40.   Parvathaneni Upendra, *Gatham-Swagatham*—Part II (Hyderabad: Satyarideema Prachuranalu, 2006), p. 115.

41.   B. Satyanarayana Reddy, who hails from Mahabubnagar District, was a former socialist who joined the TDP in 1983. He was appointed as the governor of Uttar Pradesh during the National Front government.

42.   A chit fund company is a financial institution engaged in the business of managing savings schemes for its members.

43.   Margadarsi Chit Fund, whose turnover surpassed Rs 10,000 crore in 2018, is considered the main cash cow of Ramoji Rao's businesses, and hence targeted by several politicians.

44.   The headline 'Prashnottarala Pai Peddala Galabha', appeared on 10 March 1983 in *Eenadu*.

45.   S. Venkat Narayan and Amarnath Menon, 'I Have Failed in Rooting Out Corruption', *India Today*, 31 January 1984.

46.   The ordinance on the abolition of part-time hereditary village officers was issued a few days before the first anniversary of the government, on 8 January 1984.

47.   Y. V. Reddy, *Advice and Dissent: My Life in Public Service* (Noida: HarperCollins, 2017).

48.   Atul Kohli, *Democracy and Discontent: India's Growing Crisis of Governability* (New York: Cambridge University Press, 1990), pp. 89–90. Interestingly, Kohli quoted K. Raju, the district collector, to criticize the NTR government's moves. Raju later joined the Congress party and was presently an adviser to Rahul Gandhi.

49.   Nadendla Bhaskara Rao, *Walking with Destiny* (Hyderabad: Sarvadharma, 2008), p. 183.

50.   Ibid., p. 260. *Eenadu*, however, was as critical, if not more, of the TDP government as any other newspaper. But because of its overall anti-Congress stance, the paper continued to be seen as pro-TDP.

51. NTR first travelled to the US in June 1984.

52. I. Venkata Rao, *Oke Okkadu* (Hyderabad: Monica Publications, 2014), p. 93.

53. 'Rashtrabhivruddiki kendram sahakaram', *Andhra Patrika*, 17 August 1984; 'NTRku NBR sawaal [NBR Challenges NTR]', *Andhra Patrika*, 18 August 1984.

54. Sumit Mitra, 'Dismissal of NTR Ministry Planned, Nadendla Bhaskara Rao Nurtured with Care of an Assassin', *India Today*, 15 September 1984.

55. Sanjoy Hazarika, 'Another Gandhi Opponent Is Forced Out of State', *New York Times*, 17 August 1984.

56. The strength of various parties in the assembly at this time stood thus: TDP 201, Congress 57, PDF 7, CPI 5, CPI (M) 4, BJP 4, Majlis 5, Rashtriya Sanjay Manch 2, Janata Party 1, NDP 1, Independents 7. Vacant 1.

57. 'NTRku NBR sawaal [NBR Challenges NTR]', *Andhra Patrika*, 18 August 1984.

58. Parvathaneni Upendra, *Gatham-Swagatham*—Part I (Hyderabad: Satyarideema Prachuranalu, 2006), p. 138.

59. 'I Was Not Consulted by Governor: P.M.', *The Hindu*, 22 August 1984.

60. Raju Santhanam, 'Film Clips of NTR Press Conference, Meeting with President Zail Singh Under Scrutiny', *India Today*, 15 September 1984.

61. Ibid.

62. Ibid.

63. Ibid.

64. Nani Palkhivala, *We, the Nation: The Lost Decades* (New Delhi: UBS Publishers, 1994), p. 60.

65. Ram Lal later left the Congress party and floated Jan Kranti Party, which he subsequently merged with the Janata Dal. It was embarrassing for NTR when he became part of the National Front, but he did not press the issue. Ram Lal died in 2002.

66. Amarnath K. Menon, 'Andhra Pradesh Drama Starring N.T. Rama Rao Promises to Be a Crucial Test of Democracy', *India Today*, 30 September 1984.

67. 'Assemblylo Gandaragolam [Pandemonium in Assembly]', *Andhra Patrika*, 13 September 1984.

68. 'Bagareddy rajinaama [Bagareddy Resigns]', *Andhra Patrika*, 14 September 1984.

69. R.J. Rajendra Prasad, *Dateline Andhra and an overview of Political Movements in Andhra* (Hyderabad: R.S. Prasad, 2010), p. 257.

70. William K. Stevens, 'Outrage Over an Opponent's Removal', *New York Times*, 16 September 1984.

71. Sanjoy Hazarika, 'Another Gandhi Opponent Is Forced Out of State', *New York Times*, 17 August 1984.

72. 'Ippudu kaneesam talalaina lekkapattaru, appudadi ledu [At least Heads Are Being Counted Now]', *Andhra Patrika*, 16 September 1984.

73. Girilal Jain, 'Undo the Damage', *Times of India*, 24 August 1984.

74. Andhra Pradesh High Court, *Nadendla Bhaskara Rao vs Government of Andhra Pradesh*, 19 September 1988. Justice Krishna Iyer later resigned as inquiry commissioner and was replaced by Justice Chandrasekhara Menon. Meanwhile, the NTR government appointed the Agarwal Commission to inquire into allegations of corruption against past and present chief ministers, ministers, MPs and others. On a petition filed by Nadendla, the High Court quashed the appointment of the Menon Commission.

75. As many as twenty-two dissident TDP MLAs supporting Nadendla joined the Congress before the 1984 December Lok Sabha elections.

76. P.C. Alexander, *Through the Corridors of Power—An Insider Story* (New Delhi: HarperCollins Publishers, 2004), p. 207.

77. Inder Malhotra, *Indira Gandhi: A Personal and Political Biography* (New Delhi: Hay House India, 1989).

78. R.N. Kulkarni, *Sin of National Conscience* (Mysore: Kritagnya, 2004), p. 128.

79. Goné Prakash Rao Interview, IDream News, YouTube Video, https://www.youtube.com/watch?v=tuw-_gc5qhA.

80. P.C. Alexander, *My Years with Indira Gandhi* (New Delhi: Vision Books, 2018), pp. 35–36.

81. 'NTR did not campaign for national Opposition parties in 1984 polls in accordance with the word he had given to Rajiv,' said H. J. Dora (*NTRtho Nenu*). According to him, the agreement was

reached in a secret meeting between Rajiv and NTR in November 1984.

82. NTR requested to be allowed to use an official helicopter in view of his fragile health, but the Election Commission refused permission, saying that only the PM was exempted from this condition.

83. Srikakulam and Rajampet elections were countermanded due to the death of independent candidates. When polls were held on 28 January, both the seats were snatched by the TDP.

84. The only other candidate for the BJP who won in the country was A.K. Patel from Mehsana in Gujarat.

85. The CPI got 1.70 lakh votes, while the CPI (M) got 1.20 lakh votes, together polling more than the Congress party's 2.61 lakh votes.

86. Amarnath K. Menon, 'TDP's Astounding Victory Makes It the Largest Opposition Party in the New Parliament', *India Today*, 15 January 1985.

Act III

1. Y.V. Reddy, *Advice and Dissent: My Life in Public Service* (Noida: HarperCollins, 2017), p. 111.

2. Ibid., p. 110.

3. Ibid.

4. K.R. Venugopal, *Deliverance from Hunger, the Public Distribution System in India* (New Delhi: Sage Publications, 1992), p. 179.

5. Interview with retired IAS officer C.D. Arha in 2018.

6. K.R. Venugopal, *Deliverance from Hunger, the Public Distribution System in India* (New Delhi: Sage Publications, 1992), p. 181.

7. Prathipati Abraham, *From Powerless Village to Union Power Secretary: Memoirs of an IAS Officer* (New Delhi: Concept Publishing, 2009), p. 159.

8. Information from *Telugu Nata, Velugu Baata*, AP Information and Public Relations Department publication.

9. NTR called the Vijayawada bus station 'Satavahana Prayana Pranganam', but later the Congress government named it after Nehru.

10. Alivelu G., Srinivasulu K., and M. Gopinath Reddy, 'State Business Relations and Performance of Manufacturing Sector in Andhra Pradesh', Centre for Economic and Social Studies, Working Paper No. 82, January 2010.

11. G. Ram Reddy, 'Andhra Pradesh Open University [now Dr B.R. Ambedkar Open University]', in Ian Mugridge, ed., *Founding the Open Universities: Essays in Memory of G. Ram Reddy* (New Delhi: Sterling Publishers Private Limited, 1997), pp. 109–16.

12. Dr Koneru Ramakrishna Rao, 'NTR: Education Chief Minister of Andhra Pradesh', Souvenir (Hyderabad: NTR Memorial Trust, 2013), p. 97.

13. A. Mathew, *Higher Education Policy in Andhra Pradesh* (New Delhi: National Institute of Educational Planning and Administration, 2018), pp. 17–18.

14. 'Aaru nelalu chaduvu, aaru nalalu samaja seva, vidyarhulaku NTR kotha pathakam [Six Months Education, Six Months Community Work, NTR's Plan for Students]', *Andhra Patrika*, 8 July 1986.

15. Dr Nagabhairava Koteswara Rao, *Nandamuritho Naa Gnaapakalu* (Guntur: Vamsee Prachuranalu, 2001), p. 27.

16. R.V. Vaidyanatha Ayyar, *History of Education Policy Making in India 1947–2016*, (New Delhi: Oxford University Press, 2017).

17. N.T. Rama Rao, 'Role of Higher Education', *Speeches of Dr N.T. Rama Rao*, Vol. 5 (Hyderabad: Govt of AP, 1989), p. 146.

18. Koneru Ramakrishna Rao, 'NTR: Education Chief Minister of Andhra Pradesh', Souvenir (Hyderabad: NTR Memorial Trust, 2013), p. 99.

19. Ibid., p. 97.

20. Amarnath Menon, 'AP Govt Ask Tirumala Tirupati Devasthanams to Transfer Surplus Funds to the Treasury', *India Today*, 31 March 1983.

21. Supreme Court of India judgment, Executive Officer, *TTD, Tirupati vs A.S. Narayana Deekshitulu & Others*, Interlocutory Application No. 12 in Writ Petition (C) No. 638 of 1987, 9 May 1997.

22. Supreme Court of India judgment, *Shri A.S. Narayana Deekshitulu vs State of Andhra Pradesh & Ors*, 19 March 1996. The Jagan Mohan Reddy government in residual Andhra Pradesh brought

back the hereditary system in temples in 2019, quoting an AP High Court judgment in a subsequent case.

23.   Amarnath Menon, 'Tirupati to Be Given Grandeur and Special Status of a Holy City on the Lines of Vatican', *India Today*, 31 May 1984.

24.   'Kondaru Ekkuva Samaanulaa? [Are Some People More Equal]', *Andhra Patrika*, 20 October 1987.

25.   Santosh Kumar Sakhinala, 'Monumentalizing History: Statues, Regional Memory and the Politics of Representation', *Imagenaama* (Quarterly web-journal of CIViC [Centre for Indian Visual Culture]), 2013.

26.   Ibid.

27.   The pro-Telangana activists brought down eleven statues and threw some of them into Hussain Sagar during what was called the Million March on 10 March 2011. Many other statues were disfigured. They were replaced subsequently, along with a new installation of tribal rebel leader Komaram Bheem, in 2012.

28.   NTR's speech on the inauguration of the statues, reproduced by the Telugu daily, *Eenadu* on 11 March 2011.

29.   T.R. Seshadri, *From Raigiri to Rock of Gibraltar, Buddha Statue: The Story that Rocked the Nation* (Hyderabad: T.R. Seshadri, 1994), p. 41.

30.   Staff Reporter, 'Buddha Statue Arrives', *Deccan Chronicle*, 16 November 1988.

31.   'Buddhudante anta mamakaram endukante [This Is Why Such Regard for Buddha]', *Andhra Patrika*, 15 November 1988.

32.   NTR's overtures towards Buddhism offended Kanchi Sankaracharya and orthodox Hindus, according to N. Innaiah. N. Innaiah, *Political History of Andhra Pradesh* (Hyderabad: Centre for Inquiry India, 2009), p. 170).

33.   Catherine Becker, *Shifting Stones, Shaping the Past: Sculpture from the Buddhist Stupas of Andhra Pradesh* (New York: Oxford University Press, 2014), p. 166.

34.   Ibid.

35.   Interview with C. Narayana Reddy in 1998. It is, however, surprising that NTR was not aware of this very popular poem,

especially because he recited it in his film *Mahamantri Timmarusu* (1962) in which he essayed the role of Krishnadevaraya.

36. N.T. Rama Rao, 'Role of Higher Education', *Speeches of Dr N.T. Rama Rao,* Vol. 5 (Hyderabad: Government of Andhra Pradesh, 1989), p. 142.

37. Satavahanapuri was the temporary city erected for the Mahanadu event, named after the Satavahanas, the earliest Andhra kings.

38. Nagabhairava Koteswara Rao, *Nandamuri Tho Naa Gnapakalu* (Guntur: Vamsee, 2001), p. 33.

39. Narendra Luther, 'And Still I Long for Hyderabad', *The Telangana Struggle for Identity,* ed. Velchala Kondal Rao, (Hyderabad: Telangana Cultural Forum, 2010), p. 41.

40. All major Telugu newspapers—*Andhra Patrika, Andhra Jyothy, Andhra Prabha*—took several years after the formation of Andhra Pradesh in 1956 to come to Hyderabad. *Eenadu* also started publication in Visakhapatnam first. Till the 1980s, Vijayawada was the publishing centre for Telugu newspapers and books.

41. Karen Isaksen Leonard, *Locating Home: India's Hyderabadis Abroad* (Stanford: Stanford University Press, 2007), p. 32.

42. Urdu and Hindi are still widely understood in Hyderabad.

43. Hyderabad and Ranga Reddy Districts have a large Andhra population even after the bifurcation.

44. 'Udyogulakanna prajale mukhyam [People Are More Important than Employees]', *Andhra Patrika,* 30 November 1985.

45. Amarnath K. Menon, 'Non-gazetted Officers in Andhra Pradesh Go on Strike, NTR Refuses to Give In', *India Today,* 31 December 1986.

46. Supreme Court of India, B. Prabhakar Rao & Ors, etc. vs. State of Andhra Pradesh & Ors, etc., 19 August 1985.

47. H.J. Dora, *NTRtho Nenu* (Hyderabad: Emesco, 2011), p. 70. Also, P. Upendra, *Gatham-Swagatham* Part I (Hyderabad: Satya Rideema Publications 1992), p. 146.

48. The council, which was abolished on 30 May 1985, was sought to be revived by the Congress government in 1989, but the National Front government at the Centre refused. It was finally revived in March 2007, following the move by the Rajasekhara Reddy government. The Jagan Mohan Reddy government once again

resolved in 2020 to abolish the Legislative Council in the residual Andhra Pradesh.

49. The ceasefire continued for a few months before the relations flared up once again.
H.J. Dora, *NTRtho Nenu* (Hyderabad: Emesco, 2011), p. 70.
'Rajiv, NTR Niryuddha Sandhi [Rajiv, NTR agree to cease hostilities]', *Andhra Patrika*, 15 May 1985.

50. K. Balagopal, 'Anti-Reservation, Yet Once More', *Economic and Political Weekly*, Vol. 21, No. 36, 6 September 1986, p. 1572.

51. It was suspected that a section of employees who tried to attack the chief minister had political connections. Another section of employees condemned their actions. The NGO leaders offered an apology to NTR. Subsequently, the government appointed an inquiry commission by retired justice A. Gangadhara Rao to go into the incidents that took place in the secretariat on 4 September 1984. Four employees in the chief minister's office who protected NTR—Hemachandra Prasad, Laxminarayana, Narasaiah, P.L. Raju—were rewarded with promotion.

52. 'Sankshema pathakala amalupai kortula staylu [Courts Halting Welfare Programmes]', *Andhra Patrika*, 19 April 1986.

53. Ajay Sahni, 'Naxalism, the Retreat of Civil Governance', South Asia Terrorism Portal, accessed 16 February 2018, http://www.satp.org/satporgtp/publication/faultlines/volume5/Fault5-7asahni.htm.

54. Ibid.

55. Amarnath Menon, 'Blow for Naxalites in Andhra Pradesh', *India Today*, 31 May 1986.

56. H.J. Dora, *NTRtho Nenu* (Hyderabad: Emesco, 2011), p. 37.

57. K. Balagopal, 'Encounter Killings: Aftermath of Supreme Court Judgment', *Economic and Political Weekly*, Vol. 21, No. 40, 4 October 1986, p. 1735.

58. K. Balagopal, 'A Year of Encounters', *Economic and Political Weekly*, 14 January 1989.

59. Association for the Protection of Democratic Rights, 'Civil Liberties in India-Yearbook—1985', accessed 16 February 2018, http://archive.li/5bIF7#selection-735.240-735.395.

60. Statement by K.G. Kannabiran, president, AP Civil Liberties Committee (APCLC) on 9 April 1985. http://www.unipune.

ac.in/snc/cssh/humanrights/02%20STATE%20AND%20
ARMY%20-%20POLICE%20REPRESSION/A-%20
Andhra%20pradesh/9.pdf.

61. *Civil Liberties in India-Year Book—1985*, edited by Debasis
     Bhattacharya (Calcutta: Association for the Protection of
     Democratic Rights, 1986), http://archive.li/5bIF7#selection-
     735.240-735.395.

62. An unknown organization called Prajabandhu claimed responsibility.
     It was widely believed to have been propped up by the police.
     'Kidnap chensindi policele [It Were the Cops Who Kidnapped]',
     Andhra Patrika, 1 September 1989.

63. PUDR, 'Civil Rights under NTR Regime', Delhi, September
     1989, accessed 16 February 2018, http://www.unipune.ac.in/snc/
     cssh/HumanRights/02%20STATE%20AND%20ARMY%20
     -%20POLICE%20REPRESSION/A-%20Andhra%20pradesh/
     18.pdf.

64. The NTR government requested K.G. Kannabiran, who was
     with the APCLC, to intervene and act as a mediator to resolve
     the crisis. 'This type of intervention was a first for a human rights
     organizations in this country,' said Kannabiran.

65. 'Naxalsku salam kottoddu [Don't Bow before Naxalites]', *Andhra
     Patrika*, 22 August 1989.

66. 'Stupala punarnirmanam aagadu [Will Not Stop Naxalite
     Memorial Construction]', *Andhra Patrika*, 22 August 1989.

67. 'Ayudhalu vaddannaaru, ippudemantaru [Why I Said We Need
     Weapons]', *Andhra Patrika*, 4 September 1989; 'Naxalstho Congi
     milakhat [Congress Nexus with Naxalites]', *Andhra Patrika*, 3
     September 1989; 'Naxals samasayapai kendram sahaya nirakarana
     [Centre's Non-cooperation over Naxalite Issue]', *Andhra Patrika*,
     10 September 1989.

68. 'Ayudhalu vaddannaaru, ippudemantaru [Why I said We Need
     Weapons]', *Andhra Patrika*, 4 September 1989.

69. D.M. 'John' Mitra, who was a joint director of the National Crime
     Records Bureau, voiced this opinion in his article 'The Relevance
     of Technology in the Fight against India's Maoist Insurgency',
     Global ECCO, accessed 19 February 2018, https://globalecco.
     org/277.

70. Greyhounds have contributed substantially to the decline of Naxalite influence in the erstwhile AP. They have since become a model force for anti-Naxal operations in the country.

71. K. Balagopal, 'A Year of Encounters', *Economic and Political Weekly*, 14 January 1989.

72. Of the ninety-eight people killed in police firings, none, according to the official account, were connected with the Naxalite movement. So was the case with 107 of the 112 people who died in police custody. People's Union for Democratic Rights (PUDR), Delhi, September 1989.

73. *Civil Rights Under NTR Regime*, People's Union for Democratic Rights, Delhi, 1989. http://www.unipune.ac.in/snc/cssh/HumanRights/02%20STATE%20AND%20ARMY%20-%20POLICE%20REPRESSION/A-%20Andhra%20pradesh/18.pdf.

74. Amarnath K. Menon, 'Public Furore Compels Andhra CM NTR to Order Judicial Inquiry into Police Custody Deaths', *India Today*, 31 October 1986.

75. Letter written by Kapil Bhattacharya, president, Association for Protection of Democratic Rights on 19 September 1984. http://archive.li/5bIF7#selection-695.0-695.59

76. 'Naxalstho Congi milakhat [Congress Nexus with Naxalites]', *Andhra Patrika*, 3 September 1989.

77. The CPI (M) leaders of the state claimed they had evidence that Channa Reddy as state Congress president had a secret deal with Naxalites under which they ensured Congress (I) victory in forty-one assembly seats in the 1989 elections. In lieu of this, Channa gave them free rein after he became the chief minister, leading to breakdown in law and order, alleged CPI (M) leaders Bodepudi Venkateswara Rao and Koratala Satyanarayana.

78. Interview with Prof G. Haragopal in 2019.

79. S. Venkat Narayan, *NTR: A Biography* (New Delhi: Vikas Publishing, 1983), pp. 88–89.

80. Ibid.

81. Amarnath Menon, '1984 to Be Boom Time for Telugu Press', *India Today*, 15 November 1983.

82.   Narayan, Menon, 'How Is One-time Telugu Film Superstar N.T. Rama Rao Faring in His Political Incarnation?', *India Today*, 31 January 1984.

83.   Justice M. Krishna Rao, 'Report of the Single Member Commission of Inquiry on the Decision to Allot Land to Maharshi Veda Vishwa Vidya Peetham at Vijayapuri South', Government of Andhra Pradesh, 21 August 1985, p. 8. The land allotment to Mahesh Yogi did not happen in the end.

84.   Ibid.

85.   'Innaallu Prajalaku Pettevadu, Ippudu Tane Topi Dharinchadu [Made Public Fools All this While, Now Turned Himself a Joker]', *Zamin Ryot*, 11 July 1986, p. 1. This is a rough translation of a longish article.

86.   Interview with *Eenadu* cartoonist Sridhar in 2019.

87.   Contemporaries recalled R.J. Rajendra Prasad, *The Hindu* Hyderabad correspondent, was one of the few reporters whom NTR recognized.

88.   K. Balagopal, 'Censorship by Force a "Telugu" Prescription for the "Yellow" Virus', *Economic and Political Weekly*, Vol. 22, No. 26, 27 June 1987, p. 1023.

89.   Ibid.

90.   Ibid., p. 1022.

91.   Ibid.

92.   Andhra Pradesh Legislative Assembly, 'Statement Placed on the Table by Chief Minister', 14 December 1987.

93.   Amita Malik, 'Sight and Sound', *Indian Express*, February 1983.

94.   In recent times, Chandrababu Naidu was sought to be lampooned in some Telugu films.

95.   Actor Krishna joined the Congress and contested as an MP candidate. Vijaya Chander and Prabhakar Reddy were directly associated with the Congress party. All the films reflected the Congress's criticism of NTR.

96.   Nagabhairava Koteswara Rao, *Nandamuri Tho Naa Gnapakalu* (Guntur: Vamsee, 2001), p. 81.

97.   The Congress mobilized Harijans in the aftermath of various incidents such as Karamchedu, Neerukonda and Padirikuppam.

The party brought national leaders to the state who spoke about the TDP's alleged atrocities against Harijans.

98. Justice Y. Venkateswara Rao, 'Report of the Commission of Inquiry into Padirikuppam Harijanawada Fire Mishap', Andhra Pradesh Government, 15 May 1983.

99. K. Balagopal, 'The Karamchedu Killings: The Essence of the NTR Phenomenon', EPW, Vol. 20, No. 31, 3 August 1985, p. 1299.

100. Ibid.

101. According to *India Today*, cash grants and other concessions to the widows of those killed in the outrage came faster than usual. They were either given permanent government jobs in the hostels for poor students run by the government in Chirala or at other offices in and around Chirala. Amarnath K. Menon, 'Harijans in Karamchedu Village in Andhra Pradesh Fight Doggedly for Justice', *India Today*, 31 July 1987.

102. Supreme Court of India, *State of AP vs Rayaneedi Sitharamaiah & Ors*, 19 December 2008.

103. Justice D.P. Desai, 'Report of the Commission of Inquiry on the Clashes that Took Place at Karamchedu Village, Prakasam District', General Administration Department, Government of Andhra Pradesh, 31 August 1987.

104. 'Karamchedu Kathaku Maro Vyakhyanam [Another Angle in Karamchedu Story]', *Andhra Patrika*, 30 July 1987. The population of the village at the time was 10,000. The majority of the population belonged to the Kamma caste.

105. Justice D.P. Desai, 'Report of the Commission of Inquiry on the Clashes that Took Place at Karamchedu Village, Prakasam District', General Administration Department, Government of Andhra Pradesh, 31 August 1987, pp. 2, 6, 7. The judge felt the Dalit leaders were behind the decision. The absence of testimony of Kamma villagers was attributed to their being either in prison or missing from the village due to the police hunt.

106. The accused in the Karamchedu case were not immediately brought to justice because '. . . the prime perpetrator in the bloodshed was Daggubati Chenchuramaiah, a close relative of the Chief Minister NTR', said Sambaiah Gundimeda in *Dalit Politics*

in Contemporary India (New York: Routledge, 2016). Many other accounts repeat the same as a fact.

107. Interview with NTR's son-in-law Daggubati Venkateswara Rao in 2019.

108. Patricia Gossman, *Police Killings and Rural Violence in Andhra Pradesh* (New York: Human Rights Watch, 1992), p. 19.

109. K. Balagopal, 'The Karamchedu Killings: The Essence of the NTR Phenomenon', *Economic and Political Weekly*, 3 August 1985, p. 1299.

110. Amarnath Menon, 'Andhra Pradesh CM N.T. Rama Rao Finds It Difficult to Live Up to His "Good Guy" Image', *India Today*, 30 November 1985.

111. Mahanadu was held in January this year, contrary to the regular practice of conducting the meeting in May.

112. '7 ekarala kosam rajakeeyallo cheranu: Akkineni [Will Not Join Politics for 7 Acres: Akkineni]', *Andhra Patrika*, 9 November 1985.

113. Girilal Jain, 'The Republic of Lawyers: Why Andhra Aroused the People', *Times of India*, 19 September 1984.

114. 'Mantra tantra vidyallo naku viswasam ledu [Don't Believe in Occult]', *Andhra Patrika*, 27 April 1985.

115. Ibid.

116. 'I Want to Be a Saint in Politics: N.T. Rama Rao', *India Today*, 31 August 1986.

117. H.J. Dora, *NTR tho Nenu* (Hyderabad: Emesco, 2011), p. 113.

118. Ibid.

119. 'Ee vesham saswatham [This Is Permanent Attire]', *Andhra Patrika*, 13 July 1986.

120. Ashghar Ali Engineer, 'Making of Hyderabad Riots', *Economic and Political Weekly*, 9 February 1991, pp. 271–74.

121. Asghar Ali Engineer, a human rights activist, said in EPW ('Making of the Hyderabad Riots', 9 February 1991), 'There was a comparative lull in communal violence in Hyderabad during the Telugu Desam rule because of the Majlis support.' The credit was given to Majlis (MIM) apparently because it did not want to disturb the alliance partner. The fact was that NTR was friendly with all Opposition parties including BJP and MIM initially but

moved away from them once their communal colours came out. MIM was no more a friendly party to the TDP by the end of 1983. After the communal riots of September 1983, the ruling TDP kept away from MIM which moved closer to Congress. In fact, contrary to what Engineer said, MIM captured the Hyderabad mayor seat with the support of the Congress in 1985. MIM also supported Nadendla Bhaskara Rao in the 1984 coup against NTR.

122. Brijender Singh Panwar, 'Deccani Sikhs Prospering in an Alien Land', *Tribune*, 6 July 2002.
123. Steve Coll, 'Buddha of the Lake Bottom', *Washington Post*, 9 April 1990.
124. One case was related to Mullapudi Venkata Krishna Rao, who was elected from Tanuku in East Godavari District, and another to Kalamata Mohan Rao, who defeated the Congress candidate in Pathapatnam seat in Srikakulam District.
125. 'Telugu Viswavidyalamlo Jyothisha Peetham [Astrology a Subject in Telugu University]', *Andhra Patrika*, 23 January 1986.
126. Played by Kaikala Satyanarayana sporting the familiar afro-style wig of Sathya Sai, the character is shown as a charlatan.
127. Author's interview with C.D. Arha (retired IAS) in 2018 in Hyderabad.
128. Harihara denotes the unity of Vishnu and Shiva as different aspects of the same Ultimate Reality called Brahman.
129. NTR's sons were Jayakrishna, Saikrishna, Harikrishna, Mohana Krishna, Balakrishna, Ramakrishna and Jayashankara Krishna, and his four daughters were Lokeswari, Purandeswari, Bhuvaneswari and Uma Maheswari.
130. NTR precedes Yogi Adityanath, the chief minister of Uttar Pradesh, in his saffron costume by at least three decades. But in their secular outlook, they are opposites.
131. NTR announced an increase in BC reservations in July 1986, and began sporting the new headgear before embarking on a series of public meetings in districts to highlight the new measure.
132. Amarnath Menon, 'I Want to Be a Saint in Politics: N.T. Rama Rao', *India Today*, 30 August 1986.
133. T.N. Nian and Amarnath Menon, 'Reform Should Be Taken to Purify Politics: N.T. Rama Rao', *India Today*, 31 August 1986.

134. Y.V. Reddy, *Advice and Dissent: My Life in Public Service* (Noida: HarperCollins, 2017), Chapter 9, 'My Days with NTR', Kindle.

135. NTR expressed displeasure several times at the Centre's intervention whenever his government acted against the All India Service officers in the state.

136. The concurrent list is a list of items given in the Seventh Schedule to the Constitution of India. It includes the power to be considered by both the Central and state governments. However, the Central law prevails when there is conflict over these items.

137. 'Party adhyakshudiga NTR tirigi ekagriva ennika [NTR Re-elected Unanimously as Party Prez]', *Andhra Patrika*, 28 May 1988.

138. 'Nijayiti rujuvu chesukondi, leda tappukondi [Prove Your Innocence or Quit]', *Andhra Patrika*, 4 April 1987.

139. A.G. Noorani, *Constitutional Questions and Citizens' Rights* (New Delhi: Oxford, 2005).

140. Amarnath Menon and Prabhu Chawla, 'Andhra Pradesh: Locking Horns', *India Today*, 28 February 1987.

141. Amarnath Menon, 'Andhra CM Rama Rao Seeks Intervention of PM and President to Discipline Gov Kumudben Joshi', *India Today*, 28 February 1987.

142. Prabhu Chawla, 'President Zail Singh Questions Govt's Decisions, Much to PM Rajiv Gandhi's Embarrassment', *India Today*, 28 February 1987.

143. 'Judgeela empikalo rashtrala paicheyi [States Should Have a Role in Judges' Selection]', *Andhra Patrika*, 11 January 1989.

144. Report of the Sarkaria Commission, available at http://interstatecouncil.nic.in/report-of-the-sarkaria-commission/.

145. Shekhar Gupta, 'Victory of Asom Gana Parishad Ushers in a New Era of Hope and Change in Assam', *India Today*, 15 January 1986.

146. Chidanand Rajghatta, 'NTR on Chaitanya Ratham Storms Haryana', *Telegraph*, 15 June 1987.

147. Prabhu Chawla, 'N.T. Rama Rao Catapulted into the New Throne of Just-floated Seven-party National Front', *India Today*, 31 August 1988.

148. Upendra claims that while Arun Nehru and Madhu Dandavate supported NTR's election as Front chairman, Biju Patnaik cautioned him against bringing NTR into national politics.

Act IV

1. 'TeDe vidhanalaku Viswamitre spoorthi [Viswamitra Is Inspiration for TDP]', *Andhra Patrika*, 19 July 1989.
2. 'Viswamitra nirmanam sigguchetu [CM Making Viswamitra Film Shameful]', *Andhra Patrika*, 10 June 1989.
3. 'Gangaku addu Rama Rave [NTR Obstructing Telugu Ganga]', *Andhra Patrika*, 16 June 1989.
4. 'NTRpai aropanalanu sakshyalatho nirupista [Will Prove Allegations against NTR]', *Andhra Patrika*, 1 August 1989.
5. Andhra Pradesh High Court, *Vidadala Harinadhababu and Etc., vs N.T. Ramarao, Chief Minister*, 31 August 1989.
6. Ibid.
7. 'Menaka chintatho sabha chenthake rara? [Won't He Come Till He Finds His Menaka?]', *Andhra Patrika*, 6 March 1989.
8. Andhra Pradesh High Court, *Dronamraju Satyanarayana vs N.T. Rama Rao and Ors.*, 1987.
9. K. Chandrahas, *The People's Scientist Dr Y. Nayudamma* (Hyderabad: Pegasus India, 2013), pp. 157, 58.
10. Koneru Ramakrishna Rao, *Elements of Parapsychology* (North Carolina: McFarland and Company, 2007), p. 279.
11. V. Gowri Rammohan, 'K.R. Rao: The Man and His Mission', *New Frontiers of Human Science, a Festschrift for K. Ramakrishna Rao*, ed. V. Gowri Rammohan (McFarland & Company, 2002).
12. Dr Kakarla Subba Rao, *A Doctor's Story of Life and Death* (New Delhi: Ocean Paperbacks, 2000), p. 56.
13. Amarnath K. Menon, 'Andhra Pradesh Lok Ayukta Sambasiva Rao Marks the End of an Impressive Tenure', *India Today*, 15 December 1985.
14. P.V.R.K. Prasad, *Asalem Jarigindante* (Hyderabad: Emesco, 2010), p. 169.

15. Prof K. Ramakrishna Rao, *Souvenir* (NTR Memorial Trust: 2013), p. 97.

16. Ibid.

17. This was so at least till the emergence of the BJP as a major political force.

18. Kapu leaders who held *Kapunadu* meetings several times during 1987 and 1988 had the single-point agenda of sticking charges of caste bias against NTR and TDP. They were encouraged in this campaign by the Congress.

19. Interestingly, Srinivasulu Reddy, while he was a minister, defended the government saying, 'The Reddys are seething with jealousy as a Kamma has occupied the chief minister's chair after 35 years.'

20. K. Balagopal, 'Rise of Gangsterism in Politics', *Economic and Political Weekly*, 4 February 1989, p. 229.

21. S. Venkat Narayan and Amarnath Menon, 'I Have Failed in Rooting Out Corruption: N.T. Rama Rao', *India Today*, 31 January 1984.

22. P.S. Ramamohan Rao, 'A Police Failure—Its Fallouts and Lessons', *Reflections and Reminiscences of Police Officers*, ed. Sankar Sen (New Delhi: Concept Publishing, 2006).

23. Amarnath Menon, 'Landmark Writs Admitted against Andhra Pradesh Chief Minister N.T. Rama Rao', *India Today*, 30 November 1987.

24. Andhra Pradesh High Court, *Dronamraju Satyanarayana vs N.T. Rama Rao and Ors.*, 2 November 1987.

25. Ibid., 2 January 1988.

26. Ibid.

27. Ibid.

28. Ibid.

29. Amarnath Menon, 'Andhra Pradesh HC Finds CM N.T. Rama Rao Prima Facie Guilty of Misusing His Position', *India Today*, 31 January 1988.

30. Andhra Pradesh High Court, *Dronamraju Satyanarayana vs N.T. Rama Rao and Ors.*, 2 January 1988.

31. Amarnath Menon, 'Andhra Pradesh HC Finds CM N.T. Rama Rao Prima Facie Guilty of Misusing His Position', *India Today*, 31 January 1988.

32.   Ibid.

33.   R.J. Rajendra Prasad, *Dateline Andhra and An Overview of Political Movements in Andhra* (Hyderabad: R. S. Prasad, 2010), pp. 297–98.

34.   'An Amazing Verdict', *Indian Express*, 4 January 1988.

35.   Amarnath Menon, 'Details of Some of the Significant Cases Filed against N.T. Rama Rao', *India Today*, 15 September 1989.

36.   'Sankshema pathakala amalupai staylu, NTR vimarsa [NTR Criticises Court Stays on Welfare Programmes]', *Andhra Patrika*, 19 April 1986.

37.   'Federal vyavashtalo Emi Cheyyaali? [What Can We Do in Federal System?]', *Andhra Patrika*, 27 November 1987.

38.   Rayalaseema is a dry and backward region in AP. From time to time, Opposition parties tried to rake up agitation demanding better irrigation facilities to the region.

39.   'Karuvu choodatanika, bala pradarsanaka, pradhani raaka? [Was the PM's Visit for Show of Strength or for Drought?]', *Andhra Patrika*, 9 September 1987.

40.   Amarnath Menon, 'A Caste War Erupts', *India Today*, 31 January 1989.

41.   The total number of people killed in the incidents were thirty-nine, according to government figures.

42.   'When Vijayawada Became "Beirut" on Boxing Day', *The Hindu*, 31 December 2015.

43.   P.S. Ramamohan Rao, 'A Police Failure, Its Fallouts and Lessons', *Reflections and Reminiscences of Police Officers*, ed. Sanker Sen (New Delhi: Concept Publishing, 2006), p. 115.

44.   'Tagalabadi potunna Vijayawada [Vijayawada in Flames]', *Andhra Patrika*, 27 December 1988.

45.   P.S. Ramamohan Rao, 'A Police Failure—Its Fallouts and Lessons', *Reflections and Reminiscences of Police Officers*, ed. Sankar Sen (New Delhi: Concept Publishing, 2006), p. 109.

46.   D. Parthasarathy, *Collective Violence in a Provincial City* (New Delhi: Oxford University Press, 1997).

47.   K. Balagopal, 'Rise of Gangsterism in Politics', *Economic and Political Weekly*, 4 February 1989, p. 229.

48.   P.S. Ramamohan Rao, 'A Police Failure—Its Fallouts and Lessons', *Reflections and Reminiscences of Police*, ed. Sankar Sen (New Delhi: Concept Publishing, 2006), p. 109.

49.   'NTR Admits Failure of Police', *Deccan Chronicle*, 10 January 1989.

50.   K. Balagopal, 'Rise of Gangsterism in Politics', *Economic and Political Weekly*, Vol. 24, No. 5, 4 February 1989, p. 228.

51.   Chegondi Hararama Jogaiah, *60 Vasanthala Naa Rajakeeya Prasthanam* (Vijayawada: Crescent Publications, 2015), p. 72.

52.   P.S. Ramamohan Rao, 'A Police Failure—Its Fallouts and Lessons', *Reflections and Reminiscences of Police Officers*, ed. Sankar Sen (New Delhi: Concept Publishing, 2006).

53.   Ratna Kumari, who was elected to the assembly on a Congress ticket for two terms in 1989 and 1994 from Vijayawada East after Ranga's death, later joined the TDP. On the other hand, the prime accused, Devineni Rajasekhar, who was elected to the assembly for four terms on a TDP ticket between 1983 and 1994, joined the Congress on the eve of the 1999 assembly election. While Ratna Kumari was denied a ticket by the TDP, Rajasekhar lost the 1999 election. Since then, the caste-based mafias lost much of their dominance in Vijayawada. In 2019, Vangaveeti Radhakrishna, son of Vangaveeti Ranga, who sailed all along with non-Telugu Desam parties, joined the TDP.

54.   Justice C. Sriramulu, 'Report of the Commission of Inquiry on the Death of Mallela Babji at Vijayawada', Government of AP, 1992, p. 43.

55.   Statement by the home minister in the Andhra Pradesh assembly.

56.   Amarnath Menon, 'Justice Sriramulu Probe Results into Babji Letters May Prove Crucial for N.T. Rama Rao', *India Today*, 15 July 1988.

57.   Justice C. Sriramulu, 'Report of the Commission of Inquiry on the Death of Mallela Babji at Vijayawada', Government of AP, November 1987, p. 223. Interestingly, Justice C. Sriramulu was admitted into the TDP by Chandrababu Naidu when he was the party chief and the chief minister in December 2002.

58.   Ibid., p. 135.

59.   Ibid., p. 115.

60.   Amarnath K. Menon, 'I Have Entered Politics Only to Serve the People, Not to Make Money: N.T. Rama Rao', *India Today*, 30 September 1987.

61.   Korada.com, 'Jayaprakash about NTR', YouTube, 18 January 2016, https://www.youtube.com/watch?v=MxIWTLgbcV0.

62.   Mohan Kanda, 'The Phenomenon Called NTR', *Hans India*, 13 December 2016.

63.   The ad was published in 1995 to welcome NTR after his return from a foreign tour. The incident was mentioned in Cheekolu Sundaraiah, *Prajalu . . . Prabhutvam . . . Oka IAS* (Hyderabad: Emesco, 2014), pp. 108–09.

64.   'Tyagajeevulake pattam katta [I Have Inducted Selfless People]', *Andhra Patrika*, 16 February 1989.

65.   'Apoorva Sirachcheda Rajakiya Drama Rao', *Andhra Patrika*, 19 February 1989.

66.   'NTRpai aaropanalanu sakshyalathos saha nirupista [Will Prove Allegations with Evidence]', *Andhra Patrika*, 1 August 1989.

67.   Shekhar Gupta and Bhaskar Roy, 'CAG Report on Bofors Gun Deal Revitalises Opposition, Puts Congress (I) on the Defensive', *India Today*, 15 August 1989.

68.   'Veera jawanulaku tuppupattina videsi mara tupakula? [Why Sub-standard Guns to soldiers?]', *Andhra Patrika*, 16 August 1989.

69.   'Delhi margam tokkedi ledu [Will Not Go to Delhi]', *Andhra Patrika*, 22 October 1989.

70.   'Andhra Pradesh Voters Reject Rama Rao's Eccentric Politics and Incompetence', *India Today*, 15 December 1989.

71.   Out of the fifteen independent victors for the assembly, many were Congress and TDP rebels, who subsequently rejoined their respective parties.

72.   This is how the TDP allies fared: CPI won eight, CPI (M) six, BJP five, JD one and MIM four seats.

73.   Writer Nagabhairava Koteswara Rao recounted the incident. *Nandamuritho Naa Gnaapakalu* (Guntur: Vamsee Prachuranalu, 2001).

74.   Amarnath K. Menon, 'Andhra Pradesh Voters Reject Rama Rao's Eccentric Politics and Incompetence', *India Today*, 15 December 1989.

75.   P. Upendra, *Gatham-Swagatham* Part I (Hyderabad: Satya Rideema Publications, 1992), pp. 177, 78.

76. 'Channa kritagnatalu [Channa's Thanks]', *Andhra Patrika*, 28 November 2020.

77. P. Upendra, *Gatham-Swagatham* Part I (Hyderabad: Satya Rideema Publications, 1992), p. 202.

78. Ibid., p. 203.

79. Justice M.R.A. Ansari, 'Report of the Commission of Inquiry to Inquire into the Incidents that Followed after the Assassination of Sri Rajiv Gandhi on 21-5-1991', General Administration Department, Andhra Pradesh, Hyderabad, 19 July 1992.

80. Ibid.

81. P. Upendra, *Gatham-Swagatham* Part I (Hyderabad: Satya Rideema Publications, 1992), pp. 217–19.

82. R.J. Rajendra Prasad, *Dateline Andhra and An Overview of Political Movements in Andhra* (Hyderabad: R.S. Prasad, 2010), p. 338. There was furore in the state assembly later that K.P. Reddaiah, one of the TDP rebel MPs who supported the P.V. government, was generously paid Rs 1.25 crore additional amount under a contract by the state electricity board.

83. P. Upendra, *Gatham-Swagatham* Part II, (Hyderabad: Satya Rideema Prachuranalu, 2000), p. 13.

Act V

1. *Major Chandrakanth*, released on 23 April 1993, was NTR's last but one film. His last film was *Srinatha Kavi Sarvabhowmudu* on a Telugu poet, acted and produced by him and directed by the Bapu–Ramana duo. It was released on 21 October 1993.

2. 'Lakshmi Parvathi angikariste pelladutha [If She Consents, Will Marry Lakshmi Parvathi]', *Eenadu*, 11 September 1993.

3. I. Venkata Rao, *Oke Okkadu* (Hyderabad: Monica Books, 2000), pp. 171, 72; 'Sevalu chesi pranam posindi [She Gave Me My Life Back]', *Udayam*, 11 September 1992.

4. 'Marriage Won't Affect Political Life: NTR', *The Hindu*, 12 September 1993.

5. Harikatha, said to have originated in coastal AP, is a composite art form composed of storytelling, poetry, music, drama, dance and philosophy and is most prevalent in AP and Karnataka.

6.   Despite this fact, Parvathi was heckled following her marriage
     with NTR as some 'cheap' Harikatha artiste. Folk artistes, while
     admired by many, rarely enjoyed high social status.

7.   'Troubled Times of NT Rama Rao', *Hans India*, 12 January 2004.
     'The poor man went to bed without food, I was told the following
     day. Few in the family bothered to call on him or inquire about
     his welfare.'

8.   NTR had already suffered a fracture to his right shoulder during
     his acting stint due to which he was not able to use his right hand
     effectively. Probably for this reason, even as Lord Krishna, he
     would lift his left hand to bless, attracting criticism by purists.

9.   N. Lakshmi Parvathi, *Telugu Tejam: NTR Rajakiya Jeevitham*
     (Hyderabad: Unnam Brothers Publications, 2017). This political
     biography in Telugu provides Lakshmi Parvathi's point of view.

10. R.J. Rajendra Prasad, *Dateline Andhra* (Hyderabad: R.S. Prasad,
     2010), p. 360; N. Lakshmi Parvathi, *Telugu Tejam: NTR Rajakiya
     Jeevitham* (Hyderabad: Unnam Brothers Publications, 2017), p. 191.

11. N. Lakshmi Parvathi, *Telugu Tejam: NTR Rajakiya Jeevitham*
     (Hyderabad: Unnam Brothers Publications, 2017), p. 186.

12. The film, produced and directed by NTR and released on 28 May
     1992, flopped at the box office.

13. N. Lakshmi Parvathi, *Telugu Tejam: NTR Rajakiya Jeevitham*
     (Hyderabad: Unnam Brothers Publications, 2017), p. 191.

14. Ibid., pp. 187–89. The allegation was that Parvathi had relations
     with a security officer working for NTR and another boy from
     a family known to Parvathi. According to Parvathi, the trial was
     carried out by NTR himself. While the security officer backed out
     even before facing NTR, the mother of the boy was taken to task
     by NTR for spreading lies.

15. N. Lakshmi Parvathi, *Telugu Tejam: NTR Rajakiya Jeevitham*
     (Hyderabad: Unnam Brothers Publications, 2017), p. 191.

16. Ibid., p. 186. Parvathi received her divorce papers on 15 April
     1993. It appears that NTR and Parvathi married secretly in 1992
     (as claimed by Parvathi) even before she received her divorce
     papers. That could be one of the reasons why the marriage was not
     made public till September 1993.

17. Ibid., p. 191.

18. NTR attended the 9th TANA (Telugu Association of North America), held at Nassau Coliseum, Long Island, New York, as the chief guest and addressed the main conference.

19. 'N.T. Rama Rao's Relationship with His Live-in Biographer Lakshmi Siva Parvathi Snowballs', *India Today*, 30 June 1993.

20. 'Krishna Kumari Is No More', *Deccan Chronicle*, 25 January 2018.

21. 'Troubled Times of N.T. Rama Rao', *Hans India*, 12 June 2014.

22. A.B. Anand, 'Veeragandham Venkata Subba Rao Interview, Facts about NTR and Lakshmi Parvathi's Marriage', YouTube, 11 December 2017, https://www.youtube.com/watch?v=PZPVoNZ0l9A.

23. N. Lakshmi Parvathi, *Telugu Tejam: NTR Rajakiya Jeevitham* (Hyderabad: Unnam Brothers Publications, 2017), p. 186.

24. 'Congress, TDPla valle na pranalaku muppu (Fear for My Life from Congress, TDP)', *Eenadu*, 26 September 1992.

25. 'Rajakeeyalaku Parvathi Dooram', *Eenadu*, 20 September 1993.

26. 'Rajakeeyalloki Lakshmi Parvathi? Desamlo Tarjana Bharjana', *Eenadu*, 27 September 1993.

27. 'Rajakeeyalloki Pravesinchanu', *Eenadu*, 30 October 1994.

28. R.J. Rajendra Prasad, *Dateline Andhra* (Hyderabad: R.S. Prasad, 2010), p. 356.

29. N. Lakshmi Parvathi, *Telugu Tejam: NTR Rajakiya Jeevitham* (Hyderabad: Unnam Brothers Publications, 2017).

30. 'Desaniki Sorry Cheppu [Say Sorry to the Party]', *Eenadu*, 19 June 1994.

31. 'Renukaku Bahishkara Dandana [Renuka Expelled]', *Eenadu*, 26 June 1994.

32. After her expulsion, Renuka went on to form the TDP II and continued to be a Rajya Sabha member till 1998. Chandrababu Naidu took her back into the TDP soon after toppling NTR. She was appointed as the minister of state for health and family welfare in the United Front government supported by the TDP in 1997. Her elevation was apparently not to the liking of Chandrababu who pitched for actresses Sarada (elected to the Lok Sabha) or Jayaprada (elected to the Rajya Sabha). Renuka subsequently fell out with Chandrababu and joined the Congress in 1999,

got elected twice to the Lok Sabha in 1999 and 2004, and held ministerial positions in the Manmohan Singh government from 2004 to 2009.

33. 'Andhra Pradesh CM K. Vijaya Bhaskara Reddy Faces Tough Times Ahead', *India Today*, 31 October 1992.

34. 'Andhra Pradesh: N.T. Rama Rao Sells Fantasy Built on Subsidies and Doles', *India Today*, 15 January 1994.

35. Shekhar Gupta and Amarnath K. Menon, 'Showman's Drama', *India Today*, 15 December 1994.

36. Shekhar Gupta and Amarnath K. Menon, 'Rao Is Our Shame', *India Today*, 15 December 1994.

37. 'Ika Grihanike Parimitam, Lakshmi Parvathi', *Eenadu*, 10 December 1994.

38. 'Vatti Matalu Kaadu, Chethala CMni', *Eenadu*, 14 December 1994.

39. 'N.T. Rama Rao's Victory May Signal the Beginning of a Veritable Mahabharata', *India Today*, 15 December 1994.

40. Editorial, *Eenadu*, 16 May 1991.

41. N. Lakshmi Parvathi, *Telugu Tejam: NTR Rajakiya Jeevitham* (Hyderabad: Unnam Brothers Publications, 2017), p. 235.

42. Daggubati Venkateswara Rao, *Oka Charitra—Konni Nijallu* (Hyderabad: Nivedita Publications, 2009), p. 97.

43. Dr Kakarla Subba Rao, *A Doctor's Story of Life and Death* (New Delhi: Ocean Paperbacks, 2000), p. 122.

44. 'When Balamurali Struck a Blow for Fine Arts', *The Hindu BusinessLine*, 23 November 2016.

45. R.P. Singh, who was chief of the intelligence department, during NTR's time.

46. Parvathi said NTR had earlier offered Harikrishna a seat for assembly elections, but he did not show interest. Now, NTR did not want to give a ticket as he was wary of the 'forces behind Harikrishna'.

47. N. Lakshmi Parvathi, *Telugu Tejam: NTR Rajakiya Jeevitham* (Hyderabad: Unnam Brothers Publications, 2017), p. 284.

48. 'Palanalo Parvathi Jokyaniki Kallem [Rein in Parvathi's Role in Administration]', *Eenadu*, 5 August 1995.

49. Author's interview with V. Appra Rao, a retired IPS officer.

50. 'Ivigo kathora vastavalu [These Are the Bitter Truths]', *Eenadu*, 21 January 1995.

51. N. Lakshmi Parvathi, *Telugu Tejam: NTR Rajakiya Jeevitham* (Hyderabad: Unnam Brothers Publications, 2017), p. 287.

52. While Ramoji Rao projected NTR's action of giving permission to closed distilleries as perfidious, a little after NTR was overthrown, the Chandrababu government completely reversed total prohibition without a murmur from Ramoji or *Eenadu*.

53. 'Telugu Desamlo Musalam [Flare Up in Telugu Desam]', *Eenadu*, 23 August 1995.

54. 'Desam MLAla Madhya perutunna antaram [Increasing Differences among TDP MLAs]', *Eenadu*, 18 August 1995.

55. Dadi Veerabhadra Rao, a senior leader who was a minister in the NTR cabinet, in a TV interview said that NTR had appeared quite confident believing the assurance of an astrologer that Chandrababu would never become the chief minister.

56. 'Nyayam kosam nannanaina yedirista [Will Defy My Father for Justice]', *Eenadu*, 22 August 1995.

57. Author's interview with IPS officer R.P. Singh, the chief of the intelligence department.

58. N. Lakshmi Parvathi, *Telugu Tejam: NTR Rajakiya Jeevitham* (Hyderabad: Unnam Brothers Publications, 2017), p. 300.

59. 'Telugu Desamlo Musalam [Strife in TDP],' *Eenadu*, 24 August 1995.

60. R.J. Rajendra Prasad, *Dateline Andhra* (Hyderabad: R.S. Prasad, 2010), p. 363.

61. Interview with Dr Yarlagadda Lakshmi Prasad in February 2019.

62. NTR said these words to Dr Jayaprakash Narayan, his secretary.

63. 'Bani marchina madam [Madam Changes Tune]', *Eenadu*, 25 August 1995.

64. 'Cheelika vargam neta Chandrababu [Chandrababu Is Leader of Splinter Group]', *Eenadu*, 25 August 1995.

65. Andhra Pradesh High Court, *N.T. Rama Rao vs His Excellency, the Governor of Andhra Pradesh*, 22 December 1995.

66. Among those who reportedly tried to find a way out of the power tussle were Jayaprakash Narayan (a secretary in CMO) and Durga Prasad (a state intelligence sleuth), besides lawyer J. Chelameswar,

a friend of Daggubati and a long-time associate of NTR (and later judge of Supreme Court of India).

67. 'Chandrababu Stakes Claim', *The Hindu*, 26 August 1995.

68. 'Tammullu Randi, Annagaru Chalu Pondi [Brothers, Come Back, No Sir, Sorry]', *Eenadu*, 25 August 1995.

69. 'Congress MP Renuka Chowdhury Full Interview', iDream News, YouTube, 17 July 2017, accessed 11 September 2018.

70. Daggubati Venkateswara Rao, *Oka Charitra—Konni Nijalu* (Hyderabad: Nivedita Publications, 2009), p. 106.

71. 'I Never Intended to Harm Anyone: Parvati', *The Hindu*, 27 August 1995.

72. 'Fresh Mandate Only Option, NTR Tells Governor', *The Hindu*, 26 August 1995.

73. Andhra Pradesh High Court, *N.T. Rama Rao vs His Excellency, the Governor of Andhra Pradesh*, 22 December 1995.

74. 'Rajinikanth Supports Chandrababu Naidu', *The Hindu*, 27 August 1995.

75. Rajini said though he was opposed to the role played by Lakshmi Parvathi, the situation changed after her apology. 'NTRtho Rajini bheti', *Eenadu*, 3 December 1995.

76. 'NTR Urges People to Weed Out the Corrupt from Politics', *The Hindu*, 28 August 1995.

77. 'AP Crisis: Mediation Makes Little Headway', *The Hindu*, 28 August 1995.

78. 'AP Crisis: Mediation Makes Little Headway', *The Hindu*, 28 August 1995. Ramachandra Rao, who single-handedly fought dozens of cases against NTR in courts, including the one in which NTR was found prima facie guilty on seven counts, was surprisingly made advocate general by NTR after the TDP came into power in 1994.

79. 'Removal of AG: Court Keeps Order in Abeyance', *The Hindu*, 31 August 1995.

80. 'AP Crisis: Mediation Makes Little Headway', *The Hindu*, 28 August 1995.

81. 'Honour Awaits You at National Level', *The Hindu*, 30 August 1995.

82. 'Parvati Main Target at TD Meeting', *The Hindu*, 30 August 1995. The rural bus services in Andhra Pradesh at the time were painted red.

83.	'Sidelights', *Eenadu*, 31 August 1995.

84.	N. Lakshmi Parvathi, *Telugu Tejam: NTR Rajakiya Jeevitham* (Hyderabad: Unnam Brothers Publications, 2017), pp. 314–15.

85.	Ibid.

86.	Damodaram Sanjeevaiah, a Dalit Congress leader, took over as the chief minister in January 1962 at the age of thirty-eight.

87.	'Court Verdict in Chandrababu Naidu's Appointment as Andhra CM Proves Another Blow to NTR', *India Today*, 15 January 1996.

88.	Jayaprakash Narayan, 'Lok Satta Party President Dr Jayaprakash Narayana Interview', Telugu Popular, YouTube, 2017.

89.	AP Assembly Proceedings, 7 September 1995, accessed online: https://archives.aplegislature.org/documents/archives/ A-000546_07-09-1995.pdf.

90.	'Cine glamourku kalam chellindi [Days of Cine Glamour Are Over]', *Eenadu*, 21 November 1995.

91.	NTR's youngest son Jayashankar Krishna who was also present at the time, in Daggubati's own words, not only stiffly opposed his brother-in-law going to Viceroy Hotel, but also castigated Daggubati in harsh words for not listening to him.

92.	Andhra Pradesh High Court, *N.T. Rama Rao vs His Excellency, the Governor of Andhra Pradesh*, 22 December 1995.

93.	Ibid.

94.	Subhash C. Kashyap, 'Farce and Fraud in A.P.', *The Hindu*, 4 September 1995.

95.	Editorial, 'Mr Rama Rao's Exit', *The Hindu*, 1 September 1995.

96.	Yarlagadda Lakshmi Prasad was elevated to Rajya Sabha by Chandrababu on Harikrishna's recommendation in 1996.

97.	G. Alivelu, K. Srinivasulu and M. Gopinath Reddy, 'State Business Relations and Performance of Manufacturing Sector in Andhra Pradesh', Centre for Economic and Social Studies, 2010.

98.	R.J. Rajendra Prasad, 'Rama Rao Refuses to Quit State Politics', *The Hindu*, 31 August 1995.

99.	K. Balagopal, 'Politics as Property', *Economic and Political Weekly*, 7 October 1995, p. 2484.

100.	N. Lakshmi Parvathi, *Telugu Tejam: NTR Rajakiya Jeevitham* (Hyderabad: Unnam Brothers Publications, 2017), pp. 252–54.

101. 'Lok Satta Party President Dr Jayaprakash Narayan', Telugu Popular TV, YouTube, 18 April 2017, accessed on 5 September 2018, https://www.youtube.com/watch?v=NMis7JX4F-0.

102. Dr Kakarla Subba Rao, *A Doctor's Story of Life and Death* (New Delhi: Ocean Paperbacks, 2000), p. 122.

103. Author's interview with R.P. Singh, a retired IPS officer.

104. Kalpana Kannabiran, 'Gender in Mainstream Politics: Case of Telugu Desam Party', *Economic and Political Weekly*, Vol. 32, No. 22, 31 May–6 June 1997, pp. 1236–39.

105. 'AP Crisis: Mediation Makes Little Headway', *The Hindu*, 28 August, 1996.

106. Newspapers—both supporters and critics of the TDP—played up the sycophancy around Lakshmi Parvathi. I. Venkata Rao, *Oke Okkadu* (Hyderabad: Monica Publications, 2010), p. 221.

107. P. Upendra, *Gatham-Swagatham* Part II (Hyderabad: Satya Ridhima Prachuranalu, 2006), p. 58.

108. The journalist I. Venkatrao also mentioned his name in this regard.

109. 'Daggubatiini Deputy CM chestananaledu: Babu [Never Promised Deputy CM Post to Daggubati]', *Eenadu*, 1 November 1995.

110. According to the legend, Krishna killed Sisupala on committing his 101st sin.

111. Technically there is no tenth planet in Hindu astrology but there is a saying 'Jamatha Dasama Graham', which means one's son-in-law is a tenth planet, the cause of problems in one's life.

112. Y. Kasipathi and N. Sitaramaraju, 'NTR Aakhari Veelunama [The Last Will of NTR]', *Vaartha*, 7 January 1996.

113. 'Still the Darling of the Masses', *The Hindu*, 18 January 1996.

114. 'N.T. Rama Rao Passes Away', *The Hindu*, 19 January 1995.

115. 'A Courageous Leader, Says Jayalalitha', *The Hindu*, 19 January 1995.

116. 'A Loss to Democratic Forces: Jyoti Basu', *The Hindu*, 19 January 1995.

117. 'Vacuum Created at National Level: Advani', *The Hindu*, 19 January 1995.

118. 'N.T. Rama Rao, 72, Is Dead; Star Status Infused His Politics', *New York Times*, 19 January 1996.

119. Tim McGirk, 'Obituary: N.T. Rama Rao', *Independent*, 19 January 1996.

120. Daggubati also says in his book that NTR was using steroids.

121. 'Parvathi Did Not Go to NTR's Rescue', *The Hindu*, 27 January 1995.

122. 'NTR tudi ghadiyala mystery [NTR's Last Moments Mysterious]', *Eenadu*, 22 January 1996.

123. Dr Kakarla Subba Rao, *A Doctor's Story of Life and Death* (New Delhi: Ocean Paperbacks, 2000), p. 123.

124. N. Lakshmi Parvathi, *Telugu Tejam: NTR Rajakiya Jeevitham* (Hyderabad: Unnam Brothers Publications, 2017), p. 384; Daggubati Venkateswara Rao, *Oka Charitra—Konni Nijalu*, (Hyderabad: Nivedita Publications, 2010), p. 115.

125. Ibid.

126. I. Venkata Rao, *Oke Okkadu* (Hyderabad: Monica Publications, 2010), p. 176.

127. N. Lakshmi Parvathi, *Telugu Tejam: NTR Rajakiya Jeevitham* (Hyderabad: Unnam Brothers Publications, 2017), pp. 356–57.

128. Ibid., p. 357.

129. Ibid., p. 359.

130. Ibid., p. 362.

131. The winner, official TDP's Budda Sailaja, got 63, 277 votes.

132. 'I don't know why the leadership feels shy of NTR's legacy. Look at the AIADMK, the leadership feels proud of MGR's legacy,' he told Rediff.com on 14 January 1999.

133. Daggubati Venkateswara Rao, *Oka Charitra—Konni Nijalu* (Hyderabad: Nivedita Publications, 2010), pp. 116, 17. Daggubati said that Reddy, after the results, called up to tell him that he gave Rs 5 lakh each to the MLAs through Lakshmi Parvathi.

134. Chandrababu remains the longest-serving chief minister of combined Andhra Pradesh—a period of eight years and eight months—from September 1996 to May 2004. Y.S. Rajasekhara Reddy would have claimed the credit had he escaped accidental death during his second term in 2009 in a helicopter crash.

135. K.C. Suri, 'Telugu Desam Party: Rise and Prospects for Future', *Economic and Political Weekly*, 3–10 April 2004, p. 1487.

136. Chandrababu's son Lokesh is married to Balakrishna's daughter Brahmani. Lokesh was made a minister in the Chandrababu government, while Brahmani takes care of Heritage Foods, a Nara family concern.

Epilogue

1. S. Venkat Narayan, *NTR: A Biography* (New Delhi: Vikas Publishing, 1983), p. 93.

2. 'NTR oohallo maro prapancham [Brave New World of NTR]', *Andhra Patrika*, 13 October 1987.

3. T.N. Ninan and Amarnath K. Menon, 'Reform Should Be Taken to Purify Politics: N.T. Rama Rao', *India Today*, 31 August 1986.

4. 'Pratipakshala Aikyata Sadhinchi Teerutam [Will Achieve Opposition Unity]', *Andhra Patrika*, 19 May 1988.

5. B.K. Eswar, *Vijayachitra Gnapakalu* (Chennai: Vijaya Publications, 2016), pp. 151–53.

6. Shekhar Gupta and Amarnath K. Menon, 'Narasimha Rao Has Mortgaged the Country to the Foreigners: N.T. Rama Rao', *India Today*, 15 December 1994.

7. Ibid.

8. Yaga Venugopla Reddy, *Naa Gnapakaalu* [My Memories] (Hyderabad: Emesco Books, 2017), p. 165.

9. N.T. Rama Rao, 'National Front', *Speeches of Dr N.T. Rama Rao—Volume 5* (Hyderabad: Government of Andhra Pradesh, 1989), p. 171.

10. L.K. Advani, *My Country, My Life* (New Delhi: Rupa & Co., 2008), p. 443.

11. N.T. Rama Rao, 'Vision of My India', *Speeches of Dr N.T. Rama Rao—Volume 5* (Hyderabad: Government of Andhra Pradesh, 1989), p. 270.

12. 'Rashtrapati palana vidinche nibhandanala punasameeksha [Need to Review Provisions for President's Rule]', *Andhra Patrika*, 21 August 1983.

13. *Andhra Patrika*, 'Pritipakshala Aikyataku Raktam Dharaposta [Will Sacrifice Life for Opposition Unity]', 14 January 1984.

14. N.T. Rama Rao, 'Vision of My India', *Speeches of Dr N.T. Rama Rao—Volume 5* (Hyderabad: Government of Andhra Pradesh, 1989), p. 269.

15. Girilal Jain, 'Editorial: Mr. Rama Rao's Politics', *Times of India*, 31 May 1983. Retrieved from: https://www.girilaljainarchive.net/1983/05/editorial-mr-rama-raos-politics/.

16. L.K. Advani, *My Country, My Life* (New Delhi: Rupa & Co., 2008), p. 443.

17. Korada.com, 'Jayaprakash Narayan about NTR', YouTube, 18 January 2016, accessed on 7 September 2018, https://www.youtube.com/watch?v=MxIWTLgbcV0.

18. *Andhra Patrika*, 'Pritipakshala Aikyataku Raktam Dharaposta [Will Sacrifice Life for Opposition Unity]', 14 January 1984.

19. Madhu Trehan, 'We Are Requesting Hyderabad Be Made as a Free Port and International Airport: NTR', *India Today*, 15 July 1984.

20. Shekhar Gupta and Amarnath K. Menon, 'Narasimha Rao Has Mortgaged the Country to the Foreigners: N.T. Rama Rao', *India Today*, 15 December 1994.

21. 'NTR oohallo maro prapancham [Brave New World of NTR]', *Andhra Patrika*, 13 October 1987.

22. 'Asinchina Rashtrabhyudayam, Viplavam Sadhinchalekapoya [Failed to Achieve Expected Development, Reforms]', *Andhra Patrika*, 2 March 1986.

23. 'Entho Sadhinchalanukunna, Emi Cheyyaleka Poya [Wanted to Achieve So Many, but Failed]', *Andhra Patrika*, 27 May 1986.

24. 'Sanyasini na daggara emundi ichenduku [I Am a Sanyasi, Nothing to Give]', *Andhra Patrika*, 10 November 1983.

25. Renuka Chowdary's video interview with this author.

26. 'Kendra vaikharipai NTR avedana (NTR Anguished over Centre's Attitude)', *Andhra Patrika*, 28 April 1986.

27. Narendra Luther, *A Bonsai Tree—An Autobiography* (New Delhi: Niyogi Books, 2017), p. 153.

28. Y.V. Reddy, *Advice and Dissent: My Life in Public Service* (Noida: HarperCollins, 2017), p. 102.

29. Mohan Kanda, 'The Phenomenon Called NTR', *Hans India*, 13 December 2016.

30. P. Abraham, *From Powerless Village to Union Power Secretary* (New Delhi: Concept Publishing, 2008), p. 159.

31. Bhabani Sen Gupta, 'Rama Rao Has Built Telugu Desam into a Political Party with a Pyramidal Architecture', *India Today*, 15 April 1984.

32. Manish Phadke and Prerna Chatterjee, 'Bal Thackeray, the Cartoonist Who Could Stop Mumbai at Will', Print, 23 January 2019, https://theprint.in/theprint-profile/bal-thackeray-the-cartoonist-who-could-stop-mumbai-at-will/181871/; Aarefa Johari, 'Back to the '60s: The Shiv Sena's Tradition of Violence Is As Old As the Party Itself', Scroll.in, 29 October 292020, https://scroll.in/article/761832/back-to-the-60s-the-shiv-senas-tradition-of-violence-is-as-old-as-the-party-itself; Dipankar Guta, 'The Appeal of Nativism: A Study of the Articulation and Perception of Shiv Sena's Ideology', *Sociological Bulletin*, Vol. 29, No. 2, September 1980, pp. 107–41.

33. 'KCR Targets Andhra Corporate Schools, Colleges', *The Hindu*, 5 September 2011; 'KCR's Remarks Trigger 'Biryani' War', *Times of India*, 3 February 2011; 'Telangana Agitators Attack 40 Andhra Buses', *Times of India*, 4 October 2011.

34. P.S. Ramamohan Rao, 'NTR—Phenomenon and Paradox', *Souveni*r (Hyderabad: NTR Memorial Trust, 2013), p. 39.

35. Ibid.

36. Straight Talk with Telakapalli Ravi, 'Dr Jayaprakash Narayan Reveals Interesting Things about NTR', *Telugu Popular TV*, 28 May 2018.

37. 'Engili metukulaku aasapadamu [Not Looking for Your Charity)', *Andhra Patrika*, 16 May 1988.

38. 'Pratipakshala Aikyata Sadhinchi Teerutam [Will Achieve Opposition Unity]', *Andhra Patrika*, 19 May 1988.

39. Y.V. Reddy, *Advice & Dissent: My Life in Public Service* (Noida: HarperCollins, 2017), p. 114.